D1121326

THE LOCAL CHURCH

THE LOCAL CHURCH

TILLARD AND THE FUTURE OF CATHOLIC ECCLESIOLOGY

CHRISTOPHER RUDDY

A Herder & Herder Book
The Crossroad Publishing Company
New York

BX
1746
.R795
2006

The Crossroad Publishing Company
16 Penn Plaza – 481 Eighth Avenue, Suite 1550
New York, NY 10001

Copyright © 2006 by Christopher Ruddy

All rights reserved. No part of this book may be reproduced, stored in a retrieval system, or transmitted, in any form or by any means, electronic, mechanical, photocopying, recording, or otherwise, without the written permission of The Crossroad Publishing Company.

Printed in the United States of America

The text of this book is set in 10/12 Sabon.

Library of Congress Cataloging-in-Publication Data

Ruddy, Christopher, 1970-
The local church : Tillard and the future of Catholic ecclesiology / Christopher Ruddy.
p. cm.
"A Herder & Herder book."
Includes bibliographical references and index.
ISBN 0-8245-2347-4 (alk. paper)
1. Church. 2. Catholic Church – Doctrines. 3. Tillard, J.-M.-R. (Jean-Marie-Roger), 1927-2000 I. Title.
BX1746.R795 2005
262′.02 – dc22
2005028300

ISBN 13: 978-0-8245-2347-3

1 2 3 4 5 6 7 8 9 10 10 09 08 07 06 05

JKM Library
1100 East 55th Street
Chicago, IL 60615

In memory of

Jean-Marie Roger Tillard, O.P.
September 2, 1927–November 13, 2000

"For here the saying holds true,
'One sows and another reaps.'
I sent you to reap that for which you did not labor.
Others have labored, and you have entered into their labor."
(John 4:37–38)

and

To my mother and father

"With all your heart honor your father,
and do not forget the birth pangs of your mother.
Remember that it was of your parents you were born;
how can you repay what they have given to you?"
(Sirach 7:27–28)

Contents

Acknowledgments

It is only fitting that a study of eucharistic ecclesiology should begin by giving thanks. I am grateful above all to the late Jean-Marie Roger Tillard. He was a most gracious host at the Couvent Saint-Jean-Baptiste in Ottawa, welcoming me to prayer with the Dominican community and giving me all of the time that I needed for questioning and conversation, despite the unrelenting spread of his cancer. His energy and the sheer joy of his faith were remarkable, and I am blessed to have known one of the giants of twentieth-century Catholic theology and ecumenism. This work is a small act of thanksgiving for his life and work (and faith and order!).

I thank Lawrence Cunningham and Brian Daley, S.J., both of the University of Notre Dame, for their guidance of this project from its beginning. Larry was encouraging, efficient, sane, and wise. Brian remains not only my friend, but my "father in faith" (1 Cor 4:15). Both men reveal that the life of the mind and the life of the heart perfect each other.

I wrote much of this book while in residence at Corpus Christi Church in Manhattan, and so I thank its parishioners and most especially their pastor, the Rev. Raymond M. Rafferty, for his generosity, vision, and hospitality.

I am grateful, too, to friends:

The Rev. Robert Imbelli of Boston College for his wisdom and witness to theology done in the service of the church;

The staff of *Commonweal* magazine, especially Paul Baumann and Patrick Jordan, for incisive and humorous conversation during the writing of this book;

Steven Granato, for his manifold generosity;

Jerry Ryan, for his support, critique, and ecumenical witness;

John Jones, the editorial director of the Crossroad Publishing Company, for his untiring advocacy and support of this and other projects;

My parents, Cathey and Richard Ruddy, to whom this book is dedicated. I have come to know God through their love for me. Their support has been unwavering, and this book is a small effort to pay off an unrepayable debt.

Finally, I thank my wife, Deborah. Gracing my life with deep faith and uncommon love, she reveals that "nothing will be impossible for you" (Matt 17:20).

Introduction

JEAN-MARIE ROGER TILLARD AND THE THEOLOGY OF THE LOCAL CHURCH

IN RECENT YEARS an unprecedentedly public and contentious conversation has taken place at the highest levels in the Catholic Church. In venues ranging from *Festschriften* and Vatican conferences to the German and American media, Cardinal Walter Kasper and Pope Benedict XVI (then Cardinal Joseph Ratzinger),[1] first-rate theologians who are, respectively, the president of the Pontifical Council for Promoting Christian Unity and the former prefect of the Congregation for the Doctrine of the Faith, have respectfully but firmly disagreed about the nature of the local and universal churches and their proper relationship, and about the pastoral implications of that relationship. Although granting that they agree on many points, Pope Benedict has claimed that Cardinal Kasper's position is a "sharp critique" and "attack" containing some "groundless" fears about Roman centralization.[2] Kasper, on his part, has gone so far as to state that Benedict's critique of his views "is a profound misunderstanding that amounts to a caricature."[3]

What is at stake here? Following Vatican II, both men agree that in each local church "the one, holy, catholic, and apostolic church of Christ is truly present and active" (*Christus Dominus* #11). The local church is accordingly not a mere branch office of the Roman headquarters, nor, as *Lumen gentium* #27 shows, is the local bishop a "vicar of the Roman Pontiff"; conversely, the universal church is more than the sum or federation of autonomous local churches. Moreover, both theologians affirm that there is a mutual interiority, or perichoresis, between the local church and the universal church; they are inherently ordered to each other.

The two men disagree, though, on what might seem the abstract matter of ecclesial priority: which comes first, the local church or the universal church? Benedict holds that the universal church ontologically and temporally preexists the local churches. Ontologically, diversity is possible only on the basis of a prior unity of being. Temporally, the event of Pentecost reveals that the church was first universal and only subsequently local. To hold otherwise, he warns, is to open the door to a sociological conception of the universal church as a federation of local communities, emptied of cosmic and theological import.

Kasper refuses to assign priority to either the local church or the universal church, arguing instead for their simultaneity. While agreeing with Benedict that the church preexists creation in having "its foundation in God's eternal will for salvation," he nonetheless holds that such preexistence refers not simply to the universal church (as Benedict argues) but also to its expression "in and from" the local churches.[4] Moreover, from its historical beginnings, the Christian church has existed as inseparably local and universal: the Pentecostal church in Jerusalem was already both local and universal. In like manner, a believer today, for example, is baptized simultaneously into the universal church and into a concrete local church.

The debate over the relationship between the local and universal churches may seem to be the esoteric realm of theologians and bishops, but, as Kasper notes, it has profound implications for several concerns, including the exercise of the papacy, the nature of the episcopate, and the ecumenical quest for full visible unity among the Christian churches. For instance, Catholicism's failure to exhibit in its own life the proper relationship of unity and diversity — a relationship that avoids the extremes of uniformity and promiscuous pluralism — will scare off Orthodox and Protestant churches and communities unwilling to be absorbed by an overly centralized Catholicism. Within the Catholic Church, the debate can have substantial impact upon matters of liturgy, evangelization, inculturation, the appointment of bishops, and the role of synods and episcopal conferences. It likewise makes a significant difference whether the pope is seen primarily as the "universal bishop" of the universal church or as the one who exercises his unique Petrine and Roman ministry within the communion of his fellow bishops and their churches; the first view tends toward a monarchical, Roman centralization, while the second allows greater scope for other bishops and appears more adequate to scriptural, traditional, and ecumenical concerns.[5]

The Kasper-Benedict exchange is only the most dramatic and public example of the challenges of the ongoing reception of Vatican II in the Catholic Church and the Christian church as a whole — a reception that, in some ways, is only beginning decades after that council's close. Guided by the council and its incipient ecclesiology of communion, which roots the church's life in the communal life of the Trinity and sees such communion expressed and effected most fully in the eucharistic celebration, Catholicism has recovered a sense of the true and full ecclesial reality of each local church. Vatican II's Decree on the Pastoral Office of Bishops in the Church (*Christus Dominus*) expresses the matter concisely:

> A diocese is a section of God's people entrusted to a bishop to be guided by him with the assistance of his clergy so that, loyal to its pastor and formed by him into one community in the Holy Spirit through the Gospel and the Eucharist, it constitutes one particular church in which the one, holy, catholic, and apostolic church of Christ is truly present and active.[6]

Although careful to note that no local church exists solely in and for itself and, through its bishop, "is bound to be solicitous for the entire church,"[7] the council affirms — however embryonically — that each local church is not an administrative unit or a branch of the "home office" in Rome, lacking its own proper ecclesial reality, but rather that the "Church of Christ is really present in all legitimately organized local groups of the faithful which, united with their pastors, are also called churches in the New Testament."[8] Thus situated within a framework of communion with the triune God and fellow churches, the theology of the local church is pivotal to the council's ecclesiology.

In the forty years since the close of Vatican II, the church has confirmed the worth and centrality of this conciliar ecclesiology of communion. Convened to celebrate and reflect upon the council, the 1985 Extraordinary Synod of Bishops stated that Vatican II was a "gift of God to the church and to the world,"[9] and that the "ecclesiology of communion is the central and fundamental idea of the council's documents."[10] In subsequent years, both John Paul II[11] and the Congregation for the Doctrine of the Faith[12] have asserted the primacy of communion ecclesiology for Catholicism. Moreover, theologians as influential and diverse as Leonardo Boff, Yves Congar, Henri de Lubac, and Joseph Ratzinger have similarly made it the focus of their reflection, and several renewal movements such as Communion and Liberation have sprung up under its inspiration.

The content and implications of the ecclesiology of communion and, a fortiori, the theology of the local church, however, remain ambiguous — as evidenced, for example, by the many divergent ecclesiologies offered by various theologians. It is also increasingly clear that the fuller reception of the conciliar ecclesiology will take several more decades, possibly centuries. In his 1981 article "The Church of God Is a Communion: The Ecclesiological Perspective of Vatican II,"[13] the French Dominican ecclesiologist Jean-Marie Roger Tillard outlines several areas of tension in the conciliar ecclesiology, all arising, he argues, from a clash between a juridical ecclesiology and an ecclesiology of communion: the tension between (papal) primacy and collegiality, and that between "pyramidal" and "synergistic" models of ecclesial authority and structure. Underlying these two areas of tension is the more fundamental one between the local church and the universal church: What and where is the Church of God?

Although Tillard — perhaps contemporary Catholicism's foremost ecclesiologist — does not explicitly draw the conclusion, it seems that the theology of the local church represents both a cornerstone in, and a stumbling block to, the church's reception of Vatican II. In a positive vein, it offers a vision for the realization of the church's deepest identity: a community of faith and sacrament grounded in the Trinity's life-in-communion, incarnated in a particular culture or region, and culminating in the eucharist, for the praise of God and the service and unity of humanity. More problematically, questions concerning episcopal collegiality, papal primacy, the role of the bishop in both the local and universal churches, inculturation, ecumenism, and the reception of faith and doctrine all flow, at least in part, from the theology of the local church and the consequent difficulty of interpreting and assimilating the council's emergent ecclesiology. To cite just one example, how well do Roman Catholicism's current procedures of selecting bishops respect both the bishop of Rome's special *sollicitudo omnium ecclesiarum* and the integrity of each local church? If the council is to be received fruitfully as a "gift of God to the church and to the world," and if the church is to resolve pressing issues of mission, service, ministry, and authority, then the theology of the local church needs to be elaborated with depth and clarity, and — more importantly — realized in the concrete, daily life of the church.

Where, then, can we fruitfully turn for resources on these crucial questions? My thesis is that Tillard's writings offer the most coherent, comprehensive, and convincing ecclesiology developed to date for addressing the life of the Catholic Church and its reception of Vatican II — a task impossible apart from his contribution. This book strives to introduce Tillard's thought to an English-speaking audience where he is little known, and to evaluate that thought and to identify several trajectories — for example, the relationship of primacy and synodality-collegiality, inculturation and the process of reception — that offer promise for the future of the church. This work will succeed, then, to the extent that it (1) presents clearly Tillard's thought on the theology of the local church, (2) analyzes and evaluates this thought, and (3) shows its essential contribution to the life of the church today, particularly to the reception of Vatican II.

Biography

Jean-Marie Roger Tillard's theology of the local church is the culmination of a life's work in theology and ecclesiology.[14] Born on September 2, 1927, at St. Pierre-et-Miquelon, French territorial islands near the southwestern coast of Newfoundland, he professed vows as a Dominican in 1950 and earned degrees in philosophy from the Angelicum in Rome and in theology from Le Saulchoir, the French Dominican *studium generale,* in 1957. Noted for its application of a historical method to the study of theology in general, and Thomas Aquinas in particular, Le Saulchoir's faculty included such giants as Marie-Dominique Chenu and Yves Congar. Tillard was particularly influenced by Pierre Camelot's patristic studies (especially on Augustine), Hyacinthe Dondaine's courses on the *Summa theologiae*'s trinitarian doctrine, and Jean Tonneau's integration of Aquinas's moral theology and theological anthropology. No less important was Le Saulchoir's distinctively Dominican milieu: its rhythm of liturgy, contemplation, and study profoundly marked his thought, while his classmates included such future theologians as Bernard-Dominique Dupuy, Claude Geffré, and Jacques Pohier.

His first book, *L'Eucharistie, Pâque de l'Église* (1964),[15] which grew out of his doctoral studies, set forth the primary themes of his life's work: the centrality of the eucharist to church life and theology ("the eucharist makes the church; the church makes the eucharist"); a deep interest in liturgy; a thorough knowledge of scripture and the tradition, especially Irenaeus, Augustine, and Thomas Aquinas; and, most important for this study, the ecclesiology of communion, which he had learned from his studies of the Fathers and from his Dominican teachers and brothers, most especially Congar. This work is also notable for the manner in which it anticipates (the text was completed in 1962) Vatican II's eucharistic and pilgrimaging ecclesiology.

Having returned in 1957 to Canada to teach dogmatic theology, Tillard devoted his energies throughout the 1960s to two broad areas: ecclesiology and the renewal of religious life (particularly in relation to evangelical obedience and poverty).[16] Drawing upon contacts made in Rome during the council, he became deeply involved in ecumenical labors. In 1968 he was part of the first group of Catholic observers at the World Council of Churches (WCC) assembly in Uppsala, where he worked with John Meyendorff and John Zizioulas on its document on worship. Subsequent years saw his appointment to the First Anglican–Roman Catholic International Commission (ARCIC-I, 1969), his election in 1978 as vice-president of the WCC's Faith and Order Commission (where he played an instrumental role in developing its 1982 report, "Baptism, Eucharist, and Ministry"), and his appointment as a charter member of the Joint International Commission for the Theological Dialogue between the Orthodox Church and the Roman Catholic Church (1979). In recent years, he continued to serve as a member of ARCIC-II — his hand is evident, for example, in "Church as Communion" (1991) and "The Gift of Authority" (1999) — the Orthodox-Catholic dialogue, and the Roman Catholic–Disciples of Christ dialogue. Perhaps most significantly, he was rumored to be the primary drafter of Pope John Paul II's pioneering 1995 encyclical on ecumenism and the papacy, *Ut unum sint*. After a two-year struggle with cancer, Tillard died in Ottawa on November 13, 2000. His confrere Michel Gourgues said in a eulogy that "even if some things in the life of the church could sometimes provoke his impatience, his disappointment, or even his indignation, Jean-Marie Roger Tillard loved this Church — like his Order — as one loves a person, that is to say, passionately." The following day, preaching at the funeral Mass, Tillard's prior, Yvon Gélinas, praised him as "a man of faith — lively, audacious, critical, generous faith — who has imprinted in our memory and our hearts the sign of the grandeur of faith and the price of fidelity."

The seeds sown in *L'Eucharistie* and his ecumenical work have borne fruit with particular range and depth in a series of lengthy studies (some running over 570 pages). Beginning with *L'Évêque de Rome* (1982) and continuing through *Église d'églises* (1987), *Chair de l'Église, chair du Christ* (1992), and, most definitively, *L'Église locale* (1995),[17] Tillard has drawn upon scripture, tradition (especially the patristic era and Aquinas), and modern and contemporary ecclesiology in order to develop an ecclesiology of communion in which the local church gathered around the eucharistic table with its bishop is recognized as the church of God in its fullness,[18] that place where the catholicity of the church is fully realized in the double plenitude of divine gift and human-cultural depth:[19] the local church is the church of God sinking its roots into the "fleshly earth."[20] From this fundamental vision of divine gift and human response, he develops a coherent understanding of the local church as a sacramental community built on faith and baptism,[21] realized most fully in the eucharist,[22] served through ordained ministry,[23] and called to mission in the world. Furthermore, he argues that the local church is fully the church of God only when it recognizes its intrinsic, necessary communion with other local churches, a communion expressed particularly in synodality, episcopal collegiality, and the exercise of primacy — most notably (and problematically) the universal primacy of the bishop of Rome.[24] In short, the theology of the local church has become the focal point and structuring principle of Tillard's thought, and this book will explore its contribution to the life of the church and its theology.

Overview

The focus of this book will be Tillard's primary ecclesiological works — *L'Eucharistie, L'Évêque de Rome, Église d'églises, Chair de l'Église, chair du Christ,* and *L'Église locale.* The first two chapters will provide historical context for his theology of the local church, drawing upon Orthodox and Catholic theologians of the nineteenth and twentieth centuries. The third, fourth, and fifth chapters will be expository and analytical, treating the major themes and issues of his thought. Chapter 6 will serve as a summation and evaluation of Tillard's theology of the local church, as well as a constructive proposal for some possible trajectories of his thought. For the sake of economy, at each stage I focus on a given theme in its relation to the theology of the local church; for example, the eucharist will be examined primarily for how it constructs and sustains the local church, and not for an exploration of transubstantiation or of the Eastern and Western forms of the epiclesis.

Clarification of Terms

Although this book is not a study of Tillard's ecclesiology of communion as such, that ecclesiology is the basis of his theology of the local church, and so a brief summary may be helpful. Present already in his first major work, *L'Eucharistie,* the ecclesiology of communion was since continually developed and refined, becoming both more specific (*L'évêque de Rome*) and more expansive (*Église d'églises*) in scope. Communion is the central concept of his theology and ecclesiology, for it structures his thought on faith, the sacraments, liturgy, ministry, hierarchy, service, and mission. In *Église d'églises* he puts it concisely:

> Communion with God (himself trinitarian communion) in the goods of salvation acquired by Christ (whose incarnation was a communion, realized between God and humanity) and given by his Spirit, fraternal communion of the baptized (recreating the connective tissue of a torn humanity), all made possible by communion with the once-for-all (irreversible) event of Jesus Christ that throughout the centuries guarantees communion with the apostolic witness and that the eucharist (the sacrament of communion) celebrates. That is the church in its substance, and from this the Catholic tradition has always lived.[25]

Seen in this light, the point of departure for an ecclesiology of communion is "the central event in the life of the visible church, namely, the eucharistic celebration of the local church, when presided over by the bishop himself, surrounded by his presbytery, the deacons, and the Christian people."[26] This sacrament of communion in Christ's dying and rising, in turn, gives rise to the church's mission to the world, its sharing in the "joys and hopes, the grief and anguish of the people of our time."[27] In all things, the church of God is to be a sign and servant of God's plan to join all peoples—Jew and Gentile alike—in communion with God and with each other through Jesus Christ. Moreover, Tillard's ecclesiology of communion has its own vocabulary: words such as "symphony" (unity in diversity), "osmosis" (reciprocal influence), "symbiosis" (relation that preserves each person's or function's specificity), and, especially, "synergy" (common task realized together).[28] In this context, *koinonia* is not an ecclesial model, such as sacrament or herald (to use two of Avery Dulles's models), "but precedes them all," for it involves the divine life-in-communion that makes the church exist.[29] It thus serves as the framework for Tillard's theology of the local church.

Second, Tillard writes of the "local church" (*l'Église locale*) instead of the "particular church" (*l'Église particulière*). Although both terms refer to the "diocese... in which the one, holy, catholic, and apostolic Church of Christ is truly present and active,"[30] his choice of terms is not arbitrary, but has serious implications for how one conceives the relationship of the diocese to the church universal, and for how the diocese interacts with the cultures, geographies, and histories—in short, the humanity—of its surroundings. "Local church," in his mind, better conveys the thoroughly catholic nature of the church of God, through its emphasis on that church's engagement with all of creation and humanity. Therefore, while acknowledging that Vatican II alternates inconsistently between the two terms, and that the Code of Canon Law entirely ignores "local church," Tillard states:

> To retain the expression "local church" is therefore, in remaining faithful to scripture, to dwell in the profound intuition of the ecclesiology of communion, which links the Church to the work of God in creation. For the Church is not

> superimposed on this [work]. It is, by the creative Word and Spirit, the work of grace in the realism of the "earth of men and women." The "two hands of the Father" are at work in one as well as the other.[31]

"Local church," then, conveys the "fullness of the gift of God"[32] in a way that "particular church," by definition, cannot.

Third, Tillard opts as well to write of the "theology of the local church," instead of the "ecclesiology of the local church." Apart from its redundancy, the latter phrase often fails to address the necessarily theological framework upon which any responsible ecclesiology must be built. In Tillard's view, much contemporary ecclesiology, whether "conservative" or "liberal," remains mired in a Counter-Reformation, Bellarminian mind-set that focuses narrowly on hierarchical authority and the "visible" aspects of the church, that is, what might, quite loosely, be called its "plumbing" or "mechanics." While addressing such concerns in great detail (for example, in his analyses of papal primacy and infallibility at the two Vatican councils), Tillard situates them in the overarching framework of his theology of communion, rooted originally and ultimately in Triune communion: "This communional being constitutes the [local church's] essence. And, its relation to the communion of the Father, the Son, and the Spirit indicates its rootedness even in the eternal reality of the mystery of God."[33] At least in principle, such grounding helps one avoid a theologically meager ecclesiology.

I offer one final note. As this work is primarily a study of Tillard's theology of the local church in light of Vatican II, Anglican, Orthodox, and Protestant theologies as such will not be studied at length, except where needed or when specifically related to Tillard's ecumenical endeavors, for example, the documents of ARCIC I and II. My hope, however, is that this book will, in some measure, be of service to all Christians in their common quest for full, visible eucharistic unity among the churches.

Chapter One

THE DEVELOPMENT OF THE THEOLOGY OF THE LOCAL CHURCH IN NINETEENTH- AND TWENTIETH-CENTURY ORTHODOXY

JEAN-MARIE TILLARD'S theology of the local church has roots in the ecclesiological renewal of the nineteenth and twentieth centuries in Catholicism and Orthodoxy, both strands of which have influenced each other. Modern Orthodox theology stands under the towering influence of the nineteenth-century Russian thinker Alexei Khomiakov (1804–60), whose notion of *sobornost* — an untranslatable Russian neologism derived from *sobirat,* meaning "to bring together," and often rendered as "catholicity," "communion," or "conciliarity" — freed Orthodox theology from its legalism and scholasticism and envisioned the church as a community of love, in which unity and freedom cohere and are brought to fullness. Drawing upon his insights and extending them through a more thorough return to scripture and tradition, the Russian diaspora of the twentieth century, centered in Paris at the Institut Saint-Serge, developed a renewed eucharistic or local ecclesiology, most notably through the work of Nikolai Afanasiev (1893–1966).[1] Afanasiev's seminal contribution was his patristic insistence that the church is fundamentally eucharistic and that "each eucharistic community reveals not part of Christ but the whole Christ."[2] This insight, which may be considered the fundamental principle of all theologies of the local church, led, however, to an at times one-sided emphasis upon the full ecclesial reality of each local church and a consequent occlusion of its necessary communion with other local churches.

Afanasiev's ideas were adopted and refined by several of his students, most prominently John Meyendorff (1926–92) and Alexander Schmemann (1921–83). Central to each of them has been increased attention to the need for, and nature of, ecclesial structures and institutions (for example, the role of primacy and synodality), as well as a continued understanding of catholicity as primarily the fullness and integrality of God's gift to the Church, and only secondarily as geographic or cultural extension (a conception that is fundamental to Tillard's ecclesiology). Such an understanding enables them to affirm both that the local church is truly catholic in its own right, and that catholicity involves not uniformity, but the flourishing of unity in diversity.

It is the Greek John Zizioulas (b. 1931), however, who has brought the Orthodox ecclesiological tradition to perhaps its fullest, most comprehensive development to date. His works — particularly *Being as Communion*[3] — have established him as the foremost Orthodox ecclesiologist and theologian of the local church. Adopting the basic principles of Afanasiev's eucharistic ecclesiology, he avoids — on grounds of the simultaneity of the one and the many in the Trinity — Afanasiev's prioritizing of the local church over the universal church. He holds instead that the local and universal churches inhere in each other through a kind of perichoresis: just as the unity of the Trinity is located in the communion of the divine persons, so too is the unity of the universal church located in the communion of the local churches; each local church, while possessing the fullness of eucharistic life, is thus intrinsically related and oriented to the other local churches. In Zizioulas's thought, the Orthodox ecclesiological renewal finds its most balanced and rich expression in a theology of the local church that integrates life and structure, locality and universality.

This chapter will examine this modern rebirth of Orthodox theologies of the local church. Rather than exhaustive analysis of each figure listed above, our focus will be on several pivotal thinkers — Khomiakov, Afanasiev, and Zizioulas — each of whom is significant both intrinsically and in relation to Tillard's own thought. I will place each in historical context and sketch their contributions to the theology of the local church. My goal here — and in the next chapter — is to situate Tillard's theology of the local church in its historical, ecumenical, and contemporary contexts, for, apart from reference to these underpinnings, our understanding of his thought and its own development is impoverished.

Alexei Stepanovich Khomiakov (1804–60): Slavophilism and Sobornost

"The first original theologian of the Russian church,"[4] Alexei Khomiakov is the seminal figure in the modern renewal of Orthodox theology and ecclesiology. Born in 1804 to a wealthy, refined family, he was immersed in both European and Russian culture and was as fluent in English, French, and German as in Russian. In the wake of Peter the Great (1672–1725) and his Western-inspired reforms of Russian society and church, upper-class Russian intellectual society of Khomiakov's time was divided broadly into two groups, each influenced by European thought (most notably the Idealism of Schelling and Hegel), but differing in their attitudes toward Russia's future. The first group, the Westernizers, believed that Russia's political and social development depended upon a rejection of Russian despotism and a consequent embrace of Western civilization, most notably its conceptions of individual freedom, rationality, and industrial development. The second, the Slavophiles, argued that Russia, in uncritically accepting such ideals, had scorned its own heritage and fallen prey to the West's rationalism and legalism, and so they wished to develop a distinctly Russian civilization based partly on a return to a pre-Western and pre-Petrine society.[5]

The father of the Slavophile movement, Khomiakov was at first more of a social and cultural philosopher than a theologian, whose initial inspiration for the renewal of Russian society was derived from an idealized conception of Russian peasant life and the Slavic temperament. He saw in the *obshchina* — the Russian peasant commune — the seeds or framework for the regeneration of Russia.[6] In opposition to the perceived individualism and social chaos engendered by the French and Industrial revolutions, he believed that this small commune, in which people lived close to the land and made decisions collectively, created an atmosphere in which interdependence and freedom were mutually reinforcing. Moreover, the commune expressed the even more fundamentally communal nature of the Slavic and especially Russian temperament, which distinguished it from other cultures, particularly the West and its individualism.[7] At this early stage of his thought, Khomiakov's interest in Orthodoxy arose from its integral role in Russian culture: social and cultural concerns preceded and determined religious ones.

Soon, however, he turned his attention to more properly theological and ecclesiological matters, and, synthesizing culture and religion, arrived at his fundamental thesis: only Orthodoxy, through its ideal of mutual love, can hold together unity and freedom.[8] This ideal is his celebrated notion of *sobornost*,[9] which conceives of the church as a gathering or assembly, a living communion of mutual love, wherein unity and freedom are brought to fulfillment. Four aspects of *sobornost* are essential: communion, divine unity–high ecclesiology, catholicity, and its opposition to the forms of Western Christianity.[10]

In the first place, authentic Christian existence takes place solely in communion: if one "withdraws himself from communion with [the church], he perishes himself."[11] The church is an organic, "living body," whose primary characteristic is the communion established by love. "The crown and glory of the Church,"[12] love sets the believer free from sin, establishes him or her as an adopted child of God, binds each one to the others, and is both the condition and the consequence of all of the church's worship and works. Communion serves also as the matrix for knowledge and salvation. Christian knowledge comes from faith, which is given only in and through the church; left to his or her own powers of reason, the human person cannot grasp divine truths.[13] So, too, is salvation possible only within its boundaries, as it involves an incorporation into the Body of Christ.[14] Finally, in a step which will be of crucial importance to subsequent Orthodox ecclesiology and its theology of councils, Khomiakov's understanding of communion leads him to hold that authority rests ultimately with the entire faithful; there can be no question of a hierarchical teaching authority standing above or apart from the believing community, for any such distinction would rend the living body of the church and destroy its organic communion: "in performing his sacramental service [the bishop's] action proceeds not from himself, but from the whole Church, that is, from Christ living within her."[15] Khomiakov thus eschews any notion of authority as legal, juridical, or structural: a communion of love has no place for such realities.

Second, this communion's unity is rooted in God's own unity. Khomiakov writes, "The Church is one. Her unity follows of necessity from the unity of God; for the Church is not a multitude of persons in their separate individuality, but a unity of the grace of God."[16] This divine unity leads, in Khomiakov's hands, to a very high ecclesiology, wherein the distinction between the earthly, visible church and the heavenly, invisible church exists only on the part of human perception (a notion deeply in debt to Byzantine liturgy): there is but one church, rooted in the unity of God, and the visible church participates fully in the life of the invisible one.[17] A further corollary of his high ecclesiology is the church's complete sinlessness and inerrancy. In words that would make the most fervent Ultramontanist blush, Khomiakov claims:

> It is impossible that there should have been a time when she could have received error into her bosom.... The Church knows nothing of partial truth and partial error, but only the whole truth without admixture of error.... And the Church herself does not err, for she is the truth, she is incapable of cunning or cowardice, for she is holy.... Never is she either disfigured or in need of reformation.[18]

Third, this divinely united communion is catholic: its unity embraces the fullness of both divine gift and human existence. In contrast to what Khomiakov considers to be Catholicism's quantitative sense of catholicity, Orthodoxy embraces a more qualitative sense, which emphasizes, above all else, that "every action of the Church, directed by the Holy Ghost, the Spirit of life and truth, sets forth the full completeness of all His gifts — of faith, hope, and love."[19] Such divine fullness leads to a consequent embrace of all humanity, not primarily in a sheerly geographical sense — for example, the church is on every continent, in so many nations — but rather in that it takes up the totality of all human existence and cultures. In his "Lettre au rédacteur de l'union chrétienne, à l'occasion d'un discours du Père Gagarine, Jésuite," which rebuts the Jesuit's charge that the Slavonic church wrongly rendered "catholic" as *sobornoi* in its translation of the Nicene-Constantinople Creed, Khomiakov answers that the translators deliberately and rightly rejected geographic universality in favor of the sense of "assembly" or "unity in plurality."[20] More precisely, *sobornoi* reflects the belief that

> the catholic Church is the Church which is *according to all,* or *according to the unity of all,* the Church of perfect unanimity, the Church where there are no more nationalities, no more Greeks or barbarians, where there are no more differences of conditions, neither masters nor slaves, it is the Church

> prophesied by the Old Testament and realized by the New [Testament], in short, the Church as Saint Paul defined it.[21]

Similarly, in *The Church is One,* he writes that the church "belongs to the whole world and not any particular locality; because by [it] all mankind and all the earth, and not any particular nation or country, are sanctified"[22] and also that "when the Church shall have extended [itself]... the fullness of the nations shall have entered into [it]."[23] In each instance, then, Khomiakov consistently emphasizes that the catholicity proper to *sobornost* is primarily fullness of life, both divine and human, and only secondarily geographic expansion—a point that will immensely influence both Orthodox and Catholic thought in the twentieth century.

Fourth, as a meshing of pure Orthodoxy and the Slavic-Russian genius, *sobornost* stands in opposition to what Khomiakov characterizes as Western individualism. Accordingly, Catholicism and Protestantism, although often thought to be radically opposed, are but "two sides of the same coin":[24] they destroy Orthodoxy's harmony of unity and freedom through their respective legalism and individualism. Catholicism replaces the internal witness of love with an external authority of law,[25] and Protestantism replaces the unity of an organic community with individualism and congregationalism (a mere aggregate of individuals).[26] In short, Rome sacrifices freedom for illusory unity; Protestantism, unity for illusory freedom.[27] And, despite these differing emphases on unity and freedom, Protestantism is actually the logical outcome of Catholicism: the arrogance of the papacy in setting itself up as an authority standing above the church (as in the *filioque* controversy, where, according to Khomiakov, the Western church, in the person of the pope, altered the Creed without consulting the East) leads inevitably to the Protestant denial of tradition and community in favor of the individual's solitary conscience (and culminates in the rationalism and secularity of the Enlightenment).[28] In this context, even Roman legalism—which seems to privilege the community over the individual—is an ironic expression of individualism, for laws exist apart from and over the community, and eventually set the individual over against the community.[29] Only Orthodoxy, through its notion of *sobornost,* which holds together unity and freedom in mutual love, can preserve the church's truest and deepest identity:

> This [objective] world can be found not in the activity of isolated individuals, not in their fortuitous accord (the dream of the Reformers), not in an exterior rapport of slavery (the folly of the Romans): it is found only in the intimate union of human subjectivity with the real objectivity of an organic and living world, of a holy unity whose law is neither an abstraction nor a human invention, but a divine reality: God himself in the revelation of mutual love. This is the Church.[30]

How, then, does all of this relate to our consideration of the theology of the local church? Positively, Khomiakov's conception of catholicity as fullness of life and as unity in diversity enables him to affirm that all human goods, cultures, and nations are capable of being assumed by the church: *sobornost*'s catholicity is universal, not uniform. Moreover, his emphasis on the love that unites Orthodoxy, rather than the legalism of Catholicism, undergirds this catholicity, as love does not destroy or seek to limit difference (as does law), but rather enables it. Love aims at fullness of life, and therefore it welcomes locality.

There is, however, a deep irony at the heart of his thought on the local church: it is at once too local and too universal. In the first place, he overvalues locality through his uncritical exaltation of Slavic and Russian culture. His initial ideas and writings draw heavily and primarily upon a thoroughly romanticized conception of Russian life and culture, especially in regard to peasant communities and the Slavic temperament. Little mention is made of the feudalism and serfdom so prevalent in his culture, nor does he depict the Slavs in anything but the most glowing of terms: they are gentle, peaceful, hospitable, familial, naturally religious and Christian.[31] Most devastatingly, John Romanides, while praising Khomiakov's ecclesiology for its rejection of Western ecclesial thought and for its attention to the foundational principles of love and freedom, argues that it is insufficiently based on biblical and patristic theology, which stresses — among other themes — that baptism involves a struggle against sin and death, a struggle that prevents an uncritical assimilation of human cultures and values. This theological lacuna, in turn, leads Khomiakov to "adapt [himself] to a contemporary German philosophy of social life as organism and [to] imagine that the Russian peasants were the Orthodox *par excellence* because of something inherent in the national character."[32] In short, although Khomiakov came to insist that Orthodoxy gave rise to Russian culture, rather than the reverse, it remains that his theology and ecclesiology are often uncritically bound up with peculiarly Russian concerns and lead to an exaggerated valuation of locality and culture.

Complementing this flawed sense of locality is an equally flawed one of universality, which sets at odds unity and locality. In his "Letter to Gagarine," Khomiakov writes that the church that is "one according to all or according to the unity of all, the church of free unanimity," is also the one "where there are no more nationalities, no more differences of conditions."[33] And, concluding *The Church is One,* he goes still further:

> When the Church shall have extended herself, or the fullness of the nations shall have entered into her, then all local appellations will cease; for the Church is not bound up with any locality; she neither boasts herself of any particular see or territory, nor preserves the inheritance of pagan pride: but she calls herself One Holy Catholic and Apostolic; knowing that the whole world belongs to her, and that no locality therein possesses any special significance, but only temporarily can and does serve for the glorification of the name of God, according to His unsearchable will.[34]

In each of these passages, Khomiakov asserts, however unwittingly, that the church's universality is the fruit of a unity so complete that it ultimately excludes locality or difference. His choice of "temporarily" in the latter passage points to his inability to distinguish (and not separate) adequately the earthly and heavenly churches, which has the consequence of allowing no real, significant place for earthly or human conditions: so strongly focused on heaven and the kingdom, he is often indifferent or blind to more immediate realities, be they of culture or history; in his hands, the church's transtemporal nature tends to suppress history, rather than suffuse it.[35] Furthermore, his deficient, even contradictory sense of catholicity undercuts his understanding of universality and locality. Although he clearly states in the "Letter to Gagarine" that *sobor* means "unity in plurality,"[36] just several sentences later he writes the above-mentioned lines, "the Church [is] where there are no more nationalities, no more differences of conditions." He leaves open the question of whether this transcendence eliminates or integrates difference, but it remains that locality and catholicity are in tension, even opposition. In sum, one might say that for Khomiakov the church spreads across the world and encompasses all peoples within itself, but does not set down deep roots (except, perhaps, in Russia). Such is the irony of the Slavophile's ecclesiology.

Khomiakov's wavering over locality is but one of his ecclesiological and theological difficulties. His use of scriptural and patristic resources is relatively thin, while his reflections on the church begin (and sometimes end) more from his personal experience than from historical study.[37] Equally troubling is his treatment of the eucharist and its role in the church's communion and unity. Based on abstract notions of divine unity (and a largely absent trinitarian theology, in which christology has a minimal role), the church's eucharistic character is largely ignored; his treatment of the eucharist focuses almost exclusively on transformation of the bread and wine into the body and blood of the Lord, but fails to draw any connection to its role as both the bond and the sign of the church's unity.[38] Nonetheless, Khomiakov's *sobornost* ecclesiology, which does not adequately address the local church, enabled its future development by re-envisioning the church as a communion of mutual love rooted in God's own love and paved the way for future ecclesiological developments, of which he — "the theologian *par excellence* of the Slavophile movement"[39] — would be the spiritual and ecclesial father.

Nikolai Nikolaevich Afanasiev (1893–1966): The Local Church is Eucharistic

Nikolai Afanasiev is perhaps the most important figure in the modern renewal of the theology of the local church. In works stretching over a thirty-year period, and ranging from canon law to ecumenism, the Russian

Orthodox theologian and priest drew upon scripture and the Fathers, especially Ignatius of Antioch, in developing a eucharistic ecclesiology, which conceived of the local church — the eucharistic assembly gathered around the table with its bishop — as the church of God in its fullness. Often expressed in a deliberately explosive and polemical manner, his conviction that the eucharist must determine the shape of the church's life, ministry, and structures would decisively alter the course of twentieth-century Orthodox and Catholic ecclesiology, directly influencing such theologians as Yves Congar, John Meyendorff, Alexander Schmemann, Jean-Marie Tillard, and John Zizioulas.

Afanasiev was born in Odessa in 1893 and studied mathematics in college. The events of 1917–18 were a watershed for him, as he witnessed both the Russian Revolution and the restoration of the Moscow Patriarchate. After fighting as a White Russian against the Communists, he left Russia for Serbia in 1921; his experience of the destruction wrought by the Revolution upon the Russian church not only was personally scarring but also would "form a continuing leitmotiv in his ecclesiology . . . the issue of the relations between Church and civil society."[40] For the next four years he studied theology in Belgrade, where he received a rigorous historical and patristic formation under his mentor, A. P. Dobroklonsky, and ultimately wrote his thesis on "The Power of the State in Ecumenical Councils."[41] Moreover, beyond this deep patristic grounding, Afanasiev's years in Serbia marked him with a lifelong revulsion for the jurisdictional conflicts engendered by the Diaspora of the Russian church.[42]

After several years of high school teaching, he moved in 1930 to Paris to teach canon law at the Institut Saint-Serge, an Orthodox seminary that had been founded in 1925 by several theologians of the Russian Diaspora. The 1930s were "the most brilliant epoch of the history . . . of the Institute,"[43] and Afanasiev found himself immersed in a vital environment, wherein two schools of thought dominated. The first, represented above all by Serge Bulgakov, sought to go "beyond the Fathers" through a synthesis of patristic tradition with modern philosophy. The other, headed by Georges Florovsky, pursued a "return to the Fathers" and emphasized the "permanent and eternal value of *Hellenic* categories for Orthodox theological thought."[44] Although influenced by Bulgakov's turn to ecclesiology, Afanasiev clearly belonged to the *ressourcement* school; his future ecclesiological work would bear a deeply patristic imprint. He would remain at Saint-Serge for the rest of his life, and subsequent years saw the publication of many works, including *Church of the Holy Spirit* (1950) and *The Lord's Supper* (1952), as well as increasing involvement in the ecumenical movement, culminating in his participation as an official observer at the fourth and final session of Vatican II, which witnessed the mutual lifting of the excommunications of 1054 by Pope Paul VI and Ecumenical Patriarch Athenagoras.

Afanasiev's writings had been ecclesiological from the start, but it was only with his arrival at Saint-Serge and its deeply "eucharistic climate"[45] that he came upon his central insight: the church is radically eucharistic in its life and structures, to the extent that it is even created by the eucharist ("the eucharist makes the church"). Furthermore, the eucharist, in making Christ fully present to the eucharistic assembly, makes of the local church the church of God in its fullness; the local church is not simply a part of the universal church, but is its full realization in a given place. This eucharistic ecclesiology, as he terms it, was the practice of the ancient church and is seen most seminally in Ignatius of Antioch. It stands in radical opposition to universal ecclesiology, which conceives of the church as a "single organic whole,"[46] the Body of Christ, in which the local churches are parts of the universal whole. Beginning in 1934 with an essay in Russian on "Two Types of Ecclesiology" and continuing until his death, he constructed his thought largely on the contrast between these eucharistic and universal ecclesiologies, a contrast to which we now turn.

Universal ecclesiology has its roots, according to Afanasiev, in Cyprian of Carthage. Concerned about the maintenance of (visible) unity in an ever-growing and increasingly fractious church, the African bishop, a Roman by training and instinct, found his perhaps unconscious inspiration in the Roman Empire, which united the disparate provinces in the person of the emperor.[47] Cyprian found a more immediate foundation for his ecclesiology in Paul's image of the body and its limbs: the body is an organic whole, made up of limbs that cannot exist on their own. From this image Afanasiev derives the basic principle of universal ecclesiology:

> The church which exists in empirical reality is considered as being a single organism, which is the mystical Body of Christ. In this same empirical reality, this organism appears as being divided into parts, the local churches, that is to say, the communities of the faithful having a bishop as their head.[48]

In short, each local church is a *part* of the one, universal church, possessing ecclesial reality through its participation in the whole. And, as the unity and fullness of the church exist only on the universal level, each part, by definition, manifests such attributes only incompletely.[49]

How, then, is the unity of the universal church maintained? The episcopacy is both the sign and the safeguard of the church's unity: just as God is one, Christ is one, and the faith is one, so, too, is the episcopacy one, for "the chair of Peter is one, in which the origin of unity has been established."[50] As a successor of Peter, each bishop is a sign of unity only to the extent that he remains in communion with the other bishops; it is primarily belonging to the episcopal college, and not being head of a local church, that determines the bishop's function and role as sign of unity. The bishop, then, is the visible, "distinctive empirical sign" of the unity of the universal church, a sign that the local church belongs to the *Catholica*.[51] And, in turn, the church is united to the degree that the bishops remain in agreement; in this sense, the episcopacy is not simply the sign of unity, but also productive of it. The unity of the universal church and the unity of the episcopacy mutually reinforce each other.

Afanasiev, while wholly disagreeing with this universal ecclesiology (for reasons we will soon examine), nonetheless admits its logical consistency and argues that it demands a doctrine of primacy. He therefore faults Cyprian — and his latter-day followers — for failing to take universal ecclesiology to its logical conclusion: if each church should have one head, then the one universal church should have one bishop at its head: there should be only one bishop in the entire church. Instead, Orthodoxy and Catholicism have inverted this principle, holding that there are "many bishops in the [one] Church and each of them is at the head of a part of the church."[52] Orthodoxy puts the bishops as a single whole (the council) at the head of the universal church, while Catholicism makes one of them — the pope — the head. In respective fashion, both stop short of the logical, inevitable result of a fully universal ecclesiology: a kind of radical Ultramontanism, in which the pope alone is truly a bishop, while the other bishops are such only in name, serving in reality as his administrative assistants;[53] primacy is singular and absolute, resting in the Roman pontiff. That this is clearly a deformation of a sound doctrine of the church — eviscerating as it does the theology of the local church — leads Afanasiev to a consideration of another model: eucharistic ecclesiology.

Although often thought to be a modern development, eucharistic ecclesiology, Afanasiev claims, is the practice of the church of the first three centuries and finds its most fundamental expression in the letters of Ignatius of Antioch. Where universal ecclesiology's basic principle is "each local church is a *part* of the church of God," eucharistic ecclesiology holds that "each local church is the church of God in its *fullness,*" that is, the local church is truly fully one, holy, catholic, and apostolic.[54] This ecclesial fullness has its source in the fullness of Christ's presence in the eucharist, for each eucharistic celebration makes present the whole Christ, not simply part of Christ: where Christ and the eucharistic assembly are, there is the church.[55] Thus the sign of the local church is "the eucharistic assembly in which the Church of God finds its most complete expression,"[56] and its principle of unity is the eucharist. In addition, the nature of the eucharistic assembly necessarily includes the office of bishop, as there can be no eucharist without a president; episcopal ministry is, at root, eucharistic presidency in the local church of God. Where universal ecclesiology tends to place the bishop above his church by identifying him primarily with the episcopal college, eucharistic ecclesiology situates him within the eucharistic assembly, as its head, and only as its head does he become a member of the college. Accordingly, when "we speak of the eucharistic assembly, we speak of the bishop," and, in this manner, the bishop joins the eucharist as the "distinctive empirical sign" of the church.[57]

Moreover, lest one object that a multiplicity of authentic, full local churches of God would destroy the unity of the church, by rendering impossible the *one* church of God, Afanasiev states that Euclidean arithmetic is not, as it were, ecclesiological or eucharistic arithmetic: one plus one does not equal two, but one: "The plurality of the eucharistic celebration does not abolish its unity, just as the plurality of local churches does not abolish the unity of the Church of God. In ecclesiological matters, unity and plurality do not exclude each other, but on the contrary mutually complete each other."[58] One might add that neither does the plurality of bishops exclude their unity. In short, one and the same eucharist is celebrated throughout time and space, and one and the same church of God is fully present in each local church, because the Body of Christ is indivisibly present.[59]

That each local church, possessing fully the attributes of the church of God, is intrinsically autonomous ("contain[ing] in itself everything necessary to its life") and independent ("not depend[ing] on any other local church or bishop outside of itself")[60] does not, however, shut it off from communion with other local churches; self-sufficiency does not entail isolation. Each local church is connected to other churches on at least four levels: eucharist, reception, council, and priority. In the first and most fundamental place, because each eucharistic celebration makes fully present the *one* church of God, it follows that whatever happens in one church happens to all; the unity engendered by the eucharist binds together every church in the one, indivisible Body of Christ.[61] Second, through a process of reception, the local church accepts (or rejects) the actions or witness of another local church: one church bears witness to the witness of another, thereby affirming (or denying) that its actions accord with God's will for the church.[62] Third, a church council is not simply a potentially effective structure of communion, but a concrete expression of *sobornost* ("gathering together") and is thereby an integral part of the church's very nature.[63] In line with this Khomiakovian influence, Afanasiev insists that every council needs to include all sectors of the church and be received subsequently by the churches: a council is not a purely clerical affair, nor do its decisions have intrinsic authority; truth alone is the criteria, and inerrancy belongs to the church as a whole.[64] The post-Nicene church erred, in his view, by replacing the process of conciliar reception with juridical fiat, thus compromising the integrity of each local church.[65] Fourth, and perhaps most problematically, although each local church is absolutely equal in value because of its eucharistic fullness, some local churches have greater authority and exercise a priority of love and witness through their divine election.[66] In contrast to universal ecclesiology, wherein the bishop stands above his church and exercises his power over it and others (through councils and — depending upon the local church — metropolitan, patriarchal, and/or universal primacy), eucharistic ecclesiology renounces the imposition of primatial power in favor of a twofold priority of authority and love, which accrues to the church and to its bishop, through the church; primacy and priority are thus mutually exclusive.[67] Such a "church-in-priority," as Afanasiev terms it, realizes in a greater manner the presence of the church of God and thus can bear especially compelling, but never coercive, witness to God's will for the church.[68] Among the churches-in-priority, the church of Rome is the one that, in Ignatius of Antioch's words, presides in love. Although the church of Jerusalem was originally the church with the greatest authority, owing to its central role in salvation history, by the beginning of the second century, Rome, on account of the authority it held from the witness of Peter and Paul, had begun to emerge as the arbiter of apostolic faith, a church whose reception of a given decision or act was decisive for the churches as a whole;[69] Rome is greatest in love, not in power. Afanasiev logically concludes his treatment of Roman priority — and, by extension, his eucharistic ecclesiology — with the affirmation that the church of God should be directed by a local (not universal) church, the church of Rome, whose authority springs not from law or obligation, but from the witness of a love unto death.

The flaws in Afanasiev's ecclesiology fall into two primary categories: theological presuppositions and understandings of locality. Concerning the former, one first must question the harsh, even false antinomies his theology sets up between love and law, grace and law, love-harmony and institution, priority and primacy. Khomiakov's emphasis on mutual love to the exclusion of law is clearly evident here, as is Rudolf Sohm's dualism of law and spirit, as Meyendorff aptly notes.[70] Catholicism and, increasingly, Orthodoxy acknowledge that such dichotomies are overstated, even dangerously erroneous: structures are not necessarily inimical to mutual love, nor do law and rights necessarily conflict with the church's life in grace and truth. In this vein, a Catholic scholar has noted that Afanasiev's narrow focus on the liturgical celebration of the eucharist prevents him from seeing the eucharistic implications for the church's mission in the world, a mission of evangelization, transformation, and liberation that needs ecclesial structures to be truly effective;[71] structures and institutions can be vehicles of grace, even if the temptation always exists to turn them into ends in themselves. Second, Afanasiev's reading of Cyprian as the forefather of universal ecclesiology has been challenged by other scholars.[72] Without entering into an extended discussion, clearly any treatment of Cyprian has to take into account his practice of, and support for, conciliarity, an ecclesial practice with deep roots in the Northern African tradition. Third, as has been perceptively noted, Afanasiev's sense of history "seems to have stopped . . . at the end of the third century, when Christians had come to a real awareness that they were a worldwide religion and a significant force in the world."[73] One need not mount a defense of Constantinian Christianity to affirm that the increasingly global spread of Christianity necessitated a recasting of the church's structures of communion and harmony, and that the relative intimacy of a Mediterranean and Middle Eastern church could not be simply extrapolated to a larger church. Ironically, Afanasiev, whose strong eschatological awareness made him keenly aware of the relativities of history, may have absolutized the life and structures of the ante-Nicene church.

Afanasiev's conceptions of locality deserve scrutiny as well. In the first place, even granting Michael Plekon's argument that Afanasiev's critics have wrongly attacked his supposed "hyper-localism,"[74] it remains that the latter's repeated descriptions of the local church as autonomous and independent are ambiguous at best, confirmatory of criticism at worst. Where universal ecclesiology asserts that the universal church ontologically and temporally precedes the local church, Afanasiev's eucharistic ecclesiology appears to give the priority to the local church, thereby affirming that the local church can exist independently of other churches and that its ecclesial integrity obviates any such intrinsic link; the bonds of communion belong to the local church's *bene esse,* not its *esse.* One must grant, at least, that Afanasiev should have used such terms more carefully and precisely, especially since they concern the heart of his thesis. Moreover, the sad irony is that a one-sided emphasis on autonomy and independence can lead precisely to the jurisdictional conflicts and in-fighting he found so distasteful and even sinful in the Russian Diaspora and throughout Orthodoxy as a whole. Second, although he certainly brings out the church's essentially local nature in a manner inconceivable to Khomiakov's universalism, he nonetheless fails to see that such locality is not simply eucharistic, but cultural as well, embracing the whole range of human activity. One might say that, for Afanasiev, the church is in a place, but not of a place; his experience of nationalism and ecclesial autocephaly may have kept him from a fuller awareness of how human culture is the raw material of redemption and can enter into the life and customs of a truly local church; here, modern Catholic theology and ecclesiology has much to offer. In this sense, his theology of the local church remains incomplete, as it has a constricted conception of locality and catholicity.

Although still little known even in many theological circles, Afanasiev's recovery of the centrality of the eucharist for the church's life and structure has exercised a decisive influence on ecclesiological and ecumenical matters. As Aidan Nichols puts it, "a higher theology of the local church (*any* local church) can hardly be imagined: each is the whole Church in its own place, the total ecclesial mystery."[75] His eucharistic, patristic, and local ecclesiology corrected Khomiakov's weaknesses in these very areas, while at the same time preserving the latter's *sobornost* ecclesiology with its emphases on love, unity, and freedom. Afanasiev directly influenced Meyendorff, Schmemann, and Zizioulas, while also affecting the debates and documents of Vatican II.[76] In large measure, then, his eucharistic ecclesiology has set the terms of the contemporary ecumenical conversation. Admittedly one-sided in content and needlessly polemical in style at times, his insistence on the fullness of the local church's sacramental life is "perhaps the most original contribution of post–World War II Russian theology"[77] and remains a source to which all contemporary ecclesiology and ecumenism need return, even if it must ultimately be surpassed.

John Zizioulas (b. 1931): The Simultaneity of the One and the Many in Communion

Drawing in part upon the ecclesiologies of Khomiakov and Afanasiev, while seeking to overcome the exaggerated universalism of the former and the exaggerated localism of the latter, John Zizioulas has developed what stands as the most systematic and integrated Orthodox theology of the local church. Although Greek, Zizioulas has a deep affinity with Russian Orthodox theology and is acknowledged today by many as the premier ecclesiologist in all of Orthodoxy; his *Being as Communion* (1985) is perhaps the pivotal work of contemporary Orthodox ecclesiology, thoroughly integrating trinitarian, christological, ecclesiological, anthropological, and sacramental thought through the perspective of an ontology of communion. Ecclesiology has been his lifelong interest, extending back to his 1965 doctoral dissertation for the University of Athens, *The Unity of the Church in the Eucharist and the Bishop during the First Three Centuries,* and continuing to the present day with programmatic essays such as "The Church as Communion" and "Communion and Otherness."

Bound up with this interest in the church is Zizioulas's commitment to ecumenism. For several years in the 1960s and 1970s he was the executive secretary of the World Council of Churches' Faith and Order Commission and, in 1968, with John Meyendorff and Jean-Marie Tillard, worked on its document on worship. He remains active in the World Council of Churches, delivering, for instance, a keynote address in 1993 at the Faith and Order Conference at Santiago de Compostela. He has been a central participant as well in Orthodox-Catholic dialogue through both his formal involvement in the Joint International Commission for Theological Dialogue between the Orthodox and Catholic Churches from its inception in 1980 and his informal contacts and friendships, most especially with Jean-Marie Tillard, with whom he drafted several of the Dialogue's agreed statements. Currently metropolitan of Pergamon, he teaches at King's College, London, and at the University of Thessalonica and remains active ecumenically.

Throughout this career, three elements have structured his ecclesiology — God as Trinity, the reciprocal influence of Christ and the Spirit, and the theology of the local church — all cohering around the concept of communion. Zizioulas's ecclesiology begins with the insistence that if the church is the church *of God,* then we must first ask what kind of God this is: the mystery of the church is inconceivable apart from the mystery of God.[78] The central theme of Zizioulas's thought is communion, which has its source and pattern in the personal nature of God as Trinity. Drawing especially upon Athanasius and the Cappadocians, he argues that God *is* communion, a relational being who is always one and three simultaneously. Rejecting what he considers to be Western individualism in philosophy (Boethius's definition of the person as an "individual substance of rational nature") and theology (the scholastic division of the doctrine of God into the tracts "de Deo uno" and "de Deo trino"), Zizioulas holds that God's essence is *koinonia;* where the West defines the person as an individual, whose unique identity consists in its separation from another person, the East, as he sees it, stresses that the person is a relation, whose identity is found only in communion with other persons; one's uniqueness is found paradoxically in one's relatedness. Accordingly, in the patristic tradition, God is not an individual substance, who subsequently enters into communion, but is from the outset personal and relational:

> The ontological "principle" or "cause" of the being and life of God does not consist in the one substance of God but in the *hypostasis,* that is, *the person of the Father.* The one God is not the one substance but the Father, who is the "cause" both of the generation of the Son and of the procession of the Spirit.... Thus God as person—as the hypostasis of the Father—makes the one divine substance to be that which it is: the one God.[79]

God, therefore, is a communion of persons, in which identity and otherness mutually inhere; God is not first "one," then "three," but always both simultaneously. Each divine person has its distinctive mission, while also having such personal identity only through relation to the other divine persons; for example, the Son is Son precisely in his relation to the Father, for his person is what he receives from the Father. The Trinity thus reveals that otherness is not threatening to, but constitutive and generative of, unity and communion: the one and the many exist in perfect communion, wherein personal distinctness is realized only in mutual relation and vice versa.[80] This ontology and pattern of divine communion is, for Zizioulas, the only one possible for the communion of the church of God.

Moreover, because the church of God is also the Body of Christ and the Temple of the Holy Spirit, it follows for Zizioulas that ecclesiology must be formed as well by the integration and synthesis of christology and pneumatology, by the missions of the Word and Spirit. In contrast to any unwitting christomonism, Zizioulas argues that Christ's own identity is inconceivable apart from the Spirit; the Spirit is not simply the Spirit of *Christ,* but equally the *Spirit* of Christ. In the synoptic Gospels, for example, Jesus' identity as the Christ is made possible only through the working of the Spirit, be it by Jesus' conception in Matthew and Luke or by his baptism in Mark.[81]

The pneumatic constitution of Christ leads, in turn, to an eschatological and corporate christology. In the first place, Zizioulas states that if the Son becomes history through the incarnation, the Holy Spirit transcends or liberates from history by inaugurating the end-times: the Holy Spirit makes Christ an eschatological being, the Second Adam who is the first-fruits of salvation.[82] Second, a pneumatic christology leads to a corporate christology, in which the Holy Spirit, as the agent of communion, "de-individualizes" Christ and irreversibly links him to the community;[83] in short, there can no longer be a head without a body, no one without the many.[84] Moreover, a corporate Christology offsets even a "soft" christomonism in which the "one" of Christ preexists — and becomes only subsequently — the "many" through the Holy Spirit. Because the Holy Spirit is ontologically constitutive of Christ, it is futile — and destructive — not only to separate christology and pneumatology, but even to subordinate one to the other.[85] Their relationship must be both integrated and simultaneous.

Therefore, because the Holy Spirit is ontologically constitutive of Christ, it follows that it is also constitutive of the church.[86] As Zizioulas cleverly phrases it, if Christ *in*-stitutes the church as the Body of Christ, the Holy Spirit *con*-stitutes it both corporately and eschatologically at Pentecost.[87] That is, the Holy Spirit does not animate an already existing church (as in a "Last Supper" ecclesiology), but, as the principle of communion, makes it to be; the Spirit is less an ecclesial dynamism than an ecclesial essence, thoroughly integrating the one and the many, the head and the body, in the event of communion.[88] Moreover, Pentecost also makes the church an eschatological community, an icon of the Kingdom, whose "diagram," as Zizioulas writes, is "given in the Upper Room."[89] The Holy Spirit, as we have already described it, makes present the end-times in which, as the events of Pentecost reveal, the many are gathered as one and remain united in their difference: there is no one without the many, nor a one that precedes the many, but rather a simultaneity of the one and the many. In a christologically and pneumatologically integrated ecclesiology, then, there can be no question of priority. The one church and the many local churches cohere, for the "one Christ event takes the form of *events* (plural), which *are as primary ontologically* as the one Christ event itself."[90]

It remains now to examine how this trinitarian economy of communion is expressed in the church's central event: the eucharistic synaxis, which is at once communal and eschatological, local and catholic. The church is fundamentally the mystery of humanity's participation in the trinitarian life; ecclesial communion has no other source than divine communion. Zizioulas, following the early church, especially Ignatius of Antioch, sees such communion expressed most fully in the local church, which, celebrating the eucharist in a given place under the presidency of its bishop, makes Christ fully present and unites the church to all other local churches.

Three elements are primary for Zizioulas's theology of the local church: eucharist, episcopacy, and conciliarity. The central principle of the theology of the local church is that each eucharistic celebration makes Christ fully present, thereby bringing into communion the one and the many, the local and the universal, the human and the divine. Zizioulas makes this point clearly and programatically at the beginning of his essay "The Local Church in a Perspective of Communion":

> The basic ecclesiological principle applying to the notion of the local Church ... is that of the identification of the Church with the eucharistic community. Orthodox ecclesiology is based on the idea that wherever there is the eucharist there is the Church in its fullness as the Body of Christ. The concept of the

> local church derives basically from the fact that the eucharist is celebrated at a given place and comprises by virtue of its catholicity all the members of the Church dwelling in that place.[91]

The eucharistic celebration, as this definition indicates, is local and catholic. Its locality is both geographical and cultural. Geographically, the church of God is always rooted in a given place, as the Pauline letters indicate: the church of God at Corinth, the church of God at Antioch. It cannot exist in the ether, as it were, but is always present when the eucharistic community is gathered "in the same place," a recurrent phrase in the New Testament. This gathering of the local church also incarnates itself in local culture and life, "tak[ing] root in a particular local situation with all its natural, social, cultural and other characteristics."[92] Such inculturation must be a discerning one, however, for the world is "fallen and disintegrating" and stands in need of the unity and redemption offered by the eschaton and eucharist; Zizioulas avoids here, for instance, Khomiakov's uncritical assimilation of Russian and Slavic culture.[93]

The local eucharistic community is catholic on several levels. In the first place, its catholicity is christological: the church is the body of Christ, and every eucharist makes the whole Christ fully present in the body. Echoing both the Fathers and Afanasiev, Zizioulas writes that each eucharistic community reveals "not part of Christ but the whole Christ and not a partial unity but the full eschatological unity of all in Christ. It [is] *a concretization and localization of the general.*"[94] In short, where the catholic Christ is, there is the catholic church. Second, christological catholicity is possible only if placed in the context of the eschatological communion fostered by the Holy Spirit.[95] In particular, the catholicity or fullness of presence characteristic of the Body of Christ is possible only by a constant epiclesis, or invocation of the Holy Spirit, who, as Zizioulas never tires of repeating, creates communion.[96] In calling out for the descent of the Spirit upon the gifts, the eucharistic community also calls out for its descent upon the church itself. And so the church's catholicity is not a static possession — a temptation of a christomonic ecclesiology — but a dynamic reality for which the community must ceaselessly pray.[97] Third, eucharistic catholicity is anthropological. Patterned on divine communion, the eucharist is respectful, even encouraging, of otherness. The eschatological communion engendered by the eucharist transcends all human division and brings all of creation into communion with God and itself; it is a foretaste of the Kingdom.[98] The eucharistic and ecclesial form of unity is communion, not uniformity or absolute difference, and the inclusiveness of the Kingdom — sacramentalized or iconicized in the eucharistic community — leads Zizioulas to criticize the practices of a private eucharist (a contradiction in terms) and a eucharist celebrated for a limited group such as students or children, for their erosion of communion.[99] Again, communion and catholicity demand the continuous integration of the one and the many.

Understood in this christological, pneumatological, and anthropological framework, then, it becomes evident that the church is necessarily local and catholic, and that this catholicity "does not mean anything else but the *wholeness* and *fullness* and *totality* of the Body of Christ 'exactly as'...it is portrayed in the eucharistic community."[100] The eucharist thus appears not as one devotion among others, or simply as a cultic activity, but as "the foyer which concentrates in itself the entire mystery of salvation and spreads it throughout all the dimensions of ecclesial life,"[101] making present Christ and the Kingdom. Imaging the simultaneous oneness and multiplicity of both the Trinity and the pneumatic Christ, the eucharistic community cannot but be a communion of the One and the Many at the same time.[102] And, in sum, a eucharistic ecclesiology cannot but be a theology of the local, catholic church.

At the head of the local church is the bishop, who, as its "head and center," exercises a ministry of unity.[103] Because the church's unity is a gift given by God through the eucharist and the Spirit of communion, the bishop does not create unity, but rather oversees and protects it: he is the "one in whom the 'many' united...become 'one.' "[104] Responsible for the communion of the "many," he must promote the otherness that is constitutive of communion, while also ensuring that such diversity be supportive of ecclesial unity; Zizioulas writes that "all diversity in the community must somehow pass through a ministry of unity,"[105] if it is not to lead to division.

The preeminent exercise of the bishop's ministry of unity is his presidency of the eucharistic assembly, which itself has the effect (or *res*) of unity; in this, his presidency is the culmination and fullness of the communion of the "one" and the "many."[106] Furthermore, the nature of the eucharistic assembly shows that episcopal ministry must always be exercised within, and not above, the local church; the "one" must not be placed outside of the "many," even though the bishop is always the "first."[107] In other words, communion requires an organic bond between the minister and the community. Finally, episcopal ministry is at once local and universal.[108] Locally, the bishop is of course the minister of unity, quintessentially so in the eucharist, which is the sacrament of unity. Universally, the bishop is part of the episcopal college, through which he is connected with other bishops in time (with the apostles, the previous occupants of his chair, and those who will preside) and space (with all the bishops of the other local churches in the world).[109]

The simultaneity of locality-universality and unity-multiplicity in the eucharist (the one eucharist celebrated in many eucharists) and the episcopacy (the bishop is both head of a local church and member of the episcopal college) points, in turn, to the essentially conciliar or synodal nature of the church. Conciliarity is the " '*sine qua non conditio*' for the catholicity of the Church,"[110] because through it every local church is recognized as fully ecclesial, that is, catholic. On the theological level, conciliarity is an expression of God's own communion, in which oneness and multiplicity reciprocally involve each other, and of human participation in such communion through the eucharist (which, again, is always the one eucharist celebrated in many churches).[111] Structurally, conciliarity gives institutional expression to such communion by affirming that (1) each local church, as a eucharistic community, is equal in dignity to other churches and has a right and duty to participate in a council, and (2) such conciliarity respect the integrity and legitimate otherness of each local church.[112] A council, then, arises from the demands of communion and seeks to treat those matters which pertain to the communion *between* the local churches. The council thus is not a superstructure above the local churches, but rather an "internal" sign and instrument of their communion. Zizioulas thus finds the term "universal church" misleading, as it seems to posit a reality existing apart from or above the local churches. Instead, he sees the church's unity or oneness as the communion of churches, in which each local church is the church of God in its fullness, although not exhaustively: "Each eucharistic community [is], therefore, in full unity with the rest by virtue *not of an external superimposed structure* but of the whole Christ represented in each of them."[113]

On account of this simultaneity of the one and the many in divine communion, Zizioulas rejects any notion of ecclesial priority, be it of the local or the universal church. On the one hand, he thinks it is clear that the conciliar and eucharistic nature of the church prohibits any kind of universal priority in which the many would be collapsed into or subjugated by, and not integrated within, the one; this, he argues, has been the perennial temptation of Roman Catholicism. On the other, arguing primarily against Afanasiev, he rejects local priority, because it would place the many before the one — or assert that a local church could exist independently of ecclesial communion — and consequently compromise each local church's essential relation — through eucharist and ordination[114] — to other churches; the relationship between local churches would then be one of confederation, not communion. Put perhaps too simply, ecclesial conciliarity is neither curial nor confederal, but communional.

Finally, the conciliarity or synodality of the church necessitates a ministry of primacy within the various groupings of churches: the bishop within his local church, the metropolitan within the local churches of a given region, and, ultimately, the papacy within the communion of all local churches.[115] Throughout his treatment of primacy and conciliarity, Zizioulas returns to the thirty-fourth Apostolic Canon,[116] which affirms that the bishops of a region must recognize "one" (*protos*) as their head (*kephale*) and do nothing apart from him, while the "one" must always act in concert with the "many." The papacy is obviously the most contentious form of primacy, but Zizioulas, with several qualifications, upholds its necessity.[117] First, it must not interfere in the internal jurisdiction and affairs of the local churches. Second, the primatial prerogative belongs to the local church of Rome and, through it alone, to its bishop. Third, the primacy must be exercised within, not above, communion and conciliarity. Just as the local bishop must stand within his local church, so too must the primate stand within the communion of local churches. Placing him outside of it ruptures communion between the one and the many. In an ecclesiology of communion, then, pyramidal conceptions of local and interlocal authority, ministry, and structures have no place, for they make such authority extrinsic to communion and erect structures outside such communion.[118] As the simultaneous communion of the one and the many, the church is intrinsically conciliar and primatial — each calling forth and requiring the other.

The merits of Zizioulas's theology of the local church are evident, especially in relation to Khomiakov and Afanasiev. While retaining Khomiakov's emphases upon the bonds of communion and love that comprise the church's deepest identity as *sobornost,* he follows Afanasiev in correcting Khomiakov's relatively sparse scriptural and patristic foundation, excessive universalism, and deficient eucharistic theology; Zizioulas's work is undoubtedly a patristically determined local and eucharistic ecclesiology. Moreover, while clearly adopting the central themes of Afanasiev's eucharistic ecclesiology — the eucharist as ecclesially constitutive, the local church as the fullness (and not as part) of the church of God — he corrects several of its abuses.[119] In the first place, Zizioulas's argument for the simultaneity of the local and universal churches is solidly rooted in trinitarian theology (which is not as well developed in Afanasiev) and enables him to avoid Afanasiev's prioritizing of the local church. This simultaneity, in turn, helps Zizioulas to articulate more clearly the bonds and institutional structures — both eucharistic and episcopal — of communion between the local churches. There is little question here of Afanasiev's ambiguity over the "autonomous" and "independent" nature of the local church. It remains, I believe, that while Afanasiev undoubtedly holds *that* each local church must be in communion with other churches, he remains unclear as to *how* this communion is to be realized or sustained. By contrast, Zizioulas is able to affirm both that each local eucharistic community with its bishop is fully the church and that the local church's eucharistic, conciliar, and episcopal essence makes Afanasiev's use of "autonomous" and "independent" misleading at best, indicative of "self-sufficiency" at worst.[120] Finally, in distinction to Afanasiev's largely eucharistic notion of locality (the eucharist is celebrated in a given locality, in a given local church), Zizioulas develops better the cultural nature of the church's locality, embracing — not uncritically, as baptism involves in part dying to the world — the cultures of the world and its people. The church's mission to the world is one of incarnation, inculturation, and recapitulation,[121] and each local church carries out that mission by ensuring that

> the saving event of Christ [take] root in a particular local situation with all its natural, social, cultural, and other characteristics which make up the life and thought of the people living in that place.... If it is to be truly local... it must

absorb and use all the characteristics of a given local situation and not impose an alien culture on it.[122]

And yet, difficulties remain in his theology of the local church, perhaps due more to his Orthodox ethos than to his Orthodox theology. Foremost among these is his realized eschatology and its implications for catholicity, locality, and ecclesiology. His conception of the catholicity brought about by the Holy Spirit — the one who makes present the eschaton in history — comprises not only the presence of the whole Christ, but also the transcendence of all human division in Christ; Christ is the one in whom "there is no Jew or Greek . . . " This may, however, have the unwitting effect of relativizing local, cultural, and social differences to the degree that they seem to disappear entirely in the eschaton.[123] The question thus remains whether the transcendence of difference unwittingly leads to uniformity rather than unity. If God's eternal being is eternally threefold, then why should a redeemed and integrated humanity be any less diverse, even in the Kingdom? In other words, does Zizioulas's eschatology preclude any enduring and ultimate place for the human otherness he otherwise defends so eloquently?

In terms of ecclesiology, a realized eschatology risks identifying the church and the Kingdom to the extent of obscuring that the church remains an imperfect community journeying in history. Zizioulas willingly acknowledges the church is on pilgrimage in history, but does not seem to follow this history to its consequences. His "maximalistic ecclesiology" need not lead to triumphalism,[124] but it does render the church susceptible to pride and self-satisfaction, and it can overlook the fact that the church's eucharists are often signs of ecclesial and cultural division, not unity. Although the "first-fruits" of the Kingdom, the church remains a community marked by sin and is "not yet" the Kingdom in its fullness; eschatology has not yet fully eclipsed history. As a theologian and now as an Orthodox bishop, Zizioulas is keenly aware of these problems, so these difficulties in his thought may perhaps be ones of emphasis or tendency, rather than of substance. At any rate, a realized ecclesiology demands of the church a deep humility and repentance that goes beyond purely individual responsibility.[125]

Lastly, he remains unclear about the nature and structures of authority in the church, tending to see primatial — especially papal — jurisdiction as inevitably interference in the affairs of the local church.[126] One may hear echoes of Khomiakov and Afanasiev, with their distinction between love and law — a distinction that often tends toward separation. Zizioulas does not commit such errors — and his careful writings on councils, succession, and primacy bear witness to his appreciation of the need for structures of authority in the church — but he fails, at least from a Catholic perspective, to see how papal primacy is interior to each local church; that while such primacy must not usurp the integrity, rights, and prerogatives of each local church, it also can contribute to each church's proper functioning. The need for papal primacy to be exercised, as Zizioulas argues, in a synodal and communional manner does not necessarily conflict with its involvement in a given local church, if that church's actions harmfully affect the communion of all the churches; when acting with the "many," the "one" is not an interloper in the life of the local church. Communion, in fact, demands such primacy.

We can say, by way of conclusion, that ecclesiology is the crown of Zizioulas's theology, the "tip of the iceberg," as it were, since it rests on a deep theological and ontological base of communion — much of which is not apparent at first glance. The local church, through its eucharistic celebration, is the sacrament or icon of divine communion and is relational in identity, structure, ministry, authority, mission, time, and space; nothing escapes the integration wrought by the communion of the one and the many in the Trinity.[127] His theology of the local church is not without its faults, as has been indicated, but it does succeed in uniting the local and the universal, the conciliar and the primatial, the institutional and the charismatic, to a degree unequaled in Orthodox thought. And it is a theology that enables him to draw upon the best of Khomiakov and Afanasiev, while also to enter into a fruitful dialogue with other Christian communities, especially Catholicism. His friendship and labors with Jean-Marie Tillard bear witness to such a dialogue, and the development of the theology of the local church in Catholicism is our next concern.

Chapter Two

THE DEVELOPMENT OF THE THEOLOGY OF THE LOCAL CHURCH IN NINETEENTH- AND TWENTIETH-CENTURY CATHOLICISM

THE SEEDS of a renewed theology of the local church in Catholicism were sown by the nineteenth-century Tübingen theologian Johann Adam Möhler (1796–1838), whose *Unity in the Church* synthesized German Idealism and the ecclesiology of the church's first three centuries.[1] He recovered a sense of the church as a living organism or body animated by the Holy Spirit, and his deeply patristic — especially Ignatian — sense of episcopacy and catholicity opened a path for the development of a theology of the local church. With the exception of Dom Adrien Gréa's *De l'Église et sa divine constitution* (1885), however, the local church remained virtually unexamined for decades.[2] Only with the scriptural and historical *ressourcement* of the twentieth century, particularly through its retrieval of the image of the Mystical Body of Christ, did matters begin to stir again.

Emile Mersch (1890–1940), Lucien Cerfaux (1883–1968), Ludwig Hertling (1892–1980), Sebastian Tromp (1889–1975), and Pope Pius XII (1876–1958) in *Mystici Corporis Christi* all opened a path for the great flowering of communion ecclesiologies in the 1940s, 1950s, and 1960s. Among those prominent in this regard were Yves Congar (1904–95), Henri de Lubac (1896–1991), and Jérôme Hamer (1916–97); Congar's work especially bore the clear imprint both of Möhler's thought and of ecumenical contacts with Orthodoxy. Vatican II itself set forth an emergent ecclesiology of communion and theology of the local church (for example, *Sacrosanctum concilium* #41; *Lumen gentium* #1–4, 23, 26; *Christus Dominus* #11), and, in the post-conciliar era, Leonardo Boff (b. 1938), Pope Benedict XVI (b. 1927), and Jean-Marie Tillard have been among the most prominent exponents of the movement, albeit with often highly different — even contradictory — emphases.

In a sense, then, it is therefore more accurate to speak of theologies of the local church and ecclesiologies of communion. All, however, share a vision of the local church as a sacramental community, whose being is grounded in the communal life of the Trinity and realized most fully in the eucharist. This chapter will examine the renewal of theology of the local church in modern Catholicism through an exploration of three seminal theologians and events: its roots in the work of Johann Adam Möhler, its growth in the writings of Yves Congar, and its magisterial recognition in the documents of Vatican II. Contemporary theological interest in the theology of the local church invariably touches upon these three persons and events.

Johann Adam Möhler (1796–1838): Tübingen and the Fathers — The First Modern Catholic Ecclesiology of Communion

Johann Adam Möhler is the catalytic figure in the renewal of modern Catholic ecclesiology. In response to the increasingly juridical ecclesiologies emerging out of the late Middle Ages and the Counter-Reformation, represented classically by Robert Bellarmine (1542–1621), and to the legacy of the Enlightenment, Möhler set forth the first modern Catholic ecclesiology of communion. His major ecclesiological works, *Unity in the Church* (1825)[3] and *Symbolism* (1832–38),[4] synthesized patristics and modern philosophy in presenting the church as a communion both human and divine, rooted in God's own life and finding visible expression in the sacraments and ordained ministry. Although his thought underwent significant change by the time he wrote *Symbolism,* moving from a more pneumatological approach to a more christological one, its signal contribution remained constant: it restored to Catholic ecclesiology a properly theological and supernatural grounding, one rooted in the missions of the Son and the Holy Spirit, in contrast to the more juridical and sociological ecclesiologies of his time.[5] And so, although he wrote little on the theology of the local church, his ecclesiology of communion nonetheless set in motion a process that would bear fruit at Vatican II and beyond.

Möhler was born in 1796, during a period of extraordinary change in European history: the Enlightenment was underway, Romanticism and Idealism were emerging, and the effects of the French Revolution were only beginning to be felt. After an early philosophical and theological apprenticeship in Ellwangen, Germany, he completed his theological studies at Tübingen and was ordained a priest in 1819. Following a short period of pastoral work, he returned to Tübingen in 1820 and began teaching church history, metaphysics, and canon law. Soon appointed a lecturer (*Privatdozent*) in church history, he undertook in 1822–23 the then standard study trip to various theological faculties, of which Berlin most impressed him. There he encountered the Protestant church historian Johann August Neander, whose knowledge of and respect for the Fathers, sense for the spiritual realities within history, grasp of the unity or wholeness of all existence, awareness of the "commonly lived experience of Christian truth over the centuries,"[6] and affirmation of Tübingen's insights into the working of the Holy Spirit in the hearts of the believing community were all decisive for the young theologian.[7] Returning to Tübingen, Möhler resumed teaching and began the work that would lead to the publication of *Unity in the Church* in 1825. Throughout these early years of study and research, he drew upon several streams of thought. Above all, Tübingen gave him, notably through his teacher Johann Sebastian von Drey (1777–1853), a theological approach emphasizing historical research, dialogue with secular philosophy and culture, and the renewal of a vital Christianity and church.[8] In turn, this constructive engagement with tradition and culture led Möhler to an encounter with Romanticism and Idealism; the former appears in his work as a concern for community and the primacy of life over thought, the latter through attentiveness to subjectivity, the relationship of the one and the many, and the organic nature of community.[9] Subsequent years saw the publication, in 1827, of *Athanasius der Grosse und die Kirche seiner Zeit, besonders in Kampfe mit dem Arianismus* (Athanasius the Great and the church of his time, especially in the struggle with Arianism), a key transitional work which led to a deeper christological orientation in his ecclesiology, and *Symbolism* in 1832. Weakened by poor health, he resigned his teaching post in 1838 and was unable to complete the fifth revision of *Symbolism* before his death that same year.

Möhler did not develop a substantial theology of the local church as such, but he did set forth the principles of an ecclesiology of communion that would enable its future development, notably in the works of Congar and in Vatican II. *Unity in the Church,* considered today to be his most insightful work, presents the church as a living organism of love, animated and sustained by the Holy Spirit given at Pentecost. Five aspects of the *Unity* will be crucial for the development of the theology of the local church: a properly theological and pneumatological ecclesiology, the intrinsically communal nature of Catholicism, ecclesial unity as unity in diversity, qualitative catholicity, and episcopacy as the service of unity. Foremost is his resolutely theological, especially pneumatological, ecclesiology, which envisions the church as an organic whole, whose principle of life is the Holy Spirit. In the *Unity* he stresses that Catholic ecclesiology, in its polemics against the Reformation and Enlightenment, has typically emphasized one-sidedly the church's visible and associative nature; the classic, if now overused, instance is Bellarmine's definition of the church as a community as visible as the Kingdom of France or the Republic of Venice. Möhler does not deny such visibility, going so far as to write that "the formation of the visible Church is . . . the greatest act of believers,"[10] but argues that the church's deepest nature is spiritual, proceeding from God's own life through the Holy Spirit:

> Before the time of Christ the Spirit that forms, quickens, and unites the totality of believers descended only haltingly and sporadically, here and there, on individuals. As a result no common, spiritual, or religious life could be established: everything was a special and peculiar case. Following the great and miraculous descent of the Spirit upon the apostles and the whole Christian congregation, which with this descent properly began in a true and living way

> at this time, the same divine Spirit would never again leave believers, would never come again but would *continually be present.* Because the Spirit fills her, the Church, the totality of believers that the Spirit forms, is the unconquerable treasure of the new life principle, ever renewing and rejuvenating herself, the uncreated source of nourishment for all.[11]

This passage encapsulates the essence of Möhler's early ecclesiology of communion: the pneumatic, Pentecostal origin and nature of the church, its organic character as "embodied love,"[12] and thus its dynamic, living nature. The church is visible, but only as the expression of the life of the Spirit. Furthermore, although less developed in the *Unity,* the church is also christological, in that believers are united to each other and to God through their reconciliation in Christ.[13] And, as both the Son and the Holy Spirit have the mission of leading the community of believers back to the Father, the church is therefore fundamentally a communion in the triune, divine life.[14]

Second, sharing in this divine communion, the church is intrinsically communal in its life and thought. In the first place, the Christian's life comes only through the church and the Spirit which forms it;[15] no one becomes a Christian by his or her own effort. Rather, the believer is first attracted by the witness of another, hears the Word preached by another, is baptized by another, and receives communion from another.[16] The believer's thought is equally communal. Möhler holds that thought springs from life, that Christianity is a life before it is a concept, and that this life claims the whole person.[17] Accordingly, knowledge of Christ and the church is possible only from within the believing community.[18] The outside observer can grasp only an isolated, cold, abstract concept and is unable to integrate it within the living thought of the church, i.e., tradition. Moreover, since God can be known only in the whole, heresy results from the egotism and selfishness of the one who takes the individual principle to an extreme, preferring his or her own counsel and insight to that of the church.[19] Mistakenly believing that a detached, "free" "objectivity" apart from faith is necessary for true knowledge,[20] the heretic "attempt[s] to discover Christianity by mere thought... without consideration for the common Christian life and that which arises from it."[21]

Möhler's rejection of heresy does not, however, lead him to ecclesial and doctrinal uniformity. The church's unity is rather a unity in diversity, which embraces legitimate and productive differences. Such difference is inscribed in the very constitution of the church through the action of the Holy Spirit, who distributes different charisms to the various members of the Body. The Spirit engenders communion, not uniformity.[22] Furthermore, Möhler helpfully distinguishes between antithesis and contradiction: the former creates a productive tension which issues forth in clarification and greater knowledge, while the latter leads only to disunity and sectarianism. For instance, one encounters in the New Testament a variety of theological and stylistic approaches: Paul is speculative and dialectical, while John is mystical and interior; the two do not contradict, but complement, each other and bring out the other's strengths.[23] Heresy, however, leads to contradiction by isolating a doctrine and making it a putative rule of faith.[24] Tertullian, to use another of Möhler's examples, prized sexual abstinence — certainly a potential virtue — to the extent of condemning marriage; Clement of Alexandria, in contrast, saw both as divine charisms and allowed for a rightful diversity, seeing each discipline as the antithesis of the other.[25] In sum, the Spirit's gift to the church is life, and life as a spiritual organism composed of different charisms. Diversity in life and thought is thus part of Christianity, and is to be promoted to the extent that it is tested against, and received by, the believing community.

The church's theological, communal, and plural dimensions cohere in its catholicity. In contrast to a quantitative catholicity, which emphasizes the sheer numbers of believers or the worldwide reach of the church — classically expressed in Augustine's battles with the Donatists — Möhler, drawing upon Ignatius of Antioch, Clement of Alexandria, and Cyprian, stresses a qualitative catholicity, focusing on the wholeness and fullness of God's presence in the church. Theologically and pneumatically, "since the Spirit of the whole is in every part of the great whole because it will be the same in each part, it is called Catholic."[26] Communally, catholicity is the "organic coherence of all believers."[27] And, plurally, the Catholic Church possesses "unity in diversity in such a way that it cannot be dissolved without the parts that make up the whole being destroyed by such dissolution."[28] One sees in Möhler's discussion a particularly fine illustration of how his patristic *ressourcement* enabled him to reach back beyond Counter-Reformation ecclesiology's preoccupation with the church's visibility and geographic universality, so as to recover a more theological and spiritual understanding of the church. Although Möhler does not himself develop the implications of qualitative catholicity for the theology of the local church, his work will, especially through Congar, prove to be one of the most important elements in its future development.

Finally, ecclesial communion finds special expression and visibility in the episcopacy. Möhler examines the church's ordained ministry in a nuanced manner, somewhat surprising for the order of its presentation. Rather than beginning, as did many tracts of his time, with Peter's reception of the keys and then proceeding downward from papal power to the bishops, he moves in the opposite direction, building upward from the local bishop to the metropolitan and, finally, to the episcopal college and to the papacy. The bishop is primarily the visible expression and guarantor of ecclesial unity. His office is an expression and "image" of the believers' desire for unity:

> The bishop is thus the uniting of believers made visible in a specific place, the love of believers for one another made personal, the manifestation and living center point of the Christian disposition striving toward unity. Because the perception of this union is continually given in the bishop, he is the love of

> the Christians themselves coming to consciousness and the means to make this firm [original passage italicized].[29]

His office is not one of rights or of powers, but of service: he has "responsibility for the whole congregation" and is "a servant of all."[30] In addition, although he "does not act on the orders of the people" as a mere delegate would,[31] he stands always *in* the community, never above or apart from it; there is an organic compenetration between the bishop and his church, as expressed by Cyprian's claim that "the bishop is in the Church, and the Church is in the bishop."[32] Moreover, the episcopacy as a whole builds up and represents the unity of the "great visible whole"[33] that is the church; it is not itself the essence of the church, but the expression of the "concentration of love" or "embodied love" that constitutes the church.[34] And, ultimately, the pope is the "living image" or "personally existing reflection" of both the episcopacy's and the entire church's unity.[35] At every level of authority, then, Möhler's balanced exposition is remarkable for its time. He avoids maximalist claims of episcopal and papal authority and consistently places the episcopacy within the community and at its service. As a ministry of unity, the unity that is the very principle of Catholicism, the episcopate is the capstone of Möhler's ecclesiology of communion.

Möhler would never reject the fundamental insights of the *Unity,* but he soon came to refine them. His study of Athanasius led him to see that the *Unity* was susceptible to pantheistic and anti-hierarchical misinterpretations, and also lacked a substantial christological base. The work that resulted from these labors, *Athanasius* (1827) gave a decided — and lasting — christological emphasis to his theology,[36] which would then be developed more fully in *Symbolism* (1832, five editions through 1838). This latter work especially, although retaining strong organic and communional qualities,[37] may be seen as an effort to highlight those elements underemphasized or underdeveloped in the *Unity:* the christological, human, visible, exterior, quantitative, and hierarchical. Two quotations suffice to establish its basic framework:

> By the Church on earth, Catholics understand the visible community of believers, founded by Christ, in which, by means of an enduring apostleship, established by him, and appointed to conduct all nations, in the course of ages, back to God, the works wrought by him during his earthly life, for the redemption and sanctification of mankind, are, under the guidance of the spirit, continued to the end of the world.
>
> Thus, to *a visible society of men,* is this great, important, and mysterious work entrusted. The ultimate reason of the visibility of the Church is to be found in the *incarnation* of the Divine Word.... The Deity, having manifested its action in Christ according to an *ordinary human fashion,* the form also in which His work was to be continued, was thereby traced out. The preaching of his doctrine needed now a *visible, human* medium.... The Church, [Christ's] permanent manifestation, is at once divine and human — she is the union of both.[38]

> The episcopate, the continuation of the apostleship, is accordingly revered as a Divine institution: not less so, and even, on that very account, the Pope, who is the center of unity, and the head of the episcopate. If the episcopate is to form a corporation, outwardly as well as inwardly bound together, in order to unite all believers into one harmonious life, which the Catholic church so urgently requires; it stands in need of a centre, whereby all may be held together and firmly connected.[39]

Several differences from the *Unity* are immediately apparent in these passages. Möhler has obviously moved from a pneumatocentric ecclesiology to a christocentric one, thereby stressing the church's human elements of visibility and exteriority; the church's life and structures stand under the logic of the Incarnation. Second, the hierarchy's divine institution by Christ contrasts with the *Unity*'s argument that the episcopacy is generated by the inner need and impulse of believers for unity. Third, the *Symbolism*'s ecclesiology is strongly universalistic, centered in the papacy and conceiving of the particular churches as a "helpless, shapeless mass" tending toward dissolution and contradiction.[40] Only the pope as "visible head" can secure the unity of the various parts of the church; the pope thus appears more as the foundation of ecclesial unity, rather than as its crown or summit. Fourth, Möhler envisions authority pyramidally, flowing downward from the apostles to the bishops and from the pope to the bishops, and insists on the infallibility that accrues to such authority; one reads that, in the absence of tradition and authority, there would be "no certainty and security, but only doubt and probability."[41] He accordingly emphasizes the doctrinal aspect of the bishop's authority much more strongly than he did in the *Unity;* the bishop appears in the *Symbolism* more as teacher than as shepherd or servant (although such teaching authority is certainly in the service of unity).[42]

Because of his premature death, Möhler never had the opportunity to develop more fully the ecclesiological synthesis of pneumatology and christology. As a result, a certain one-sidedness pervades his entire work: *Unity in the Church*'s imbalanced pneumatological emphasis can obscure the distinction between the Holy Spirit and the communal spirit of believers and also diminish the institutional nature of the church, while the *Symbolism*'s christomonism tends toward the divinization of the earthly church and exaggerated claims of ecclesial authority. Moreover, neither work presents an explicit theology of the local church. The *Unity* gestures in this direction through its presentation of the bishop and his diocesan community, but one looks in vain for a consideration of the eucharistic and cultural dimensions of locality. Both works, be they organic or institutional, present a universalistic ecclesiology.

And still, Möhler's ecclesiological achievements remain formidable. Foremost is the theological foundation he restored to ecclesiology after centuries of controversy-induced neglect; he perceived correctly that the mystery of the church is inseparable and unintelligible apart from the mystery of God.

This theological renewal led him, in turn, to the ecclesiology of communion; the Christian God is triune, and the church participates in God's own communion through the missions of the Son and the Holy Spirit. Third, although set forth only in the *Unity,* Möhler planted the seeds for a renewal of the episcopacy by refusing to separate the bishop from his community and insisting upon the diaconal essence of his authority. Lastly, his theological method was at once traditional and modern, drawing upon the best of the Fathers as well as the currents of modern thought. It was precisely this dual movement of *ressourcement* and *aggiornamento* that would be adopted by the great Catholic theologians of the twentieth century and by modern Catholicism's greatest event, the Second Vatican Council.

The great irony of Möhler's thought is that his two major works engendered such different legacies. The *Symbolism,* which had far greater impact than the *Unity* in the century following his death in 1838, helped to shape the Roman School, whose members — most notably Giovanni Perrone (1794–1876), Carlo Passaglia (1812–87), Johann Baptist Franzelin (1816–86), and Klemens Schrader (1820–75) — found inspiration in Möhler's idea of Christ's "continuing incarnation" in the church to espouse Roman centralization and papal authority.[43] Schrader, in particular, exercised significant influence at Vatican I. The *Unity,* which was eclipsed upon the publication of the *Symbolism,* was rediscovered only in the 1930s through the labors of such figures as Pierre Chaillet, Yves Congar, and Josef Rupert Geiselmann. Each found in it a vital, organic, traditional, and spiritual ecclesiology of communion, so often lacking in the neoscholastic manuals of the time. Although, as Congar wrote, the *Unity* succeeds more by its "intuitions" than its "precisions,"[44] it nonetheless served as a foundational text for the renewal of Catholic ecclesiology in the twentieth century. Its ecclesiology of communion is Möhler's contribution to the theology of the local church.

Yves Congar (1904–95): Pioneer of the Ecclesiology of Communion and Ecumenism, Herald of Vatican II

Yves Congar is the most significant Catholic ecclesiologist since Robert Bellarmine (1542–1621). His ecclesiological *ressourcement,* ranging from scripture and liturgy through Aquinas to Möhler and modern Orthodoxy, issued forth in an ecclesiology of communion at once deeply Catholic and ecumenical. One of the most influential voices at Vatican II, his pioneering work on the church, laity, church reform, ecumenism, and missionary activity entered into the common vocabulary and authoritative teaching of the Catholic Church. Similarly, his ecumenical involvement, both formal and informal, represented a breakthrough in Catholic attitudes toward other Christian communities.

Moreover, it was this confluence of ecclesiology and ecumenism that allowed him to develop one of the first modern Catholic theologies of the local church. His patristic and historical grounding made him aware of the West's rich ecclesiological heritage, while his contacts with the Russian Orthodox émigré community in France helped him to grasp more fully the local, catholic, and sacramental — especially eucharistic — nature of the church. This meeting of East and West provided the matrix for his exploration of the theology of the local church. Although the local church was never the center of his thought, as with Afanasiev, and thus never received extensive analysis, Congar nonetheless viewed it as a promising subject, offering new insight into communion, catholicity, sacramentality, and the relationship of collegiality and primacy. Our study of his ecclesiology will be limited to the pre-conciliar era for two reasons. First, as the next section of this chapter examines the Second Vatican Council, his thought is of interest here insofar as it precedes and anticipates Vatican II. Second, his post-conciliar theology, while evolving as is natural after an event of such magnitude, remained in deep, fundamental continuity with his earlier efforts; its development is largely organic and the differences are ones of degree, not of kind.

Congar was born in 1904 in the Sedan, a northern French region of mixed ethnicity and religion — a factor of central importance for the future ecumenist — whose inhabitants were known for their austerity, sense of duty, and strong work ethic.[45] Having entered the Dominicans in 1925, he was ordained a priest in 1930, and spent his ordination retreat meditating on John 17; it was there that he recognized and committed himself to the vocation of church unity. His master at Le Saulchoir, the French Dominican theologate, was Marie-Dominique Chenu, who pioneered the historical study of Thomas Aquinas and a historical method for theology in general;[46] Chenu also introduced Congar to the work of Möhler, who would prove to be a decisive influence.[47] He soon established ecumenical contacts, especially with the Orthodox during a year of postgraduate study at the Institut Catholique in Paris.[48] His first book, *Chrétiens désunis* (1937; ET, 1939), set forth the principles of a modern, irenic ecumenism, sensitive to the contributions of Orthodoxy, Anglicanism, and Protestantism to Christianity. Moreover, many of its central themes — the Trinitarian and christological roots of ecclesiology, qualitative catholicity, Orthodox and Anglican contributions to ecclesiology — would recur throughout his entire life and work. Seeking to restore the "true face of the church" through a return to the biblical, patristic, and liturgical sources of Christianity, he founded the *Unam Sanctam* series, whose early contributions included Henri de Lubac's *Catholicisme,* the French translation of Möhler's *Einheit in der Kirche,* and Albert Gratieux's two-volume study of Alexei Khomiakov's life and thought. After spending five years in prisoner-of-war camps during World War II, he returned home to an era of great liveliness in the French church: the worker-priest movement was at its height, as were the Young

Christian Workers movement (Jeunesse Ouvrière Chrétienne) and the so-called *nouvelle théologie.* In 1950, he published *Vraie et fausse réforme dans l'Eglise,* which, for its exposition and analysis of the conditions for authentic church reform, one commentator has called "perhaps the most constructive, and especially the most historically important" work of his career.[49] While still papal nuncio in France, Angelo Roncalli, who later became John XXIII, reportedly read the book and asked, "A reform of the church, is it possible?"[50]

Under increasing curial scrutiny for his ecclesiological and ecumenical labors — beginning in 1952, he was required to submit all of his writings to a Roman censor — he released in 1953 *Jalons pour une théologie du laicat* (ET, 1957), before finally being removed from his teaching post at Le Saulchoir in 1954 and sent into exile,[51] first to the École Biblique in Jerusalem (where he wrote *Le mystère du temple,* not published until 1958 because of censor problems) and then to Cambridge, where, of all things, he was commanded to limit his contacts with Anglicans. This was a time of intense bleakness and suffering, in which he came to experience the Cross.[52] Allowed to go to Strasbourg in 1956, he resumed his labors and, in 1960, was named — along with de Lubac — as a member of the preparatory commission for the ecumenical council recently announced by Pope John XXIII. He helped to organize several preparatory and exploratory studies, for example, *L'Épiscopat et l'Église universelle* (1962), which were published in *Unam Sanctam.* His contribution to the council was one of the most decisive — equaled perhaps only by de Lubac and Karl Rahner. His hand is evident in *Lumen gentium* (its themes of the church as the people of God, mystery, and communion; theology of the laity and episcopacy), *Dei verbum* (its insistence that scripture and tradition are not two separate sources of revelation, i.e., "partim... partim...," but together flow from the Word of God), *Gaudium et spes, Ad gentes divinitus, Apostolicam actuositatem, Presbyterorum ordinis,* and *Unitatis redintegratio,* to name only the most prominent. While the council was in session he released *Tradition et Traditions* (2 vols., 1960, 1963; ET, 1966). Immediately after the council he set to work on *Unam Sanctam*'s commentary on the conciliar documents, ultimately releasing over twenty volumes — and thereby justly earning the title of "*the* theologian of Vatican II par excellence."[53] The 1970s and 1980s were a period of continued labors, culminating in his three-volume *Je crois en l'Esprit saint* (1979–80; ET, 1983), a landmark work on pneumatology and ecclesiology. In 1984, Congar left the Dominican house of Saint-Jacques in Paris and entered l'Hôtel des Invalides, as his neuromuscular disorders, from which he had suffered for decades, made more extensive care necessary. Created a cardinal by Pope John Paul II in November 1994,[54] he died in Paris on June 22, 1995, and his funeral Mass was celebrated there at the Cathedral of Notre Dame.

Congar's theology of the local church is built on an ecclesiology of communion and catholicity and manifested especially in the church's sacramental life and ministry. Its foundation is communion, which has its origin, pattern, and end in God's own life. A 1935 essay on Möhler speaks of the church as "a mystery...a mysterious communication of divine life to humanity and the world, an intimate communion of souls with each other and with God in Christ,"[55] while *Chrétiens désunis* examines the church's unity from the threefold stance of Trinity, humanity, and Christ. The church, in the first place, is the *Ecclesia de Trinitate.* It is not "properly a society of men associated with God, but divine society itself, the life of the family *of God* reaching out to humanity and taking it up into itself."[56] In fact, he goes so far as to say that the church is the "community of those souls living *the very life* which is *trinitarian life.*...The church is *life with God.*"[57] Second, this movement of God to humanity is mirrored by the movement of humanity to God in the *Ecclesia ex hominibus.* Trinitarian communion takes form and is structured through visible, earthly realities. Third, these reciprocal movements of "from above downward" and "from below upward" unite in the *Ecclesia in Christo:*[58] humanity partakes in divine communion through partaking in the life of Christ in the sacraments, most particularly baptism and eucharist.[59] Finally, these three churches are elements in the "unique organic reality" that is at once a visible society and the Body of Christ, a communion in which humanity shares in God's own communion through the mediation of Christ.

The ecclesiology of communion set forth in *Chrétiens désunis* would only deepen in subsequent years, as Congar drew more deeply upon both Eastern and Western traditions. Works such as *Vraie et fausse réforme dans l'Église* and *Jalons pour une théologie du laicat* unfolded in a framework of communion and, in 1960, only two years before the beginning of Vatican II, he wrote that the concept of communion was the "future" of ecclesiology, and that one of its "most promising tasks" was the development of a "*theo*-logy of communion, that is to say, the model and principle that it has in the mystery of God himself."[60] It is not coincidental that the opening paragraphs of *Lumen gentium* are an exposition of the trinitarian nature of the church.

Catholicity is the extension and realization of ecclesial communion in both its divine and human aspects. In *Chrétiens désunis* Congar presents a primarily qualitative conception of catholicity, which he defines as the "universal capacity of [the church's] unity."[61] While not denying its quantitative sense, i.e., number of believers and/or their geographic expansion, he holds that catholicity is primarily Christic and cultural: catholicity is "the fullness of Christ, his expansion and realization in humanity....It is, for each one personally and for all humanity, gathering, accomplishment, and fullness in unity."[62] Christ will gather up all peoples and cultures in a work of purification and recapitulation, thereby leading all creation to divine unity. As the assimilation of the human "many" by the divine "one," unity thus exists prior or anterior to diversity, and, at times, is threatened or even contaminated by it.[63] An unresolved tension exists here between unity and diversity—in terms of their potential relation and dissolution—

which results from Congar's understanding of diversity as a "provisional and secondary reality in regard to unity";[64] he tends at times to see unity as transcending diversity, rather than as expressed in it. I would add that he fails to apply fully his Trinitarian theology of communion, in which diversity and unity mutually inhere in communion, to catholicity. Against his intentions, then, Congar's conception of catholicity in *Chrétiens désunis* may lead to uniformity, rather than a unity in diversity.

Subsequent works refined this qualitative understanding of catholicity,[65] but it was only several decades later that Congar articulated a truly balanced catholicity, in which unity and diversity mutually inhere in each other. His 1961 essay, "Unité, Diversités et Divisions," is paradigmatic in this regard, for he applies his trinitarian theology of communion to catholicity. Congar writes here of a "kind of mutual interiority of unity and diversity.... The principle of this interiority, which is also its model and end, [is] the holy Trinity, the perfect communion of the three persons in unity."[66] The church accordingly "imitates" the Trinity, which leads to an understanding of ecclesial unity not as uniformity or even assimilation, but as "rich with abundant diversity.... The church is fullness, it is at once unity and diversity."[67] Unity, for Congar, is no longer anterior or superior to diversity. Thus the "great demand of communion is openness, a disposition of welcome, gift, exchange,"[68] by which the gifts of God "take living root" in history and culture.[69] On the eve of Vatican II, then, Congar envisions catholicity as the quality by which the whole (of God's life and gifts) is (potentially) present in each of the parts (of humanity and creation)—a point of great importance for the theology of the local church.

The local church unfolds in Congar's ecclesiology as that place where communion and catholicity are manifested. While not offering a theology of the local church as systematic or as comprehensive as his work on the laity or church reform, Congar nevertheless authored several pivotal historical and ecumenical studies on the topic. His basic framework in each is the tension between universal and local ecclesiologies: the former being Western and taking as its point of departure the universal church, the latter being Eastern and beginning with the concrete local community. The framework first appears at length in *Neuf cents ans après* in 1954, and takes clearer form in his 1962 essay "De la communion des Églises à une ecclésiologie de l'Église universelle." In this latter essay he distinguishes himself explicitly from the extreme localism of several Russian Orthodox theologians, namely, Nikolai Afanasiev and Paul Evdokimov, which often relativizes or dispenses with the life and structures of the universal church. Nonetheless he freely admits that there is "something incontestable" in their local-eucharistic ecclesiologies, something that Catholics can "recognize unhesitatingly, in fidelity to our own tradition."[70] The result of Congar's labors is what might be called a localized universal ecclesiology, which attempts to integrate Eastern localism and Western universalism in a structured communion.

We may note at least four levels to this nascent theology of the local church: the cultural and ecclesiological differences between East and West, the ecclesial fullness of local church, the communion of local churches, and the relationship of the local church to the universal church. Congar begins his thought on the local church with the premise that the roots of the ecclesiological differences between Orthodoxy and Catholicism are not primarily theological, but cultural: the "*mystery of the church* is fundamentally the same in both the East and the West."[71] Western Christianity was formed in part by the legacy of the Roman empire, which inclined toward centralization, juridicism, and universality. Accordingly, the Western-Roman Christian conceived of the church firstly as "a universal reality to which [he was] joined, even a great family or great organization whose center is the [pope]."[72] This movement toward universality led, at various times in Catholicism's history, to ecclesial uniformity and a virtual absolutization of papal power over the local churches. In contrast, Eastern Christianity, according to Congar, began in a variety of cultures and maintained its linguistic and ritual diversity. The local churches were primary and united not by Roman centralization, but by bonds of communion, which were tenuous at times. "Church," for the East, thus meant primarily the concrete local community, "which [was] familial, ethnic, national, cultural, in short, human at the same time it was spiritual and even divine."[73] At times, notably in the Muslim invasions, such particularism led to defensiveness and nationalism, thereby obscuring the bonds of communion uniting the various local churches.

Despite these cultural-ecclesiological differences, however, the West does affirm that the "church" refers as well to the local community. For both East and West, the local church, a community gathered around its bishop,[74] is the church of God in its fullness. Accordingly, the local church is primarily a mysterious, sacramental reality, which is founded on faith, guided by apostolic ministry, and realized most fully in the eucharistic celebration.[75] Moreover, this local church is itself truly catholic, "less as universality, than as the presence of the whole in each part, the experience of the whole in the local community";[76] Scholasticism's conception of the "homogeneous body," in which the nature of the whole is realized in its each of its parts, indicates that such notions of locality and catholicity have a place in the Western ecclesial tradition.[77] In short, each local, catholic church possesses the fullness of God's gifts — faith, sacraments, ministry — incarnating them in a milieu distinctly its own.[78] While not exhausting the reality of the church of God, each local church makes it truly and fully present — a point on which East and West agree.

Third, each local church exists in communion with other local churches. This communion is primarily sacramental, secondarily societal and juridical. In its deepest reality it is founded upon an "identity of professed faith and celebrated sacraments" between local churches.[79] Baptism and the eucharist join Christians not simply to their local churches but also to the universal church,[80] while the collegiality of bishops gives particular expression to such universal communion. On the sacramental level, each local church is equal in status and worth; even the pope, as bishop of Rome, is sacramentally equal to his fellow bishops.

Sacramentality, however, does not exhaust ecclesial communion. The church is not solely a communion of local churches, but also a society or organism, in which the total or universal church is itself a unity and has its own divinely instituted structures of governance, existing apart from the local churches.[81] Congar argues that Catholicism thus goes beyond Orthodoxy — particularly Afanasiev — in insisting that this communion of local churches is preceded and sustained by the universal church.[82] This priority of the universal church has its roots in apostolicity and the subsequent relationship between collegiality and primacy. In the first place, the apostles were not twelve individuals, but "The Twelve," a body or college in which unity precedes diversity. The bishop, as successor of the apostles, is therefore first a member of the episcopal college and only second the head of a local church;[83] in like manner, the universal church precedes the local churches. Second, just as Peter was the head or first of the apostles, so too is the pope the head of the bishops by divine institution. Although sacramentally equal to other bishops, he nonetheless has a unique responsibility for the church as a whole.[84]

This tension between collegiality and primacy or, as Congar phrases it, between the ecclesiologies of communion and universal-pontifical power, is subject to abuse. Orthodoxy, along with Gallicanism and Anglicanism, deny — explicitly or implicitly — a separately existing life and structure of the universal church above the local churches and their communion. Papal primacy, if it is recognized, is seen solely as a "power *in*" the church;[85] its power is executive rather than constitutive, and the papacy is simply the "image and guarantee of unity," not its instrument.[86] On the other hand, a universal-pontifical ecclesiology risks overemphasizing the societal and juridical, thereby neglecting the sacramental and mystical. It has the tendency of "treating the church as the diocese of a single bishop, turning unity into uniformity, [and] effectively making the pope the sole hierarch of divine law, a sort of super-bishop and even a super-priest in the sacramental order."[87] Placing the pope outside or above the episcopal college, it thus views papal primacy almost entirely as "power *over*" the church, independent of the bishops.

In contrast to either extreme, Congar argues that a balanced Catholic position on the papacy

> does not affirm a power *over* which would not also be a power *in*. The ecclesiology of pontifical power, as an "episcopal" power qualitatively superior to the ensemble of churches and faithful, should be expressed in union with a theology of communion.[88]

In other words, Congar seeks the integration of the ecclesiology of communion and the local church — common to Orthodoxy and the ancient church — with the universal ecclesiology that developed over centuries in the West. This localized universal ecclesiology, as I inelegantly termed it earlier, thus may be summed up in two basic principles. First, the deepest reality of the church is sacramental, but always expressed through societal and juridical forms. Second, the local church, while possessing in its faith, sacraments, and apostolic ministry the fullness of the church of God, is nonetheless preceded and enveloped by the universal church. The tension between these two statements points to the central weakness of Congar's theology of the local church: the question of priority between the universal church and the local churches.

While the strengths of Congar's theology of the local church are manifest — a theological grounding of communion, a qualitative catholicity embracing diversity, a recovery of the church's sacramental-eucharistic nature — his major fault, the priority of the universal church, results from his failure to apply fully these strengths to the local church. In both his theology of communion and catholicity, as we have seen, he gradually realized that unity and diversity are simultaneous: the doctrine of Trinity shows that God is at once three and one, while catholicity comes to mean, not unity expanding into diversity, but a unity-in-diversity. In each instance, he moved from *first* the "one" and *then* the "many," to their *simultaneity:* the one and the many are interior to each other. Moreover, partly under the influence of Orthodox theology,[89] Congar developed an ecclesiology of communion and a theology of the local church that gave primacy to the church's sacramental, mysterious nature: the church's own life both derives from and symbolizes God's life in communion.

However, while rightly criticizing any move to local priority, Congar failed to see that the priority of the universal church is equally erroneous. Correct in arguing that the universal church is not the *result* of the communion of the local churches, he could not grasp that the universal church does not exist above or apart from such communion, but *is* that communion; while not exhausted by any given local church, the universal church nonetheless exists only in and through these local churches. The Trinitarian parallel is clear: God's oneness does not precede God's threeness, but is always threefold, and vice versa. In short, out of a rightful concern for visible, structured, worldwide communion — in contrast to the (possible) excesses of *sobornost* and eucharistic-local ecclesiologies — Congar failed to extend his theology deeply enough into his ecclesiology: an ecclesiology of communion does not need to be complemented by one of universal-pontifical power, but contains within itself the resources for an integration of oneness and multiplicity, unity and diversity, primacy and collegiality, universality and locality.

In his conclusion to *Le Concile et les conciles,* a 1960 collection of papers written in preparation for the ecumenical council announced the previous year by Pope John XXIII, Congar notes:

> The health of [a council's] labors comes from the authenticity of its efforts concerning both the questions posed to it and the response that it must draw from the depths of its apostolic heritage. The church does not contemplate itself for the pleasure of gazing upon itself, but solely in order to ensure the fidelity of its response. It does not define for the pleasure of defining, but solely in order to respond to the demands of the times.... The next council should be one where the church, in scrutinizing itself with the questions of the age, defines itself in a most open and generous manner, not so much in and for itself, as in its relationship to the world and in the relationship others have with it.[90]

When he wrote these lines, Congar was a largely ignored member of the council's preparatory commission, unable to contribute much to the neo-scholastic schemas being drawn up mostly by curial theologians. Little did he know that many of the topics he proposed for consideration in this essay — for example, collegiality, the ecumenicity and historicity of councils, the relationship of scripture and tradition to councils and conciliar authority, Orthodox and Protestant thought — would become some of the council's central concerns, or that he himself would become one of its most influential theologians.[91] The council's vision of the local church, inspired in large measure by Congar, is our next topic.

Second Vatican Council (1962–65): Seeds of Renewal of the Local Church

The Second Vatican Council is arguably the most significant Christian event since the Reformation, and its full import will be realized only after continued reception by the Catholic Church and other Christian communities. Although the council was essentially an ecclesiological one, setting forth Catholicism's self-understanding through a recovery of the fullness of Christian tradition and a response to the signs of the times, it did not itself develop a fully coherent ecclesiology, let alone a theology of the local church. Whether one sees this lack of coherence as the result of a juxtaposition of two markedly different ecclesiologies[92] — one juridical, the other communional — or as a search for consensus, which simply established basic principles and left open the future resolution of difficult questions,[93] it remains that the conciliar ecclesiology is a transitional one, and that one must be careful in making broad statements about it.

The council's theology of the local church reflects this ambiguity. While marked by a predominantly universalistic ecclesiology, the conciliar documents, in a number of passages, do establish some basic, embryonic principles for a theology of the local church — principles perhaps more important as catalysts for subsequent ecclesial reflection than for their influence at the council itself. This theology of the local church has its roots in the council's ecclesiology of communion and catholicity and finds particular expression in several statements on the eucharist and episcopacy. These four elements — communion, catholicity, eucharist, and episcopacy — will thus serve as the framework of our examination.

Because of the consensual and synthetic nature of the conciliar documents, no single ecclesiological image or theme has preeminence. The first chapter of *Lumen gentium,* "The Mystery of the Church," puts forth, for instance, a number of images — for example, kingdom of God, Body of Christ, sheepfold, farm, building, spouse — without declaring a preference for any single one. While "People of God" is perhaps the most prominent and visible image in the document as a whole,[94] and "Body of Christ" appears regularly as well, neither is dominant nor do they exclude others.[95] An increasing number of theologians and bishops, however, have come to hold that communion is an integrating theme, perhaps *the* integrating theme of the conciliar ecclesiology, more as an "umbrella" or integrating concept able to embrace the images of People of God, Body of Christ, Temple of the Holy Spirit, and so on, than as simply another contesting image.[96] Leaving aside the validity of this argument, I wish to examine briefly the central role played by communion, for it is the matrix of the council's theology of the local church.

Vatican II uses "communion" on several different levels.[97] Foremost, it is *vertical* or *trinitarian.* As the opening paragraphs of *Lumen gentium* make clear, the church originates in, and is patterned on, the divine communion that is the Trinity. Expressed in the call of the Father to covenant and in the missions of the Word and Spirit, trinitarian communion is the foundation of all ecclesial communion.[98] Second, it is *horizontal* or *human,* in relation to fellow believers and, more broadly, humanity.[99] Third, it is *eucharistic,* in that the eucharist brings believers into communion with God and with each other.[100] Fourth, communion is *local,* where each particular community is united through the eucharistic celebration under its bishop.[101] Fifth, it is *universal,* where the local churches both constitute and are constituted by the one, worldwide church; the church is, in some sense, a communion of churches.[102] Sixth, it is *ecumenical,* in that, while the church of Christ "subsists" in the Catholic Church, other churches and ecclesial communities share in "some, though imperfect communion" with it, to the degree that they preserve authentic faith, baptism, eucharist, and apostolic ministry.[103] While these six dimensions do not exhaust ecclesial communion — the incarnational, eschatological, visible, and invisible are several others — they are the foundation of the council's ecclesiology of communion and thus the building blocks of its theology of the local church.

Vatican II's sense of catholicity is as expansive as its understanding of communion. Primarily qualitative, catholicity strives for "fullness in unity,"[104] which is achieved by a twofold movement: a "downward" one of inculturation, and an "upward" one of recapitulation or transformation in Christ. Through both movements the church seeks to "redemptively integrate"[105] in Christ the breadth and depth of humanity and its achievements.

The goal of catholicity is primarily the transformation and recapitulation of earthly and human goods in Christ. The church "fosters and takes to itself, in so far as they are good, people's abilities, resources, and customs. In so taking them to itself it purifies, strengthens, and elevates them."[106] Ultimately, this transformation is recapitulated in Christ, who will be "all in all."

This upward movement first requires, however, a descent or implanting of the church in a given culture or people; one might say that grace requires some "nature" with which to work. Although a quantitative-universalistic sense of catholicity is present in the conciliar documents — for instance, the People of God "is to be spread throughout the whole world and to all ages in order that the design of God's will be fulfilled"[107] — they give preference to catholicity's qualitative-cultural aspects: the church does not simply spread *across* the face of the earth, but, more importantly, sinks its roots *into* the earth. Thus the church does not engage society and culture as an *arriviste,* merely giving a subsequent blessing or ratification upon a purely human endeavor, or as an unrelenting critic, but is present from the outset in a work of transformation. That is, the church and Christianity do not simply either overlay or condemn a culture, but rather enter into it, in a process whereby church and culture undergo a mutual transformation.[108] This is the logic of inculturation and adaptation, and the council shows how this process affects the entire spectrum of human endeavor: society, political life, culture, family, liturgy, ecumenism, to name only a few dimensions. Accordingly, in a passage representative of numerous others, the council declares that the Christian people

> must give expression to this newness of life in their own society and culture and in a manner that is in keeping with the traditions of their own land. They must be familiar with this culture, they must purify and guard it, they must develop it in accordance with present-day conditions, they must perfect it in Christ so that the faith of Christ and the life of the church will not be something foreign to the society in which they live, but will begin to transform and permeate it.[109]

Therefore, while the church is never to identify itself exclusively with any culture, it paradoxically belongs to all cultures and peoples and is manifested in and through them.[110] It is for this reason that *Lumen gentium* defines catholicity in its broadest sense as "fullness in unity," while *Ad gentes divinitus* expresses the same idea with greater lyricism through the biblical-patristic contrast of Babel and Pentecost: "On [Pentecost] was foreshadowed the union of all peoples in the catholicity of the faith by means of the church of the New Alliance, a church which speaks every language, understands and embraces all tongues in charity, and thus overcomes the dispersion of Babel."[111]

Finally, this catholic unity-in-diversity is not simply socio-cultural, but also ecclesial. On the simplest level of adaptation, *Sacrosanctum concilium,* the council's first document, clearly supports the need for, and desirability of, liturgical inculturation.[112] On a deeper level, *Lumen gentium, Ad gentes divinitus, Unitatis redintegratio,* and *Orientalium ecclesiarum* all affirm that the diversity of local churches can contribute to the catholicity of the Christian communion as a whole: "This multiplicity of local churches, unified in a common effort, shows all the more resplendently the catholicity of the undivided church."[113] In the council's qualitative understanding of catholicity, then, the opposite of catholicity is not locality or diversity, but uniformity. "Redemptively integrated," diversity builds up the catholicity and communion of the church of Christ. This insight is of great significance for Vatican II's theology of the local church.

The council's theology of the local church is a small, mostly implicit chapter of its ecclesiology of communion and catholicity. Only a few paragraphs of the council's documents explicitly treat of the local church, and these are often poorly integrated into the documents in which they are found; for instance, the first paragraph of *Lumen gentium* #26, which is one of the pillars of the theology of the local church, was a late "interpolation" into a preexistent text, and thereby exercised little explicit structural or thematic influence upon the council's ecclesiology.[114] Moreover, the council's ecclesiology remains predominantly universalistic and pontifical: chapter 3 of *Lumen gentium* contains sixteen assertions of the bishops' subordination to the Roman pontiff, assertions that almost always follow on the heels of affirmations of the role and dignity of the bishops. It is, as Kilian McDonnell has stated, a "very nervous, defensive chapter."[115] If one speaks of Vatican II's theology of the local church, then, it must be admitted that it has more of the seed than of the fruit, more of the sketch than of the formal portrait. These seeds and sketches are found in the council's eucharistic ecclesiology, its teaching on the episcopacy, and its understanding of the relationship of the local and universal churches.

In the first place, the council consistently affirms the centrality of the eucharist in the church's life. *Sacrosanctum concilium,* for instance, states that "the [eucharistic] liturgy is the summit toward which the activity of the church is directed; it is also the source from which all its power flows,"[116] and *Christus Dominus* holds that "the eucharistic sacrifice is the center and culmination of the entire life of the Christian community."[117] Moreover, Vatican II affirms that the eucharist is the primary defining mark of ecclesiality: not only does the church make the eucharist, but the eucharist also makes the church. *Presbyterorum ordinis* thus declares that "no Christian community is built up which does not grow from and hinge on the celebration of the most holy eucharist,"[118] while *Lumen gentium* #26 and *Christus Dominus* #11 — the two pillars, as it were, of the council's theology of the local church — give more expansive indication of this eucharistic essence:

> This church of Christ is really present in all legitimately organized local groups of the faithful which, united with their pastors, are also called churches in

> the New Testament.... In them the faithful are gathered by the preaching of the Gospel of Christ, and the mystery of the Lord's Supper is celebrated "so that, by means of the flesh and blood of the Lord the whole brotherhood and sisterhood of the body may be welded together." In any community of the altar, under the sacred ministry of the bishop, a manifest symbol is to be seen of that charity and "unity of the mystical body, without which there can be no salvation." In these communities, though they may often be small and poor, or dispersed, Christ is present through whose power and influence the one, holy, catholic, and apostolic church is constituted.[119]

> A diocese is a section of God's people entrusted to a bishop to be guided by him with the assistance of his clergy so that, loyal to its pastor and formed by him into one community in the Holy Spirit through the Gospel and the Eucharist, it constitutes one particular church in which the one, holy, catholic, and apostolic church of Christ is truly present and active.[120]

In these paragraphs the council affirms that the eucharist is the foundation of the church's essence and unity; it even stands as the "the source and summit of all preaching of the Gospel."[121] In short, the eucharist makes the church to be.

Second, this local church, formed by the Gospel and eucharist, is fundamentally episcopal. As the citations above indicate, the council identifies the local church not with the parish, but with the diocese, for the bishop is the one who possesses the fullness of orders and exercises it in the service of unity.[122] Thus the local church is primarily the eucharistic community gathered by and under its bishop, and his role as preacher and teacher of the Gospel finds its culmination in eucharistic presidency. Furthermore, by his sacramental ordination, the bishop receives and exercises the powers appropriate to his office. He is not a mere delegate of the pope, but has "proper, immediate, and ordinary" power in his local church.[123] In making such statements, however counterbalanced they may be by declarations of pontifical sovereignty, the council helped to recover the sacramental nature of the church and its ministry: in its eucharistic celebration, the local church, under its bishop, genuinely manifests the church of Christ.[124]

In addition, bishops are joined to each other through bonds of collegiality. Each bishop, through his sacramental ordination and hierarchical communion with other bishops and the pope, is incorporated into the episcopal college and as such is "to be solicitous for the entire church."[125] In fact, because they view the bishops primarily as "successors to the apostles,"[126] both *Lumen gentium* and *Christus Dominus* give precedence to the collegial dimension of episcopacy and only secondarily consider the bishop as head of a local church;[127] the difficulties this position presents for a theology of the local church will be discussed below. Furthermore, the council's endorsement of episcopal conferences serves as another expression of collegiality and catholicity; the former through gathering bishops together, the latter through giving expression to the needs, desires, and problems of a given region or nation.[128]

Third, as this uneasy yoking of the collegial and local dimensions of episcopacy indicates, Vatican II left unresolved the relationship between the local churches and the universal church. *Lumen gentium* #23 is the key passage in this regard: it states, in part, that the "particular churches... are modeled on the universal church; it is in and from these [particular churches] that the one and unique catholic church exists." While affirming the mutual inclusion and interiority of the local churches and the universal church (a not insignificant contribution to a theology of the local church), these lines do not directly address or resolve the question of priority; the two statements are simply juxtaposed, without any attempt to clarify their logical and temporal relationships. One is left wondering *how* such inclusion occurs.

It is reasonable, however, to argue that the council's ecclesiology remains universalistic-pontifical. *Lumen gentium* and *Christus Dominus* clearly situate their ecclesiologies within a universalistic framework. The ecclesiology of each begins, for instance, with the universal church, whose paradigm is the apostolic college, rather than the local, eucharistic community.[129] More tellingly, Vatican II's conception of the papacy is almost entirely universalistic. To put it bluntly, the council's pope is the Roman pontiff, not the bishop of Rome, and his power is primarily power *over* the church, not power *in* the church (to borrow Congar's phrasing).[130] The pope is called "the perpetual and visible source and foundation of the unity of both the bishops and the whole company of the faithful,"[131] and great care is taken to show that he reserves the right to act on his own authority, apart from the episcopal college.[132] On the grounds of such statements, Hermann Pottmeyer has argued that Vatican II's assertions are even more papally maximalistic than those of Vatican I. Out of a fear of the "nightmare of shared governance" between the pope and the bishops, the conciliar minority—comprised of a significant curial presence, intent on preserving its own power—"succeeded in having the pope's independence and freedom of action stressed in a way that had not been emphasized even in the Vatican I definition [of papal primacy and infallibility in *Pastor aeternus*]."[133] In short, Vatican II remains tethered to a strongly universalistic ecclesiology, in which a maximalistic papacy, not the communion of eucharistic communities, is the dominant note. The theology of the local church remains a minor, even suspended note.

Vatican II's theology of the local church thus has both methodological and substantive faults. Methodologically, the "interpolative" nature of *Lumen gentium* #26—and the ad hoc nature of like-minded passages such as *Lumen gentium* #23 and *Sacrosanctum concilium* #41—give evidence of the council's failure to allow the local church to structure the conciliar documents; they remain universalistic. And, in turn, this methodological lacuna reveals a deeper substantial fault: the council's failure to address the question of ecclesial priority in a theologically nuanced manner. *Lumen gentium* #23 rightly asserted the mutual inherence and reciprocity of the local and universal churches but did not give a properly theological grounding to such relationship. By not integrating its Trinitarian theology with its ecclesiology, the council failed to model the relationship of the local and universal churches on the Trinitarian communion of the "one" and the "many," in which neither has priority. As a result, the council's ecclesiology gives priority to the "one" over the "many," and sets forth a heavily universalistic ecclesiology, which results in a maximalist view of papal primacy and an unbalanced theology of the episcopate, in which the bishop is first a member of the episcopal college and secondly — but not necessarily — head of a local church; both the papacy and episcopacy are distanced from their sacramental-ecclesial essence. In short, a juridical ecclesiology triumphs over an ecclesiology of communion, and the question of priority, which seemed at first to be a minor, even esoteric academic exercise, shows itself to be of the highest importance for the life and ministry of the church.

Despite these shortcomings, Vatican II did make significant, if tentative, advances in its theology of the local church, advances all the more notable for the highly contested atmosphere in which they arose. The council's great contribution to the theology of the local church is its affirmation of the authentic ecclesial reality of each local church. Because the church is primarily a mysterious and sacramental community, and secondarily a juridical one, in which "the eucharistic sacrifice is the center and culmination of the entire life of the Christian community,"[134] the local eucharistic community makes present the one, holy, catholic, and apostolic church. Second, this eucharistic ecclesiology is thoroughly local. In documents such as *Sacrosanctum concilium, Ad gentes divinitus,* and *Orientalium ecclesiarum,* the council affirmed that the church takes root and flesh in particular cultural and social contexts: the church is not simply *in* a place, but is *of* that place and is itself transformed by such an encounter: its liturgy, evangelization, and social mission should always bear the mark of a legitimate, thorough inculturation. In some sense, the local church must be that place where divine gift and human response meet. Third, although obvious problems remain in its conception of the episcopacy and the papacy, the council's doctrine of collegiality does represent a genuine advance, one that can rein in papal and curial centralization and restore the rightful place of all the bishops in the governance and care of the church. Collegiality is an exigency of the church's nature as communion, not a flawed or devious attempt to "democratize" the church or to establish a politicized balance of power. Finally, apart from these concrete achievements, the council also set in motion a kind of ecclesial trajectory, providing the seeds for future growth. Walter Kasper, for one, has described this movement as one of increasing "co-responsibility" in the church, by which believers and communities come to full subjectivity and action,[135] while Jean-Marie Tillard sees in the recovery of the local church and the ecclesiology of communion the overcoming of pyramidal models of authority and mission by synergistic ones that activate the gifts and charisms of local communities and their people.[136]

Whatever one thinks of these proposals, the necessarily incomplete and unfinished work of any council leads to a concluding thought. Much as Vatican II resumed and completed the interrupted work of Vatican I, which set forth a theology of papal primacy and infallibility without being able to finish the planned schemas on the episcopacy, might not a future council or synod complete and extend Vatican II's work on episcopal collegiality and papal primacy by setting forth a systematic theology of the local church? As Catholicism struggles to become a "world church," in Karl Rahner's words, and as Vatican II continues to be received by the Catholic and other Christian churches, questions of primacy, collegiality, ministry, inculturation, and mission will only continue to proliferate. Without an ecclesiology adequate to the fullness of the Christian tradition and the demands of contemporary cultures and societies, that is, a theology of the local church, Catholicism will be rendered increasingly sclerotic and impotent, unable to spread the riches of the Gospel to those who stand in need of them. The church would then fail to bear witness to Christ, the light of the nations.

Chapter Three

The fundamental principles of Jean-Marie Roger Tillard's theology of the local church

In the foreword of *Église d'églises,*[1] Jean-Marie Tillard writes, somewhat wryly, that "our purpose is therefore modest, to reveal . . . the vision which is found at the root of the article of the Nicene-Constantinopolitan creed: 'We believe in one, holy, catholic, and apostolic Church.' "[2] Guided by this creedal framework, *Église d'églises* sets forth a systematic ecclesiology of communion, which takes as its point of departure the event of Pentecost: "It does not seem exaggerated to us to affirm that [Pentecost] . . . thus appears if not as the origin of the church . . . at least as the epiphany of its nature."[3] *L'Église locale,*[4] Tillard's *magnum opus,* develops this ecclesiology still further into a theology of the local church, through its conviction that this Pentecostal church of God is fundamentally and necessarily a local church. Established as the church of God in its fullness by the *ephapax* outpouring of the Holy Spirit at Pentecost, which seals Christ's sacrifice upon the cross and issues forth in the commissioning of the apostles, this church arises only in a definite place: Jerusalem, the city that stands at the center of salvation history for both Jews and Christians. Incarnating in a concrete, local community the fullness of God's gift through the Son and in the Holy Spirit, the church of Jerusalem is therefore at once local and catholic; the two imply each other. And the fullness of the divine gift in this local church allows Tillard to state, "even when it was only the community at Jerusalem, the Pentecostal church was already fully the catholic Church of God."[5] Subsequent local churches will not add to the church of God, but will instead enter into the fullness of grace given to it in Jerusalem at Pentecost.

The Pentecostal church of Jerusalem is the source and paradigm of Tillard's theology of the local church and ecclesiology of communion. Accordingly, this chapter will analyze the Pentecostal form of his ecclesiology and its implications for the church's locality, universality, unity, holiness, catholicity, and apostolicity. Although this chapter's divisions are unavoidably somewhat artificial — how does one, for example, distinguish the church's belonging to God from its holiness? — they nonetheless will lend conceptual clarity to our study.

Pentecost

Tillard places Pentecost at the heart of his theology and ecclesiology. At first glance, this decision may seem somewhat arbitrary: why not begin, for instance, with the call of the disciples or the Last Supper, each of which has obvious ecclesiological import? Moreover, as Tillard admits, the New Testament, apart from Luke-Acts, is largely silent about Pentecost. In light of such respective plurality and paucity, why and how can he claim that "the event of Pentecost dominates and conditions the vision of the church that gradually will be integrated into the Christian consciousness"?[6]

Tillard grants that his choice is a personal one, grounded in his reading of scripture and especially the Fathers.[7] It is, nonetheless, based on a comprehensive understanding of the economy of salvation, particularly the mystery of Jesus Christ, who is at once the realization of the "hope of Israel" and the head of a reconciled creation.[8] In contrast to either the community of disciples (which can appear as an aggregate of individuals relating directly to Jesus, with little horizontal connection to each other) or the Last Supper and the piercing of Jesus' side on the cross (although eucharistic, both events precede the resurrection), Pentecost is the pivotal ecclesial event of this divine economy, for it fulfills the covenant formed by the giving of the Law at Sinai (fifty days after Passover) and forms into a church those who were witnesses to the saving death and resurrection of Christ (fifty days after Easter).[9] Joining together the covenant with its irreversible accomplishment in reconciliation and communion, Pentecost reveals the church's place at the heart of salvation history. Such confluence is, in part, *why* Tillard structures his ecclesiology with Pentecost. We turn now to *how* Pentecost operates in his thought as eschatological fulfillment and communion.

Pentecost opens a "new era in salvation,"[10] forming the church and making present by the Holy Spirit the good news of salvation, but it does so only in continuity with the hope of the Jewish people. It is not accidental, for instance, that Peter's Pentecost discourse begins with an invocation of the prophet Joel and his words of the "last days," wherein God's Spirit will be poured forth on all flesh and salvation will be present to all who call upon God's name (Acts 2:17–21, quoting Joel 2:28–32). The eschatological newness brought by the Holy Spirit is more of a continuity than an entirely new reality,[11] and so Pentecost represents the fulfillment of what began with the theophany at Sinai, when God entered into covenant with God's people and gave to Moses the Decalogue.[12] The parallels between Sinai and Pentecost are evident. Taking place fifty days after Passover, when God spared the Israelites and led them from Egyptian oppression, the theophany to Moses occurs after a period of temptation in the wilderness, and makes the Israelites a people precisely by bringing them into covenant with God; deliverance and community are inseparable. Pentecost likewise is a passage from fearful dispersion into unity: fifty days after Easter, the Pasch of Jesus, the Holy Spirit descends upon the people and makes present the "last days" for all who call upon God's name.

Therefore, as the "theophany of the new covenant,"[13] Pentecost accomplishes the work begun in the Sinai desert by extending this salvation to all people.[14] The many languages spoken at Pentecost are one example of this universality, but it is perhaps most evident in the role played by the Twelve.[15] At once symbolizing the twelve tribes of Israel and commissioned to go forth to all nations, they are to fulfill God's promise that Abraham would be the father of all the nations.[16] The "mother-cell" of the church,[17] the apostles alone are the eyewitnesses that this covenant has been fully accomplished in the resurrection of Jesus and the sending of his Spirit upon the Christian community. Their apostolic witness to the fulfillment of God's salvific plan is intrinsic to the Pentecostal event and will remain at the heart of Christian faith.

The Holy Spirit who inaugurates the "last days" does so, though, only by reconciling all peoples and bringing them into communion with God and with each other; eschatology and communion are inseparable. In this regard, Tillard notes that it is not accidental that the first description of Christian community occurs in the context of Pentecost and stresses precisely its *koinonia* or mutual concern.[18] The Holy Spirit functions, then, as the agent both of the eschaton, making the power of Christ's resurrection present to the community, and of communion, introducing believers into the reconciliation effected by his death and resurrection.[19] As Acts relates, the Pentecostal community, having received both forgiveness of sins through baptism in the name of Jesus Christ and the gift of the Holy Spirit, manifests such divine reconciliation and communion through the communion of its members with each other in eating, praying, and almsgiving; communion with God and communion with humanity are indivisible.

Furthermore, as the "giver of life," the Holy Spirit gives life in communion, whereby human differences are integrated into a common faith. The classic, patristic contrast to Pentecost is the story of Babel, where the confusion of languages symbolizes human sinfulness and the resultant division. Pentecost reveals that the antidote to Babel is not uniformity, however, but unity. It answers Babel's confusion by

> the reunification of humanity in an understanding of the apostolic witness [particularly of Peter] and, by this witness, of the divine message. . . . In the feast of Pentecost the multitude of languages, the symbol of the barrier erected between peoples, is joined in the common understanding of the apostolic Word. Such is the work of the Spirit of the "last days."[20]

In a paradox that Tillard probes over and again, Pentecost reverses Babel precisely by encouraging difference and, through the Holy Spirit, integrating it in a unity of faith and common life: "Babel will cease, especially where human reconciliation takes form, because, in faith and baptism, men and women will be put under the mastery of the Spirit of the Lord."[21]

Communion does not absolutize difference, nor does it reduce difference to uniformity, but rather forms it into a unity-in-diversity;[22] the church is a "communion of 'differences.'"[23] Pentecost thus provides the theological grounding—the Magna Carta, one might say—of communion and difference, revealing the Holy Spirit of God to be the one who introduces human diversity into divine communion.

The essential elements of Pentecost, then, are three: the Holy Spirit, the apostolic witness, and communion.[24] Eschatological accomplishment and communion meet in the Christian community's experience of the Holy Spirit at Pentecost. As a once-for-all event, Pentecost will be the continuing source—and not simply model or point of departure[25]—of all subsequent ecclesial life and grace; later communities will not add to this grace, but rather enter into it.[26] Thus indwelt by the plenitude of the grace of the Holy Spirit, the Pentecostal community is the realization of the holy people (*Qahal*) of God, which is none other than the church of God already in its fullness.

Church of God

What does it mean, however, to call the Pentecostal community of Jerusalem the "church of God"? Risking the obvious, one needs to look first at the meaning of "church," and second at that of "of God." In the first place, much as the mystery of the Christian church is bound up with the mystery of the people of Israel, so is the New Testament's use of the Greek *ekklesia* rooted in the Old Testament's *qahal.* The Hebrew *qahal,* in its broadest sense, means the "gathering of the believing People, convoked by God, for the important act of its life, an 'assembly of God.'"[27] In contrast to the Hebrew *'am,* which refers simply to the People of God in its totality, *qahal* refers specifically to this People as a "gathering in its faith, ordinarily expressed by a common liturgical act."[28] Still more specifically, the *qahal* has its roots in the covenant formed by the promulgation of the Law at Sinai.[29] It is thus a "people of the covenant," created by a divine call or initiative, and set apart in holiness.[30] This sense of belonging gives rise to a tension. On the one hand, a sharp boundary is often drawn between those who are within the assembly-covenant and those who are excluded for not having "journeyed out of Egypt" (see Deut 23:3–4); the *qahal* allows for no degrees of belonging: one is in or one is out. On the other hand, although the *qahal* originates in a particular history of salvation, several sections of scripture and certain Jewish schools held that the Law, and thus the People, were destined for all peoples.[31] This tension between exclusion and inclusion, particularity and universality will mark Jewish and, later, Christian, existence.

The New Testament ordinarily uses the Greek *ekklesia* to name the church. The original meaning of the word is largely political: "an official assembly of a social group, the gathering in the same place of the citizens of a political community."[32] *Ekklesia* takes on a properly theological sense first through the Septuagint, which generally translates *qahal* with *ekklesia*. The New Testament continues this usage, although naturally in a more specifically Christian sense. Its adoption of the Septuagint likely indicates the early Christian community's awareness of the continuity of the divine convocation that began with Abraham and Sinai and emerged in its fullness at Pentecost.[33] Tillard, as we have seen, insists on the organic, salvific continuity between Israel and the church. In events as central to its being as the Last Supper and Pentecost, the church knows itself to be rooted "in 'the same mystery' (Rom 11: 25) as Israel, a *church of churches,* the church of the *qahal*. . . . It is impossible to understand the church without having understood Israel."[34] For Christians, clearly, Jesus himself is the realization of the hope of Israel (John 15), the long-awaited messiah.[35] The *Ekklesia* is thus the assembly of those who believe in Christ, the fruition at Pentecost of the divine initiative that began in the *qahal* at Sinai.[36]

This church is "of God" through at least a fourfold relation to God. First, the church, as we have just described, is the object and result of a divine initiative; its origin is "of God," not "of humanity."[37] In the second place, as part of a lengthy history of salvation that connects the church with Israel, this divine initiative arises more broadly and properly from the action of God (the Father) than of Christ. Paul writes of the "church of Christ" but once (Rom 16: 16), as he does also with those churches "which are in Christ" (Gal 1: 22).[38] Third, this initiative results not in an extrinsic, contractual relationship, but truly joins the church to God; it belongs to God as his holy possession.[39] Fourth, and most profoundly, the church both reflects and shares in God's own life. Put simply, God is triune communion,[40] and all ecclesial reality and communion can be grasped only in light of this trinitarian communion.[41] The church has no life which is not ultimately trinitarian and, therefore, "of God." All characteristics or marks of the church are therefore first "divine," and secondly "human."[42] Therefore, to speak of the "church of God" is to name that assembly which, at Pentecost, brings to fruition the economy of salvation begun with the *qahal* and already participates in God's life through Christ and in the Holy Spirit.

Jerusalem

The Pentecostal church of God emerges, not accidentally but salvifically, in Jerusalem, and is at once fully local and universal. Receiving the fullness of the *ephapax* grace of the Holy Spirit,[43] the church at Jerusalem is situated at the heart of a particular, definite history of salvation for both Jews and Christians. In the first place, it is in Jerusalem that God brings to completion the *qahal* or assembly that began in the desert centuries before with the calling and formation of the Jewish people.[44] Second, Jerusalem is the heart of Israel, that place where Abraham offered up Isaac in sacrifice and is promised by God the nations as an inheritance,[45] God established his dwelling and temple, and final judgment will be delivered.[46] Third, for Christians, it is where Jesus' life reaches its climax in his death and resurrection.[47] Fourth, by this resurrection, the *katholou* of the plan of God is accomplished: Jesus, by the blood of the cross, knocks down the dividing wall between Jews and Greeks and achieves the saving communion of all (Eph 2:11–22);[48] is it coincidental, as Acts 15 recounts, that the meeting between Peter and Paul on the recognition of Gentiles takes place in Jerusalem? And, ultimately, for both Jews and Christians, Jerusalem represents the realization of human destiny, for it is the holy, eschatological city: the "new Jerusalem," which will not destroy but perfect all that preceded it;[49] it is the final destination of the pilgrim church.[50] For these reasons, Tillard argues that the church's foundation at Jerusalem is not accidental, but historically and eschatologically necessary. The "mother of all churches" is thus itself the child of a long history centered in Jerusalem.

Moreover, the church's foundation in Jerusalem shows that the church is inherently both local and universal: announcing a salvation destined for all the nations, the church does so only through particular histories and places. This tension between the universal and the particular is encountered at the depths of the divine plan, from which flows the church of God at Pentecost.[51] The church's locality, therefore, is not a negative reality to be avoided or restrained (as if it led inevitably to nationalism or to the re-creation of Babel) or even a neutral one to be tolerated (thereby contributing nothing to the accomplishment of God's plan for humanity), but instead belongs to the very will and design of God to recapitulate everything in Christ.[52] At the beginning of *L'Église locale,* Tillard writes:

> A strange situation, that of the Church of God! From Israel it inherits an essential relation to the earth . . . because the earth belongs to the plan of God, and not solely because it constitutes the "place" of human destiny. It is not accidental that in the Bible Adam draws his origin and his name from *adamah* (Gen 2:7, 3:19; Job 34:15; Qoholeth 12:7), the earth. Between him and [the earth] is a strange history of solidarity. Mother-earth, but also the earth that a sinful humanity involves in its folly. . . . What would the Adam of the Bible be without reference to the earth?[53]

This inheritance is a mixed blessing, which makes the church vulnerable to idolatry and accommodation. However, it also enjoins the church to sink its roots into the "fleshly earth" and draw sustenance from it. Accordingly, the church is necessarily local, for its essence draws upon its encounter with history and culture; scripture, liturgy, tradition, and theology all bear witness to such engagement.[54] Thus, to speak of the church of Jerusalem as a "particular" church is "impossible":[55] the Jerusalem church is not a mere part of a larger, universal whole, but rather is a genuinely local church, manifesting the fullness of the *ephapax* grace of Pentecost in and through a given place's history and culture, a place that is, in fact, at the center of salvation history.[56]

And yet, although existing only in Jerusalem, this church is also universal. On the day of Pentecost it already speaks many languages, and it is to spread to all the nations the good news that "all who call upon the name of the Lord shall be saved" (Acts 2:21) — Jews and Gentiles alike. Similarly, Tillard sees in Acts 2:39 — "For the promise is for you, for your children, and for all who are far away, everyone whom the Lord our God calls to him" — the fulfillment in Christ of the promise made by God to Abraham that "by your offspring shall all the nations of the earth gain blessing for themselves" (Gen 22:18).[57] And furthermore, the narrative structure of Luke-Acts itself presents the church as the fulfillment of the Promise and of Israel, which then spreads throughout the world, symbolized especially by Peter's and Paul's journeys to Rome, the capital of the empire (and, by extension, the world); the fullness of the divine gift given to the local church of Jerusalem is destined for the entire world.

To sum up briefly, we have seen that Pentecost is the manifestation or epiphany of the church of God. As the accomplishment of the *qahal* begun in Sinai with the promulgation of the Law to Moses, this church emerges in Jerusalem — the holy, eschatological city — endowed once-for-all with the fullness of the Spirit of Christ, and is called to spread this gift to all peoples. Shaped by its formation in Jerusalem, this local church is fully the church of God, and subsequent churches will share in such fullness.

We shall now examine Tillard's presentation of the "marks" of the church of God, which he attributes properly to each local church. We will look first at how the church of Jerusalem manifests these qualities, and second at how they function in his theology of the local church as a whole. In both instances, the eschatological and communional role of the Holy Spirit is central.

Unity

Grounded in the event of Pentecost, each of the marks of the church — unity, holiness, catholicity, and apostolicity — is caught up in an eschatological tension.[58] Both divine gift and human task, each mark is "already" and "not yet" realized; the church, in its life and its reflection, must avoid seeing itself as either triumphant realization or a purely human construct. To speak of the *one* church of God, then, is to acknowledge that its unity is irrevocably given by God and yet broken by human sinfulness.

The church's unity is, in the first place, a reflection of divine unity.[59] God's unity, as Trinity, is communion: a mutual sharing or unity-in-diversity, which excludes both uniformity and division.[60] Accordingly, the unity proper to the church of God is communion, both vertically (a sharing in God's own communion) and horizontally (a sharing with fellow believers and communities), and it is expressed paradigmatically in the event of Pentecost. On that day, of course, the church of God is fully established at Jerusalem by the *ephapax* outpouring of the Holy Spirit upon the community. This local church of

Jerusalem is thus the *one* church of God, not because there are not yet any other churches, but rather because it already possesses the entirety of the church. The oneness of the Church therefore is not quantitative, but rather qualitative, in that it pertains to the wholeness and integrity of God's gift to the Church.[61] Having given it the fullness of grace, God will create no other Church: there is only the *unica Ecclesia*,[62] and subsequent churches will not add to, but enter into, the grace of the Pentecostal church.[63] Communion, the church's only form of unity, "means entry into an integral participation in a *full and definitive* (already eschatological) gift of God, made first of all to a local community."[64]

The church's Pentecostal unity subsequently manifests itself in several forms. First, the Holy Spirit, the "giver of life," forms believers into a communion by bringing them "into the real possession of one and the same life, coming from animation by one and the same Spirit."[65] Moreover, as the source and agent of communion, the Holy Spirit introduces every church into the fullness of Pentecost. As the miracle of the Jerusalem community's common understanding of many languages shows, the unity brought by the Spirit is not uniformity, but a communion of differences bonded together.[66] Such communion enables the church to be simultaneously one church and many churches — incarnating the same Pentecostal grace in a diversity of locales:

> [The local churches] are found wholly seized in the grace of [the church of Jerusalem's] *ephapax,* thanks to the "visit of God" to a rent humanity. Each of them is therefore the One, Holy, Catholic, and Apostolic Church of God. They do not establish it in forming the sum of its realizations. Each *is* the Church in being the authentic presence of the *ephapax* of the apostolic Church in one of the places and times where humanity lives its destiny. The Church is not multiplied. The Spirit integrates into the fullness of Pentecost the *places* of human destiny.[67]

Second, the Holy Spirit brings about such life-in-communion by introducing believers into the body of Christ through baptism. After Pentecost, Christ and the church are inseparable;[68] one belongs to Christ the head only by belonging to his body, the church. Through his cross and resurrection Christ destroyed the wall of division, reconciling all humanity — Jew and Gentile alike — by bringing it into communion with God and with each other. Baptism introduces the believer into this communion through a parallel dying and rising in Christ. Tillard draws freely here upon Aquinas's position on the simultaneity of forgiveness-redemption and sanctification-communion: one is forgiven and brought to new life by being incorporated into Christ and his body.[69] In the *Summa theologiae,* for example, Aquinas writes:

> By baptism man is brought again unto the spiritual life, which is proper to the faithful of Christ.... Now life is only in those members that are united to the head, from which they derive sense and movement. And therefore it

> follows of necessity that by baptism man is incorporated in Christ, as one of his members.[70]

> Since the pains of Christ's Passion are communicated to the person baptized, inasmuch as he is made a member of Christ, just as if he himself had borne those pains, his sins are set in order by the pains of Christ's Passion.[71]

Baptism, as the believer's entrance into Christ, thus serves as the foundation of ecclesial unity, a foundation so strong that it survives schism.[72]

Third, ecclesial unity, formed by the communion of the Holy Spirit and founded in baptism, is brought to its fullest expression in the sacrament of communion: the eucharist, whose primary effect or *res* is the unity of the church.[73] The eucharistic synaxis, because it is a gathering "not only 'around' Christ Jesus but 'in him,' " is the deepest *koinonia* with God and with humanity possible on earth.[74] And once again, one encounters the paradox of communion: there is at once only one eucharist and yet many eucharists; the same real presence is manifested in many eucharistic assemblies.[75]

Therefore, because the church and its unity are given fully by God at Pentecost, there can be, in one sense, no question of "more" or "less" church, "more" or "less" unity. Subsequent believers and churches will enter into this gift through the Holy Spirit, life in Christ, and the eucharist. No increase in grace or the church of God is possible or necessary.

However, although fully endowed by the primordial, Pentecostal gift of God,[76] this *unica Ecclesia* has not remained *una Ecclesia;* because of human sinfulness, the church, as the title of one of Tillard's articles states, is "broken in pieces." Moreover, the scandal of such division is not primarily pragmatic in its hindrance of united witness to the world, but theological, because it is an abuse of God's gift of communion.[77] The church's division would lead to resignation or despair, were one to forget that, though broken, the one church of God still exists and that all Christians share in such unity through their baptism. In contrast to much Orthodox theology, which holds that baptism is valid only in a church celebrating a true eucharist,[78] Tillard draws upon the affirmations of Vatican II[79] and the ecumenical movement[80] to argue that baptism is the basis of ecclesial communion:

> The one and only Church of God is already present, though very often in an abnormal way, everywhere an authentic baptism is celebrated by a community trying, in good conscience, to be faithful to the apostolic faith. Sometimes one or many of the means of sanctification are either absent or badly understood.... Nevertheless, either glowing or faded, healthy or wounded, either with all its capacities or in a quite humble way, the one Church of God is there. It may be veiled, hidden, diminished, decadent, disfigured, *cathedra pestilentiae*, "more corrupt than any Babylon or Sodom" (as Luther said in his *Open Letter to Pope Leo X*). Nevertheless, as Luther himself professed, one cannot cease to believe in the faithfulness of God for

all those who put their hope in Christ. God likes to exercise his power "*sub specie contraria.*" The Spirit never erases the Church.[81]

Thus, if the church of God's unity is imperfect, it is nonetheless real. And, ultimately, the restoration of full, visible unity will require mutual conversion, a dying to ecclesial self for the sake of greater ecclesial life and unity.[82] Therefore, because the church's unity is eschatological, the ecumenical task of the church demands that "onto this community of destiny [be] grafted a community of mission."[83] The gift of unity given at Pentecost to the church of Jerusalem anticipates the final unity of the heavenly Jerusalem.

Holiness

Holiness is perhaps the church of God's most important mark, for it involves the church's election by God and its "sharing in God's own glory" and communion;[84] the church's holiness is thus theological before it is ethical. Any conception of its holiness must therefore begin with the statement that God alone is holy, and that the church is holy only insofar as it participates in God's holiness; it has no holiness of its own apart from God. Moreover, because holiness concerns humanity's destiny, it is closely tied to salvation, with which it is ultimately synonymous, for both involve life-in-communion (salvation will be studied at length in chapter 4; it will be developed here only insofar as is necessary). To speak of holiness, then, is to speak of the fullness of God, the human person, and the church. It is also to speak of sin and the church's lack of holiness. In this section, we shall present briefly Tillard's understanding of holiness, examine the church of Jerusalem's holiness, and consider the holiness of the church of God as it exists between Pentecost and the Parousia.

Holiness is primarily divine election and a belonging to God and only secondarily a matter of human conduct. One thinks readily of 1 Peter 2:9, which affirms that believers are "a chosen race, a royal priesthood, a holy nation, God's own people," as well as of Ephesians 5:25–27, which states that Christ gave himself up for the church "in order to make her holy by cleansing her with the washing of the water by the word." The church is holy, then, because it belongs to God — it is the church *of God* — through divine election, rather than through human choice or effort. In this sense, its holiness is indefectible, for human weakness and sin cannot overpower God's own holiness.[85] Moreover, on its deepest level, such belonging involves a participation or communion in God's own life: the church and its members are not simply associated *with* God or *alongside* God, but called to dwell *in* communion with God through Christ and in the Holy Spirit, and, ultimately, to share eternally in God's glory. All ecclesial holiness has its origin and destiny in triune communion.[86]

Second, the church's theological holiness gives rise to its ethical holiness.[87] Irrevocably sanctified by God, the church seeks to respond to this gift of communion by living accordingly; the gift of communion becomes the task of communion, one in which believers often fall short, "because creatures who belong to [God] will still be marked by their fragility."[88] Nonetheless, despite the scandal given by such lack of ethical holiness, the church of God remains sustained by God's own abiding holiness, which is a gift more than it is a possession.

The church of Jerusalem exemplifies the theologically and ethically holy Christian community. At Pentecost, the Holy Spirit powerfully abides in it, endowing it once-for-all with the fullness of divine life. It belongs to God, for the community of Pentecost "represents the emergence — finally! — of the 'community of God' after the Fall, on account of what has been accomplished in and through Jesus the Nazorean. It is, therefore, the work of the grace of God."[89] Its holiness results from the forgiveness of sins through baptism and the gift of the Holy Spirit, who acts as the agent of both eschatology and communion. This theological holiness, the emergence of the "last days" through the formation of divine and human communion, manifests itself further in the church's acts of communion: prayer, the breaking of bread, almsgiving, common possession of goods, healings (Acts 2:42–47). Despite such holiness, however, the community is not yet the absolute fullness of communion, which awaits the end of time; Jerusalem, although the "holy city," is not yet the "heavenly city," and so the church of Jerusalem lives in hope.

L'Église locale is not a naïve work, but its strong focus on the event of Pentecost — in the hope of conveying the fullness of God's work in the church and the world through Christ and the Holy Spirit — tends to minimize ecclesial sin and division. For a fuller sense of the church of God's eschatological "in-betweenness," its graced and wounded being, we need to turn to Tillard's other works, most notably *L'Eucharistie*.

The holiness of the church of God on earth is marked by eschatological tension. It is, on the one hand, already complete in some manner, because of the outpouring of the Holy Spirit. On the other, it is also clearly the "not-yet," in that it is both incomplete, yearning for eschatological fullness, and sinful, acting against such fullness by creating division and violating communion. Its sinfulness is an incontrovertible fact, and its fragility ever-present.

Tillard describes this tension most fully in *L'Eucharistie, Pâque de l'Église,* through his conception of the "two moments"[90] of salvation — redemption and communion — which he applies to both the individual believer and the church. The pattern is first seen in the pasch,[91] or passage, of the Exodus: a "deliverance from oppression" and a "projection into a wondrous universe.... Hence, salvation is at once the shore of Egypt, the shore 'of servitude' (Ex 2:23), and the shore of the Promised Land, the shore of hope and of life."[92]

For the Christian believer this saving passage occurs initially in baptism, and is perfected through the eucharist and the "sacrifice of a holy life."[93]

Baptism alone, through the simultaneous effects of forgiveness of sins and incorporation into the body of Christ,[94] brings about the initial passage into Jesus' death and resurrection.[95] This life *in* Christ begun by baptism reaches its earthly climax in the eucharist. As both a dramatic participation in Christ's definitive Pasch and the ordinary, progressive deepening of this holiness, the eucharist is a present sharing in divine communion that anticipates the believer's perfect holiness. Furthermore, the growth in holiness wrought by baptism and eucharist issues forth in what Tillard calls the "sacrifice of a holy life,"[96] an offering of service, mercy, and self-dispossession which culminates in the praise of God — all anticipating eternal life wherein "all of our action will be Amen and Alleluia."[97] At each moment — baptism, eucharist, holy life — the believer is delivered from sin and brought into salvation and communion, a life of sharing in God's holiness that will reach its eschatological fullness in the Parousia.

The church itself, and not simply its members, shares in this passage. The "earthen vessels" of which Paul wrote refer not simply to individuals but to communities and the church as well — a church that is, as Augustine noted, a *corpus permixtum*, not a *corpus bipartitum*.[98] Thus, the church's holiness is not a possession with which it may be satisfied, but a gift which invites human response and often finds human sinfulness. In this regard, the church of God's "moments of salvation" parallel the believer's: "purification" and "glorification," each effected preeminently in the eucharist, the celebration of Jesus' passage from death to life.[99]

In words remarkable for their time — *L'Eucharistie* was completed in 1962, on the eve of Vatican II — Tillard describes the church of God in its earthly passage as "pilgrim" and "wandering,"[100] rather than the then more common "militant."[101] Where the latter term tends to see the earthly church's holiness as awaiting only its definitive fulfillment and locates the church's struggle against sin solely in relation to a sinful world, the former terms locate such struggle within the church itself and conceive of its holiness as something both already possessed and often compromised; the danger is that the church militant risks imagining itself to be already the church triumphant. For this reason, Tillard stresses that the church is paschal not simply because its life flows from Christ's sacrifice on the cross, but because it proceeds by way of suffering and trial, living between history and the eschaton, between Pentecost and the Parousia.[102] In words that anticipate *Lumen gentium's* powerful declaration that "the church . . . at once holy and always in need of purification, follows constantly the path of penance and renewal,"[103] he writes:

> The decisive battle is won in the paschal act of Christ, but . . . the fight is pursued in the daily acts of each faithful until the great victory of the Parousia. Such is the concrete situation of the Church Pilgrim. It is not a situation of peaceful repose, but of continual passage from the world of sin to the world of God. . . . In short, it is an essentially paschal situation.[104]

Such passage is effected most especially in the eucharist, the "paschal food"[105] of the church as it breaks with sin and enters into communion. Holiness is therefore preeminently eucharistic, for it is through the sacrament that the Holy Spirit "unites the personal body of the Lord with his ecclesial body and its members with each other,"[106] thereby "snatching [the pilgrim church] a little more away from death"[107] and making the church holy. Apart from Christ, the holy one, the church has no holiness.[108]

The paradox of the church of God's holiness, then, is that the church is called "to be what it has become"[109] through its communion with Christ: a holy communion of salvation. Grasped by the sanctifying power of Pentecost, yet straining toward eternal life, the holiness of the church is both theological gift and ethical responsibility.

Catholicity

In the foreword to *L'Église locale,* Tillard writes:

> It matters therefore, this time at the very heart of the Catholic community, to specify what the local church is in reality. It is necessary to show that in it the Gospel is realized in its entirety, to explain clearly that it is not the radicalization of "difference" and how it does not endanger "catholic" reconciliation.[110]

Subtitled "The Ecclesiology of Communion and Catholicity," *L'Église locale* argues that the church's experience of communion is an experience of catholicity, both of the fullness of God's own communion and of its spread throughout all creation. Tillard's central insight into catholicity, inspired by the Fathers and by the Russian Orthodox émigrés of Paris, is that it is primarily qualitative, rather than quantitative. Derived from the Greek *kath'olou* — "according to the whole" — catholicity refers first to the fullness of the divine gift given to the church of God at Pentecost and its penetration into diverse human cultures and places, and only secondarily to the church's geographic universality.[111]

A modified version of Avery Dulles's schema in *The Catholicity of the Church* of the four dimensions of catholicity aids in understanding Tillard's theology of catholicity.[112] First and most important is the "height" of catholicity, which emphasizes the fullness of God's gift to the church in Christ and the Holy Spirit; it concerns the mystery of God's trinitarian fullness in the church. Second is catholicity's "depth," in which this divine gift seeks to "plunge its roots"[113] into the soil of diverse human cultures. Third, the "breadth" of catholicity emphasizes geography: the church's universal mission to the entire world. Finally, catholicity's "length" refers to its extension through history: the church's pilgrim, eschatological nature and the communion of saints. With this framework we will look first at the early church's understandings of catholicity, second at the paradigmatic catholicity of the local church of Jerusalem, and third at the catholicity of the entire church of God.

Tillard's understanding of catholicity is formed in large part by the Fathers of the church, who developed a balanced vision of catholicity that emphasized both its qualitative and quantitative aspects.[114] Never used by scripture to describe the church,[115] "catholic" is used first in this sense by Ignatius of Antioch (c. 35–c. 107), although its precise meaning — be it geographical expansion, communal perfection, Christ's transcendent reality uniting all the faithful, the integrity of faith against heretics — remains unclear. The *Martyrdom of Polycarp* (c. 160) speaks of geographic universality, but the dominant sense of catholicity soon comes to refer in Polycarp (c. 69–c. 155) to the fullness of truth possessed by the church over against heretics or, in Clement of Alexandria (c. 150–c. 215), to the apostolic church modeled on divine unity. Later, in the East, Cyril of Jerusalem (c. 315–87) gives a rich, balanced account, highlighting the fullness of the church's truth and doctrine, but also affirming its universality.

It is Augustine, however, whose vision of catholicity is the early Western church's most influential and expansive. In response to the Donatist crisis, he strongly emphasizes the geographic universality of the Catholic Church in opposition to the Donatists of northern Africa; the *Catholica* is the *Ecclesia toto orbe diffusa*. Tillard argues, though, that the significance of Augustine's anti-Donatist struggle has tended to overshadow his deeper, qualitative sense of catholicity:

> Expansion throughout the *entire* universe has meaning only to the degree that it corresponds to the spread of the *entire* salvific truth and to *all* peoples. The fundamental mistake of Donatism is precisely not that of rendering impossible the local omnipresence of the *Catholica* (which the communities of the *pars Donati* avoided) but of constituting two *populi,* thus breaking the "*communio totius orbis*" in salvation. The integrality of salvation (in the fullness of truth and the authenticity of sacramental life) and expansion (in the totality of places where humanity lives its history) are broadly linked in the Augustinian vision of catholicity.[116]

The strongest corresponding image of catholicity is that of the church as the *totus Christus,* which embraces all humanity in the fullness of Christ the head, most definitively in the eucharist.[117] In short, Augustine develops a truly catholic sense of catholicity, comprising both the qualitative and quantitative, each of which is located ultimately in Christ's own catholicity.

Augustine's fine balance was upset, however, with the West's increasing identification of catholicity with universality. Aquinas, in his exposition of the Creed, defines catholicity as being primarily universal in its extension to all the nations, secondly as embracing all peoples (male and female, Jew and Gentile), and thirdly as spanning all ages.[118] His quantitative conception is correct but incomplete, as it lacks a corresponding qualitative sense.

Furthermore, in reaction to the Reformation, Catholic apologetics and theology began to stress that the Catholic Church alone possessed the creedal marks of the church.[119] For instance, in contrast to a then largely European Protestantism, Catholicism emphasized that it alone was truly catholic or universal in its geographic extension into the new world and in its sheer numerical superiority. Through the influence of such polemics, Catholicism expounded an increasingly constricted notion of catholicity, and a balance would be recovered fully only in the twentieth century through the work of Congar and others.

Tillard seeks to reaffirm this fullness of the church's catholicity through a seemingly paradoxical consideration of the church's locality. Drawing upon the Fathers, the insights of twentieth-century Catholic theology — especially Yves Congar and the documents of Vatican II — and also upon the work of such Russian Orthodox theologians as Georges Florovsky and Nikolai Afanasiev, Tillard joins a qualitative catholicity to a theology of the local church to argue that the church of God is inseparably local and catholic. He goes so far, in fact, as to state that it is catholic precisely because it is local: the fullness of the divine gift given at Pentecost takes root only in the diverse cultures, geographies, and histories of humanity. In short, Tillard privileges the "height" of catholicity, and sees it as the font from which flow catholicity's "depth," "breadth," and "length."

In the first place, catholicity is "height," the *fullness* and *integrality* of the divine, Pentecostal gift to the church of God. At Pentecost the church, although only in Jerusalem and not yet spread to the nations, is already truly and fully catholic: it "bears the fullness, the integrality, the *katholou* of the gift of God. It is thus the community where the divine *oikonomia* attains its moment (*kairos*) of fullness."[120] Accordingly, there will be no more catholicity in all of the subsequent churches of God than in that of Jerusalem, for

> catholicity is found, not only in its origin but also in its essence, in the grace of *a* local church, the apostolic church of Jerusalem. It will be no more dense in the gathering of all the churches of God "spread throughout the world" than in the eucharistic synaxis of Jerusalem, because it will involve a communion of all these churches in the "once-for-all" of the event of Pentecost.[121]

In other words, following the logic of communion,[122] additional churches will neither add to nor increase the catholicity of the church of God, but instead enter into the *katholou* that is already fully present in the local church of Jerusalem.[123] Catholicity therefore has its source in God, not humanity, and each local church partakes fully of the divine gift.

Second, the church of Jerusalem's catholic "height" is realized only in an equally catholic "depth." The interpenetration of catholicity's "height" and "depth" leads Tillard to affirm that the church is catholic precisely because it is local. Such a stance sounds paradoxical to contemporary ears, because of the virtual identification by much theology and preaching of catholicity and universality; in such a framework catholicity often seems to be defined precisely by its opposition to the local and the particular: catholicity is held to be what transcends or abolishes differences. As Joseph Komonchak has remarked, though, too often Catholicism has identified the church's catholicity with a "merely abstract universality"[124] and unity, and therefore "tension with catholicity almost defines the nature of the local church."[125] Ecclesial diversity is thus seen as a (potential) threat to ecclesial unity and catholicity.[126] When, however, catholicity is seen as a unity-in-diversity (communion), as the fullness of the one church taking root in many localities and cultures, then all such conflict drops out.[127] Local churches, far from being threats to the church of God's unity and catholicity, then become their very expression.[128] The event of Pentecost, as Tillard argued repeatedly, shows the dichotomy or even contrast of unity and diversity, of catholicity and locality, to be false, even dangerous. In short, locality does not compete with catholicity, but instead expresses it fully.

Therefore, as the role of Jerusalem and locality in Tillard's ecclesiology has been discussed previously, a brief summary will suffice here. Steeped in the history of Israel, the church of God inherits a relationship to the land, and must sink its roots in the "fleshly earth" if it is to incarnate the divine gift it receives "from above." In some sense, it would have been impossible for the church of God to have been manifested first other than in Jerusalem. As the *katholou* of the covenant formed at Sinai, the Pentecostal church is paradoxically realized only within a quite particular economy and history of salvation.[129] Jerusalem, as the holy and heavenly city, thus enters into the very identity of the church of God, making the church of Jerusalem not simply a particular church, but a local one which bears the marks and history of its place. In other words, the church of Jerusalem manifests its catholicity not simply by being in Jerusalem, but by entering fully into its history and culture.

In sum, although at Pentecost the church of God is only in Jerusalem, and has not yet spread to other nations (the breadth of catholicity) or reached the end of history (the length of catholicity), it is already entirely catholic. While not the full accomplishment of the eschaton, the local church of Jerusalem fully and integrally manifests the divine gift given to it at Pentecost and is therefore catholic.

However, the church of Jerusalem, while *fully* the church of God, is not the *whole* church of God.[130] As the church journeys through history, the gift of catholicity becomes the task of catholicity; the catholicity given at Pentecost, although irrevocable, is subject to growth and to decay, and awaits its definitive realization in the eschaton. Because the "height" of catholicity has already been examined, we need say only that the divine gift given in Jerusalem is not simply the origin of church's catholicity, but its substance.[131] Other local churches do not increase the church of God's catholicity, but rather share in its *ephapax*, unsurpassable fullness.

Nonetheless, as the church of God spreads beyond Jerusalem, this grace needs to be incarnated continually in the various dimensions of human existence: the cultural, the geographic, and the historical. In the most comprehensive sense, Tillard places this catholic incarnation in both a human and cosmic framework. Humanly speaking, catholicity embraces all peoples, Jews and Gentiles, in communion. It is best witnessed in the intermingling in martyrdom of the blood of Peter and Paul:

> [In Rome] is found...the attestation par excellence of the catholicity of the Christian faith, for this catholicity — we have emphasized this at length — does not mean solely the universality of faith. It concerns a more particular universality: that which includes in a single whole at once the People of the old Covenant and the pagan nations. No one has shown this better than the author of the letter to the Ephesians. In this plan, Peter and Paul are inseparable.... In their complementarity [Peter, the apostle to the Jews; Paul, the apostle to the Gentiles] they knit together the totality of humanity according to God, the *kath'olon* formed of the Jews who have been the chosen People and of the pagans entering into the communion of this election.[132]

More broadly, Tillard draws upon Ephesians and Irenaeus to argue that the goal of the divine plan is recapitulation: all creation is to be gathered up in the catholicity of Christ the Head.[133] Ultimately, nothing will escape such catholic reconciliation.

And on the most concrete level, the eucharist is the preeminent means by which catholicity penetrates and suffuses both humanity and creation: making Christ fully present in the Spirit (height), one and the same eucharist is celebrated in the liturgies of many cultures (depth), extends to all places and nations (breadth), and remembers the past while anticipating the future (length).[134] Through the eucharist, the fullness of divinity meets the fullness of humanity in catholic communion:

> From every age, from every social condition, from every group, from every race, from every culture, men as well as women, repentant sinners as well as saintly persons, clergy as well as laity, enemies as well as allies in civic life, they form therefore *in truth* only one Body, all inserted into the reconciling power of the one whose death on the cross and the resurrection "they announce" (1 Cor 11:26). Their gathering — the synaxis — not only "around" Christ Jesus but "in him" is thus the deepest expression possible of their *koinonia* at once with the Lord and with each other. It renders [this *koinonia*], in the strictest sense, visible and tangible.[135]

Although the eucharist embraces and sums up all of humanity and its projects, it does not however exhaust the realization of the church's catholicity. The depth of catholicity is realized as well in evangelization and inculturation — a process not limited to missionary lands, but active in every local church and its efforts to incarnate the Gospel in the "fleshly earth" of its region.[136] Evangelization "concerns the proclamation, incarnation, and expression of the Word in the cultures proper to diverse human groups,"[137] while inculturation is "the crucial process through which the Church as such *receives* into its own flesh the realities of the Creation or the fruits of human skill, together with the pains and efforts of people striving to transform the human condition into what their conscience teaches them it has to be.... It realizes the catholicity of the Church."[138] Both tasks aim for what Vatican II calls the "purifi[cation], strengthen[ing], and elevat[ing]" of human cultures and goods.[139] Against the risk of accommodation or even syncretism,[140] each local church must not simply mirror culture, but carefully discern that its inculturation preserves the church's faith and contributes to an authentic catholicity as a "fullness in unity"[141] or a "communion of differences."[142]

Furthermore, each local church not only transforms culture, but is itself transformed by such engagement.[143] As a communion of local churches, the church of God is built on a communion of differences: liturgies, creeds, devotions, theologies — each of which is the product of a given culture or community. One need look only at the diversity of ecclesiologies in the New Testament, the various Eastern and Western liturgies, the theological schools of Alexandria and Antioch, or the church's many creeds.[144] Such differences do not merely "color" each local church, but enter into its very identity. In short, Tillard's theology of inculturation — presented only briefly here — is both an exegesis of Vatican II's notion of catholicity as well as its ecclesiological development through a reflection on how the church of God itself is transformed in and through the local churches that manifest it fully.

The quantitative dimensions of catholicity — breadth and length — stand in service of the qualitative: catholicity stretches across space and time so that divine fullness may penetrate more deeply into humanity and creation. The breadth of the church of God's catholicity is readily apparent. It seeks the fulfillment of God's promise to Abraham that his "offspring [will be] as numerous as the stars of heaven" and that through them "shall the nations of the earth gain blessing for themselves" (Gen 22:17–18). It likewise responds to the risen Christ's commissioning of the apostles to "go therefore and make disciples of all nations" (Matt 28:19). Such breadth is, still more broadly, both recapitulative and eucharistic.

Length is catholicity's fourth and final dimension. In its broadest sense it concerns the intersection of time and the eschaton, and therefore the church's struggle to actualize its primordial, Pentecostal gift. Although *L'Église locale* is structured and dominated by the event of Pentecost, and so tends toward a very "high" or realized ecclesiology, Tillard also emphasizes that the church on earth is a pilgrim church. As with its holiness, the church in its catholicity bears the triumphs and failures of the past, presently lives in-between history and the "last days," and looks with hope toward the future. Just as the pilgrim church "at once holy and always in need of purification, follows constantly the path of penance and renewal,"[145] so too does its catholicity thus unfold in time, not triumphantly or uninterruptedly, but with pauses and regressions and successes. It seeks the fullness of the divine gift given at Pentecost not by rejecting the past for the radically new (*neon*), but by seeing the future as the fulfillment (*kainon*) of the past, especially of the covenant made at Sinai;[146] Avery Dulles writes, in similar fashion, of "that continuity in time without which there is no true catholicity."[147] Furthermore, this continuity stretches beyond time into eternal glory: the pilgrim, catholic church journeys not by itself, but with the communion of saints. In a passage that merits quotation at length, Tillard writes:

> I bear in my life of faith today the drama of Israel, the fruit of the costly discussions of Nicaea and Chalcedon, what Francis of Assisi mined of the mysteries of evangelical poverty, what thousands of obscure believers have affirmed of the power of hope in their responses to persecutors. And our successors will, in their time, be enriched by what African and Latin American Christianities in their contexts are working out before our eyes. The communion of saints is not relegated to the register of merits or of prayer. It already involves the fundamental plan of faith.[148]

The church of God shares not simply in earthly joys and sorrows, but also in the catholicity of the saints, whose holy fullness is communicated to pilgrim believers. Partaking of divine and human communion, this eschatological catholicity may be summed up, then, quite simply as the "creativity by which the power of Easter embraces the work of Creation."[149] The church of God, in its catholicity, is, and strives to be, nothing less than the "catholicity of the very *agape* of God."[150]

Apostolicity

The apostolicity of the church of God refers both to its origin in the apostolic community as well as to its ongoing continuity with the faith and ministry of that community. Above all, it refers specifically to the witness borne by the apostles concerning the words and deeds of Jesus Christ, especially his death and resurrection — the central reality of Christian life. Subsequent generations will come to know about God and Jesus only through this apostolic witness, and so it is the key to ecclesial identity and its continuity.

The church of God first emerges, of course, in Jerusalem, gathered in the name of Christ and sealed by the Holy Spirit at Pentecost. This beginning is specifically apostolic, for the apostles alone are capable of bearing eyewitness to Christ's resurrection and the salvation that it brings.[151] Founded upon this once-for-all witness, the church of Jerusalem is the "mother-cell" of the entire church of God. Moreover, as the "Twelve," the apostles stand at the crossroad of time and eternity, in continuity with the twelve tribes of Israel and prefiguring the heavenly Jerusalem (on the twelve foundations of its wall "are the twelve names of the twelve apostles of the Lamb" [Rev 21:12–14]).[152] The apostles testify to the "last days" inaugurated by the Holy Spirit at Pentecost, and, although not the source of communion (the Holy Spirit is), they are nonetheless its "visible foyer."[153] Eschatology and communion meet in their witness.

Because the apostolic witness is both unrepeatable and complete, subsequent churches — according to the logic of communion[154] — will not add to the church's apostolicity, but enter into it.[155] The apostolic church thus is not simply the "point of departure"[156] or "initial cell"[157] of the church of God, but is the "yardstick"[158] and, more profoundly, the continuing presence of "the truth of its *martyria* and of the *exousia*, the authority, needed to make that witness effective."[159] Since each local church "lives only as it is clasped perpetually in the embrace of the apostolic community,"[160] its apostolic connection is essential if it is to remain in communion with the apostolic faith and practice throughout history.

Unfortunately, apostolicity has often been constricted in polemics and theology to the notion of apostolic succession and the church's claim that it possesses a historically unbroken chain of ordained ministry reaching back to the Twelve. Although the historic episcopate is a doctrine shared by Anglicanism, Catholicism, and Orthodoxy, it does not exhaust the church of God's apostolicity. Drawing upon his ecumenical and patristic labors, Tillard places apostolicity in a broader framework, which has two interrelated dimensions: apostolic continuity and apostolic succession.[161] As these issues will be discussed more fully in the analysis of the episcopacy in chapter 4, a brief summary will suffice at this point. Apostolic continuity, which concerns the fidelity of each local church as such to the apostolic heritage in all of its fullness (for example, faith, sacramental life, mission, service to the poor), envelops apostolic succession, which concerns primarily the succession of ministry, particularly the bishop's integration into the episcopal college. Communal faithfulness and ordained ministry are symbiotically linked so as to ensure that the church of God is faithful to the witness and faith that it has received from the apostles.[162]

In the generations succeeding the death of the apostles, the apostolic witness takes the form of memory in the church's life. Memory is one of the central categories of Tillard's theology and ecclesiology, shaping in particular his understanding of eucharist, faith, ministry, salvation, scripture, and tradition. Neither a static reality nor the "sediments of the past," memory is rather the "soil from which [the church's] life ceaselessly draws."[163] In more concrete terms, the church's memory is its remembrance — in liturgy, in faith, in service — of what God has done in Jesus Christ, a memory which, paradoxically, anticipates the future; memory is therefore a living reality. "Tradition" is simply another word to describe the church's life in this apostolic memory of Jesus' life, death, and resurrection:

> Tradition (*paradosis*) is in effect the perpetual memory, preserved by the Spirit, of *the acta et dicta* of the Lord Jesus, of what he was and also of the understanding that the Apostles had of the work that God accomplished in him. It is therefore communion — yet again the word recurs — throughout the ages, with what constitutes the experience of the Apostles.[164]

Furthermore, the apostolic memory and tradition are fostered not only through the apostolic continuity of each local church, but more particularly through ordained ministry. Such ministry is fundamentally a "ministry of memory."[165] The bishop, whose ministry is one of oversight, is specifically charged with this ministry. As a successor to the apostles, each bishop receives the charge of watching over the apostolic witness. More precisely, since the apostolic witness is *ephapax* and therefore intransmissible, the bishop watches over the apostolic faith and witness not, properly speaking, as the successor, but as the vicar of the apostles and their faith and ministry.[166] He ensures that his local church is the "authentic presence of the *ephapax* of the apostolic church in one of the places and times where humanity lives out its destiny"[167] precisely by ensuring that his church remembers and proclaims its continuity with the apostolic witness.

Finally, through such memory, apostolicity returns ineluctably to the central event of the church's life: the eucharist. Each eucharist seals the local church's communion with the apostolic church, for the eucharist is where one "proclaims and celebrates the reality which constitutes the very heart of the apostolic witness":[168] Jesus' saving death and resurrection. Such eucharistic apostolicity is the surest and deepest sign of each local church's apostolic continuity,[169] for through it the church " 'remembers' a future which is already at work in human history."[170] Each apostolic eucharist re-presents Jesus' death and resurrection, which is the church of God's memory and hope, its origin and its destiny.

Conclusion

Thus, as one, holy, catholic, and apostolic, the church of God at Jerusalem is at once local and universal, incarnating in a cultural, geographical, and historical context the fullness of the gift of God given once-for-all at Pentecost. If the church is catholic because it is "the bearer of the *katholou,* the entirety of the plan of God for his People, at the end of a long journey through the centuries of history . . . the realization in its entirety of what was entailed in the call (or convocation) of God that first resounded over Israel,"[171] then the local church is the "fruit of the *katholou* of the Gospel of God in the totality of place . . . a double fullness (*katholou*): that of the gift of grace, and that of the human reality affected [by it]."[172] Far from splintering the church or needing to be held in check by the centralizing power of the universal church, then, each local church is the full — although not exhaustive — manifestation of the church of God in a given place and culture, arising from the intersection of the earth and its eschatological future.[173] The tension of the earthly Jerusalem cannot be resolved, however, short of the heavenly Jerusalem, and so each local church is both the first-fruits of salvation and a pilgrim community; its graced being is both glorious and fragile. The local church's life of faith, sacrament, and ministry — its concrete way of living out this Pentecostal gift — is our next concern.

Chapter Four

The local church is a communion of faith and sacrament

Where the preceding chapter dealt with the overarching vision and formal marks of the local church in Jean-Marie Tillard's ecclesiology, the present one provides its material complement: faith, baptism, eucharist, and ordained ministry. In its own tentative theology of the local church, Vatican II joined such formal and material elements concisely:

> This church of Christ is really present in all legitimately organized local groups of the faithful which, united with their pastors, are also called churches in the New Testament.... In them the faithful are gathered by the preaching of the Gospel of Christ, and the mystery of the Lord's Supper is celebrated "so that, by means of the flesh and blood of the Lord the whole brotherhood and sisterhood of the body may be welded together." In any community of the altar, under the sacred ministry of the bishop, a manifest symbol is to be seen of that charity and "unity of the mystical body, without which there can be no salvation." In these communities, though they may often be small and poor, or dispersed, Christ is present through whose power and influence the one, holy, catholic, and apostolic church is constituted.[1]

This passage unites, within a framework of communion, the local church's creedal identity, faith, and sacraments. However, it and the council in general do so without precision or depth. Concerned primarily with the renewal of the church as a whole, Vatican II did not develop a coherent, mature theology of the local church.

Tillard's ecclesiology seeks to further the reception of the council through the development of such a theology of the local church. "Visibly gathered first and foremost by the Word of God"[2] and reaching its "normative expression par excellence"[3] in the eucharistic celebration presided over by its bishop, the local church is for Tillard a communion of faith and sacrament. In *Chair de l'Église, chair du Christ,* he writes:

> At the foundation of the Church of God, Word and sacrament form a single whole. Without the Word and the faith it elicits, a sacrament is nothing more than an empty rite; without the Eucharist, the Word cannot lead the believer to the depths of the "mystery." It is not by accident that the reaffirmation of

the ecclesiology of communion at Vatican II coincided with the rediscovery of the role of the Word and the renewal of mission.[4]

Echoing Vatican II's insight that the church is fed by the "double table" of word and eucharist,[5] this passage affirms that the church's faith and sacramental life call forth one another: the sacraments make visible and effective the "mystery" of reconciliation in Christ that is proclaimed and believed by the church. Accordingly, although the subject of faith may initially seem to be related more to a general or universal ecclesiology than to one of the local church — and hence outside the scope of this work — it forms an essential part of any examination of the theology of the local church: the sacramental life of the local church is unintelligible, even magical and superstitious, apart from that church's faith.

This chapter therefore will study how the local church is shaped by and shapes its faith and sacramental life. Faith, as the foundation of the church of God, is necessarily our first concern: its nature as the "good news of salvation," whose end is communion of life in the Kingdom of God (faith's "what"); its ecclesial and personal subjects (faith's "who" and "where"); and its reception in tradition, canon, creed, worship, and spirituality through the interplay of the *sensus fidei* and episcopal ministry (faith's "how"). Next, we will examine how the faith of the local church issues forth in baptism, eucharist, and ordained ministry. Throughout, a constant theme will be the communion with God, humanity, and creation that is the origin and destiny of the local church's faith and sacraments — the communion that is, according to Tillard, the "key idea of the council."[6]

Faith

"Word and faith are always first"[7] in the church of God, for the Word of God calls the church into being and establishes the faith that is made fruitful in sacrament and service. This faith has both objective and subjective dimensions. The two are inseparable, but the objective aspect is primary, its content — "what God has accomplished for humanity in Jesus Christ"[8] — giving rise both to its profession by the community and the believer and to its ecclesial reception in tradition, scripture, and liturgy; the church professes not itself, but God and God's deeds. In brief, "the Church of God has for its rock faith,"[9] and thus even "[the epistle of] James attests to the fecundity and absolute priority of faith."[10]

The Content of Faith: The Good News of Salvation Is Communion

At the origin of Christian faith is the Word of God. Referring first to the eternal Word from which the revealed Word springs forth, the Word of God more generally concerns the divine initiative that "breaks the silence"[11] between God and humanity caused by original sin. Tillard prefers the expression "Gospel of God" to "Word of God," however, for the former conveys a more vital, dynamic understanding of divine revelation.[12] Where "Word" may unwittingly conjure up notions of abstract theory or over-intellectualized teaching, "Gospel" conveys a living reality: the Good News of Salvation in Jesus Christ. Expressed most concisely in Mark 1:15 — "The time is fulfilled, and the Kingdom of God has come near. Repent, and believe in the good news" — the Gospel of God is:

> the Good News that, since the dawn of history, God has always sought to sound out humanity suffocating in its distress. Israel has been chosen with a view to the realization of this project of God. And if the community confesses Christ Jesus as Savior, it is precisely because in him this Gospel of God is accomplished.... It is this presence, never perfectly clear but nonetheless indisputable, of a Word of hope overflowing the destiny of Israel as such in order to include it in a vaster divine plan that we call the Gospel of God.[13]

Not simply a written word,[14] then, the Gospel is the "way of salvation,"[15] joined to the joys and sorrows of the world, and stretching from Abel to the end of time.[16] Preaching this Gospel of God, the local church becomes "a graft of communion on the wounded body of a rent city and humanity."[17]

Salvation is, literally, health, and so Tillard's use of "graft" and "wound" language to describe salvation is not accidental.[18] He understands salvation broadly as the accomplishment of the plan — or "mystery," as in the Pauline letters to the Ephesians, Colossians, and Romans — of God for all humanity (Jew and Gentile alike) and creation to share in God's life through Jesus Christ. This salvific plan is built on two fundamental truths: first, that God offers salvation to all, and, second, that such salvation is acquired by Christ and made present by the Holy Spirit.[19] God's plan has been operative from the beginning of creation, finding its first expression in the covenant with Israel. Jesus Christ, as the "hope of Israel,"[20] is the realization of the covenant, but his church remains in continuity with Israel and the entire economy of salvation.[21]

This salvific economy and plan can be summed up in one word: communion.[22] The dominant theme of Tillard's theology and ecclesiology, communion stretches from his earliest writings on the eucharist to his most recent theology of the local church. We may distinguish three aspects of communion in his thought: its content, its means, and its place.

Humanity, individually and communally, is saved by being brought into the communion of God's own life. The content of such communion is threefold, encompassing God, humanity, and creation. In its deepest sense, communion is divine-theological: it involves God's own trinitarian life and human participation in that life (e.g., John 17:20–26, 1 John 1:3, 2 Pet 1:4). Second, such trinitarian communion is not simply the model, but the source, origin, and place of human communion:[23] life with God necessarily involves life with others. The interpenetration of divine and human communion finds its ultimate expression in John 17:21, wherein Jesus prays to the Father: "I ask . . . that they may all be one. As you, Father, are in me and I am in you, may they also be in us."[24] Third, because there is a fundamental continuity between creation and salvation, communion is cosmic; all creation, as Ephesians and Colossians reveal, is destined to be gathered up into divine communion — and thereby saved — through Christ the Head.[25] Communion is thus the "stuff" of the good news of salvation, and the church of God the herald and sacrament of that saving communion.[26]

It is obvious, however, that the fullness of communion willed by God does not yet exist, that the plan of God is frustrated by human sin. The drama of sin is that the human person

> has become an isolated being, creating a broken world where individuals interact without forming authentic bonds of communion. Humanity is thus condemned not to exist in truth. It is reduced to becoming scarcely more than a collage of individuals. Personhood is not realized there. . . . The struggle for the person is a struggle against "egomania," the quest for singularity is satisfied only in a welcome and much sought after solidarity.[27]

If the human person, the image of the triune God, is to realize the interpenetration of communion and singularity that marks divine life, then sin — the "rupture of communion"[28] — must be overcome. Accordingly, in the work of salvation, communion is effected through a movement or "pasch" from sin to grace, "a passage from a sinful condition (with all it implies) to a condition of love (with all it implies), a passage from the world of sin into the world of God."[29]

This passage involves the means of forgiveness-redemption, reconciliation-communion, and, ultimately, recapitulation in Christ.[30] As argued in the previous chapter, Tillard's first book, *The Eucharist,* sets forth the basic framework of salvation that will inform all of his subsequent work: the "two moments"[31] of forgiveness-redemption and reconciliation-communion, each of which is personal and ecclesial. Drawing upon Aquinas's baptismal theology, he holds that the two moments are not consecutive, but simultaneous. That is, the believer is not first forgiven and redeemed and only subsequently incorporated into the body of Christ, but rather he or she is forgiven and redeemed precisely by being brought into communion with Christ the Head and participating in both his death and his resurrected life.[32] In a similar manner, the church itself passes through the "two moments," most powerfully in its eucharistic celebration, whereby the "pilgrim church" is led ever closer to its eternal home.[33]

Alongside the imagery of the Exodus-Pasch and the Johannine "one in us," Tillard uses two other scriptural images to convey the nature of salvation: Christ's abolition through the cross of the wall of hatred between Jews and Gentiles (Ephesians), and the recapitulation of all creation in Christ the Head (Ephesians and Colossians). Ephesians 2:11–22 speaks of how the cross of Christ effects the realization of God's plan, the "mystery" in which

Jews and Gentiles are reconciled to form one body, in which the Gentiles "are no longer strangers and aliens, but . . . citizens with the saints and also members of the household of God" (Eph 2:19).[34] Lest such reconciliation be construed as simply a gentle, idyllic process, Tillard stresses that Ephesians does not identify communion as a "gathering of friends. It is — this is much different — the encounter in Christ of reconciled men and women. It is communion in the victory over hatred (*echthra*). This victory is acquired by the Cross of Christ."[35] Ultimately, reconciliation forms part of the process of recapitulation, whereby all of creation is gathered into the fullness of Christ (Eph 1:10, 22–23; Col 1:19–20).[36] Against those who might see recapitulation as a kind of "continuing incarnation" or "continuing Christ," Tillard states that it concerns:

> the seizing of humanity in its totality — creation *in initio,* flesh and blood, clay, failure before Satan, nations, saving words of God, history, the Spirit present in man, friendship with God, "the enmity of man" — in the body of the flesh of the Word of God. Such is the church: *communion restored* by reconciliation in Christ of humanity with *all* of itself, *all* of its destiny and its origin, even with *all* of the cosmos, and above all with God.[37]

Accordingly, while not effecting an identification of God, humanity, and creation, recapitulation affirms their radical indwelling. Thus, whether salvation is understood as personal or ecclesial, God gives not simply an "inheritance" or created effect, but "himself in a mysterious communion of life."[38] The good news of salvation — communion — is that God is not simply a God *for* us, but a God *with* us.

The place of this communion is both the church of God and the Kingdom of God. Tillard describes the salvific role of the church of God in several ways. It is at once a "pilgrim church" en route to the heavenly Jerusalem and already a "communion of life" with Father, Son, and Holy Spirit; the "Body of Christ" and the "People of God"; the "*Qahal* of God" begun by the covenant at Sinai and the "accomplishment of the Gospel of God."[39] It is the "flesh of Christ,"[40] in which the "fullness of Christ" emerges in the "fabric of concrete humanity."[41] And, as the "space of reconciliation"[42] opened by Christ's sacrifice on the cross and made visible in the eucharist, the church is the "recreation of the humanity-that-God-wills,"[43] that is, a humanity-in-communion.

However, the church of God does not exhaust the communion offered by God. Following Vatican II's declaration that the earthly church is "the seed and beginning of [the] kingdom,"[44] Tillard calls the church of God the "sacrament of the Kingdom."[45] It thus exists, in Oscar Cullmann's classic terms, between the "already" and the "not-yet" of the Kingdom; it is both the first-fruits and a *corpus permixtum.* Therefore, although inseparably linked to the church,[46] the Kingdom is more expansive than the church. While manifested paradigmatically in the worship and daily life of the church, the Kingdom is also present already in all men and women who seek truth, love without limits, work for justice and peace, and protect the human dignity of the poor and the marginal.[47] This recognition of God's presence in the lives and deeds of all peoples, not simply professed Christians, has a double effect. In the first place, it prevents ecclesiocentrism and sectarianism, which tend to a narrow, even exclusive, conception of God's salvific activity. Second, in a fuller sense, the wideness, as it were, of the Kingdom bears witness to the wideness of God's grace and presence in all of creation. Communion, the end of salvation, finds its home in the Kingdom:

> The Kingdom is the manifestation, in a *communion* of praise and happiness, of the fullness of mercy and grace offered by the Father and the Spirit, in Jesus Christ. And it is such not as an addition of individuals, but as *koinonia*, the *communion* of Christians among themselves and with the heavens, all *communing* in the eternal *communion* of the Father and the Son in the Spirit. There, the church's *communional* being finds at last its "place."[48]

In conclusion, Christian faith is the Good News that the plan of God for all humanity and creation has been realized in the Pasch of Jesus Christ:[49] sin is forgiven and its alienation eradicated, the human person is saved through being reconciled with God, neighbor, and creation, and the nature of this reconciliation is communion — a sharing in God's own communion of life. In short, the salvation announced by the Gospel is communion; its sacrament, the church of God; its ultimate fulfillment, the Kingdom of God.

The Subjects of Faith: Church and Believer

The objective content of faith finds its necessary complement in the subjects who receive, profess, transmit, and even form it. As befits an ecclesiologist — and especially one whose central theme is communion — Tillard stresses that Christian faith is inseparably communal and personal, and that it is the faith of the church as such that precedes and makes possible that of the believer. This section shall examine first the communal and personal dimensions of faith, as well as their relationship.

To say that Christian faith is ecclesial means that the church is not simply the instrument of faith, but also its subject and locus. It is the church as such which receives, forms, and transmits the Gospel of God: it "is the welcome of a Good News given 'once-for-all' and guarded by the Christian community throughout the ages."[50] One might say that the Gospel is always a word not simply for the church, but a word by and in the church.[51]

In the first place, faith is given by God to the church as a whole, in order to give life and structure to the community; the Gospel is a word for the church. In both testaments of scripture, God relates primarily to believers as a people, through covenant and church; the entirety of Christian existence is communional from beginning to end.[52] Second, the church not only receives the Gospel of God, but also forms it; the Gospel is a word by the church. The church thus belongs to the "origin"[53] of the Good News, for the Gospel is, under divine inspiration, the product of early Christian communities and bears their imprint. Tillard comments:

> Faith comes only from God; but the Word of God which gives rise to it wills to pass through the covenant. The revelation of a gratuitous salvation springs forth from God as a "source of living water," but [only] after slow steeping in the rock of human history.[54]

To illustrate his point, Tillard uses the example of Luke's Gospel, whose writer was not a contemporary of Christ and who drew upon the testimony of the first Christian communities and local churches: those narratives specific to his Gospel — the prodigal son, the good Samaritan, the Emmaus resurrection appearance — reflect the heritage and concerns of those churches;[55] further examples (the Johannine community's engagement with Judaism) are readily apparent.

Third, just as the Gospel of God is in part the result of ecclesial discernment, so it is the church as a whole that alone is capable of discerning fully its meaning; the Gospel is a word in the church.[56] It is "only in the Church that the Gospel of God is present and offered in fullness," for the church has been given by the Holy Spirit the "means of divine grace" with which to transmit and interpret its meaning.[57] Chief among these are the *sensus fidei* and the certainty (*asphaleia*) necessary to discern what is essential to the church's faith; although the church as a whole is endowed with these gifts, the episcopate is specially charged with ensuring the church's fidelity to the Gospel.[58] The necessity of communal and ministerial discernment thus rules out any recourse to the principle of *sola scriptura,* whereby the individual interprets the Gospel apart from the community or the local community interprets it apart from other churches.[59] As a word for, by, and in the church, the Gospel is fully professed and interpreted only through the church.

The church's faith nonetheless requires the free assent of each believer; there can be no question of coerced assent or totalitarianism. Instead, welcome, trust, sacrifice, and self-dispossession are the dominant characteristics of personal faith.[60] In a beautiful passage, Tillard describes God's affirmation, in Jesus Christ, of human integrity:

> The God of Jesus Christ does not want to consider man as a mere beggar who could only open his hand and receive. In the delicacy of his love he respects human freedom and its responsibilities: he gives himself, but in making covenant, in binding the faithful in the new Covenant realized in Jesus. This demands a human engagement, a response of rightness, engaging all the human values informed by love. Just as Jesus, because he was true man, assumed in himself all human values, making of them the instrument of his salvific work in submitting them lovingly to the design of the Father, the Christian must, with all his life, respond to the divine initiative.[61]

Ultimately, "in faith, the Christian welcomes the limitless agape of the Father's plan."[62]

The communal and personal dimensions of faith find their synthesis in Tillard's conception of the "Two yesses" of the believer. The first "yes" involves personal assent to the kerygma, wherein the believer affirms what "Christ is *for her;*"[63] it pertains primarily to the will. The second "yes" is an act of the intelligence, whereby the believer assents to the faith of the church as it has existed throughout centuries, to the church's understanding and practice of the kerygma: "The 'yes' said to what Christ is *for this believer* is thus inserted into the 'yes' the Church says to what Christ is *for this Body.*"[64] Personal faith, in other words, is "communion in the faith borne by the entire Body, the insertion of the individual Amen into the great choir of the Church."[65] Communal faith therefore does not exclude personal faith, but rather precedes, enables, and supports it. The faith of the church as such is primary and, though this treasure is too often borne in clay vessels, it bears witness throughout history to the reality of saving communion.

The Process of Faith: Reception, Sensus Fidei, *and Magisterium*

The content of Christian faith is appropriated and developed by communities of believers through the process of reception. Involving the interplay of the *sensus fidei* (the "entire people's supernatural sense of faith,"[66] as Vatican II defined it) and the teaching authority of the episcopate, reception refers in Tillard's work most specifically to a church's integration into its life of a doctrine or practice that is faithful to the Gospel,[67] but it more broadly embraces the development of the church's tradition, canon, creeds, spiritualities, theologies, and devotions. In reception, then, the objective and subjective dimensions of faith find their synthesis in the life of the church; it is how the church's faith is received and transmitted by communities and believers. This section will examine first the nature and scope of reception and, second, the process of reception through the interaction — sometimes tense — of the *sensus fidei,* the episcopate, and theology.

Reception has become, in the last forty years, an increasingly central ecclesiological issue, for both the ecumenical movement and the ongoing assimilation of Vatican II have impressed upon the Christian churches the need for a dual process of fidelity and growth in regard to the Word and Gospel of God.[68] Tillard defines reception as

> the process by which the content of this Word, but such as it is specified and defined by those who have by virtue of their ordination the exercise of magisterium in the church, is impressed on the Christian conscience, takes flesh there, becomes one of the points of doctrine that the *sensus fidei* will henceforth "recognize" or not "recognize" in such an opinion, affirmation, or movement. And if "reception" does not give to the hierarchical magisterial declaration its truth, it nonetheless gives definite confirmation that in this declaration truth is found. Thus, by communion, truth "is made."[69]

As this definition indicates, reception is not a purely subjective process by which a given church "creates" its own truth, since its reference point always remains the apostolic witness.[70] Nor does reception usurp the rightful role of the episcopate in the determination of doctrine. However, reception does involve the interplay of continuity and growth — particularly in each local church's encounter with its culture and history — by which the church discerns the authenticity and the fullness of its faith.

Tillard posits at least five primary characteristics of reception. In the first place, the basic dynamism of reception is that of *semper ipsa, nunquam eadem* (roughly, "always the same thing, never in the same manner").[71] "Mark[ing] the entire life of the Church,"[72] this tension arises from the constant interaction of the content of the church's faith (the apostolic witness and memory) and the different cultures, geographies, and histories in which it is expressed; reception is thus necessarily catholic, for its result is not uniformity, but unity-in-diversity.[73] Second, the community as such is the agent and subject of reception; the episcopate, while exercising a role of oversight and authoritative judgment, nonetheless stands within the community and in its service. Perhaps echoing Yves Congar's image in *Vraie et fausse réforme dans l'Église* of "the periphery and the center,"[74] Tillard holds that the community as a whole is the source of initiative and growth (*nunquam eadem*), while the episcopate acts largely as the principle of conservation and continuity (*semper ipsa*).[75] The two stand in intrinsic need of each other.

Third, the criterion — the *semper ipsa* — of reception is the apostolic witness, which norms all ecclesial reception, be it the formation of scriptural canon, doctrine, creed, or liturgy. The apostolic witness, as the previous chapter explained, is the eyewitness testimony of the apostles to Jesus' death and resurrection — the central mystery of Christian faith. Unrepeatable and given "once-for-all" to the church of God, such witness must nonetheless be received anew by every generation and community. Tradition, "communion . . . throughout the ages with what constitutes the experience of the Apostles,"[76] is another name for this overarching process of reception. One finds illustration of the interplay between apostolic witness and reception, for example, in the formation of scripture, canon, and creed.[77]

Fourth, reception is intrinsically plural in its "products" and means. The manifest variety of Gospels, liturgies, creeds, theologies, devotions, and schools of discipleship give ample evidence of such plurality. Thus, since reception touches every dimension of ecclesial life, Tillard insists that it not be conceived solely in intellectual and doctrinal terms, but also in artistic, musical, poetic, and prayerful ones: "Quite often what the Churches do not dare to say in their official documents is said more freely in their hymn-books."[78] Moreover, because it occurs only within concrete, local churches and cultures, ecclesial reception necessarily involves a process of inculturation by which each church "*receives* into its own flesh the realities of the Creation or the fruits of human skill, together with the pains and efforts of people striving to transform the human condition into what their conscience teaches them it has to be."[79] Inculturation therefore realizes the church's catholicity and communion through its unifying reception and embrace of diversity.

Fifth, reception always takes place within the concrete sacramentality of the church. As Christian truth is not primarily speculative, but personal and living, it is discerned and received best in the ordinary life and worship of communities and believers. This "Catholic ethos," as Tillard terms it, is characterized by precisely such concreteness and prudence; it distrusts abstraction and prefers to be pastoral.[80]

Reception thus refers to that process by which the apostolic faith is incorporated into the life of the churches through a dual movement of continuity and growth. This basic dynamic — *semper ipsa, nunquam eadem* — unfolds through the interaction of the local church's *sensus fidei* and the episcopal magisterium, with indispensable critical assistance from theology.

The starting point is the *sensus fidei,* which *Lumen gentium* #12 defines as "the entire people's supernatural sense of the faith." A divine gift, this *sensus* ensures that the church as a whole — "from the bishops to the last of the faithful" — is infallible and "cannot be mistaken in belief."[81] Admitting that the *sensus* is hard to define with any logical precision, Tillard nonetheless builds upon the council, assaying the following definition:

> Consequence of the Spirit's presence which inspired the prophets, Jesus, and the apostles, [the *sensus fidei*] is a sort of flair, a "spiritual" sense, an "intuition" (*instinctus*), by which, in a life faithful to the Gospel, one grasps *instinctively* what is in harmony with the authentic meaning of the Word of God or what deviates from it.[82]

Several points are immediately pertinent. In the first place, the *sensus fidei* is primarily a lived enterprise, whose authenticity flows from fidelity to the Gospel, not from a mere reading of texts or from statistical sampling. It is seen best in the saints, who "by their lives are the best exegetes of the Word."[83] Second, the *sensus fidei* belongs not to the individual believer, but only to the community as such. It is a gift given in communion, and the believer participates in that gift through baptism into the community; idiosyncrasy and illuminism are excluded. Third, the *sensus fidei* exercises a prophetic function within the church and for the world. Inextricably linked to the cultures and histories in which it is situated, the church both critiques and is critiqued by its situation; it seeks through its "prophetic antennae" to discern its unchanging faith in ever-changing circumstances.[84] Finally, lest this communal, evangelical *sensus* degenerate into fideism or integralism, it needs to be subjected to questioning and judgment. The first task belongs largely to theologians, the second to the episcopal magisterium; we begin with the latter.

In regard to the *sensus fidei,* the episcopate exercises a ministry of authoritative judgment. While each bishop remains within (and not above) his church, he nonetheless receives through ordination the authority and power to preach and teach Christian faith truthfully. Enveloped within a more fundamental "ministry of the Word,"[85] which maintains the local church in communion with the authentic content of the church's faith, the hierarchical magisterium (whose ordinary minister is the local bishop in communion with his fellow bishops) seeks to clarify and explicate the community's *sensus fidei* through reference to the apostolic faith.[86]

The relationship of the *sensus fidei* and the magisterium, at once symbiotic and tensive, is rooted in the same logic that governs all reception: *semper ipsa, nunquam eadem.* Sounding a recurrent theme of communion and catholicity, Tillard writes:

> The *diakonia* of the bishop thus permits the symbiosis of fidelity and creativity, the two fruits of the Spirit's action, thanks to which the *katholou* (the integrality) of the faith lives and is translated through assuming the diversity of the "human." For the firmer the attachment to essential values, the freer the mode of expression.[87]

This exchange thus is not unilateral, which would consist solely of the community submitting its expressions of faith to magisterial judgment, but mutual: the community receives confirmation (or not) of its *sensus fidei* from the magisterium, while the magisterium genuinely receives from the community an incultured faith.[88] Therefore, in contrast both to a Khomiakovian understanding of reception (all authority in the community *tout court*)[89] and to an ultramontane one (all authority in the hierarchy [especially the pope] *tout court*), Tillard notes that, although magisterial *authority* comes from God and not from the faithful, it draws its *credibility* from their sense of faith; the tension must not be collapsed if the church is to remain vital. Tillard holds that the best analogy for this symbiosis is perhaps the eucharistic anaphora, wherein the bishop or priest prays the epiclesis and words of institution and the assembly responds with its "Amen";[90] the minister's words and deeds are not made valid or effective by the assembly's ratification, but such ratification seals or confirms what has been done. Such mutuality is an expression of what Vatican II, in *Dei verbum* #10, described as "a unique interplay [*conspiratio*] between bishops and the faithful... in maintaining, practicing, and professing the faith that has been handed on." And it is precisely in this *conspiratio,* involving the entire community, that the local church receives its faith both faithfully and creatively.

The relationship of bishops and theologians is a special instance of this *conspiratio* or symbiosis. Following Aquinas, Tillard speaks of the *cathedra pastoralis* and the *cathedra magistralis.*[91] The former, as we have seen, is exercised by the episcopal magisterium and has as its task the oversight of the church's apostolic faith; it is necessarily conservative in nature, seeking to ensure continuity across time and space. The latter chair is the province of theologians, and endeavors to discover the meaning of the Word of God through research and criticism — a task always exercised within the church, but at times challenging its teaching on a given issue. While both chairs exercise a ministry of truth, their approaches and mentalities differ. The bishop is concerned primarily about the unitive function of truth: ecclesial communion is his goal, and so he seeks "a balanced teaching which does not disturb peace in the community."[92] The theologian, while concerned about church unity, is more immediately "attached to the absolute rights of the truth," than to its pastoral consequences.[93] The fruits of theological research may place him or her in tension, even conflict, with the episcopate through a questioning of church doctrine and practice. At its best, however, the relationship between bishops and theologians is neither parallel (as the episcopate alone possesses the *charisma veritatis certum*) nor competitive, but a communional one, a *conspiratio* by which the local church lives in truth. Such (productive) tension between theologians and the magisterium points, ultimately, to the church's need for patience in its reception of the faith:

> The Church of God remains united in its "devotion" to the divine Truth.
>
> This needs patience and forbids rapid decisions or short-cuts. But in God's design, time is an essential factor. The Catholic Church knows by experience how difficult it is to correct a too hasty decision. This is why it is its tradition to teach a truth slowly articulated through a consensus of which the *cathedra magistralis* (exegetes, dogmaticians, canonists, moralists, . . .) as well as the *sensus fidei* of the whole people of God including "people in the pews" are the builders, together with the *cathedra pastoralis*.[94]

Tillard has acknowledged that some may find this vision of reception and symbiosis too "optimistic," too "hypothetical."[95] Where and how, after all, is such a process realized? Vatican II stands, in his estimation, as one such event of ecclesial reception.[96] Its conciliar decrees represented, in large part, the reception by the magisterium of decades — even centuries — of patient, often condemned, theological labors and popular movements. *Sacrosanctum concilium*, for instance, was the fruit of the European and North American liturgical movements; *Dignitatis humanae* that of John Courtney Murray's reflections on the American experience; *Lumen gentium* that of such theologians as Yves Congar, Henri de Lubac, Gerard Philips, Karl Rahner, and Otto Semmelroth. The exceptional graces of the council should not obscure, but reveal, the essential, even mundane, processes of reception by which the church of God's faith in the good news of salvation is incarnated — through each local church — in the cultures, geographies, and histories of humanity.

Sacrament

In Tillard's thought, faith bears its fruit in the life of the local church through the lived witness and confession of communion (*martyria*), the engagement of its members in the struggles of the world (*diakonia*), and the eucharistic synaxis (*leitourgia*).[97] Although the first two of these means are indispensable, our focus in the remainder of the chapter will be the community's sacramental life. In the local church, faith and sacraments are in osmosis, for the sacraments are fundamentally sacraments of the community's faith.

On the one hand, they are not magical rites, but depend upon the free response of the believer's faith for their efficacy; they are sacraments *of the faith*. On the other, the sacraments express, deepen, and complete one's faith; they are *sacraments* of the faith and make that faith visible and effective. The local church lives from this communion of faith and sacrament.

Baptism

In the church of God, "everything depends ... on a theology of baptism,"[98] for baptism seals the believer's faith, joins one to Christ and his church, and orders one's life in that communion. If eucharist is the most important of the sacraments, baptism is the most necessary, as it is the "door" through which one enters Christian life.[99] Tillard's theology of baptism, especially in *The Eucharist,* is built upon Aquinas's conception of capital grace, by which all grace flows from Christ the Head to the members of his body. For example, Aquinas writes:

> Now he is our Head, inasmuch as we receive from him. Therefore he is our Head, inasmuch as he has the fullness of grace.[100]

> By baptism, one is incorporated in Christ, and is made his member.... Consequently it is fitting that what takes place in the Head should take place also in the member incorporated.[101]

Accordingly, baptismal grace is both Christic and ecclesial, incorporating the believer into the body of Christ through a sharing in the passion, death and resurrection of Christ. Baptism, in short, is what makes one a Christian.

Baptism is, in the first place, the "sacrament of faith"[102] that signifies and makes effective faith. Conversely, faith is the necessary condition of baptism; without the believer's free acceptance of the church's faith, baptism is meaningless, invalid, and magical. The rite of baptism itself is preceded by the renunciation of evil and the confession of the church's faith on the part of the believer (or the believer's godparents, in the case of infant baptism).[103] Such confession, as described earlier in this chapter's discussion of faith's subjects, consists of two "yesses": the first to the Gospel of God and its kerygma, the second to the meaning and implications of this faith (as normally expressed in the profession of a creed). Baptism thus "seals the welcome of the Word of salvation."[104] It does so through the believer's incorporation into Christ and his body.

Baptism itself is, as Romans 6 proclaims, a salvific entry into the death and life of Christ Jesus. "In the ordinary economy of the Christian mystery,"[105] it alone effects a Pasch, destroying the believer's sin and projecting her or him into new life in Christ. These two moments or movements of salvation are simultaneous, as incorporation into Christ communicates to the new member the effects of Christ the Head's death (forgiveness-reconciliation) and resurrection (new life). Moreover, baptism imparts a decidedly paschal character to all Christian existence. In contrast to theologies of vocation that would locate laity primarily in the world (an incarnational approach) and clergy and religious in the church (a paschal-eschatological approach), Tillard insists that the life of every Christian is both incarnational and paschal. He quotes the (aptly named) French Groupe Pascal Thomas:

> There is therefore a sort of paschal mystery whose proper place is life in the world. In this sense, the world is not simply a reality of creation that Christians assume as such, one for which they give thanks and in which they collaborate with the creator. The world is also a place of Easter where, in union with the dead and risen Christ, Christians pass through loneliness, anguish, failure, and hopelessness without renouncing the promise of God and without ceasing to rely on his word.... One can no longer speak of a "secular specificity" solely in regard to laity in the world. It is the entire Church which has a mission at once secular and evangelical.[106]

As Aquinas's theology of capital grace indicates, baptism effects an incorporation into Christ through incorporation into his body, and vice versa; Christ and church necessarily imply each other. Baptism has two primary ecclesial effects: unity and equality. Baptism, quite simply, makes the church to be. It creates a bond with and in Christ so strong that schism cannot break it. Vatican II affirmed that all who are validly baptized belong to Christ and his church,[107] and, in so doing, it erased any lingering "Cyprianism," which would deny the validity of a separated community's baptism.[108] Developing the council's insight, Tillard insists that the ecclesial unity effected by baptism is Christic and ontological, and not simply psychological or contractual.[109] Accordingly, the divine gift of unity survives the division caused by human sin. Moreover, such common belonging to Christ should not simply be recognized, but is an imperative calling the churches to build upon that unity through service and, especially, the witness of faith.[110]

Within this ecclesial unity, baptism founds and sustains the equality and common dignity of all believers. Tillard notes approvingly that Augustine's primary designation of the Christian is *Christifidelis,* which precedes subsequent distinctions of clergy and laity.[111] Through baptism, all participate in Christ's threefold office of priest, prophet, and king. The faithful exercise such office primarily as a body, and only secondarily as individuals; for instance, Exodus 19:6 ("you shall be for me a priestly kingdom and a holy nation") and 1 Peter 2:9 ("you are a chosen race, a royal priesthood, a holy nation, God's own people") both refer to a communal priesthood.[112] In the life of the local church, this priesthood is exercised most fully in the eucharistic synaxis. Ordained ministry, wholly necessary for the life of the community, exists only for the service of this common, baptismal priesthood and never apart from it; the bishop is *Christifidelis* along with all the baptized of his local church.[113] The prophetic role of the baptized is engaged by the interplay in ecclesial reception of the *sensus fidei* and the magisterium, while the royal role is expressed in the synodal life of the local church.[114]

Therefore, by virtue of their baptismal mandate, all Christians have the right and duty — or, more deeply, are called — to participate fully in the life of the local church — a calling recognized by the 1983 Code of Canon Law, which, Tillard notes, makes all of the baptized the subjects of the church's mission.[115] One thus becomes Christian by baptism; it forgives sins and gives new life in Christ. This incorporation into Christ and his body, however, reaches its fullness only in the local church's celebration of the eucharist.

Eucharist

Baptism and eucharist are mutually ordered to each other in Tillard's thought. On the one hand, the eucharist is the synaxis of the baptized; it admits only those "saints" who through baptism have shared in Christ's dying and rising.[116] Conversely, baptism finds its source and fulfillment in the eucharist: the eucharist is not only the completion of the Christian initiation begun by baptism and a sharing in divine life-in-communion, but also the wellspring of the new life in Christ given by baptism.[117] The eucharist is thus both the "sacrament of sacraments," in which all others find their "source and summit" (*Lumen gentium* #11), and the "sacrament of the church," manifesting and effecting the communion of God and humanity — the goal of the divine plan. The eucharist, then, is the heart of Tillard's ecclesiology of communion and theology of the local church. Before exploring the role of the eucharist in the local church, however, we must first examine briefly the nature and effects of the eucharist itself.

Tillard's eucharistic theology is built upon the thesis that there is only one Body of Christ, in which the "personal" body of the Lord and the "ecclesial" body coincide sacramentally;[118] *Chair de l'Église, chair du Christ* is an extended scriptural and patristic study of such mingling. The personal or eucharistic body is, in the first place, the resurrected, glorious body of the Lord. In contrast to the position that the eucharistic body is Christ's earthly body,[119] Tillard argues that Christ's risen body alone has the life-giving power of the Holy Spirit given by the Father in the resurrection. Moreover, only the resurrected body can "recapitulate" the totality of human experience — life, death, joy, sorrow — and offer it to the Father.[120] What is given and received at the eucharist is the resurrected, transformed body, which is the "point of definitive communion of life between the Father and [humanity]."[121]

The eucharistic body is given, however, for the life of the church and the world. Accordingly, it effects an osmosis of the eucharistic and ecclesial bodies, an intuition Tillard draws from the apostles John and Paul and especially from Augustine, whose linking of the two bodies is the "most profound vision of ecclesiology in the West."[122] Tillard himself states that, after Pentecost, there can be no Head without the Body, no Christ without the church; the sacramental and ecclesial bodies are joined inseparably in and by the Holy Spirit. The Johannine and Pauline traditions offer complementary ways of looking at this *circumincessio* of the eucharistic and ecclesial bodies.

For John, the eucharistic body is the Logos, the life-giving flesh, and the ecclesial unity it works is a mutual indwelling or abiding in the Father; this view is a "high," ontological, and incarnational one, finding classic expression in the Alexandrian school, especially in Cyril of Alexandria.[123] Paul, in contrast, sees the eucharistic body as the "pneumatic body" of Jesus Christ transformed by the Holy Spirit at the resurrection,[124] and ecclesial unity as an incorporation into the body of Christ through sharing in Christ's body and blood; Paul's orientation is "ascending," historical, and paschal. While differing in certain respects, Augustine gives the Pauline tradition its most paradoxical, "audacious"[125] expression: "be what you see and receive what you are."[126] In both traditions, the *res,* or effect, of the eucharist is the same: the communion of life between God and humanity:

> "The flesh of the Church" [is] the communion of life of a humanity reconciled with the Father and with itself *en Christo.* We have seen that, by the power of the Spirit and of the Word, it is the "flesh of Christ" in the osmosis of the Lord's sacrificial flesh and of the concrete fabric of the lives of the baptized—a *circumincessio,* an osmosis, of which the eucharist is the *sacramentum.*[127]

One thus understands why the eucharistic synaxis is the heart of the local church: it is not simply what the local church does, but what it is. In gathering as the baptized around the eucharistic table with its bishop (or his presbyter), the local church fully expresses its communion with God, humanity, and creation.[128] It enters into the paschal mystery, is taken up into that divine life, and so is made a reconciled community, a foretaste and sacrament of the salvation announced in the Gospel of God.[129] Celebrating the one and only one eucharist, which stretches from the apostles to the Parousia, the local church *is* the church of God, not simply a part of that church.[130]

Accordingly, Tillard would agree with Afanasiev's claim that "the eucharist makes the church": ecclesial communion is effected and made visible in the eucharist which binds the baptized to God and to each other. However, he insists just as strongly that "the church makes the eucharist": it is the church of God that celebrates the eucharist, and only those who have entered by baptism into Christ's dying and rising can share in his body and blood; the eucharistic celebration presupposes an already existing church. The eucharist is thus both the "*sacrament* of the church" and the "sacrament *of the church.*"[131]

The communion brought about by the eucharistic synaxis extends into the entire life of the local church, a movement that Orthodoxy describes as the "liturgy after the liturgy." Tillard writes similarly of the "sacrament of the brother"[132] (see Matt 25:31–46) and the "two meals of the Lord,"[133] whereby bread is given to believers and to the poor. Perhaps most deeply, through the eucharist each local church shares in the death and resurrection of Christ, the "victim betrayed by his own, crushed by unmerited violence, nailed to a gallows,"[134] and so it shares in the suffering of all victims; although Tillard does not state so, it should therefore be clear that the eucharist of a local church in Rwanda or East Timor has a different quality in this regard than that of one in Belgium or Canada. The eucharist likewise remembers and thereby makes present both God's victory over the cross and the joy of the resurrection. In each of these dimensions — fraternal care, service to the poor, communion with humanity's victims — the local church enters more fully into communion with the joys and sufferings of the human community in which it dwells. The eucharist opens out into the "sacrifice of a holy life,"[135] and that holy life, in turn, finds its earthly fullness in the eucharistic synaxis: "for the Church of God is not simply an event, a *happening*. It is the seizing of concrete humanity in the power of the Gospel of God made real by the Spirit of paschal reconciliation."[136]

Episcopacy

At the heart of the eucharistic synaxis is the bishop. Exercising a ministry of oversight (*episkopè*) or watchfulness over the local church,[137] the bishop ensures the unity of his church and its communion with other local churches and with the Pentecostal church of Jerusalem. He labors *ad aedificationem Ecclesiae*, primarily through his ministry of the Word and his eucharistic presidency. This ministry of unity is, in turn, rooted in his charge "to keep the church — by the eucharist, the sacraments, orthodoxy, and evangelical life — in the memory of the apostolic *ephapax*"[138] of Pentecost. In this section we first examine the relationship of the bishop to the local church and the role that he exercises within it. The apostolic origin and nature of the episcopacy, which makes of it a "ministry of memory," is our second concern. Finally, we consider the exercise of this apostolic ministry through the bishop's service of the Gospel and presidency of the eucharist.

Episcopal ministry exists not simply for the local church, but also in the local church. It has its charter in baptism, the foundational grace upon which all Christian life and service is built. The bishop is therefore first and foremost a Christian (*Christifidelis* with all of the baptized, according to Augustine), and his own ministry is rooted in the common priesthood of the baptized.[139] Moreover, drawing upon Cyprian's phrase, "the bishop is in the church, and the church is in the bishop," Tillard holds that the bishop reminds his church that there can be no body without a head, while the community reminds the bishop that there is no head apart from the body; both head and body need each other for the proper exercise of their respective functions within the local church.[140]

The interplay of bishop and church is developed further in Tillard's treatment of the episcopal *sedes* and *sedens*. The *sedes* has deep ecclesiological resonance, for it represents the local church's identity and continuity with its own faith and traditions, as well as its fundamental link with its apostolic heritage; although the great tradition continues to grow, it nonetheless does so only in continuity with the ecclesial permanence embodied in the *sedes*. It thus precedes the *sedens*, the bishop who sits upon the *sedes* and thereby ensures the local church's fidelity to the living tradition: quite visibly, the bishop's chair or throne in the cathedral endures, while its various occupants do not.[141] The *sedes* has both a historical and an eschatological orientation. Historically, it represents continuity with the church of God's apostolic memory and inheritance; the church of Rome, for example, keeps alive the memory of the faith and martyrdom of Peter and Paul. Eschatologically, the *sedes* prefigures and symbolizes the twelve thrones of the Apocalypse, the "seat[s] of glory"[142] which are themselves symbols of the twelve tribes of Israel in the kingdom of God — the end of God's plan for all humanity. In the *sedes*, then, time and eternity intersect at the heart of the local church:

> At the heart of its space and its life, through the *sedes* on which its bishops follow each other, the local church knows therefore that it comes from God who, in Christ, does not cease to keep it in the apostolic witness and to lead it towards the great liturgy of the messianic feast in the Kingdom.[143]

The compenetration of church and bishop represented by the *sedes* — to the extent that a *sedens* without a *sedes* is unthinkable — raises the matter of titular and auxiliary bishops. Although not condemning such bishops, Tillard states unambiguously that they — and the "universal ecclesiology" they represent — "wound the authentic nature of the episcopacy."[144] In a universal ecclesiology, which posits the priority of the universal church over the local church, the bishop is conceived as belonging first to the college of bishops. Subsequently, but not necessarily (as in the case of titular — auxiliary and curial — bishops, who are assigned once extant, but now defunct, dioceses), a bishop may be assigned to a local church; Vatican II, we have argued, upheld in the main this theology of the episcopacy, stressing its collegial nature over its local nature.

However, in Tillard's theology of the local church, which posits the simultaneity of the local and universal churches and denies the existence of a universal church existing prior to, or apart from, the communion of local churches, a bishop is simultaneously a member of the episcopal college and the occupant of the *sedes* of a local church; a bishop existing apart from a concretely existing local church is anomalous, since the bishop is not a mere member of a "board of directors" for the universal church, but genuinely a pastor and head of a local church. Apart from reference to that local church, his oversight and his episcopacy have no real ecclesial content. Therefore, both curial and auxiliary bishops have no essential place in Tillard's theology of the local church: the former because the bishop has no connection to a presently existent local church and *sedes*, the latter because the "body" of the local church can have but one "head," and the "seat" have but one occupant. Each kind of titular bishop weakens the intrinsic bond between the bishop and the local church.

The bishop thus exercises his *episkope* only from within the local church, never apart from it. In the local church, *episkope* involves two broad, overlapping areas of activity: leadership and coordination.[145] By virtue of his sacramental ordination, the bishop has the mission and duty of shepherding his community and preserving it in the apostolic faith; he leads the local church therefore especially by ensuring its apostolic fidelity. Such leadership, however, does not exhaust the community's ministry and activity. It seeks rather to promote the "synergy" of the entire community and to coordinate its diverse charisms.[146] The bishop is not the apex of a pyramid, from which all power and initiative flow, but the one whose ministerial priesthood makes it possible for all members of the local church to exercise their baptismal priesthood.[147] He conducts the "symphony" of the local church's gifts, ordering and guiding them in light of the common good.[148]

Therefore, whether exercised as leadership or coordination, the bishop's *episkope* is a *diakonia,* rather than domination or privilege. This last sentence may well sound platitudinous, but it bears repeating that the bishop is the servant of his local church. By both his teaching and his personal example, the bishop serves his church with the goal of "gathering all believers in the apostolic word of reconciliation,"[149] a word which is a word of communion. Moreover, in so doing, the bishop's *diakonia* is not merely functional, but sacramental — in the dual sense of its ordained character and of its signification of God's own oversight of, and care for, the church of God.[150]

Episkope has its origin in the witness and ministry of the apostles. As outlined in the preceding chapter's discussion of apostolicity, the apostolic witness is "the axis of ecclesial faith and life,"[151] for it is the source and continuing presence of the church's communion with the life, deeds, and words of Christ. The bishops "succeed" the apostles not in terms of this witness — which is *ephapax,* unrepeatable — but in their "judgment" upon, and discernment of, its reception in the life of the local church;[152] they are vicars and not, in the strictest sense, successors of the apostles:

> [They] will be therefore the *vicars* charged with the radiance of what will remain *the* fundamental ministry — that of the Apostles — until the end of time, in the rhythm of history and in ever-new circumstances. [Their] task will be the conservation, explication, interpretation, realization, and transmission of the apostolic Word, in the local churches.[153]

Furthermore, because episcopal ministry is always exercised within and for the local church, each bishop ministers, in part, by "coordinating" the various initiatives and projects of the community as a whole, thus "guaranteeing that this *aggiornamento* remains in the grasp of what the apostolic community understood and transmitted of the *acta et dicta* of the Lord."[154] Accordingly, the bishop's "ministry of memory," which is even the "fundamental ministry *in* the church,"[155] remains in constant symbiosis with the *sensus fidei,* by which the dynamic of Christian tradition — *semper ipsa, nunquam eadem* — is manifested in the local church. Drawing its life and purpose from the apostolic ministry, episcopal ministry does not monopolize or suffocate communal initiative, but ensures its creative and faithful development.

The bishop's charge to maintain communion with the Pentecostal, apostolic church finds preeminent expression in his ministries of Word and eucharist. His "minist[ry] of the Word"[156] involves several activities (catechesis, exhortation, teaching), of which preaching the Gospel has pride of place (as signified, for example, by the open book of the Gospels held above his head during ordination). More broadly, such ministry concerns the "guarding of the "memory" of the church, therefore of the Word which is its content."[157] Through the sacramental grace of ordination, the bishop "succeeds" the apostles and is empowered to teach authoritatively, i.e., to discern the authentic content of the apostolic Word in ever-changing circumstances. Although his magisterial teaching always remains yoked to the *sensus fidei* of the local church, he nonetheless is specifically charged with the oversight of the apostolic deposit and the preservation of his church in the unity of truth. Through this exercise of *episkope* the bishop fulfills the prophetic dimension of his ministry and builds up his local church through the proclamation of the Gospel in its integrity and its fullness.

The bishop's oversight culminates in his eucharistic presidency, just as the life of the local church culminates in its eucharistic synaxis. In that gathering, faith and sacrament reach their mutual fullness and the local church most fully manifests its communion with God and humanity. In like manner, the bishop becomes the "master craftsman of unity" through his presidency, for the eucharist's effect is the unity of the church.[158] It is here, perhaps, that we see why the local church must be the diocese rather than the parish.[159] As head of the community, in the dual sense of "source of life" and "bearer of authority," the bishop "holds the place of God" (according to Ignatius of Antioch). In order for the eucharistic celebration to be valid, the bishop or his designate (another bishop or a presbyter) must preside, so as to ensure apostolic continuity and ecclesial communion. In this context, the eucharist of a parish is legitimate to the extent that it is celebrated in communion with the local bishop. Apart from the bishop, however, the eucharistic synaxis becomes a sign of ecclesial disunity and thus a visible contradiction of the communion willed by God, announced in the Gospel, and celebrated in the eucharist.

Conclusion

As a communion of faith and sacrament, the local church in Tillard's thought exemplifies Vatican II's theology of the local church. At the heart of both the council's and Tillard's theology of the local church is the communion of Gospel and eucharist, of faith and sacrament. Both are equally necessary for the full life of the local church. Their relationship is neither additive (faith and sacrament as two separate entities joined extrinsically) nor consecutive (first faith, then sacrament), but communional: faith and sacrament depend upon each other, and together they bring each other to fullness. On the one hand, the eucharist is the sacrament of faith: "*the* sacrament of communion, [the eucharist] constitutes the liturgical act par excellence of the confession of faith";[160] that is, the content of faith — communion — finds its fullest earthly manifestation in the eucharistic synaxis of the local church. On the other, the communion effected and signified by the eucharist sends forth the community into the world in order to evangelize and to share the good news of salvation. Communion and mission call forth each other in the life of the local church.

Furthermore, in its eucharistic synaxis — that event where the faith of the church is both proclaimed and made effective in visible communion — each local church fully manifests the church of God. It is not an incomplete part of the church universal, but, in Vatican II's words, "it constitutes one particular church in which the one, holy, catholic, and apostolic church of Christ is truly present and active." Tillard likewise sees the eucharist as the embodiment of the church's creedal identity. The eucharist makes the church one, through the communion of all believers in the one body of Christ; holy, for it joins the ecclesial body of Christ to his personal-sacramental body and thus enables the church to share in divine communion; catholic, because each eucharist is "accomplished in communion with all of the synaxes celebrated throughout the world in the course of history";[161] and apostolic, for each eucharist remembers the apostolic witness to Jesus' death and resurrection and thereby celebrates the same apostolic eucharist throughout history. In short:

> The truth, at once of the eucharist and of the local church, is determined by this communion which embraces both places and times, in direct reference to the body and blood of the Lord. Given everywhere without being divided, the body and blood of reconciliation uniting in the power of the Spirit all those who "receive" them, they manifest in the community (gathered around the eucharistic Table at which its bishop or one of his presbyters presides) the Church of God in this place and this time. At its synaxis, this community is manifested as *possessing all that which makes* the Church of God, *without being taken for the whole.*[162]

Each local church's eucharistic and communional dynamism of life points beyond itself to the communion of local churches that comprises the church of God, a church that is a "church without borders."[163] The communion of these local churches and its implications for ecclesial recognition, the relationship of the local and universal churches, synodality, episcopal collegiality, and the ministry of the bishop of Rome are the subjects of the next chapter.

Chapter Five

The church of God is a communion of local churches

Although fully the church of God, the local church does not exist, *pace* Afanasiev, autonomously or independently of other local churches. Joined to fellow churches through their communion in the one church of God established at Pentecost, it cannot exist in isolation:

> It is [the church of God], by its very nature, with other churches in communion. Its life according to its priestly, prophetic, and royal functions is the authentic dynamism of the Body of Christ only if it is enveloped in the communion of all the churches, its sisters, which throughout the universe and across the ages celebrate one and the same eucharist, in the indivisible flesh and blood of one and the same Lord, proclaim one and the same faith "received from the Apostles," under the *episkope* of one and the same apostolic ministry. Synodality overflows its boundaries, just as its synaxis embraces the ensemble of eucharists and its word expresses the *sensus fidei* of the People of God in its entirety.[1]

Sharing in a common patrimony of faith, sacrament, and ministry, the local churches are one church in many churches, each manifesting the same divine, Pentecostal gift. These local churches, already being true churches of God, thus do not seek in each other what they lack,[2] but rather recognize in each other the same one, holy, catholic, and apostolic church; that is, they see in each other the traits and characteristics of the church first given at Pentecost. They are "sister-church[es], built upon the same apostolic foundation,"[3] and such communion excludes all ecclesial self-sufficiency. In this sense, the communion of the local bishop and his church, synodality (the communion of local churches with one another), and collegiality (the communion of local bishops with one another) are all of a piece.[4]

This chapter will examine the one church of God understood as the communion of local churches, in service of God's plan for "the recapitulation threedots of all humanity by the communion of all the "nations" (with their races, cultures, destinies) *en Christo* and by him in the Father."[5] Beginning with an exploration of recognition as a sign and instrument of ecclesial communion, we will then take up the relationship of the local and universal churches (Tillard's thought will be presented in relation to Pope Benedict's, as a means of framing our analysis), synodality and collegiality, and the papacy. This chapter will thus address neuralgic issues of authority, governance, and primacy — issues at the heart of Catholic and ecumenical disagreements and conflicts. Part of our task throughout will be to show how Tillard's vision stands in both harmony and tension with Vatican II and recent magisterial documents.

Recognition

Ecclesial recognition stands at the heart of Tillard's "ecclesiology of communion and catholicity," to quote the subtitle of *L'Église locale.* It is

> one of the principal categories of an ecclesiology of communion. By *recognition* one means, in this context, the attitude by which a church discerns in the diversity of expressions or rites and in the plurality of traditions the faith and evangelical practices which are its own. In other terms, in difference . . . it perceives the same fidelity to one and the same Revelation.[6]

Such recognition begins with the conviction that each local church, genuinely the church of God, is intrinsically oriented to other local churches, not out of need, but through communion with the apostolic church established at Pentecost; its "boundaries are porous,"[7] open to all other churches, and so all ecclesial self-sufficiency is excluded. The local churches are interlocked — through one and the same faith, eucharist, and episcopate — to form only the church of Pentecost.[8] This is the logic of communion: subsequent local churches do not add to, but enter into the Pentecostal church of God; there are many churches (eucharists, bishops), yet only one church (eucharist, episcopate).[9]

Recognition does not create such ecclesial communion *ex nihilo,* which is based originally and ultimately in God (the Holy Spirit is the agent of communion), but expresses the communion of each local church, through its faith and sacramental life, with both the apostolic church of Pentecost and its sister churches: "In the Holy Spirit and by the power of the eucharist, it is mutual recognition that forms the concrete fabric of *koinonia.*"[10] It is the process or act by which a given local church acknowledges that another local church — in the varied forms taken by its inculturation of faith and sacrament — is truly the church of God. Tillard's conception of mutual recognition, then, is analogous to what John Paul II has termed "mutual inclusion," wherein

> every particular church, as a realization of the one Church of Christ, is in some way present in all the particular churches "in which and out of which the one and unique catholic Church has its existence" [*Lumen gentium* 23]. . . . The basic ecclesial choices of believers in one community must be able to be harmonized with those of the faithful in other communities in order to allow that communion of minds and hearts for which Christ prayed at the last supper.[11]

Tillard sees the struggle at Jerusalem over the necessity of circumcision for Gentiles as the paradigm of ecclesial recognition, revealing its "extremely demanding" character. When Paul and Barnabas press for the admission of the uncircumcised, they are asking not for a minor change in window-dressing or custom, but rather for a fundamental revision of Christian communal self-understanding: a movement from Christianity as a primarily Jewish movement to a more universal one, embracing all peoples; few changes could be more radical. Accordingly, the acceptance of such change by James, the head of the Jerusalem church, involves not a mere expression of good will, a "purely pragmatic plan" for common action, or a "cheap unity" based on a "lowest common denominator" of consensus,[12] but a recognition that such Gentile communities manifest the same essential characteristics of the Pentecostal church. This recognition thus enables the church to embrace a diversity that initially appeared upsetting and even potentially destructive.[13]

In like manner, recognition today permits a "Parisian to recognize his own eucharist in the Sunday celebration of a Maronite community, a Warsaw parishioner to recognize his own gospel belief in the preaching of a Brazilian base community."[14] The mutual recognition of local churches thus entails not only their individual relationships to Rome, as wheel-spokes to a hub, but equally their engagement with each other: "What good would it be for them all to be in communion with Rome if the local churches remained water-tight compartments, shut up in their differences?"[15] Rome, whose distinctive ministry is the overseeing of the communion of all the local churches, does not replace, but supports and strengthens the many bonds of ecclesial communion.

The ecclesial communion effected in the mutual recognition of the local exists ultimately for the sake of human communion. In the divine plan, "God wills, inseparably, that humanity be one and that it be so in the complex display of its diversity."[16] Recognition thereby serves the "catholicity of the divine plan,"[17] by effecting and ensuring a genuinely catholic unity-in-diversity.

Tillard's conception of ecclesial (and human) communion as built upon a recognition of catholic unity-in-diversity seems, at first glance, unobjectionable and unremarkable. Vatican II, we have seen, affirms that the legitimate diversity of local churches "shows all the more resplendently the catholicity of the undivided church,"[18] and a general theological and magisterial consensus supports it as well; few bishops or theologians would claim that unity entails uniformity.

Difficulty arises, however, when mutual recognition is applied to the relation of the local church to the universal church. The Congregation for the Doctrine of the Faith, in its letter "Some Aspects of the Church Understood as Communion" (1992), sharply warns against an "ecclesiological unilateralism," which "assert[s] that every particular church is a subject complete in itself, and that the universal church is the result of a reciprocal recognition on the part of the particular churches."[19] It states further that " 'the universal church cannot be conceived as the sum of the particular churches or as a federation of particular churches.' It is not the result of the communion of the churches."[20] The Congregation is clearly concerned about any conception of the universal church that would make it something extrinsic to the life of each local church, reduce the entire church's unity to a kind of congregationalist contract between autonomous local churches, or deny the "ontological and temporal prior[ity]" of the universal church to "every individual particular church."[21] The objects of these admonitions seem to fall into two principal groups: eucharistic or local ecclesiologies influenced by Russian Orthodox interpretations of the church fathers (especially that of Afanasiev), and liberation ecclesiologies that envision the genesis of the church in small base-communities.[22]

Joseph Komonchak has criticized the Congregation's depiction of mutual or "reciprocal" recognition. Recognition, he writes, need not be conceived of as some "second moment" in which already existing local churches "see that they all agree about certain things, and then decide to form a federation."[23] Rather, recognition is *simultaneously* constitutive of both the local church itself and the communion between all local churches; each local church knows itself only in its relationship, its communion with other churches. The question of priority — which comes first: the local church or the universal church? — is a mistaken one, to some extent.

How, then, does Tillard conceive of the relationship between the local and universal churches? Does his conception of recognition give evidence of congregationalist or localist tendencies? Where does he stand in the debate over ecclesial priority? Such questions are our next concern.

Priority or Simultaneity? The Relationship of the Local and Universal Churches

Seemingly esoteric at first glance, the question of priority in regard to the local church and the universal church is a pressing issue in the Catholic Church, full of practical import for matters of synodality, collegiality, primacy, and ecumenism. Tillard argues that Catholicism, by virtue of its conception of papal primacy and the ecclesiological influence of Aquinas's "metaphysics of the common good"[24] — in which local, particular goods give way to the universal good — has traditionally opted toward the priority of the universal church. This option is represented today most notably, and influentially, by Pope Benedict XVI, who, when he was Cardinal Joseph Ratzinger, argued for the ontological and temporal priority of the universal church, which is then established in a particular area. Conversely, under the influence of liberation theologies and their emphases on base communities, some theologians have argued for the priority of the local church. Such a position, however, has had little influence on Catholic ecclesiology.[25]

Tillard rejects the question of priority as a mistaken one, arguing that the universal church is a communion (not confederation) of local churches, a communion of communions, a church of churches: each local church exists only in communion with that universal church of churches, and the universal church exists only in, through, and from the local churches. The universal church does not exist apart from the communion of local churches, but *is* such communion; the local and the universal are simultaneous. In this sense, even to raise the question of priority betrays a misunderstanding of the relationship of the local and the universal, of unity and diversity. As a prelude to our consideration of Tillard's position, then, we will look first at Pope Benedict as an exemplar of moderate universalist ecclesiological tendencies, in order to provide the context necessary for a treatment of the relationship in Tillard between the local and universal churches.

Pope Benedict XVI: The Priority of the Universal Church

Both in his own writings and through his work as prefect of the Roman Congregation for the Doctrine of the Faith (hereafter, CDF), Pope Benedict has developed a nuanced ecclesiology of communion.[26] Contrary to popular impression and even caricature, his ecclesiology is not a repressive "hierarchology,"[27] but thoroughly sacramental, centered above all on the eucharistic celebration. Its dominant tone is mystical, even romantic, in its emphases upon the communal, the interior and intuitive, the familial. Most fundamental, perhaps, is his sense of divine gift: the church and its liturgy are to be received by men and women in wonder, rather than actively made or constructed.[28]

The heart of his ecclesiology is the communion with God and humanity that the eucharist effects and manifests. Its point of departure is the Last Supper, where Jesus institutes the eucharist and gathers people unto him. Accordingly, the "Church is Eucharist," for its celebration joins it to the death and resurrection of Jesus Christ, making present the "whole Christ" and not simply part of him. The church is likewise "gathering," for its eucharist includes peoples from the "four corners of the earth"; no one is to be excluded from such catholic reconciliation. Eucharist and gathering together constitute the *communio* that is the church. The church itself is the body of Christ where vertical (divine) and horizontal (human) communion meet, the former giving rise to the latter.[29]

The eucharist, in turn, calls forth the episcopate, the servant of unity.[30] The bishop watches over the unity of the particular church (Benedict prefers this term to "local church," holding that the geographical element is not central to ecclesiality and may, in fact, compromise the unity of the universal church.[31]), taking care to preserve the public and reconciling character of the eucharist, from which no one is excluded on grounds of race, color, sex, or class. The bishop's "oneness" thus integrates and unifies the "many," by enabling the ecclesial *communio* to be a sacrament of God's saving, reconciling work. Moreover, each bishop, as a successor to the apostles, bears responsibility for the *communio* of the universal church through space and time.[32] And in contrast to what Benedict considers to be the ecclesiological tendencies of Protestantism, the church's episcopal nature excludes any congregationalist tendencies. The church is not primarily a local community constructed "from below," but rather by divine call, of which the bishop is the representative and the guarantor of catholic unity.

The particular church, gathered in the eucharist and guided by its bishop, is therefore genuinely ecclesial, for "the Church is present as a whole wherever [Christ] is, hence, wherever the Eucharist is rightly celebrated. It follows that just as Christ is not half but wholly present, the Church is wholly present wherever he is."[33] The particular church, nonetheless, is not the whole church. If, on the one hand, the eucharistic nature of the particular churches prevents them from being viewed as "mere subdivisions of a single administrative apparatus,"[34] neither, on the other, are they "autonomous, mutually independent entities" lacking intrinsic relation to the universal church.[35] Benedict's clear object of criticism here is the eucharistic ecclesiology developed by Nikolai Afanasiev, which uses the very same terms ("autonomous" and "independent") to describe the local church;[36] Afanasiev's name appears consistently whenever Benedict mentions eucharistic ecclesiology and its correlative theology of the local church. He sees in Afanasiev a one-sided affirmation — an "ecclesiological unilateralism,"[37] as the CDF might put it — of the particular church's self-sufficiency: its eucharistic fullness obviates any necessary bonds of unity with other churches; such bonds belong to the church's *bene esse* or "pleromatic enhancement,"[38] not its essence.

In contrast, Benedict holds that each particular church is intrinsically bound to other particular churches and to the universal church precisely through that same eucharistic and episcopal essence. The eucharist of each particular church is genuine only if it expresses the catholic unity of the entire church,[39] while the bishop likewise "represents the universal Church in relation to the local church, and vice versa."[40] Each particular church must therefore be genuinely catholic, embracing not only the qualitative fullness of the eucharist but also the quantitative extension of the church into all peoples and lands. Thus joined in eucharistic and episcopal communion, "the unity of the universal church is . . . an inner moment of the local church."[41] The CDF is still more precise, speaking of the "mutual interiority" of the particular and universal churches. Accordingly, "communion with the universal church . . . is not an external complement to the particular church, but one of its internal constituents";[42] the Congregation specifies further that the Petrine ministry and primacy are therefore interior to each particular church, for they ensure the communion of the particular churches with the universal church.[43]

The question thus poses itself: within their mutual interiority, how do the particular and universal churches relate to each other? Benedict sees Pentecost as the paradigm of their relationship. On the one hand, Pentecost models the interplay of the church's unity and diversity: many languages and many cultures are made fruitful in one faith; it is a "preliminary sketch" of how the one church and the many churches call forth each other in a mutual interiority. On the other, Pentecost shows that from the church's beginning it "was already catholic, already a world Church," and so the universal church has priority over the particular church. He writes:

> what first exists is the one Church, the Church that speaks in all tongues — the *ecclesia universalis;* she then generates Churches in the most diverse locales, which nonetheless are all always embodiments of the one and only Church. The temporal and ontological priority lies with the universal Church.[44]

In nearly identical terms, the CDF states that the universal church is "a reality ontologically and temporally prior to every particular church." The universal church's priority encompasses not simply its "temporal" manifestation at Pentecost, but also its "ontological" origin preceding creation:

> Indeed, according to the fathers [Clement of Rome, Shepherd of Hermas], ontologically the church-mystery, the church that is one and unique, precedes creation and gives birth to the particular churches as her daughters. She expresses herself in them; she is the mother and not the offspring of the particular churches.[45]

Conversely, the universal priority disclosed in the Pentecost narrative rules out the priority of the particular church, in which the church at Jerusalem would be first a local one, and only subsequently become "the base for the gradual establishment of other local churches that eventually [would grow] into a federation [through reciprocal recognition]."[46] Both Benedict and the CDF have in mind especially the base communities of liberation theology; Tillard's understanding of recognition may also be an object of criticism. Benedict's — and the CDF's — abiding concern, however, is for the priority and the "givenness" of the universal church; the church and its unity remain divine gifts, not the product of human effort, however noble or earnest.

Jean-Marie Tillard: The Simultaneity of the Local and Universal Churches

Tillard affirms with Benedict the mutual interiority of the local and universal churches, concurring with Vatican II and the CDF on the mutual ordering of primacy and collegiality-synodality to each other. Unlike the pope, however, he prefers to speak of the entire church — the church of God — as the communion of local churches rather than as the universal church, and he rejects the ontological and temporal priority of the universal church to the local church, in favor of their simultaneity. Why?

Tillard's position is built upon four points. The first is a leitmotiv of our study: Trinitarian communion as the origin and pattern of ecclesial communion. Although Tillard does not draw an explicit parallel between the simultaneity of unity and difference in the Trinity and in the church, he nonetheless makes clear that the church's own being-as-communion is rooted and sustained by the Trinity's communion: "It is a Church of Churches. Grasped in all its fullness, it is a communion of communions, appearing as a communion of local churches.... This communional being constitutes its essence. And the relation to the communion of the Father, the Son, and the Spirit indicates its rootedness even in the eternal reality of the mystery of God."[47] Tillard states elsewhere that the "Church of God is revealed as modeled in the image of the *societas* of the Father, of the Son, and of the Spirit, by the power of the Spirit. The trinitarian roots of the church thus can no longer be separated from its reality as hierarchical institution."[48] The church's unity and diversity are likewise the "refraction of the divine life" as revealed in the Johannine vision of divine mutual indwelling.[49] It is reasonable to infer from such passages as these that, just as the Trinity is at once one and three, the church of the triune God is likewise simultaneously one and many.

Second, this trinitarian vision shows that diversity is an intrinsic, inner element of divine and ecclesial unity; it rules out the simple opposition of the universal and the particular. Tillard thus takes issue with Aquinas's conception of universality and particularity, whose legacy has decisively shaped Catholic ecclesiology for nearly a millennium and, Tillard argues, can be discerned in the CDF's declaration that the universal church is ontologically and temporally prior to the local-particular church.[50] According to Tillard, Aquinas's Aristotelian-influenced position is built upon a "metaphysics of the common good," in which particular goods give way to more universal (and therefore more "divine") ones; in effect, the particular and universal are defined in contrast, even opposition, to each other: "It belongs... to the nature of the common good to precede, metaphysically and logically, particular goods, [and] not to be reduced to their sum."[51] Socially and politically, for example, the good of the city cannot be deduced from the good of individual families, nor is it the mere sum of familial goods. Ecclesially, the good of the universal church is similarly of greater worth and precedence than that of smaller ecclesial communities.

Aquinas's conception of papal primacy provides an ecclesiological face to his metaphysics. As the single "City of the living God," the universal church needs "a single head guarding the [common good] in a common faith, common teaching, common end."[52] Although Christ is the true head of the church, his place on earth is taken by his vicar, the pope, and papal primacy is derived from the primacy of Christ. The pope thus "watches over the entire church [*universa Ecclesia*], in subjection to Christ."[53] Other bishops receive, in "descending" turn, their powers of jurisdiction from the pope. Although Aquinas follows Gregory the Great in refusing to call the pope "universal bishop," for each bishop retains jurisdiction over his own diocese, he does reserve concern for the common good as such to the pope alone in his role as "universal pastor."[54] The pope, therefore, has power over the whole of the church, while the other bishops rule only their own dioceses.

Tillard concludes that Aquinas's ecclesiological vision is universalist, rather than localist or synodalist.[55] Where Tillard begins with the "*ephapax* of the Pentecostal church of Jerusalem gathered around the ministry of 'Peter and the other apostles,' " Aquinas speaks of the "service of the '*bonum commune Ecclesiae,*' " by the "vicar of Christ [the pope], and in him by Christ himself";[56] where Tillard's theology of the local church, drawing upon *Lumen gentium,* affirms that each bishop shares in the "*sollicitudo omnium ecclesiarum,*" Aquinas posits a separately existing universal church overseen by a "universal pastor," whose connection to the church of Rome is secondary. In short, Tillard holds that Aquinas's "metaphysics of the common good" entails an intrinsic tension between the particular and the universal and therefore leaves little room for the local church.[57]

Tillard's theology of catholicity and the local church, on the other hand, affirms the mutual inherence and simultaneity of locality and universality. We have seen in chapter 3, for example, that Aquinas offers a classically quantitative conception of catholicity: the church is catholic by its extension to all nations, all peoples, and all ages. He virtually identifies catholicity with universality, while also opposing catholicity and locality. This definition reflects in part the universalistic cast of Aquinas's ecclesiology (and also in part the effects of schism). In contrast, Tillard makes the seemingly paradoxical argument that the church is catholic precisely because it is local, and vice versa. Developing a primarily qualitative catholicity, he holds that a genuinely catholic church takes flesh in the diversity of human cultures; catholicity reaches its fullness only through its local inculturations. It is in this light that Tillard's statement becomes clear: "In the church of God, all is inseparably singular and plural, that is to say, plural in the singular and singular in the plural.... This is not a play of words."[58] A truly catholic church is inseparably local and universal.

Third, even if divine election of the church may "precede even creation in Christ,"[59] the Pentecostal church of Jerusalem is *simultaneously* local and universal. It is neither first a local church, which then becomes universal or "catholic" as it spreads to other lands, nor is it first universal and only subsequently local. The universality of the Pentecostal church is clearly evident. "Speaking all tongues,"[60] the church embraces all nations not simply geographically, but also in their cultures, in their spirit: "This goes to the heart of human reality, which is expressed in language. In their language, people offer forth their soul. By it, they forge their culture. In it, they cement their unity."[61] The "nations" and their riches thus are embraced and united in the one church. Such universality, however, is manifested only in a concrete locale, Jerusalem, which bears the marks of a distinctive culture and salvation history;[62] this culture and history are central to God's recapitulative plan for the church and creation. In distinction to Benedict and the CDF,[63] then, Tillard insists on calling the Jerusalem church a local church.[64]

Jerusalem, as we saw in chapter 3, stands not simply for the universality of the church and the divine plan, but also for its rootedness in creation, history, and culture. The Pentecostal church of Jerusalem is not simply or even primarily universal or local, but both. Its ecclesiality depends upon their simultaneity.

Fourth, Tillard holds that the "universal" church — the church of God — *is* the communion of local churches, not a separate entity existing apart from, above, prior, or subsequent to the local churches and their communion:

> The local church as *koinonia* of faith, love, and hope — the church where each bishop presides — is not simply a part of the Church of God. It is the Church of God in one of her manifestations in the here and now. The eucharistic synaxis brings about the emergence of the Church of God in this place and this historical situation. The eucharistic community is not the fragment of the mystery of the universal Church, but an appearance of this Church in communion with the Father and in the communion of brotherhood, through the Spirit of Christ the Lord. This is why each local community bonded into itself by the Eucharist finds that by that very fact it is "in full unity" with the other local communities, wherever they may be in the world: not "by virtue of a superimposed external structure, but by virtue of the whole Christ who is present in each one of them" [Zizioulas].
>
> Now this real presence of the whole Church in each community implies that the Church of God "which is at" one place (1 Cor. 1:2) *recognizes itself* as identical with the Church of God which is at another place. Instead of thinking of the organic unity and the catholicity of the Church as the sum total of the local communities, parts together forming a whole in which they complete each other, we should think in terms of identity and *recognition.*[65]

Because the local and universal church exist in mutual interiority and simultaneity, it follows that "every local church is the church of God, to the point that even if there were only a single local church, the church of God would still exist in all its integrity — the whole church being in the church of Corinth, of Ephesus, of Rome, of Kinshasa, of Lyon."[66] For example, were the church of God to be so reduced that only the local church of Rockville Centre remained, Rockville Centre would be the "universal" church; that is, the universal church cannot be simply identified with the church of Jerusalem or of Rome, but is present wherever the church of God exists. *Pace* the CDF, there is no question here of a quasi-universal "federation" of local churches constructed through "reciprocal recognition." Rather, each local church recognizes that other local churches are authentic presences of one and the same church of God, and that the church's universal communion is manifested both within each local church and between them. Faith, baptism, episcopacy, and especially the eucharist — "at the synaxis ... through the communion of the body of Christ, each church speaks in its own language the languages of all the churches"[67] — sustain the unity and universality of the church of God, a communion of local churches.

Benedict and Tillard: Evaluation

Tillard and Benedict have much in common. Foremost are their shared emphases on the divine origin of ecclesial communion, the church's sacramental — especially eucharistic — nature, the mutual interiority of the local-particular and universal churches, and a sense of communion as a diversified unity. Their agreement is clear and substantial.

Tillard's support of simultaneity, however, is more compelling than Benedict's support of universal priority. The chief difference between the two is the nature of the universal church. Benedict's insistence on the universal church's ontological and temporal priority appears to be mistaken. In fairness, it should be noted that the CDF's subsequent clarification in 1993 of its 1992 letter, "Some Aspects of the Church Understood as Communion," explicitly rules out a common misinterpretation of that letter: the universal church as "an abstract reality opposed to the concrete reality of the particular Churches." Instead, the Congregation holds that the universal church's priority is "with respect to any *single* particular church, not to *all* the particular churches." That is, the clarification focuses on the historical priority of the universal church, and sees it manifested in the Pentecostal church of Jerusalem, a church "as local as can be, without being — in that it is the Church of Pentecost — an '*individual* particular Church' in the sense given to that term today. At Pentecost there is no 'mutual interiority' between universal and particular Church, because these two dimensions are not yet distinct." The church of Jerusalem is therefore the universal church, for it contains the "*very structure of the universal Church:* here there are the Twelve, with Peter at their head";[68] only its offspring can be properly termed particular churches.

The CDF's clarification, despite its rightful emphasis upon the universal church's concreteness and locality, nonetheless leaves untouched the 1992 Letter's insistence upon the universal church's ontological priority to creation, which does lead to abstraction, as a church cannot concretely exist without members. And it does not affirm the Jerusalem church's particularity; the universality attributed to the "Twelve" does not exhaust the church's ecclesiality, as other believers are present.

Tillard's insistence on the church of Jerusalem as being simultaneously local and universal avoids these problems. If it is true, as the CDF argues, that the many churches make present one and the same church of God (*ecclesiae in et ex ecclesia*), it is equally true that the one church of God is present only in the many churches of God (*ecclesia in et ex ecclesiis*) — even if only one local church actually exists; in other words, just as there can be no local church apart from the universal church, so too can there be no universal church apart from the local church. The CDF is correct in affirming that these two statements are "inseparable,"[69] but it fails to affirm fully the latter. Tillard therefore rightly warns that to speak of a pre-existent universal church is a dangerous abstraction, leading to a "slide from the '*Ecclesia ex* (or *in*) *Ecclesiae*' to the '*Ecclesiae ex Ecclesia universali.*'"[70] The universal church is "not a genus in its species."[71] It is the communion of the churches of God, at once universal and local.

Benedict's primarily universalistic sense of catholicity leads as well to an unwitting deprecation of the particular church(es). Emphasizing, quite rightly, the geographical and eucharistic aspects of catholicity, he nevertheless tends to identify catholicity with universality, placing it in direct tension with locality. In *Called to Communion,* for instance, he writes: "At the moment of her birth, the Church was already catholic, already a world Church.... The temporal and ontological priority lies with the universal Church; a Church that was not catholic would not even have ecclesial reality."[72] In its otherwise salutary desire to emphasize the church's intrinsic universality, this passage represents an unnecessary opposition of catholicity and locality, which then results in a diminishment — however unintended it may be — of the catholicity and ecclesiality of the particular church. In his concern over some Orthodox, Protestant, and liberation theologies which, in his view, propose unbalanced notions of ecclesial self-sufficiency, he swings too far in the other direction and fails to see that the particular church is intrinsically catholic by virtue of its locality as well as its universality.

Part of the problem here is the danger of what Joseph Komonchak trenchantly calls "merely theological"[73] ecclesiologies, which neglect the human, cultural, and local dimensions of the church and its catholicity:

> [The] church appears to float in mid-air, constituted solely by theological, divine, supernatural elements, while socio-cultural locality represents at best the natural and human variety within catholicity, indispensable *ad bonum Ecclesiae,* and at worst centrifugal tendencies.... Tension with catholicity almost defines the nature of the local church.[74]

In such a perspective, the local church by definition is incompletely catholic and lacks universality. Tillard's own thought, which sees the church as the sacrament of the recapitulation in Christ of everything human and created, joins successfully divine-high elements with human-low ones in its theology of the local church.

Finally, both theologians provide a balanced account of the episcopate in its relationship to the local and universal churches, but Tillard's is clearer and more coherent. Benedict, in a position that seems surprising in light of his support of universal priority, states:

> Individual bishops share in the government of the universal church not by being represented in some central organ but by leading as shepherds their particular churches which together form and carry in themselves the whole Church and in doing so lead the Church as a whole, whose health and right government does not simply depend on some central authority but on the right living of the individual cells both in themselves and with relation to the whole. *It is in governing the particular Church that the bishops share in governing the universal Church, and not otherwise.* The idea that it is only by

> being represented at the center that they will have significance for the whole represents a fundamental misjudgment of the nature of the Church; it is the expression of a centralism which the Second Vatican Council in fact wanted to overcome. [italics added][75]

His position is conspicuously silent on the question of titular bishops — how can a bishop without responsibility for a presently existent particular church govern the universal church? — and seems perhaps even to support a certain logical priority of headship over collegiality. Benedict thus sees the bishop as necessarily having both local and universal responsibilities, even if he leaves open how such responsibilities are to be exercised.[76]

Tillard evinces no such ambiguity. Because the universal church does not exist apart from the communion of local churches, bishops are members of the episcopal college only insofar as they are heads of local churches:

> "Universal" ecclesiology with its conception of an "episcopal college" which in a certain ecclesial manner transcends the communion of local churches — since one can be ordained a titular bishop, without belonging to a concretely existing local church (by attribution to a *sedes* that no longer exists) — wounds the authentic nature of the episcopate.[77]

This passage does not mean that Tillard views the bishop as first the head of a local church, and second as a member of the episcopal college. It does mean that the bishop's office involves both tasks simultaneously, and that the bishop is not "ordained primarily as part of a universal organ of government";[78] the college cannot exist prior to, or apart from, the communion of the local churches. If it is true that the head of a local church exercises his office in truth only in communion with other bishops (and their churches), then it is equally true that, apart from its reference to a concrete church, the bishop's office loses meaning or purpose. One wonders, for instance, how a *sedens* sits on a titular (non-extant) *sedes*! Only a vision of the simultaneity of local and universal churches, then, preserves the authentic nature of the episcopate and the local church.[79]

For all of its strengths, Tillard's argument for simultaneity does have its lacunae. In the first place, unlike John Zizioulas, he does not provide an explicitly Trinitarian rationale for simultaneity. Although Tillard affirms (1) the Trinitarian source and pattern of ecclesial communion and (2) the simultaneity of the local and universal churches, he does not clearly link the two points. It is unclear whether this lack is intentional or not, but any future ecclesiological reflection on simultaneity and priority will need to develop from a more substantial Trinitarian theology. Second, his language and rhetoric may leave him open to charges that he supports the priority of the local church. Although he doubtlessly upholds simultaneity, a cursory reading of such passages as "is this bishop of a concrete diocese... first a member of the episcopal college designated for the present time to his see, or is he the pastor of a diocesan church whose function leads him to be a member of the episcopal college?"[80] might seem to affirm local priority.

Tillard would have done well to clarify that episcopal headship and collegiality are simultaneous. These weaknesses, however, involve style more than substance and do not detract from the coherence and cogency of Tillard's argument.

Synodality and Collegiality: Structured Life in Communion and Catholicity

Synodality and collegiality do not involve, in the first instance, administration or governance, but structured life in communion and catholicity. As our examination of recognition and priority indicated, "the boundaries of the local church are porous. By its nature, it must be open to other local churches in catholic communion and bear their concerns."[81] Synodality (the communion of local churches with each other) and collegiality (the communion of bishops with each other) are means by which such interecclesial communion and catholicity are maintained and strengthened. Although they are mutually ordered to each other, Tillard holds that synodality and collegiality "fit together poorly" at present.[82] Vatican II and the Code of Canon Law, for instance, give precedence to the college over the churches,[83] while *Apostolos suos* declares that the bishop belongs firstly to the college and secondly (but not necessarily) to a particular church—thereby severing the intrinsic link between church and bishop. Tillard, of course, argues that such a view is inverted and "wounds" the nature of both the episcopate and the church. He holds instead that just as the local church precedes its bishop (*sedes* preceding *sedens*),[84] so too does the communion of local churches give rise to the collegiality of bishops.[85] Following Tillard's own ordering, then, we will look first at synodality and second at collegiality. Underscoring their sacramental bases (baptism and order, respectively), we will be mindful that "nothing in the church escapes communion, not even *exousia,* and that at all levels of its exercise."[86]

Synodality

Synodality, which gives institutional form to the communion of local churches, exists for the service of God's plan for the unity of the church and all humanity. Rooted in the common baptismal dignity and responsibility of all believers, the synod, be it local or more expansive, is the primary way by which the church "discerns in all lucidity, in the *conspiratio* of the bishop[s], ordained ministers, and all its members, the shape of its witness (*martyria*) and its life."[87] This "synodal dynamism" must not be reduced to its juridical or canonical structures, which would merely add levels of sterile bureaucracy to the church.[88] Rather, the synod must be liturgically grounded, aware that it gathers "before God" in the unity generated by baptism and the eucharist.[89] The eucharistic and episcopal character of local and general synods, in turn, objectively calls forth a genuinely catholic "communion *of* all and *in* all among *all* the members of the family of God and *all* their human *places*."[90] Through the presence of representatives of all the baptized, the synod seeks to give voice to the totality of a church (or churches) and its concrete needs and desires.

Synodality has local, regional, and worldwide dimensions, all of which are joined in a web of communion: each local synod must act in communion with those of other churches, and the actions of a regional or a worldwide synod find their reception in the local churches. Although the words "synod" and "synodal" are not used in the New Testament, synodal structures began to emerge at the end of the second century, partly under the influence of Roman law and Greek political theory, but also on account of the need for more organized action among the churches.[91] More local and regional than worldwide, these early synods nonetheless remained in communion with the entire church, most particularly through the sending of a letter—a synodal—to other churches.[92] Be it through letters or such other means as eucharistic hospitality, inscription in diptychs, and material assistance, the synodal dynamism constituted the foundation of life-in-communion in the body of Christ, both for the local church and for the church as a whole.

However, synods slowly became largely, even exclusively, clerical affairs. Under the "slow clericalization of ecclesial life," the Mass became viewed as largely the work of the priest, the magisterium often acted in a certain "solitude" vis-à-vis the rest of the church, and the synod was restricted to the clergy; the bishop no longer met with both the clergy and people (*plebs*) of his church, but only with his priests and deacons.[93] Although lay participation varied over following centuries — reaching a high point in the Carolingian era — it remained consistently marginal. Tillard sees in Vatican II the beginning of a synodal renewal and notes that the "best witness . . . of this new climate" is John Paul II, who insisted that the Roman synod he convoked in 1988 include all of the people of God.[94] It is precisely through such inclusion that the local church manifests "its very being as communion. In it the mortal sickness of communion that is the separation between clergy and other faithful is corrected and healed."[95]

Synods are therefore particularly important vehicles of reception in the church, for they ensure that each local church remains in communion with the faith and doctrine of the whole church, and that the entire church of God be enriched by the catholic unfolding of such faith and doctrine in the concrete life of each local church.[96] They are not "mere chambers for the registration of decisions taken *elsewhere*," but gatherings where the local churches pass conciliar decisions and formulae through the "filter of their lives": their cultures, questions, histories, traditions.[97] Tillard sees the development of diverse yet orthodox Christologies in the aftermath of Chalcedon as an example of such reception: the church's faith in Christ remained the same, but reflected the different "accents" of the Eastern and Western churches. This "synodal dynamism" thus fosters a genuinely catholic communion, rooted in God's own life-in-communion:

> Where is the Spirit's power from which the Church of God lives its catholicity? It exists only in the synergy and the complementarity of capacities and powers, personal and collective, that the Spirit distributes according to the Father's *Divina Providentia,* in the entire ecclesial body of the Son. Ecclesial synodality spreads out — has its ultimate foundation — under the aegis of trinitarian circumincession. It is impossible to parcel it out.[98]

Episcopal Collegiality: Episcopal Conferences and Synods of Bishops

Episcopal collegiality is a *sacramentum* of the synodality of local churches, for the bishops represent their churches and not themselves;[99] each bishop acts as a "microphone" for his church, ensuring that its voice is heard in the "ecclesial symphony" of the church of God.[100] Collegiality itself, despite its etymological origin in Roman law, is more fundamentally a fraternal entity than a canonical one. An "apostolic brotherhood" or "episcopal brotherhood" involving more than simple "collaboration, solidarity, [or] association,"[101] it is rooted in the sacramentality of the episcopate, apostolicity, and mutual recognition. As Vatican II taught definitively, sacramentality grounds the essential equality of all bishops as "vicars of Christ"; just as the many churches are but one church, so, too, do the many bishops share in one and the same episcopate — no one is "more" or "less" of a bishop than his brothers, and each bears responsibility for the care of the entire church.[102] Apostolicity refers both to the episcopal college's role as successor (or, more precisely, vicar[103]) of the apostolic college and to the bishops' maintenance of the communion of their sister churches in the one apostolic church of Pentecost; the episcopal college ensures that the church of God "lives perpetually" in the *ephapax* of Pentecost.[104] Mutual recognition involves the logic of communion: sharing in the same episcopate through sacramentality and apostolicity, bishops recognize each other as bearers of the same apostolic faith in diverse traditions and forms. They do not add together their episcopacies to form one episcopal college, but rather enter into one episcopate. Episcopal communion, like ecclesial communion, does not suppress diversity but integrates it in a genuinely catholic unity.[105]

Collegiality finds its fullest exercise in an ecumenical council or an infallible declaration, but its more common forms in the Catholic Church are episcopal conferences and synods of bishops. Episcopal conferences are, according to canon law, "grouping[s] of bishops of a given nation or territory . . . exercis[ing] certain pastoral functions on behalf of the Christian faithful of their territory."[106] Although not immediately of divine institution — neither are ecumenical councils, Tillard slyly notes — and not possessed of the college's full teaching authority as such, they nonetheless manifest episcopal collegiality (which *is* divinely instituted) and thus can act, to some degree, in the name of the episcopal college; its acts are done in the college, and are not simply acts of bishops who belong to the college.[107] Tillard wishes to get beyond administrative ("the machinery between the center and the periphery"[108]) or antagonistic (rivalry vis-à-vis the college as a whole or the Roman curia) conceptions of the conferences, in order to see them as groupings within the college in the service of ecclesial communion and catholicity. It is helpful here to remember that episcopal conferences, like all other institutions and ministries in the church, are governed by the logic of communion, not of a balance-of-power, and so are not in intrinsic tension with the authority of either Rome or individual bishops in their own churches. On the contrary, they are to strengthen the web of communion—the synodality—binding together the church.

Tillard's distinctive insight into episcopal conferences, however, is that they are agents not simply of communion, but also of catholicity: "Episcopal conferences are to be understood first not in function of the collegiality of bishops, but of the very flesh of restored humanity which is to be manifested and served, thus of the Church."[109] The collegial and catholic dimensions are obviously inseparable, but Tillard wishes to place episcopal conferences in the broader scope of God's plan for all humanity: the recapitulation and communion of all creation in Christ. Diversity, we have seen, is rooted "in the nature of salvation itself, the supreme grace of God joining humanity in its full reality...and all the work of creation through it." Conversely, "the social face of sin consists precisely in what the image of Babel symbolizes: the break between diversity (or "difference") and community. It is clear that Luke sees Pentecost as the resolution between diversity and unity."[110] Episcopal conferences, as servants of catholicity, therefore have as their mission the task of ensuring that the various enfleshments or inculturations of the Gospel remain in communion with the church of Pentecost.[111] They further ensure that the church be not simply a "theological" or "divine" reality, but also truly "human," and thereby fully respectful of God's plan for humanity.[112] It is on account of this yoking of catholicity and communion that Tillard defines the episcopal conferences as:

> the institutional form (*de jure ecclesiastico*) that, in service of the "catholic" realization of salvation (which is *de natura Ecclesiae*), the collegial mission of the episcopate (*"ex divina institutione"*) takes today in a particular ecclesial space, ordinarily national, encompassing a segment of humanity.[113]

The international synods of bishops, instituted by Pope Paul VI in 1965 as a means of giving episcopal counsel to the pope, are another exercise of episcopal collegiality. Be they ordinary, extraordinary (for example, the 1985 synod celebrating the twentieth anniversary of Vatican II's conclusion), or special (the continental synods arranged in preparation for the Jubilee year), these synods provide a forum for the exchange of views among the bishops and the pope.[114] Tillard states, with some delicacy, that they "give the impression of still being broken in":[115] they lack a regularly deliberative voice suitable to their episcopal character, freedom of expression is often constricted, and the Roman curia often overshadows the role of the bishops.[116]

Nonetheless, with a measure of both weariness and hope, he writes, "At least the synod exists."[117]

The problems arising from the structures and exercise of collegiality flow, in large part, from an incomplete appreciation of the episcopal essence common to both collegiality and primacy. Vatican II, in *Lumen gentium* and *Christus Dominus,* affirms the sacramental equality of all bishops and their common charge of leadership in the church. John Paul II's encyclical, *Ut unum sint,* is still more explicit:

> [The pope's service of unity] must always be done in communion. When the Catholic Church affirms that the office of the bishop of Rome corresponds to the will of Christ, she does not separate this office from the mission entrusted to the whole body of bishops, who are also "vicars and ambassadors of Christ" [*Lumen gentium* #27]. The bishop of Rome is a member of the "college," and the bishops are his brothers in the ministry.[118]

On these grounds, Tillard holds that "primatial authority is not monarchical. It is fraternal.... [The bishop of Rome] is not, as primate, an entity which is not part of anything else. Collegiality is not at his service: on the contrary, his mission is to foster it."[119] The bishop of Rome and his ministry of unity are our final concern in this chapter.

Papacy: Vicar of Peter, Bishop of Rome, Servant of Unity

It is telling that Tillard reserves his consideration of the papacy until the end of both *Église d'églises* and *L'Église locale.* Dissatisfied with "pyramidal" conceptions of ministry, primacy, and authority in the church — in which power and initiative flow downward from the pope to the bishops and finally to the laity — Tillard situates the papacy within the context of divine, ecclesial, and human communion and holds it to be preeminently a ministry of unity. Rooted in the episcopate, it is sacramental and synergistic, "a communion of 'energies,' of powers... [not] one among them being heavily imposed."[120] Echoing Gregory the Great, Tillard sees the pope as the "servant of the servants of God." He is to support and watch over the "symphony of gifts" in the church.[121]

In this section, a short presentation of the historical development of papal primacy will be followed by a study of Tillard's preferred titles for the pope: vicar of Peter and bishop of Rome. We will then conclude by examining the ministry of unity exercised by the pope in these roles.

Historical Development of Papal Primacy

Tillard's reading of the history of papal primacy privileges the era of the "undivided church," for its unity of faith and love grants it a certain normativity; without being anachronistic, that church's exercise of the primacy serves as a template for future development, even if it clearly does not exhaust such development. As it is beyond the scope of this study to give a detailed history of papal primacy, crucial moments will suffice to provide context for Tillard's conception of the papacy.[122] Without attesting to the direct divine institution and succession of the papacy, scripture discloses the central role of Peter. As in so many other instances, Luke-Acts is decisive for Tillard. The first half of Acts is centered on Peter's leadership of the early Christian community: his primacy derives from his witness to the resurrection, and he confesses first the community's faith in Jesus as the messiah. However, although the first of the apostles, Peter is not alone or unique; he acts with and on behalf of the Twelve and the entire community.[123] The Gospels of John and Luke confirm the special role of Peter. John, who gives a certain precedence to the beloved disciple and his witness of love, nonetheless sees Peter as the one who speaks for the disciples and as the "first pastor" who, though often personally weak and unfaithful, is to keep the community united in the goods of salvation. Luke 22 takes care to show Peter as the one who shares preeminently in Christ's suffering and glory; he will both deny Jesus and be charged with strengthening his brothers. Although mindful of the risk of an uncritical synthesis, Tillard sees a broad scriptural picture emerge: Peter's primacy, particularly after Pentecost, is not accidental, but belongs to God's plan for the church, in order to ensure that it remain in communion with the Risen One.[124]

If the New Testament itself does not attest to an explicit primatial institution or succession,[125] the early church nonetheless did develop a primatial ministry. The early church saw itself as a communion of local churches and patriarchates; one thinks, for instance, of North African conciliarity. Within this ecclesial communion, the church of Rome was regarded as the first see on account of its *potentior principalitas* (Irenaeus), its foundation upon the apostolic faith and martyrdom of Peter and Paul. As bishop of this church, the pope acted as a center of unity and court of last resort, a guarantee of continuity and communion with the apostolic faith held by Peter and Paul. If the Eastern churches had difficulty with Roman-Western jurisdiction, they did acknowledge its privileged role regarding witness and doctrine.

The papacy of Leo the Great (440–61) marks a movement from the ecclesial-synodal character of primacy to a more personal sense. The two dimensions are inseparable, but Leo, underscoring the presence of Peter in his ministry, began to take a personal responsibility for the entire church (for example, the Chalcedonian "Peter has spoken through Leo") and obscured synodality in the West.[126] By the great schism of East and West, this delicate balance was upset, and the personal dimension or primacy had become dominant, even exclusive. Marked by efforts to secure the *libertas Ecclesiae* in the face of secular political interference, primacy in the Western medieval era was shaped above all by a triumvirate of popes: Gregory VII (1073–85), Innocent III (1198–1216), and Boniface VIII (1294–1303). In the *Dictatus Papae* (1075), a collection of statements concerning papal power, Gregory propounded a maximalistic, even despotic vision of the primacy: for example, the pope alone "deserves to be called universal," "he alone may use the imperial insignia," "he may depose emperors," and "he may not be judged by anyone."[127] Innocent reserved the title "Vicar of Christ" exclusively for the pope, thereby denying the title to other bishops and placing the pope above the bishops; he thus gave precedence to the juridical over the sacramental. Boniface's bull, *Unam Sanctam,* declared it "altogether necessary to salvation for every human creature to be subject to the Roman pontiff." It further stated that the church holds both "swords" — spiritual and temporal — and so nothing escapes the *plenitudo potestatis* of the pope, who is an absolute sovereign.[128] Tillard sees in the comparison of Gregory I and Gregory VII the shift in papal primacy in miniature: the former, who sees his "honor [in] the solid strength of my brothers," speaks the "language of respect and fraternal love"; the latter "speaks the language of power."[129]

The medieval expansion (or corruption) of papal primacy was furthered in the polemics and controversies of the Reformation. Robert Bellarmine (1542–1621), one of the most balanced theologians of the era, nevertheless referred to the pope not simply as the vicar of Christ, who "represents Christ to us as he was when he dwelt among men," but as the vicar of God.[130] Several centuries after Bellarmine, Vatican I (1869–70) stands as a watershed for the development of papal primacy in the Catholic Church. Shaped by the rise of Ultramontanism, the fall of the Papal States, fears of Gallicanism and political revolution, and the dominant personality of Pius IX, the council promulgated dogmas of papal infallibility and primacy.[131] Tillard stresses, however, that the council's teaching is more balanced than often recognized. It rejects extreme views of infallibility (the pope's infallibility as the source of the church's infallibility) and primacy (the pope as absolute sovereign, who has no need of episcopal collaboration or of the *sensus fidei*), sees the pope's ministry as one of service to the unity of the episcopate and of the church, and grounds the pope's primacy in the Roman church.[132]

Nearly a century later, Vatican II reiterated its predecessor's teaching on primacy, but also affirmed the sacramentality of the episcopate and thereby developed the doctrine of collegiality (all bishops are brothers and equally vicars of Christ[133]). Chapter III of *Lumen gentium,* for example, begins its exposition of the church's hierarchical nature by presenting the apostles as the foundation of the church and the bishops as successors of the apostles; Peter is head of the apostolic college, but he always remains a member of that same college.[134] One might say that Vatican II resolved little concerning how the college and the pope interact in their service of the church.[135] However, by placing the pope within the college of bishops, the council opened up a way for the future development of papal primacy.

Building upon Vatican II and the modern ecumenical movement, Pope John Paul II's 1995 encyclical, *Ut unum sint,* brings magisterial reflection on the papacy into a new era. Without denying that the "full and visible" communion of particular churches with the church of Rome belongs to God's will for the church,[136] or that the pope must have the "power and authority" necessary to be the "first servant of unity,"[137] John Paul nonetheless issues an extraordinary, unprecedented call — even demand — to all Christian communities to help him renew the papacy: "to find a way of exercising the primacy which, while in no way renouncing what is essential to its mission, is nonetheless open to a new situation.... This is an immense task, which we cannot refuse and which I cannot carry out by myself."[138] Echoing Vatican II, he holds up as a model for renewal the undivided church, in which "the Roman see acted by common consent as moderator" in matters of faith and discipline.[139] Significantly, he eschews the use of such titles as "vicar of Christ" and "Roman pontiff," preferring instead "servant of the servants of God" and "bishop of Rome." The entire document is permeated by such bold, evangelical simplicity. Various churches, institutions, and individual theologians have already responded to John Paul's invitation,[140] but it is clear that the encyclical's reception is only just beginning and will take time to enter the life of the Christian churches.

Vicar of Peter

Among the pope's many titles, Tillard judges "vicar of Peter" to be the most adequate to the nature and mission of the papacy, the "truest, the nearest to the intuition of the Great Tradition, and the richest."[141] In the first place, who is Peter? Personally, he is weak, even cowardly in his denial of Christ, but also conciliatory on account of his own experiences of weakness and, ultimately, faithful unto martyrdom. He is, in the words of Jerome, "successor of the Sinner, disciple of the Cross," and his ministry of unity arises from his weakness.[142] Collectively, he is the first of the twelve, whose faith and witness to the resurrection build up the church. Peter is first among the twelve. He is, variously, the first to be called, to be listed among the followers of Jesus, to confess Jesus as messiah, to see the risen Lord, to proclaim the good news after Pentecost.[143] As these events indicate, Peter is not unique among the twelve. In this regard, Tillard frequently cites Augustine's Sermon 295:

> Before his passion the Lord Jesus, as you know, chose those disciples of his, whom he called apostles. Among these it was only Peter who almost everywhere was given the privilege of representing the whole Church. It was in the person of the whole Church, which he alone represented, that he was privileged to hear, *To you will I give the keys of the kingdom of heaven* (Mt 16:19). After all, it isn't just one man that received the keys, but the Church in its unity. So this is the reason for Peter's acknowledged pre-eminence, that he stood for the Church's unity and universality, when he was told, *To you I am entrusting*, what has in fact been entrusted to all.
>
> ...Quite rightly too did the Lord after his resurrection entrust his sheep to Peter to be fed. It's not, you see, that he alone among the disciples was fit to feed the Lord's sheep; but when Christ speaks to one man, unity is being

> commended to us. And he speaks first to Peter, because Peter is the first among the apostles.[144]

Tillard likewise writes:

> The other apostles are similar to him in everything except in holding the first place. His primacy is that of a true *primus inter pares,* a *primus* who is genuinely, and not merely in point of honor, first, while the *pares* are genuinely equal and do not derive their power or their mission from him. Only the Spirit of God can give these. The first (*protos*) does not absorb the others.[145]

Second, although commonly referred to as the successor of Peter, the pope is more precisely his vicar. He cannot succeed Peter as a witness to the resurrection or in the role Peter's martyrdom plays in the formation of the church of Rome. Instead, as vicar, the pope serves as the continued presence of Peter in the church. More precisely still, he is the "memory of Peter."[146] Such memory is not merely passive, but, like the eucharist, is active and makes present what is remembered. As such, the *ephapax* of Peter's life and ministry is not simply a "starting point of the pontifical ministry, but . . . a standing reality" in the life of the church.[147] Peter, then, is not just a model, but a presence, and his vicar recalls and makes present Peter (much as the master general of the Dominican order makes present Dominic, without being his replacement or reincarnation).[148] Not simply a link in a chain of succession, the vicar bears the *ephapax* presence of Peter in every generation.

The mission of the vicar of Peter, then, is to keep the church in the memory, the presence of the *ephapax* of the apostolic, Pentecostal church. He does this not in isolation, but, like Peter, as the one who strengthens his brethren and, through them, the entire apostolic church, watching over and furthering its communion through time and space.[149]

Bishop of Rome

The vicar of Peter is also the bishop of Rome. Although distinct, the two are inseparable in God's plan:

> Rome and Peter's place in the apostolic group's confession of faith are . . . intrinsically bound together . . . Without Rome and the martyrdom he suffered there, Peter would not be the *primus* prophesied by Christ's word at Caesarea. Without Peter — linked with Paul — Rome would not be the local Church to which all may have recourse for justice to be done to them and for the truth to be guaranteed or re-established.[150]

Why did Rome become identified with the primacy? Granting the city's preeminence as the center of the empire and the "capital of the world,"[151] the more substantial reason is its foundation upon the apostolic faith and martyrdom of Peter and Paul. Irenaeus has given lasting witness to Rome as the church with the *potentior principalitas.* The phrase has the general sense of "more eminent origin." Tillard raises an interesting question: Why does

Jerusalem, the "mother" church and guardian of the Lord's trophies of the cross and tomb, not have primacy? What other church could possibly have a "more eminent origin"? Tillard responds that the hierarchy of churches was determined by apostolicity, and so took shape in the various places where the Gospel took root.[152] The apostolic faith confessed first by Peter and later spread to the Gentiles by Paul found its most powerful expression in Rome. The church of Rome, where the blood of Peter and Paul flowed together and where their "trophies" remain, is thus the most eminent of the apostolic churches:

> Peter... sealed his witness—which even his confession at Caesarea expressed only verbally—in the *martyria* of spilled blood. This blood was drunk, for all time, by the soil of the local community of Rome. The church of this place thus became the church of the witness of Peter and Paul. The primacy of the local church of Rome is therefore linked to the historical event of the martyrdom of Peter and Paul because this city remains the place where their "trophies" rest forever.[153]

Still more broadly, Tillard sees in Rome the universality and catholicity of the divine plan disclosed in the letter to the Ephesians: the joining, in Peter and Paul, of Jew and Gentile. The early Roman church's strong Jewish influence gives further illustration of the catholic unity of Israel and the nations in a single covenant.[154]

The church of Rome is therefore the church of Peter and Paul, the two apostles representing the catholicity of the church. Tillard notes that this yoking is the common heritage of the East and the West. The Roman see, for instance, "has never ceased to introduce its most solemn acts [e.g., Assumption, Immaculate Conception, documents of Vatican II] with the formula *Auctoritate Apostolorum Petri et Pauli,*" and the 1970 Roman Missal reunited on June 29, the feasts of Peter and Paul.[155] Tillard's distinctive contribution in this regard is his study of how the two apostles' complementarity in mission and identity bears witness to the catholicity of the divine plan for humanity. We may organize the complementarity as shown in the table on the following page.

The primacy of the Roman church, rooted in Peter and Paul, grounds the primacy of its bishop, and not vice versa.[156] It is significant that Irenaeus, who bore the most eloquent witness to Roman primacy, made no mention of its bishop. The pope, as bishop of Rome, bears witness and represents the faith of his church. His ministry is rooted in the sacrament of episcopal ordination: the "papacy is not a sacrament, or even a degree in the fullness of the sacrament of order";[157] he is the pope because he is bishop of Rome, not the bishop of Rome because pope. If the "universal pastor," charged with a special care for all of the churches, he is not the "universal bishop" who replaces the heads of other local churches (as indicated by the German bishops' reply to Bismarck, and its confirmation by Pius IX). Furthermore, in this universal ministry, he is neither a "super-bishop"[158] nor a monarch,

Peter and Paul's Complementarity
in Mission and Identity

Peter	Paul
Jewish community	Gentile community
rootedness of church in soil of the Promise (Jerusalem)	extension of church into infinite space of the Father's love for creation (Rome)
origin of the church in the twelve tribes	the church's destiny in the whole world
fullness in Christ of covenant	absolute newness of Gospel event
continuity of tradition rooted in God's fidelity	disruptive, unforeseeable action of God
absolute fidelity to what has been said and done	total openness to what should be said and done
first witness of resurrection	last witness of resurrection
institutional	charismatic
publicly invested as apostle	mysteriously invested as apostle

who stands apart from or above his fellow bishops. The bishop of Rome is first, but not unique. In short, he is not "more than a pope,"[159] in Tillard's sharp phrasing. Who, then, is the bishop of Rome? He is "the vicar of Peter in the Church of Peter and Paul."[160] He is the one who watches over the apostolic faith that is the "most eminent origin" and inheritance of the church of Rome.

Ministry of Unity

The primary ministry of the bishop of Rome, as with any bishop, is to watch over his church and to ensure its communion with its sister churches. However, as primate and vicar of Peter, he has a special ministry of unity, arising from the Roman church's apostolic faith and memory. This ministry is threefold: ecclesial, episcopal, and human — all ultimately in service of the Father's plan to recapitulate all creation in Christ. Enjoying a real, effective primacy, the pope is not, however, the center of the church around which all must cohere (as spokes from a hub), but rather the first servant of unity: he does not create this unity, which is the work of the Holy Spirit and the eucharist,[161] but rather watches over and deepens it.[162] In short, the unity of the church is achieved thanks to Rome, not around it.[163]

The papacy is of divine institution. Tillard flatly states that it "could not be dispensed with without doing violence to God's plan."[164] However, such institution must not be understood in a fundamentalist or blueprint manner, for nowhere does the New Testament speak either of a successor to Peter or of Roman primacy; resistance by other churches to claims of direct divine institution is often based upon these grounds. Divine institution is discerned not by searching scripture literally for what is "prescribed," but by seeking what is "willed" by God.[165] This discernment unfolds in history, guided by scripture and tradition — discerning not simply what is useful, but necessary, to the life of the church. In this context, Tillard sees the papacy's service of communion as divinely willed and instituted: "If God wills the Unity of the Church, this implies a primacy at the service of Unity. A Unity that is not uniformity but a communion of Churches deeply rooted in their human soil; a primacy that is precisely at the evangelical service of the ministries sent into this human diversity."[166]

However, Tillard is aware that the shape and scope of the papacy is subject to historical growth and decay. Many present-day ecumenical difficulties stem not from the necessity or fact of the papacy, but from the manner of its exercise. As a way forward, Tillard adopts the ancient distinction, recovered in the early twentieth century by Pierre Batiffol and furthered by Yves Congar, of the pope's threefold primacy: regional (Italy), patriarchal (West), and apostolic (worldwide).[167] The key distinction, for our purposes, is between the latter two: patriarchal authority is more administrative and centralizing, whereas apostolic authority involves matters of faith and the integrity of churches.[168]

This "apostolic" primacy embraces the church, its bishops, and humanity itself. The bishop of Rome's primatial ministry of unity is, in the first place, ecclesial. He is to promote the church of God's unity in the apostolic faith, particularly through "ensuring the mutual recognition of the churches and basically the maintenance in each of them of the traits of the Church of Pentecost."[169] He does so first by watching over the church of Rome and its patrimony of faith, memory, and martyrdom. By preserving the memory of Peter and Paul — and, thereby, the apostolic, Pentecostal faith — he ensures the communion in faith and love of all the churches.[170] Tillard most frequently describes the pope as "watchman," "touchstone," or "sentinel":

> [His] most basic function will be to work out the calling of touchstone, point of reference and memorial of the apostolic faith, the proper calling of the Roman church.... A sentinel or watchman is not the commander who gives orders and decides on the attitude to take.... The well-being of the group depends on confidence in his warning: too many false alarms and they will stop taking him seriously.[171]

This oversight is essentially a ministry of mutual recognition; other churches should be able to recognize in him (and his church) the authentic, apostolic faith, and he is to recognize such faith in other churches:

> The local church thus inscribes its (catholic) *sollicitudo* for all the churches of *all* places and *all* times in a web over which the local church of Rome (the first see) and its bishop (the primate) "watch" with special title. Catholic communion has, in Rome, a "point of conscience," an "organ of recall" of the

> conditions of its unanimity in faith, "one voice" which affirms all the bishops in their fidelity to Christ. By the *"consortium fidei apostolicae"* of its bishop and of Rome's, the local church thus remains in the once-for-all (*ephapax*) of the Pentecostal church gathered around "Peter and the apostles" (Acts 2:37; see 2:14, 5:29). Its "language" (its difference) can make flourish one of the riches of catholicity without which unity is imperiled.[172]

In the preeminent expression of his episcopacy and primacy, then, the bishop of Rome, as the "memory of Peter,"[173] serves the entire church primarily by overseeing the patrimony of the local church of Rome, and, by means of this oversight, building up the one church of God in the many local churches throughout the world. His "universal" ministry is incomprehensible apart from his "local" ministry.[174]

The most concrete expression of the pope's ministry of unity is the commission to "strengthen the brethren" as head of the episcopal college. Perhaps the classic reference concerning the relationship of the primate to his fellow bishops, the thirty-fourth Apostolic Canon states:

> The bishops of every nation [*ethne*] must know who is the first [*proton*] among them, and consider him as their head [*kephale*], doing nothing without his agreement [*gnome*]; but let each do alone what concerns his own district and the country of his region. But let the first also do nothing without the agreement [*gnome*] of all. For in this way there will be harmony [*homonoia*] and God will be glorified by the Son in the Holy Spirit.[175]

Two remarks spring to mind. First, the primate is not set over against his brother bishops, but is placed "among" them and can do nothing apart from them. Second, such communal or collegial activity is not primarily administrative or pragmatic, but doxological.[176] In other words, primacy and collegiality are mutually ordered to each other and both pertain to the communional nature of God and his church.

It is in this mutual interdependence that the pope's mission of episcopal unity must be understood. The bishop of Rome neither is set over against nor replaces his brother bishops, but stands "at the heart of their collegial communion."[177] Sacramentally equal, the bishops are to be coordinated in their apostolic brotherhood (*adelphotes*) rather than merely subordinated by their head.[178] Tillard acknowledges, however, that Vatican II did not "settle the difficult question of the boundaries" between primatial and collegial authority, and never resolved how *sub Petro* relates to *cum Petro*.[179] One thinks of the aforementioned difficulties engendered by synods of bishops, which function largely as papal advisory boards, and whose deliberative power would be a papal concession; the contrast, in Tillard's pointed phrasing, is between bishops as "associates" and as "beneficiaries" of the pope's ministry.[180] The latter understanding compromises the integrity of both primate and college.

We may say, therefore, that the bishop of Rome's universal primacy is not an absolute sovereignty arrogating all power and jurisdiction to itself.[181] He instead strengthens each bishop as the vicar of Christ in his own church. Even Vatican I's *Pastor Aeternus,* a document not uninfluenced by Ultramontanism, states as much:

> The power of the sovereign pontiff in no way obstructs the ordinary and immediate power of episcopal jurisdiction, by which the bishops, established by the Holy Spirit (Acts 20:28) as successors to the Apostles, feed and govern as true pastors the flock committed to each one. On the contrary, this power is asserted, strengthened, and vindicated by the supreme and universal pastor, as Gregory the Great says: "My honor is the honor of the universal church. My honor is the solid strength of my brothers. Then am I truly honored, when honor is not denied to each one to whom it is due."[182]

Finally, the pope's service of ecclesial and episcopal unity finds its deepest purpose in God's plan to gather all humanity in Christ. As the first servant of ecclesial communion, the bishop of Rome seeks the common good of the church of God, which is the "recapitulation (*anakephalaiosis*), in full realization, of humanity through the communion of all the 'nations' (with their races, their cultures, their destinies) *en Christo* and through him in the Father."[183] Outside of the visible unity of all humanity in Christ, of which the church of God is the *sacramentum* and first-fruits, the Petrine and Roman primacy has no purpose.

Conclusion

Ultimately, church-wide institutions and ministries must be exercised in a synergistic, not pyramidal, fashion. Synodality gives voice to all of the baptized in the church, collegiality ensures that all bishops work together for the unity of the church, and the papacy seeks to activate the charisms and gifts of both the episcopate and the entire church. Each fosters the communion of the one church of God by ensuring that the church of Pentecost remains recognizable in the faith, sacraments, and life of the many churches of God.

Tillard's theology of the local church, built upon a theology and an ecclesiology of communion, is a substantial, comprehensive accomplishment. Examining its critics and its future prospects is the task of our final chapter.

Chapter Six

Evaluation and Trajectories of Tillard's Theology of the Local Church

Jean-Marie Tillard's theology of the local church is a magisterial one. One commentator has gone so far as to state that *L'Église locale* "surpasses in ecumenical importance and sheer sparkle even the works of Möhler, Congar, [George] Tavard, . . . [Michael] Ramsey, [P. T.] Forsyth, and Zizioulas."[1] Grounded in scripture and the great tradition of both East and West, in harmony with the teachings of Vatican II, Tillard's vision of communion provides an explicitly theological and catholic foundation for ecclesiological reflection, a foundation often neglected by some ecclesiologists in their focus on particular issues of ecclesial power and politics. His account of Pentecost as the heart of all ecclesial life enables a thoroughly Trinitarian ecclesiology and a divine charter for ecclesial unity-in-diversity; no less important in this regard is his insistence that the "church needs the fleshly earth" if it is to manifest the catholicity of God's plan for humanity. Tillard's conception of the local church's faith and sacramental life is similarly profound, rooted in the baptismal dignity and equality of all believers and reaching fruition in the local church's eucharist celebrated with its bishop — the church's deepest being-as-communion with God and with humanity. Perhaps most importantly for contemporary Catholic and ecumenical life, his understanding of the relationship between the local church and the universal church — and the ministry of the bishop of Rome within it — offers the most substantial and promising proposal to date for its renewal; one hears its echoes in Pope John Paul II's encyclical *Ut unum sint.* Ultimately, Tillard's theology of the local church is passionate, reasoned, and persuasive. It will contribute to the fruitful reception of Vatican II and further the ecumenical quest for visible, eucharistic unity among all Christians.

Tillard's work has not gone without criticism, however. He himself is aware of his critics. In *Église d'églises,* Tillard notes that his vision of ministry has been reproached as "abstract, idealistic . . . a romantic return to the church of the first centuries . . . tainted with Gallicanism."[2] *Chair de l'Église, chair du Christ* addresses those who would see his ecclesiology of communion as overly sacramental and patristic, as a covert importation of modern Orthodox thought into Catholicism, and as neglectful of the Western (especially Protestant) emphasis upon the individual-interior dimension of religion and faith.[3] In *L'Église locale,* he notes that a theology of the local church raises Catholic fears of nationalism, ecclesial factionalism, and the absolutization of differences — in short, the "victory of Babel over Pentecost."[4] These charges are not minor.

Much of the criticism of Tillard has been on a general plane, however, focusing on the overall shape of his ecclesiology of communion; very little has been written to date on his theology of the local church. This chapter, then, will present the main criticisms lodged against Tillard's ecclesiology, offer responses to these critiques, and conclude by exploring two trajectories — the interplay of primacy and collegiality-synodality, and inculturation — central to Tillard's theology of the local church and to the reception of Vatican II in the life of the church in the new millennium.

Critiques

The most prominent "general" critiques of Tillard's thought are those of Avery Dulles and Nicholas M. Healy. Dulles questions Tillard's supposed idealization of the early church, while Healy argues that Tillard's work offers a largely formal-ideal model of communion that acts as a cipher with which Tillard can construct an ecclesiology according to his theological-imaginative narrative, i.e., a rejection of modern Western individualism through a return to the ecclesiology of the early church.

We look first at Dulles. He suggests that "[Tillard's] ecclesiology, which tends to idealize the early centuries, may be somewhat anachronistic. At least he can be accused of failing to provide strong theoretical reasons why the forms of the patristic period should be determinative today."[5] Such anachronism accordingly has contemporary ecclesiological consequences. For instance, is the pope primarily the bishop of the local church of Rome or the successor of Peter? Is the bishop primarily the head of a local church or a member of the body "charged with the supreme direction of the universal Church"? In both instances, the former position has, in Dulles's view, stronger roots in the history of the early church, while the latter one has better support from the two Vatican councils. Dulles's critique clearly indicates that he sees Tillard's thought as too beholden to patristic forms and wishes instead to allow for what he views as ecclesiological development.

Dulles's critique thus has substantive and methodological dimensions, which are entwined — respectively, the nature of the papacy and the episcopacy, and the interplay of historical precedent and doctrinal development. Both dimensions of the critique are mistaken, however. Substantively, Dulles's critique of Tillard's supposed patristic conception of the papacy is dependent upon a false dichotomy between the pope as successor of Peter and as bishop of Rome. As we have seen, Tillard sees the pope as defined by both titles (if, nonetheless, he prefers "vicar of Peter" to "successor of

Peter"); in fact, his most comprehensive description of the pope is "the vicar of Peter in the Church of Peter and Paul."[6] However inadvertently, Dulles leads one to have to choose between the early church and the two Vatican councils. In contrast, *The Bishop of Rome* and Tillard's subsequent reflections on the papacy, are efforts to show how the two councils stand—easily and uneasily—within the great tradition. Tillard's embrace of "bishop of Rome" and "successor of Peter" is more adequate to both history and doctrine than is Dulles's dichotomy; Tillard has the advantage, moreover, of recognizing that Vatican I and II do not fully represent the mind of the entire church, and thus stand in need of completion by the insights of the churches of the Reform and especially of the Eastern churches. Dulles clearly would not posit any essential break between the early church and the Vatican councils, but he could have been more explicit in linking the two eras. Tillard evinces no such difficulty.

Dulles's methodological critique of Tillard's patristic anachronism is the more important charge, for it undergirds his substantive one. This charge seems mistaken as well. Tillard, while attributing a certain normativity to the patristic era—the "undivided church"—does not argue for a simple return to patristic structures and forms. The history of the "divided church" has not been void of genuine development and insight, and therefore any future unity will not be a simple "return," but a "renewal" and a "recognition" of faith, tradition, and doctrine. This is evident in the following passage:

> In the perspective of an "ecumenical ecclesiology" which, as we have said, takes the "confessional factor" seriously, it is clear that such a ministry [of unity] could never replace what the confessions call synodical government, conciliarity, or co-responsibility. It would be impossible to think of what the last century described as the "monarchic" exercise of authority. Equally impossible would be simply to return to the situation of the first millennium. Because—always provided our parallel confessions are re-soldered together—account must be taken of the specific features certain "confessions" in the West have acquired, which are reconcilable with the full *communion* and which cannot be eradicated by a canonical decision. Everything seems to indicate the Holy Spirit was no stranger to the appearance of these features. There is an immense difference between the meaning of the Patriarchate in the West at the time when the "crown of Patriarchs" represented the church, and the present state of the Christian West. The West is splintered. However, several of these "confessional" churches have a solid structure and an ecclesiological vision which are far from negligible. It is no accident that certain Eastern Orthodox churches are in direct dialogue with some of them, parallel to the dialogue with the Roman Catholic Church. It is possible that, between Eastern Orthodox and Romans, the ideal would be to go back, to the centuries before the break. But that is not true for the whole of the ecclesial world. And all the more so since, very often, the perspective is obscured. It is one thing to propose a vision of *exousia* and of the function of the magisterium as healthy as they were in the early centuries; it is quite another to dream of the concrete exercising of a primacy which would be the exact copy of the first centuries.

> For, whatever the vision, its implementation will always have to adapt to the context. That was already true before 1054.[7]

Tillard does not see patristic "forms" as templates or blueprints, but as part of the common heritage of East and West, and therefore as natural resources for future development.

Let us consider two examples. First, the nature of the episcopacy. Tillard's writings marshal substantial patristic support for the necessary linkage between the bishop and his local church. On these grounds, he argues, convincingly, that titular bishops deform the episcopate and should be laid to rest. Here, historical precedent has a normative, doctrinal permanence and can serve to correct subsequent aberrations. Second, the scope of papal primacy. Although some form of distinction between the pope's patriarchal and primatial roles must be upheld and/or restored for the papacy to be acceptable to other churches, the actual concrete shape of that distinction is open to development, especially in light of massive cultural, historical, and even technological changes. If the present exercise of papal primacy is not entirely acceptable to Anglicans, Orthodox, and Protestants, neither is a simple return to its exercise in the undivided church; the patristic conception of the pope as bishop of Rome and "touchstone" or "point of reference" remains normative, but simultaneously allows for the renewal of such ministry's concrete exercise. To varying degrees of success, Vatican I and II are efforts to provide such renewal. So, too, is John Paul II's encyclical, *Ut unum sint.*

Moreover, Tillard insists upon the Christian paradox that faithfulness to the past often requires a dying to certain past forms, in order to allow the past to live anew. Ecumenism — like all Christian life — demands a willingness to be converted to new identity and life, a radical openness to the divine will wherever it leads. It at once reaches back to what is enduring and stretches forward to what must be developed. Tillard, as we have seen, writes eloquently of the impossibility of a simple return to the past, even vis-à-vis Orthodoxy. He is still more eloquent in his belief that faithfulness to the past involves an often painful discernment of what is truly essential in that past:

> For in the gospel nothing is accomplished without acceptance of the principle of loss. This is true even of the Son: according to the Letter to the Philippians *kenosis* is the very heart of his mission. Here we ought to draw attention to an ecclesiology of *harpagmos.* . . . No unity will be possible unless the Churches who are richest in doctrine and theology — I do not say faith — and who are proudest of their traditions are the first to be ready to renounce, if it is necessary, some of their particular features for the sake of communion. For instance, do we have to insist on keeping the *Filioque* if this remains an obstacle to our sister-churches in the East? Must we go on adhering to certain forms of exercise of the Roman primacy if they prevent some Churches from entering into communion with the Bishop of Rome? Is there any need to perpetuate the custom of consecrating as bishops men who have no real episcopal charge,

such as nuncios or secretaries of some official bodies, if this prevents several Churches from perceiving the true nature of the episcopate?[8]

In brief, Dulles is correct in arguing that anachronism has no place in the church, as well as that historical precedent need not foreclose doctrinal and ecclesial development; past "forms" are not chains. He falls short, however, in holding that Tillard's ecclesiology is anachronistic and insufficiently attentive to the development represented by Vatican I and II. Tillard's commitment to the early church does not foreclose growth, but fosters it through ongoing conversion to its most authentic and enduring elements.

Nicholas Healy's critique is directed against what he considers to be the ideal and abstract character of many modern ecclesiologies. These posit a primary reality (*res*) — often Triune communion — and see the church as its visible manifestation (*sacramentum*). Such a "sacramental" approach leads unfortunately — and inevitably — to ideal, abstract ecclesiologies, divorced from the church's concrete reality and unable to give an account of the church's pilgrim character or its distinctiveness from the world. In place of this approach, Healy argues for a "practical-prophetic" ecclesiology, which reflects practically upon the church's situation *in via* so as to enable better "its task of truthful witness within a particular ecclesiological context."[9] Ecclesiology, in this view, is not "about the business of finding the single right way to think about the church, of developing a blueprint suitable for all times and places."[10]

If not the main target of Healy's criticism (Karl Rahner plays this role), Tillard nonetheless is criticized for a heavy, even exclusive reliance upon an abstract conception of ecclesial communion[11] (with the consequent occlusion of the church's pilgrim status[12]) and the erosion of ecclesial distinctiveness vis-à-vis the world.[13] Healy does raise a valid point concerning the dangers of ecclesiological abstraction: communion *is* intrinsically a slippery, polyvalent term, dependent upon the imagination and agenda of theologians for its concrete implications. How else, for example, does one account for the radically different ecclesiologies of communion engendered by Tillard, Elisabeth Schüssler Fiorenza, Leonardo Boff, Peter Hodgson, and Miroslav Volf?[14]

Nonetheless, Healy fails to take account of how Tillard ties together ideality and reality, abstraction and concreteness, universality and particularity in his ecclesiology of communion. Correct in depicting Tillard's ecclesiology as shaped by "patristic theology and his concern for ecumenism and community,"[15] Healy gives insufficient attention to the material, concrete content of ecclesial communion in that ecclesiology. While one can agree with Healy over the rhetorical flight of Tillard's claim that communion "alone" can serve as the foundation for ecumenical ecclesiology, his critique of Tillard is flawed on at least three grounds.

In the first place, Healy's critique has a myopic focus. It is based upon a narrow selection of Tillard's works (only two are cited, one in a footnote only) and an equally narrow reading of those works; for instance, Healy's book, published in 2000, makes no mention of Tillard's *summa, L'Église locale,* published five years earlier in 1995. Although Healy's book is not an in-depth study of Tillard's ecclesiology, it nonetheless is responsible for presenting that thought fully and positively. It unfortunately fails to do so, and so overlooks both the breadth and the specificity of Tillard's thought.

Second, although undoubtedly idealistic in its vision of ecclesial communion, Tillard's thought is equally concrete, practical, and realistic. The issue, Healy correctly argues, is not with ecclesial models, but with "how [they are] used within a complex of interpretation — of the church's history and its present concrete shape, of the contemporary context and agenda, of construals of Scripture and the like."[16] If, then, one grants that no theologian is wholly adequate to that "complex of interpretation," can one not also say that some do succeed to a great extent in joining the ideal and the concrete? Tillard's use of communion is not arbitrary, but develops its material content in conversation with the breadth of Christian tradition through the centuries and with contemporary ecclesial concerns. The role of episcopal conferences and the existence of titular bishops, for instance, have nothing of the "ideal" about them, but have immediate consequences for church life and ministry.

Furthermore, Tillard's ecclesiology has developed in response to the demands made upon him by ecumenical and curial service. It is not, as Healy describes most ecclesiologies, the work of a theologian "working virtually alone, more or less independent of much of the Christian community."[17] For example, Tillard's study of the relationship of word and sacrament derives in part from the concrete demands of ecumenical dialogue with the Disciples of Christ and of service on Faith and Order, while his exploration of the primacy-synodality relationship arises in large part from his involvement with the Anglican and Orthodox dialogues. Accordingly, contrary to Healy, his work is not a "blueprint ecclesiology," in which "good ecclesial practices can be described only after a prior and quite abstract consideration of true ecclesial doctrine."[18] Instead, Tillard does not subordinate action to reflection, or the church pilgrim to the church triumphant,[19] but seeks to keep ecclesial reflection accountable to normative tradition and contemporary contexts.

Third, Tillard's salvific universalism is not based upon a liberal "inclusivism," which waters down ecclesial distinctiveness in an otherwise admirable attempt to comprehend the salvation of all peoples. Rather, such universalism is the consequence of his commitment to the catholicity of the divine plan for the communion of all peoples in Christ the head; the first parts of both *Église d'églises* and *L'Église locale* are devoted to such elaboration and arise from sustained scriptural and patristic reflection. Moreover, Tillard makes it quite clear that such communion is effected, as Ephesians 2 reveals, through the reconciling work of Christ's death and resurrection.[20] There is no question here of sloppy inclusivism or religious indifferentism.

Baptism introduces one into the reconciliation and communion effected by Christ's death and resurrection, while others are saved as well through the Christ-event, but in a way known to God. The church of God remains, for Tillard, the place where God can be known and loved most fully and surely; the body of Christ — inseparable, since Pentecost, from its head — remains intrinsic to the economy of salvation. Healy, whose own work is marked by a concern for "truthful witness" in a world marked by "pervasive relativism,"[21] may be insufficiently appreciative of Tillard's genuinely catholic vision and its rootedness in Christian tradition.

In sum, Healy's critique, whose commendable goal is a genuinely practical ecclesiology that can transform ecclesial witness and practice, is simply not applicable to Tillard's ecclesiology. Lacking in substantial awareness of Tillard's theology and ecclesiology, Healy can make only quite general, even unsubstantiated critiques. His rightful concern for articulating the content of "communion" is betrayed by a lack of effort to seek that content in Tillard's corpus or to evaluate such content in light of scripture, tradition, and the contemporary situation.

Prospects

Tillard's theology of the local church also has been criticized on more particular grounds. Chief among these critiques are those noted by Tillard himself: Gallican and inordinate Orthodox influence on his treatment of the papacy, synodality, and eucharistic ecclesiology; the threat of ecclesial nationalism and separatism. Under the headings of primacy-synodality and inculturation-reception, we will address such criticism and use it as a springboard for exploring possible trajectories of development. While it remains clear that the deepening of faith in Christ is the wellspring of all authentic ecclesial renewal, these concerns are nonetheless central to both the ongoing reception of Vatican II and the furtherance of Christian unity. In each of them we stand at the heart of the theology of the local church.

Primacy-Synodality

Tillard's view of the interaction of papal primacy and synodality is attacked from two angles. On the one hand, its conception of the papacy is too Orthodox, Anglican, and/or Protestant, and insufficiently heedful of the two Vatican councils; it makes of the pope a mere "honorary president," even a "Catholic Queen of England."[22] On the other, its understanding of the relationship of the pope and the bishops bears traces of Gallicanism, thereby weakening the proper role of the papacy and exaggerating the rights and powers of bishops (and their churches) over against the papacy.

It is helpful at this point to recall the main points of Vatican II's teaching on the theology of the local church, the episcopate and collegiality, and the papacy. Present only in a few key passages, the council's theology of the local church is eucharistic and episcopal: the church of Christ is truly present and active in the community of the baptized formed into one people through the Gospel and the eucharist (word and sacrament) under the headship of a bishop and his ministers. Moreover, such documents as *Lumen gentium* and *Ad gentes divinitus* provide an expansive theology of catholicity, whereby the local church and its culture engage in inculturation and mutual transformation. Second, the bishop is viewed primarily as a successor of the apostles and a member of the episcopal college. He receives "proper, immediate and ordinary power" in his own diocese through sacramental ordination.[23] Although not a "vicar of the Roman Pontiff,"[24] on account of his sacramental dignity, he is to exercise such powers in hierarchical communion with the pope and his brother bishops. As a member of the episcopal college, he is charged with care for all the churches, but is not necessarily the head of a local church. Third, the pope is presented as the Roman pontiff, the successor of Peter. He is the head of the episcopal college, but retains always the power to act freely on his own initiative. As "the perpetual and visible source and foundation of unity both of the bishops and of the whole company of the faithful,"[25] he possesses supreme, full, immediate, universal, and ordinary power over all the churches.

Thus Vatican II, through its affirmation of the sacramentality of the episcopate and of the church's eucharistic essence, renewed the doctrine and practice of collegiality and provided support for the theology of the local church. However, it also affirmed papal authority and independence in a manner that seems to have exceeded even that of Vatican I. Much of this contrast may be explained by the desire to secure broad consensus among the bishops, a necessary condition for the fruitful reception and implementation of the council. However, the council's method of juxtaposing contrasting statements, without explaining their connections, also gave rise (intentionally?) to ambiguities. The most pressing difficulty, for our purposes, is the precise scope and boundaries of episcopal and papal ministry and authority. *Lumen gentium* repeatedly stresses that the episcopal college is never to act apart from its head, the pope, but places no corresponding duty upon the head. In light of conciliar teaching on the episcopate and collegiality, what does it mean that the pope has "full, supreme, and universal power over the whole church, a power which he can always exercise freely"?[26] Likewise, how does one reconcile the "proper, immediate, and ordinary" power of each bishop in his church with the "immediate and ordinary" power of the pope over the entire church? On account of such ambiguities, Tillard concludes that the "primate's rights are well-known: his duties are not,"[27] and that the council fails to provide any corresponding statement of bishops' rights vis-à-vis the primate.[28] Such is the context that any post-conciliar ecclesiology, let alone theology of the local church, must take into account.

Tillard's theology of the local church, with its attendant stances on primacy and synodality, enters into this ambiguous context. It both upholds and develops the council's ecclesiology. On the one hand, he affirms the genuine ecclesial reality of the local church, as well as its eucharistic and episcopal character. His theology of catholicity and inculturation resonates deeply with the council's declaration that the church "speaks every language, understands and embraces all tongues in charity, and thus overcomes the dispersion of Babel."[29] He stresses the sacramentality of episcopal ordination and builds upon the doctrine of collegiality, whereby the bishops form one body in service to the church. He upholds the divine institution of both the episcopate and the papacy.

Tillard's theology of the local church also seeks to balance the universalist aspects of the council's ecclesiology by exploring its juxtapositions and ambiguities. One thinks, for instance, of his clear argument for the simultaneity of the local and universal churches, and of his conception of the church of God as a communion of local churches. As mentioned above, one of the thorniest areas of contention in Vatican II's reception is the nature of papal and episcopal authority and their interaction. Tillard's thought on primacy and synodality helps advance such reception. Accordingly, we will look first at the papacy, second at synodality.

Tillard's deepest contribution to the theology of papal primacy is his insistence upon the papacy's martyrological nature.[30] Both its Petrine and Roman dimensions flow from this core of witness. Peter, we have seen, reminds each pope of his duty to evangelize, of his own sinfulness and betrayal of Christ, and of the ministry of strengthening the brethren that arises out of such failure. The church of Rome reminds the pope that he is the (1) head of a local church, in which (2) the Petrine and Pauline charisms (3) flow together in martyrdom. As the "vicar of Peter in the Church of Peter and Paul," the pope's preeminence is not that of a corporate executive or a political ruler, but of a witness to faith, even unto death.

Vatican II, however, largely neglects the martyrological dimension of primacy. It presents the Petrine aspect in a static manner — Peter is the one who occupies the first place among the apostles, and the first place in a chain of succession — and lacks any sense of Peter's weakness, need for mercy and conversion, or martyrdom.[31] Moreover, unlike Vatican I,[32] the council does not ground papal primacy in the church of Rome. Vatican II thereby betrays a certain papal maximalism or universalism, in which the pope is primarily the supreme head of a universal church situated above the local churches. The council's pope is more the Supreme Pontiff than the bishop of Rome, and the Peter that pope succeeds has no discernible personal, human qualities — quite unlike the Peter of the New Testament. The difference is enormous.

John Paul II, in contrast, has made the martyrological nature of primacy central to his pontificate.[33] Indeed, George Weigel, the pope's semi-official biographer, sees John Paul's foremost legacy for the third millennium as precisely this recasting of the pope from administrator to witness. With a bit of grandiosity, Weigel writes:

> The world and the Church no longer think of the pope as the chief executive officer of the Roman Catholic Church; the world and the Church experience the pope as a pastor, an evangelist, and a witness.... It is very difficult to imagine a twenty-first-century pontificate that deliberately returns to the bureaucratic-managerial papal model that reached its apogee in the pontificate of Pius XII.[34]
>
> John Paul II has revitalized the papacy for the twenty-first century by retrieving and renewing its first-century roots, which lie in the New Testament's portrait of Peter's unique role as the apostle who "strengthens the brethren." In doing so, John Paul has aligned the exercise of the Office of Peter with the Second Vatican Council's teaching on the nature of the episcopate, in which, the Council Fathers write, "preaching the gospel has pride of place." Bishops are, first and foremost, evangelists, not managers. As John Paul has demonstrated with effect, that is as true for the Bishop of Rome as it is for the bishop of the smallest missionary diocese.[35]

Martyrdom has been a constant theme for John Paul. In *Tertio millennio adveniente,* his 1994 apostolic letter outlining the church's preparation for the new millennium, he makes his own Tertullian's words, "The blood of the martyrs is the seed of the church," and writes, "At the end of the second millennium, the church has once again become a church of martyrs.... The witness to Christ borne even to the shedding of blood has become a common inheritance of Catholics, Orthodox, Anglicans and Protestants.... This witness must not be forgotten"; to this end he seeks to update the "martyrologies" for the universal church, as a remembrance of such faithful witness.[36]

Ut unum sint, issued in 1995, deepens such reflection[37] and, in a manner unprecedented in magisterial documents, places witness and martyrdom at the heart of its vision of the papal ministry, particularly through its reflection upon Peter and Paul:

> The bishop of Rome is the bishop of the church which preserves the mark of the martyrdom of Peter and of Paul: "By a mysterious design of providence it is at Rome that [Peter] concludes his journey in following Jesus, and it is at Rome that he gives his greatest proof of love and fidelity. Likewise Paul, the apostle of the gentiles, gives his supreme witness at Rome. In this way the church of Rome became the church of Peter and Paul."
>
> As the heir to the mission of Peter in the church, which has been made fruitful by the blood of the princes of the apostles, the bishop of Rome exercises a ministry originating in the manifold mercy of God. This mercy converts hearts and pours forth the power of grace where the disciple experiences the bitter taste of his personal weakness and helplessness. The authority proper to this ministry is completely at the service of God's merciful plan, and it must always be seen in this perspective. Its power is explained from this perspective.
>
> This [service of unity] can require the offering of one's own life.

> I, John Paul, *servus servorum Dei,* venture to make my own the words of the apostle Paul, whose martyrdom, together with that of the apostle Peter, has bequeathed to this see of Rome the splendor of its witness....[38]

As the world and the church become increasingly subject to the twin forces of globalization and ethnic strife, such primatial witness may serve as a source of resistance to human and ecclesial uniformity and division. The temptation is always strong to conform the papacy (and other ecclesial structures) to contemporaneous forms of political and economic organization, just as Roman imperial structures and modern notions of sovereignty shaped it in centuries past and present. Today, the temptation is to conceive — consciously or not — of the church as a "multinational group," which can efficiently centralize and streamline the operations of the church by making the Vatican "a center in which the sources of ecclesial life are concentrated."[39] Detached from reference to the martyrological nature of the church of Rome and its bishop, the tendency to see the pope as the "chief executive officer" of the Catholic Church will only increase. Detached from reference to the martyrdom of Peter and Paul, the pope will become a bureaucrat, managing power rather than offering witness, seeking uniformity rather than building up a communion of differences. Conversely, in the face of increasing nationalism, the distance of the pope's witness from ethnic and sectarian concerns may serve as a center of unity. Tillard's insistence upon the martyrological character of primacy, echoed powerfully by John Paul II, is essential. It will help the church be faithful to its "vocation of saying no" to all that destroys human and ecclesial communion.[40] Ultimately, such primatial witness will serve as a reminder that all ecclesial authority — even papal infallibility — is rooted, as *Lumen gentium* states, in the proclamation of the Gospel.[41]

Tillard's second key contribution is that papal primacy is "not autocratic but fraternal."[42] Neither a "super-bishop" nor "more than a pope," the bishop of Rome is always a member of the episcopal college and must never act apart from it.[43] It is imperative, therefore, that his primatial ministry be inserted in the "sacramental circle" of the church's life, especially within the episcopate.[44] This sacramental brotherhood and equality is a particularly important point for Orthodoxy, where the sacramental nature of authority is paramount. The Anglican Communion likewise sees such equality as essential to the properly collegial and synodal exercise of authority.[45] Corresponding to such episcopal equality is ecclesial equality. The church of Rome, if the first (*prima*) see, is not unique (*unica*), and the Patriarchate of the West must be placed within the Pentarchy or "crown of patriarchs."[46] Primatial authority, then, must be both collegial and synodal.

On the magisterial level, if Vatican II, in its insistence upon affirming the free exercise of papal authority, left unclear such mutual ordering and responsibilities of primatial and collegial authority, *Ut unum sint* outlines a way forward. John Paul II states: "The bishop of Rome is a member of the 'college,' and the bishops are his brothers in the ministry." It follows that his primacy, his service of unity "must always be done in communion" with his brother bishops.[47] Moreover, "in 'keeping watch' (*episkopein*) like a sentinel," the bishop of Rome strengthens his brothers so that "the true voice of Christ the shepherd may be heard in all the particular churches. In this way, in each of the particular churches entrusted to those pastors, the *una, sancta, catholica et apostolica ecclesia* is made present."[48] Both John Paul's and Tillard's conceptions of primatial-episcopal-synodal relationship indicate that it is not to be viewed as a balance of power or as a zero-sum game, but as synergy. Primacy and collegiality-synodality do not compete, but bring each other to fullness.

Third, the primatial ministry must be distinguished according to the traditional "spheres of influence," whereby the bishop of Rome exercises a threefold primacy in Italy, the West, and the entire church. In particular, the distinction between the pope as "Patriarch of the West" and "universal primate" is essential to any possibility of full communion with Orthodoxy. Needless to say, the great good of such a renewed primacy will come only at great cost to what the various Christian communions often hold most dear: their own powers, privileges, and prejudices.

Fourth, papal primacy should be understood in light of the divine plan for the unity of all humanity in Christ. This ministry of unity extends beyond the church, not in a triumphalistic manner, but out of responsibility before God and for the world. One thus understands why the bishop of Rome has increasingly become a defender of human rights, and speaks to all people of good will:

> Such a ministry is increasingly necessary, provided it does not stop the other bishops [from] expressing their own convictions. It is a service to humanity as such. The words of the bishop of Rome are called to be, by virtue of his "distance" from local conflicts, essentially a memory of the essential words of hope expressed in the gospel and challenging human conscience as such.[49]

The papacy, like the church of God, must always serve God's plan.

Fifth, the preceding four characteristics — the bishop of Rome as witness to the apostolic faith, member and head of episcopal college, primate with several "spheres of influence," and servant of the divine plan of communion — provide the proper context in which to understand the "maximalistic" affirmations of Vatican I and II, which speak of the pope's full, supreme, immediate, universal, and ordinary power, and his ability to "always exercise freely" such power. Much of the confusion and controversy over primatial authority stems from the relation of power and task: "The place and power of the bishop of Rome within the college of bishops must be understood according to this perspective. Every task (*munus*) requires the power needed to fulfill it. That is obvious. However, the power is proportionate to the task, not vice versa."[50] The bishop of Rome's task is, of course, the "service of communion between the churches."[51] He does so by acting as a sentinel or shepherd, watching over the episcopal college so that the church of Christ may be found present and active in the local churches and their communion. The pope's primatial ministry therefore should not replace the oversight of the other local bishops, but strengthen and support it.

Accordingly, the pope's power, as Vatican I and II defined it, must be understood in terms of his ministry of unity. For example, if each bishop is the "proper, ordinary and immediate pastor" of his local church, and if the pope is "endowed with the primacy of ordinary power over all the churches,"[52] are there then two competing jurisdictions in each diocese? Simply put, no. Agreeing with Aquinas that "the formal object of the universal primacy is the common good *as such*" and is to be exercised only to that extent, Tillard writes that problems occur when the common good is confused with "the sum of the particular goods of local churches."[53] The bishop of Rome's primatial "ordinary power" must therefore be defined in terms of its task: the service of ecclesial communion and the strengthening of the episcopate, not the internal (micro-)management of other local churches. His ordinary and immediate power thus does not conflict with or duplicate local episcopal power. "Ordinary" in this instance means the bishop of Rome's own proper power, which comes from his special concern for all the churches received by virtue of being bishop of the church of Peter and Paul; it is "immediate," in that such concern does not have "to go through an intermediate body."[54]

Vatican II clarified in part the meaning of "full" and "supreme," by making the episcopal college as a whole — head and members — the subject of such power.[55] "Full" means that the college possesses all of the power necessary to fulfill its tasks, while "supreme" means that no higher power exists. However, by stating that the pope may "always exercise freely" such "full, supreme, and universal power" (*Lumen gentium* #22), the council left unclear the head's relationship to the college. Tillard asks:

> Does *libere exercere* mean that the Primate can act according to his own intuition without having to verify that this is in harmony with the vision or wishes of his brother-bishops, especially when matters touching them closely are involved? Or does it mean that it may seem good to him to express what they are all thinking without needing to inform them beforehand of this move? The nuance is important.[56]

In other words, when the primate acts "freely," does he act independently of the college, and, if so, does this compromise episcopal collegiality? If he does act within the college, how does he "always exercise freely" such power? As Tillard notes, while Vatican II repeatedly stresses that the college can act only with the consent of its head, the council makes no corresponding mention of the head's responsibilities toward the college. In short, the meaning of the pope's free exercise of full and supreme power remains unsettled. As an Anglican member of ARCIC-II asked Tillard, "after Vatican II, could Paul VI in certain situations carry out actions analogous to those of Pius X, in his own right? If he could, what is the use of calling on collegiality to reassure us in our desires for communion?"[57]

Tillard gives no canonical answer to how to harmonize the ambiguities of Vatican I and II with such ecumenical and post-conciliar concerns, the "agony" (protection of the minority at Vatican II) and the "dream" (ecumenical openness) of Paul VI, the *sub Petro* and the *cum Petro*.[58] He says *that* some account of the primate's responsibilities to the college and the entire church is needed, but does not specify *what* they are. This is the neuralgic point. The answer, in his view, does not yet exist and will exist only when it emerges from the ongoing reception of Vatican II by Catholicism and other churches and ecclesial communities.[59] It is also what John Paul means when he says of the renewal of the papacy: "This is an immense task, which we cannot refuse and which I cannot carry out by myself."[60]

Tillard suggests that the resolution of the primacy-collegiality tension will not be found in canon law or doctrinal formulations alone. A "new chapter of the ecclesiology of communion" is needed,[61] and will come about only through a renewed practice of consensus, inspired by the practice of the first millennium. As the "application of the principle 'what concerns everyone must be approved by everyone,' "[62] consensus seeks the contributions of the entire church — pope, the other bishops, councils, laity, *sensus fidelium* — for the resolution of such difficult matters, for example, as the formulation of classical trinitarian and christological doctrine. As these examples indicate, the work of consensus makes rapid answers virtually impossible.[63] Rather, time is necessary, demanding an "*oikonomia* of patience."[64] In this movement, it is essential that the voices of the local churches which comprise the church of God be able to make their proper contributions, individually and collectively; primacy and collegiality-synodality must reinforce each other. Without such input, consensus is illusory.

Consensus thus rules out two extreme understandings of papal primacy. First, the bishop of Rome does not simply approve or "receive" the common opinion of the episcopate; such a conception would empty primacy of any meaning, turning the bishop of Rome into "the successor of the other apostle Simon (the one who says nothing)" or a "Catholic Queen of England."[65] Second, the primate is not the "one who really decides,"[66] in which case the other bishops would merely "receive" papal decisions; this understanding deforms the sacramental and fraternal nature of the episcopate. As the Congregation for the Doctrine of the Faith more dryly puts it, "office of coordination" and "political monarchy" are not the only options vis-à-vis papal primacy.[67]

The place of the bishop of Rome in the formation of consensus is rather to be the "patient architect of consensus, its soul and chief guarantor."[68] He is to make possible a kind of "ping-pong game, a back-and-forth movement" between bishops and their churches and the primate, in which the goal is a "common mind on fundamental issues concerning the whole church."[69] Lest this conception of primacy seem too much like the aforementioned "office of coordination," we should recall that, in its decree on ecumenism, Vatican II spoke of the Roman church as "moderator" in disagreements over faith and discipline in the early church.[70]

It must be admitted that Tillard's "solution" of consensus is not immediately satisfying in terms of concrete results or courses of action. However, it does seem able to do justice to the collegial and synodal nature of the church of God, to the at once collegial and primatial ministry of the bishop of Rome, and to the slow, even inefficient nature of God's plan:

> The Church of God is not a political body ruled by a government which is obliged to take immediate decisions, which the next regime will probably contradict or abolish. The *prudentia* of the bishop of Rome belongs to this traditional *oikonomia* of patience. Magisterial short-cuts would be dangerous initiatives. In God's design, time is an essential factor.[71]

Not least, Tillard's conception of consensus offers a way forward for the ecumenical reception of papal primacy, so desired by John Paul in *Ut unum sint.* As Tillard has written on several occasions, ecumenism demands that "we have not only *to do* together everything we can do together, but also *to be* together what our existing *koinonia* allows us to be together."[72] For instance, he suggests that Anglicans and Catholics find ways of serving the word of God together, of sharing some kind of synodal life together, of sharing prayer together — the common celebration of Good Friday and the eve of Pentecost.[73] ARCIC-II, in similar terms, speaks of possible Anglican participation in the *ad limina* visits to Rome of Catholic bishops and of mutual participation in each other's international meetings of bishops (Lambeth Conference, Roman Synod of Bishops).[74] I would suggest, building upon Tillard, that this common living together, this synodality, will permit future development and agreement on the bishop of Rome's primatial ministry and its role in fostering the consensus essential to the health of the church of God. This is not a task that can be accomplished with one stroke, nor one, as John Paul indicates, that the Catholic Church can do on its own.

This renewal, even reformation, of papal primacy will fail unless accompanied by a renewal of synodality and episcopal collegiality. In the aftermath of Vatican II, institutions such as episcopal conferences and the international synod of bishops were promoted as concrete expressions of the ecclesiology of communion. They have, however, had mixed results. Some, like the 1971 Synod of Bishops or the open, consultative practices of the United States bishops in the 1980s, were notable successes. Other synods and episcopal conferences have been burdened by unrealistic expectations or poor procedures and structures. Tillard sees such problems as not simply administrative or institutional — important as these may sometimes be — but as reflective of a rich yet incomplete conciliar ecclesiology:

> In spite of Vatican II's new reading of Vatican I, the post-conciliar Church has not yet provided itself with institutions that will enable it to adapt itself to the

> ecclesiology of communion, whose foundations *Lumen Gentium* laid without securing them deeply enough.[75]

Such foundations, apart from an incompletely collegial primacy, are a synodality and a theology of the local church obscured by a predominantly universalistic conciliar ecclesiology, and a recognition of collegiality and its sacramental character. Any ecclesial renewal and reform will have to address these foundational concerns, if the conciliar ecclesiology of communion is to flourish. Three areas are of particular importance for such flourishing: synodality, collegiality, and subsidiarity.

Perhaps the most necessary step in this regard is a renewed appreciation of synodality and its proper relationship to collegiality. At present, synodality and collegiality fit together poorly in the Catholic Church, largely because Vatican II's universalistic ecclesiology detaches the episcopate from the local churches and thereby severs the ancient, intrinsic link between bishop and church. This position reaches its clearest expression, we have argued, in John Paul II's *Apostolos suos,* which states that membership in the episcopal college precedes being head of a local church. Tillard's theology of the local church, which sees the one church of God as the communion of local churches, and thereby denies the existence of a universal church or episcopal college prior to the local churches, rejoins the bishop and the local church. The recovery of synodality therefore means the end of universalist ecclesiologies and their centralizing tendencies.

The tight link between bishop and church necessitated by synodality has concrete consequences. Chief among them is the phasing out of titular and auxiliary bishops, and a corresponding increase in the number of dioceses. The bishop's ministry of oversight is obscured and even compromised by the requirement for secretaries of Roman dicasteries and Vatican diplomats to be ordained archbishops in order to give them status; nothing in these tasks requires the grace of episcopal ordination. The ministry of oversight is eclipsed when, as was the case under Pope John Paul II, the papal secretary, prefect of the papal household, and master of liturgical ceremonies were ordained bishops (and later promoted to archbishops), seemingly as a reward for loyal service. It is no criticism of the character of those ordained for such reasons to hold that such ordinations deform the nature of the episcopate and create ecumenical difficulties.

Moreover, a greater awareness and practice of synodality will renew not only the episcopate, but also activate the charisms of all the baptized. Paralleling Tillard's thought on synodality, John Zizioulas writes that episcopal conferences "must be understood not as meetings of bishops but as meetings of churches through their bishops."[76] This properly ecclesial foundation of collegiality will enable greater participation of the laity in synodal bodies. One thinks, for instance, of the sacramental, liturgical, and ministerial vision fostered in recent years by the Archdiocese of Los Angeles under the leadership of Cardinal Roger Mahony. As the beginning of preparation for an archdiocesan synod in 2003, the cardinal and his priests called for a more inclusive and collaborative vision of ministry, based upon "baptism as the foundational sacrament of ministry and a clearer recognition that ministry is not just for the ordained."[77] While acknowledging the difficulties caused by a decline in the number of priests, they see the present time as one of great opportunity, reminding the church of its many gifts and ministries. The outcome of this initiative remains to be seen, but it does serve as a reminder of the foundational role of baptism and synodality in the church, and what is possible when the bishop and his church work together. One hopes that, in coming years, the voices of the laity will find a similar reception in national and international bodies.

Second, a renewed practice and theory of synodality will enable a renewed practice and theory of collegiality at regional, national, and worldwide levels. This renewal does not concern bureaucratic reorganization to the detriment of supposedly "evangelical" concerns, but the reinvigoration of the church's sacramental and ministerial identity. As the preceding chapter presented Tillard's critique of the present state of collegiality, we may say simply that the core of the problem is the respect accorded (or not) to the bishops as sacramental brothers and primary collaborators of the bishop of Rome in the oversight of the church of God. They, not the Roman curia, are the "guardians designated by God of 'the catholic conscience.' " While warning against the temptation of making the curia a "scapegoat" for all that ails the church, Tillard notes that the curia must serve the episcopate, rather than "control, regulate, sometimes even scold" it,[78] and he holds up the Pontifical Council for Promoting Christian Unity as a model of such service to the bishops and to the entire church.

Tillard is not alone in such criticism. Building upon the intrinsic link between synodality and collegiality, and the consequent rejection of a universal church existing apart from the communion of the local churches, Archbishop John Quinn, Richard Gaillardetz, and Thomas Reese have called for a diminishment of the curial role in the synods of bishops, which tends to compromise collegiality. The curia, in Quinn's words, too often sees itself as a *tertium quid* alongside the pope and the other bishops, rather than as their servant;[79] often, in fact, the curia places itself above the bishops, treating them as executors of curial decisions. In like manner, the strong curial presence reinforces a model of the episcopal college as a universal "board of directors" existing apart from the communion of local churches. Gaillardetz also sees the synodal practice—since 1974—of passing off to the pope the writing of a concluding document as an abdication of episcopal teaching authority and responsibility, and has suggested that episcopal conferences move in a more synodal direction, allowing for the participation of the non-ordained.[80] Reese, for his part, has criticized the synods for the bishops' excessive and unneeded "deference" to the pope: they "give the impression that the purpose of the synod is not to advise the pope but to get his advice...to provide a forum where they can affirm their loyalty. Many bishops seems so overwhelmed by the pope's presence that they think it improper to give him advice."[81] Moreover, Quinn, Gaillardetz, Reese, and Michael Fahey all have called for greater freedom of expression at episcopal synods.[82]

Other theologians have raised still further concerns. Ladislas Orsy has written of the difference between episcopal collegiality and episcopal consultation; the latter denigrates the bishops' sacramental equality and reduces them to mere "vicars of the Roman pontiff," which *Lumen gentium* #27 explicitly excludes.[83] Francis A. Sullivan, taking up John Paul II's appeals in *Novo millennio ineunte* for a "spirituality of communion" and "structures of participation," calls for the renewal of the magisterium through more frequent general councils (every fifty years), a deliberative role for bishops in the synod of bishops, collegial collaboration in the preparation of encyclicals, a renewed appreciation of the teaching role of episcopal conferences, and the summoning of "plenary councils" in which representatives of all the baptized would participate.[84] Finally, Joseph Komonchak sees in Pope John Paul II's *Apostolos suos* a devaluation — however unwitting — of consensus in regard to the teaching authority of episcopal conferences, and a consequent emphasis on the juridical nature and status of such authority; such emphasis has the unfortunate effect of hindering trust, the "precondition of effective authority."[85] In each of these critiques, a common thread emerges: the need for a recovery of the sacramental equality of the college, head and members alike.[86]

Third, an understanding of synodality and collegiality as fundamentally sacramental entities (the former rooted in baptism, the latter in order) provides the proper context for the exercise of subsidiarity in the church.[87] Often criticized as a political and social theory somewhat inimical to the church's divine origin and character,[88] subsidiarity instead finds its deepest roots in the church's sacramentality. Although Tillard prefers the term "synergy" to subsidiarity — seeing it as less juridical and more theological, more reflective of a "communion of 'energies,' of powers: not a simple addition of them, nor one among them being heavily imposed"[89] — his theology of the local church lends support to its exercise. Local churches, each truly the church of God, are not offices following the directives of central headquarters, but sacramental communities with rightful integrity and authority; bishops, by virtue of their ordination, receive the full authority and power that they need to govern their churches.

Concretely, we might ask what is to be made of the argument of *Octogesima adveniens* #4 that the church has neither the "ambition" nor "mission" of putting forth a universally valid social teaching, and that it is up to each community to discern the course(s) of action necessary in their situation.[90] Are the local churches limited to applying a body of universal teaching to their particular context, or do their concrete circumstances enter into the formation of the social teaching itself? At a minimum, it seems that a deductive teaching must be complemented by an inductive one that only the local churches can provide.

To the extent possible, then, each church and its bishop should manage its own affairs; regional or national groupings should take care of larger concerns and difficulties, and international bodies should act only when these smaller bodies either request assistance or show themselves incapable of proper action. This subsidiarity or respect need not compromise the necessary communion between churches or the interiority of papal primacy to each church, but can further the life of the local churches and their communion.

As we conclude this section, it should be stated that, in seeking to renew the relationship of primacy and synodality, Tillard places the great tradition and the Vatican councils in a productive dialogue. He in no way seeks a rejection or even abrogation of the two Vatican councils; they remain true, if necessarily limited, and must be opened out, rather than denied, if the ecumenical quest is to be conducted in truth.[91] He commends, for instance, the "vastly more prudent and sober" tone of *Pastor aeternus* vis-à-vis the extreme claims of papal infallibility propounded by the Ultramontanists.[92]

Most pressingly, such dialogue must be done with other churches and communions, if primacy and collegiality-synodality are to find their proper exercise. Both the bishop of Rome and the episcopate as a whole exist for the sake of genuinely catholic communion, i.e., unity and diversity inseparably.[93] As "The Gift of Authority" makes clear, moreover, such ministry must be understood in light of the different needs of the churches.[94] Within Catholicism, which tends toward uniformity at the expense of diversity, the need exists for a recovery of a respect for the baptismal mandate of all God's people, the integral and genuine ecclesiality of the local churches, the sacramental equality and authority of all the bishops, an understanding of episcopal conferences and synods of bishops as agents of catholicity, and the primatial service of communion through the promotion and protection of legitimate diversity—in short, a creative fidelity to the teachings of Vatican II. In other churches, often split by national or doctrinal divisions, the need exists for the development of structures of authority able to bind the entire church in truth and charity, and, more particularly, a recognition that the church of Rome—as truly first (but not unique)—can further genuine diversity through its promotion of unity in faith and communion. In sum, each Christian community needs the ministry of unity-in-diversity provided by the interplay of primacy and collegiality-synodality. The relationship of unity and diversity leads naturally to our second trajectory, inculturation and the process of reception.

Inculturation-Reception

In 1998, as preparation for the Jubilee year, the Special Assembly of the Synod of Bishops for Asia convened in Rome to examine the new evangelization in its Asian contexts.[95] The synod was notable for its sustained focus on the interaction of the Gospel and culture, a focus that gave rise to some tension between the Asian bishops and the Roman curial officials present.

In his opening report as recording secretary of the synod, Cardinal Paul Shan Kuo-hsi of Taiwan noted that, in the church's evangelizing mission, there is "a serious need for inculturating the faith in the cultures of Asia and for shedding an appearance of being carbon copies of churches in Western societies."[96] His insight was echoed in other interventions. Archbishop Leo Jun Ikenaga of Japan, for instance, spoke of his pain at the centuries-long failure of evangelization in Asia. In contrast to the rapid spread of Buddhism, Christianity has failed to flourish in Japan, largely because it has been presented in European "paternal" ways, which contrast with the more "maternal" cast of Asian culture. Both aspects are essential, for the "God of Christianity is limitless," but effective evangelization will need to give proper due to such maternal aspects:

> Asian people, influenced by European and American ways, have learned to take an intellectual and logical approach in announcing truth. But in his heart the Asian places great importance on the body, on existence, on what is practical, on nonlogical expressions and symbols. From now on, be it in our talks on faith or the evangelization of society, in order to convey firmly the heart of Christianity we must use Asian ways of expression if our message is to take hold as we respond to the need to proclaim the kingdom of God.[97]

Bishop Francis Hadisumarta, speaking in the name of the Indonesian bishops' conference, was still more explicit. Wondering why the "new evangelization is not taking off as expected," he answered that a lack of trust in God and in each other was the culprit. The Roman curia often functioned more as a "universal decision maker" than as a "clearinghouse for information, support, and encouragement," thereby compromising the trust and authority of local bishops and their conferences. Why, he asked, must liturgical translations approved by such conferences need further approbation by Rome, by "people who just do not speak or understand our language!" He asked whether the church had the "imagination to envisage the birth of new patriarchates," and said that the Indonesian bishops await "encouragement to move from adaptation to inculturation and create new, indigenous rites."[98]

While acknowledging these desires and requests, several curial officials expressed reservations. Cardinal Angelo Sodano, the Vatican secretary of state, reminded the synod that unity in Christ and in Peter is the surest sign of ecclesial identity. Granting that the members of the "human family are different in some exterior things, in the clothes they wear or in the language they speak, in the color of their skin or in social customs," the cardinal cautioned that such "centrifugal" forces need to "return immediately by a centripetal force toward the rock of ecclesial unity, which is Peter living in his successors."[99] Cardinal William Baum, then head of the Apostolic Penitentiary, was even more stark in his reading of the present situation:

> As an American bishop [formerly the archbishop of Washington, DC], allow me a word on the theme of inculturation. The Catholic Church in the United

> States has become thoroughly inculturated and enjoys the benefits and suffers from the results of an inculturation that has been all too successful. For example, it is said that the majority of American Catholics no longer adhere to the teaching of the church on many moral issues, including that on the evil of abortion and on conjugal morality. Not a few of our universities and institutions, Catholic in origin, have lost in whole or in part their Catholic identity.
>
> More recently some of my brother bishops have begun to speak not so much of inculturation, but of the need to build a new Christian culture, a sign of contradiction to the culture of death so rapidly developing.[100]

At stake in each of these interventions, both curial and residential, was what Cardinal Julius Riyadi Darmaatmadja of Indonesia, one of the synod's president-delegates, called "the effort to be a church with a truly Asian 'face.' "[101] Providing such a "face" raises a number of questions. How is the church to secure unity of faith in the Gospel of Jesus Christ while allowing for a legitimate and necessary diversity of expressions? What is the relationship between evangelization and inculturation? What is inculturation, is it necessary, and, if so, why? What are its limits, its dangers, its possibilities? Is it a matter of faith's "clothing" or its "incarnation"? How does the church inculturate in a world marked by the dual pressures of globalization and nationalism? In this situation, one must resist not only the temptation to dismiss reflexively as repressive curial calls for unity, but also the too-simple identification of inculturation with compromise or capitulation to the "culture of death." The engagement of the Gospel and cultures is too important to the church's mission to be hindered by polemics.

In taking up the subject — and problem — of inculturation, Tillard builds upon a growing body of conciliar and magisterial teaching over the past forty years. Vatican II, although often speaking the language of "adaptation," opened the door to inculturation through its rich theology of catholicity and communion. As we argued in our first chapter, the council, in such documents as *Sacrosanctum concilium, Lumen gentium, Unitatis redintegratio, Orientalium ecclesiarum, Ad gentes divinitus,* and *Gaudium et spes* conceived of catholicity as a "fullness in unity,"[102] wherein unity is realized through the exchange of gifts by churches with each other and with their cultures. Moreover, by planting the seeds of a theology of the local church, the council affirmed that legitimate diversity is an inner dimension of ecclesial unity. Uniformity — the Roman "allergy" to diversity[103] — is to be rejected.

Paul VI's apostolic exhortation *Evangelii nuntiandi* (1975), perhaps the finest document of his pontificate, represents a new level of sophistication in regard to the church's engagement with culture. Holding that "evangelization is in fact the grace and vocation proper to the Church, her deepest identity," Paul writes that "the split between the Gospel and culture is without a doubt the great drama of our time, just as it was of other times."[104] Calling for a renewed effort of evangelization, he states:

> what matters is to evangelize man's culture and cultures (not in a purely decorative way, as it were, by applying a thin veneer, but in a vital way, in depth and right to their very roots), in the rich and wide sense which these terms have in *Gaudium et spes,* always taking the person as one's starting-point and always coming back to the relationships of people among themselves and with God.
>
> The Gospel, and therefore evangelization, are certainly not identical with culture, and they are independent in regard to all cultures. Nevertheless, the kingdom which the Gospel proclaims is lived by men who are profoundly linked to a culture, and the building up of the kingdom cannot avoid borrowing the elements of human culture or cultures. Though independent of culture, the Gospel and evangelization are not necessarily incompatible with them; rather they are capable of permeating them all without becoming subject to any one of them.[105]

Furthermore, this evangelizing encounter takes place particularly in the local churches, ever mindful of their communion with the universal church:

> The individual Churches, intimately built up not only of people but also of aspirations, of riches and limitations, of ways of praying, of loving, of looking at life and the world, which distinguish this or that human gathering, have the task of assimilating the essence of the Gospel message and of transposing it, without the slightest betrayal of its essential truth, into the language that these particular people understand, then of proclaiming it in this language.
>
> The transposition has to be done with the discernment, seriousness, respect, and competence which the matter calls for in the field of liturgical expression, and in the areas of catechesis, theological formation, secondary ecclesial structures, and ministries. And the word "language" should be understood here less in the semantic or literary sense than in the sense which one may call anthropological and cultural.[106]

In these passages, Paul sets forth a vision of evangelization that is expansive in language and scope. He rejects "decoration" and "veneer," preferring to speak of "depth" and "width," of "roots" and "richness." The scope of his vision is similarly capacious, limited not to incidentals, but reaching into the heart of the church's identity: liturgy, catechesis, ministry, theology. Through the church, then, the Gospel and cultures are to be brought into transformative encounter. This encounter is inculturation, even if it dare not yet speak its name.

John Paul II, with his insistence upon a "new evangelization" embracing even those regions evangelized in centuries past, introduces the language of inculturation into magisterial teaching. Four moments are significant for our purposes. First, *Slavorum apostoli,* an encyclical written in 1985 on the occasion of the 1100th anniversary of the death of St. Methodius, outlines and celebrates at length the evangelizing mission of Cyril and Methodius to the Slavic peoples and the mutual transformation of Christianity and Slavic culture effected by it. Always mindful of communion with Rome,[107] these brothers defended the newly emergent Slavic Christianity against its

Western critics, who saw in its diverse life and practices a threat to ecclesial unity.[108] Building upon Vatican II's conception of catholicity,[109] John Paul sees the brothers' mission of evangelization as one of inculturation, "the incarnation of the Gospel in native cultures."[110] "At the same time," this inculturation "introduces peoples, together with their cultures, into her own community." John Paul highlights the brothers' creation of the Slavonic alphabet and their contributions to the Old Slavonic liturgical language. In this way, inculturation secures unity as it promotes diversity at the heart of the church's life.

Second, John Paul's most striking support of inculturation comes perhaps in his 1986 address at Alice Springs, Australia, to the Aborigines:

> The Gospel of our Lord Jesus Christ speaks all languages. It esteems and embraces all cultures....
>
> That Gospel now invites you to become, through and through, aboriginal Christians. It meets your deepest desires. You do not have to be people divided into two parts, as though an aboriginal had to borrow the faith and life of Christianity, like a hat or a pair of shoes, from someone who owns them. Jesus calls you to accept his words and his values into your own culture. To develop in this way will make you more than ever truly aboriginal.
>
> ...All over the world people worship God and read his word in their own language, and color the great signs and symbols of religion with touches of their own traditions. Why should you be different from them in this regard, why should you not be allowed the happiness of being with God and each other in aboriginal fashion?
>
> As you listen to the Gospel of our Lord Jesus Christ, seek out the best things of your traditional ways. If you do, you will come to realize more and more your great human and Christian dignity.... Your Christian faith calls you to become the best kind of aboriginal people you can be.... And the church herself in Australia will not be fully the church that Jesus wants her to be until you have made your contribution to her life and until that contribution has been joyfully received by others.[111]

Eschewing the drier language of encyclicals, this address gives dramatic support to the desirability and necessity of inculturation: Aborigines will be most fully themselves only when their Christian lives are fully their own, while the church will be fully itself only when it becomes fully Aboriginal.

Third, *Redemptoris missio,* a 1991 encyclical on evangelization and missionary activity, echoes *Slavorum apostoli,* but situates inculturation in a more comprehensive consideration of evangelization than does the earlier encyclical. It states that "through inculturation the church, for her part, becomes a more intelligible sign of what she is and a more effective instrument of mission. Thanks to this action within the local churches, the universal church herself is enriched."[112] Such authentic inculturation will always be done in communion with the universal church, lest it "pass uncritically from a form of alienation from culture to an overestimation of culture." Moreover, inculturation must also be the work of the entire community, not "exclusively the result of erudite research," in order that it be faithful to each community's Christian experience and *sensus fidei*.[113]

Fourth, celebrating the end of the Jubilee year and the beginning of the new millennium, the apostolic letter *Novo millennio ineunte* (2001) continues John Paul's insistence upon the intrinsic bond between the new evangelization and inculturation. In words that may bear traces of the Asian Synod, John Paul writes:

> In the third millennium Christianity will have to respond ever more effectively to this need for inculturation. Christianity, while remaining completely true to itself, with unswerving fidelity to the proclamation of the Gospel and the tradition of the church, will also reflect the different faces of the cultures and peoples in which it is received and takes root. In this jubilee year we have rejoiced in a special way in the beauty of the church's varied face. This is perhaps only a beginning, a barely sketched image of the future which the Spirit of God is preparing for us.[114]

In its concision, this passage may be read as a précis of magisterial reflection on inculturation. It succeeds in finely balancing, rather than opposing, the simultaneous moments of inculturation: fidelity to the one Gospel and the beauty of the "church's varied face," each dimension finding its completion in the other. Even allowing for the rhetorical flights common to such documents, these lines indicate the deepening — and promising — magisterial reception of inculturation.

Tillard develops his theology of inculturation in dialogue with this magisterial teaching and also with the theological heritage of the church. Inculturation, for him, is not a luxury, but belongs to the essence of the church's evangelization, communion, and catholicity:

> From the outset, the local — with what it bears of the cultural, the "contextual," the geographic, the religious, the historical — belongs to the material where the *Ekklesia tou Theou* is truly incarnated. Inculturation or "contextualization" should not constitute an *a posteriori* duty. It belongs to the very springing forth of the Church of God. It is woven in catholicity.[115]

Talk of inculturation, diversity, and the theology of the local church almost invariably raises Catholic concerns about phyletism and nationalism, what Tillard refers to as the "triumph of Babel over Pentecost." Such fears, however, seem largely ungrounded at this stage of the church's life, as no signs exist of schism or widespread heresy — no small tribute to the ministry of unity exercised by the pope and the other bishops.[116] However, the situation in Christianity as a whole is much different. Commenting upon the 1991 Assembly of the World Council of Churches in Canberra, Australia, Tillard held that the "question of inculturation, or more broadly, of catholicity" was "undoubtedly the neuralgic spot of the Assembly."[117] Although stating that the "inculturation of faith is an absolute necessity which no Church today can push to the side," he worried that an increasingly "non-critical inculturation" might lead to

> a new separation, possibly more irreparable than the one between East and West, or the Catholic West and Reformed West: a separation this time between the Churches of ancient Christian traditions and the Churches of countries evangelized by them.[118]

The 1998 WCC Assembly in Harare, Zimbabwe, only increased such concern. The "richly promising inculturation" taking place in Africa was being threatened by the rise of "independent" or "traditional" African national churches.[119] Rich in faith and charity, but largely unconcerned with inter-ecclesial communion, these churches threatened ecclesial unity at precisely the time of its greatest urgency:

> It is at this point that we strike again upon ecumenism, what I called the question of double or quits. This is no longer in the context of previous centuries, where the Churches' quarrels could look like family wrangles which did not endanger allegiance to Christ or to Christianity as such. Nations, societies, sometimes individuals, could pass from one Christian group to another Christian group which was judged more faithful. But today people are going *elsewhere*. They are searching *elsewhere*. They are making attachments *elsewhere*. It is no longer just a matter of re-uniting or gathering together Christ's family. It is a matter of saving this family, hauling it out of the sand where it is stuck, for its own good and the good of the humanity which needs to be gathered together.[120]

Far from being esoteric, then, the relationship of unity and diversity is a crucial one for the Christian churches, if in differing ways: Catholicism must fight an increasing uniformity of ecclesial life, while the Orthodox must combat nationalistic tendencies, and the Protestant and independent churches must resist the dissolution of ecclesial diversity into division. Tillard, in response both to the continuing reception of Vatican II and to the present malaise of the ecumenical movement, constructs his response to the question of unity-in-diversity on a threefold foundation of catholicity, inculturation, and reception.

Tillard's theology of catholicity, as chapter 3 argued, is more qualitative than quantitative in character; it seeks the "entry of *all* human richness and *all* creation in Christ" more than the geographic extension of the church.[121] Pentecost is, of course, the paradigm and ongoing presence of this catholicity in the life of the church; the Holy Spirit descends upon the church and each believer is understood in his or her own tongue: perfect unity in perfect diversity. Genuine catholicity is neither the "addition" nor the "mixing" of such differences, but the " 'taking' of the impregnation of human diversity and plurality by the power of the Spirit of the one Lord, communicated by means of a single faith, a single baptism, and a single sacramental Body and Blood."[122] "Difference" thus appears not as a mistake or as a concession, but rather as the "richness in which catholicity takes flesh"[123] and the "*splendor gratiae.*"[124]

It is clear, however, that in a world afflicted by sin, difference is also a source of division. Tillard writes that the *katholou*

> remains marked by the tension which spans the Bible, from creation myths to the letter to the Ephesians: on the one hand, the certitude of the fundamental worth of human unity; on the other, the positive embrace of diverse peoples linked to the possibility that brothers may be transformed into rivals and enemies, solidarity into jealousy and hate.[125]

The *katholou* of the church remains incomprehensible apart from the cross, where Christ renews communion by breaking down the wall of hatred separating Jew and Gentile.[126] Difference must therefore be "converted," if it is to contribute to a genuinely catholic unity.[127] The orders of creation and salvation converge in a genuinely catholic unity, rooted in the fullness of Christ's own Lordship.[128]

Inculturation arises from this catholic encounter of creation and salvation, diversity and unity, culture and Gospel. Tillard describes inculturation through several metaphors. It is the "incarnation" or "taking flesh" of the Gospel in the riches of diverse cultures,[129] the "seizing" or "taking" of cultures and divine gifts into Christ through his church,[130] the "assumption" in Christ and the Holy Spirit of concrete humanity in its joys, sorrows, hopes, and failures,[131] the "reception into its own flesh" of created — especially human — realities.[132] Conversely, such metaphors rule out common misconceptions of inculturation as mere translation, adaptation, or what Tillard dismissively (and humorously) calls "giving Greco-Latin Christianity an African or Indian sun-tan."[133]

More importantly, Tillard's theology of inculturation should not be identified with cultural accommodation or compromise, for it flows from the catholicity of God's plan for humanity, not an indifferent relativism; a properly inculturated faith will, in fact, often be a truly powerful "sign of contradiction."[134] Through his experience with the World Council of Churches, Tillard clearly recognizes the dangers of a church that submits the Gospel to the judgment of the world. Commenting on the WCC Assembly at Canberra in 1991, he warned against an emergent "non-critical inculturation," which fails on several grounds. First, it largely "refuses to take account of what has been built up over twenty centuries of living Tradition," dismissing such tradition as irrelevant to contemporary concerns of, for example, gender, sexuality, and ethnicity. Second, in its promotion of independent national churches, it risks "reproducing . . . political divisions" in the church.[135] Third, its deepest foundation is an indiscriminate embrace of difference:

> I would describe it negatively as an almost systematic rejection of any kind of hierarchy, elitism, scale or rank in evaluating and comparing. The special difference belonging to every human category and characterizing it is seen

> as not allowing for judgment by systems of "more and less." It is in itself a plenitude. So this difference should properly be lived out without a complex, building everything on it, justifying it, defending it and standing up for it. From this may be deduced, for example, that... all cultures are to be affirmed as deserving respect and recognized as having an equal dignity.... No religion will be permitted to think of itself as higher.[136]

How, then, does one properly inculturate, fostering in the local churches a truly catholic communion of unity and diversity? The response involves a process of reception. Reception is, of course, an intrinsic part of the life of every local church. Each church, in fact, arises and is sustained through the reception of divine "generative principles" (Word, Spirit, eucharist, apostolic ministry) by human "individuating principles" of history, culture, geography; apart from such reception and encounter, no church exists in reality.[137] As we argued in chapter 4, Tillard sees reception as primarily doctrinal, whereby communities incorporate into their lives magisterial teaching. More broadly, however, it involves the entirety of a church's life — its traditions, practices, and worship.

Reception is therefore inseparable from inculturation, and its primary characteristics — outlined in our fourth chapter — dovetail with the work of inculturation: its governing dynamic of *semper ipsa, nunquam eadem*; its communal subject, involving the interplay of the *sensus fidei* and the magisterium;[138] the apostolic witness as the norm of all ecclesial faith and life;[139] the plurality of its "products," in terms of content (liturgies, theologies, spiritualities) and style (not simply intellectual, but also poetic and artistic); and its concrete, sacramental ethos, which arises from the lived faith of the entire community.[140]

To these five characteristics I would add two others particularly relevant to the work of inculturation: consensus and patience. Consensus, as our examination of its role in the exercise of primacy and synodality indicated, has nothing to do with compromise or majority rule. It rather involves the participation in the church's life of all of the baptized, from the bishop of Rome to the laity, each according to one's own station. Ruling out haste and corporate efficiency, this *conspiratio* honors the Catholic "ethos," whereby "the discernment of the authentic meaning of the Word of God is never made outside the concreteness and sacramentality of the Church's life."[141] Consensus thus serves to ensure that inculturation remains an organic enterprise that, as *Redemptoris missio* states, truly expresses the entirety of a people's genius rather than foisting upon the community the results of "erudite research."[142] In receiving the contributions of the entire church, episcopal authority, far from being weakened, will be more convincing in its discernment of authentic inculturation.

Furthermore, the work of consensus — and of inculturation in general — calls for the exercise of patience. As an organic process, inculturation takes time, is rarely linear, and must be "guided and encouraged but not forced, lest it give rise to negative reactions among Christians."[143] Tillard believes that the present-day inculturation of a primarily "Western" faith requires

> A patience analogous to that of the Fathers: from the first proclamation of the faith in Asia Minor to the Chalcedonian definition, centuries of groping, of difficult studies, of painful arguments were needed. It is a matter of making an already structured and articulated faith, with the burnish of two thousand years upon it, pass into the religious heritages which fashioned the souls of these peoples. So it is necessary to discover, if we are to avoid collapsing into syncretism, both the profound harmonies and the irreducible oppositions of these two universes. Now that cannot be grasped simply by intellectual reflection.[144]

However, in an age where the explosion of communication technologies makes possible instant global exchanges, patience is perhaps the most difficult — and yet most needed — of all of the dimensions of inculturation. What happens, for example, when thought and life in India can be engaged immediately, rather than waiting the months or even years it took for the letters of a Francis Xavier or a Matteo Ricci to reach Europe from Asia? How does the necessarily slow work of incubation and discernment proceed in an interconnected, wired world? On the one hand, it permits a rapid exchange of information, thereby reducing confusion and delays; clear lines of communication are essential for building trust and communion. On the other, technology can short-circuit the time and space needed for testing and lead to Roman micro-management; a certain "benign neglect" can often be constructive, providing the "elbow room" desired by Cardinal Newman.

In short, the wisdom gained only by an "*oikonomia* of patience,"[145] so necessary to a fruitful and faithful inculturation, does not always comport well with faxes and the Internet. For better and for worse, the church does not make quick decisions, nor does it always reach consensus easily: it is hard to think in seconds and centuries at once. As recent developments in Christology and interreligious dialogue indicate, the questions concerning inculturation — and therefore also the church — will only increase in coming years.[146] "The beauty of the church's varied face" remains a promise and a challenge, a gift and a task.

Conclusion

In *Novo millennio ineunte,* John Paul II set forth a deeply lyrical and personal vision of the mission facing Catholicism in the new millennium, ranging, in characteristic style, across matters as diverse as the universal call to holiness, international debt, the future of ecumenism, the ethical dilemmas posed by biotechnology, and Vatican II as "the great grace bestowed on the Church in the twentieth century."[147] Underlying each of these aspects is the call for the church "to take up her evangelizing mission with fresh enthusiasm."[148] We, like Peter, are "to put out into the deep" (Luke 5:4), confident in the future. Somewhat unexpectedly, perhaps, the pope proposed that this new evangelization will be realized only in and through the local churches. In two passages, which deserve to be quoted at length, he wrote:

> We now need to profit from the grace received [in the Jubilee] by putting it into practice in resolutions and guidelines for action. This is a task I wish to invite all the local churches to undertake. In each of them, gathered around their Bishop, as they listen to the word and "break bread" in brotherhood (cf. Acts 2:42), the "one holy catholic and apostolic Church of Christ is truly present and operative." It is above all in the actual situation of each local church that the mystery of the one People of God takes the particular form that fits it to each individual context and culture.
>
> In the final analysis, this rooting of the Church in time and space mirrors the movement of the Incarnation itself. Now is the time for each local church to assess its fervor and find fresh enthusiasm for its spiritual and pastoral responsibilities by reflecting on what the Spirit has been saying to the people of God in this special year of grace, and indeed in the longer span of time from the Second Vatican Council to the Great Jubilee. It is with this purpose in mind that I wish to offer in this letter, at the conclusion of the jubilee year, the contribution of my Petrine ministry so that the church may shine ever more brightly in the variety of her gifts and in her unity as she journeys on.[149]

> But now it is no longer an immediate goal [the Jubilee] that we face, but the larger and more demanding challenge of normal pastoral activity. With its universal and indispensable provisions, the program of the Gospel must continue to take root, as it has always done, in the life of the Church everywhere. It is in the local churches that the specific features of a detailed pastoral plan can be identified — goals and methods, formation and enrichment of the people involved, the search for the necessary resources — which will enable the proclamation of Christ to reach people, mold communities, and have a deep and incisive influence in bringing Gospel values to bear in society and culture.
>
> I therefore earnestly exhort the Pastors of the particular churches, with the help of all sectors of God's people, confidently to plan the stages of the journey ahead, harmonizing the choices of each diocesan community with those of neighboring Churches and of the universal Church.
>
> This harmonization will certainly be facilitated by the collegial work which bishops now regularly undertake in episcopal conferences and synods. Was this not the point of the continental assemblies of the Synod of Bishops which prepared for the jubilee and which forged important directives for the present-day proclamation of the Gospel in so many different settings and cultures? This rich legacy of reflection must not be allowed to disappear, but must be implemented in practical ways.[150]

These passages are at once prosaic and striking. Prosaic, in that talk of synods and pastoral planning stirs the hearts of very few people. Striking, however, for they give pride of place to the theology of the local church: the eucharistic essence of the church, the link between evangelization and inculturation, the need for greater collegiality in synods and episcopal conferences, the involvement of all the baptized ("all sectors of God's people") in the life of the church, a genuinely catholic sense of ecclesial communion. In short, John Paul proposed a synodal and collegial church, gathered by word and sacrament and united for evangelization — the one church of God taking flesh in the many churches of God. As a new millennium begins, the need for the theology of the local church, and for Tillard's contribution to it, could not be greater.

Conclusion

The Future of Catholic Ecclesiology

Jean-Marie Tillard died on November 13, 2000. Benedict XVI was elected pope on April 19, 2005. In the intervening years, the world and the church changed greatly. One readily thinks of the terrorist attacks of September 11, 2001, followed by wars in Afghanistan and Iraq; the eruption in 2002 of the clerical sexual-abuse scandals in the American Catholic Church; the death of Pope John Paul II and the subsequent election as pope of Cardinal Joseph Ratzinger in April 2005; the near-schism provoked in the Anglican Communion by competing visions of sexuality and authority.

The future of Catholic life and ecclesiology will be shaped by developments such as these. In the light of Tillard's theology of the local church, I want to conclude by looking briefly at three issues that will be of paramount importance for Catholic ecclesiology in the coming years: the prospects of Benedict's XVI's pontificate, the future of ecumenism, and the centrality of Christ to the church and to ecumenism.

With the election of Pope Benedict XVI — seemingly impossible and inevitable at once — the Catholic Church finds itself living in an extraordinary time of transition. We have already looked at the main themes of his ecclesiology, so I wish to focus instead on some key topics that have emerged in his initial homilies and addresses — topics that share much in common with Tillard's theology of the local church. Foremost is Benedict's vision of the papacy as a ministry of witness and unity. At the Mass where he took possession of the Basilica of St. John Lateran, his cathedral as bishop of Rome, he said that "the task of all Peter's Successors [is] to be the guide in the profession of faith in Christ, Son of the living God. The Chair of Rome is above all the Seat of this belief."[1] And the day after his Mass of installation at St. Peter's Basilica, Benedict went to the Basilica of St. Paul-Outside-the-Walls to underscore the Pauline, missionary dimension of his Petrine office: "Paul proclaimed Christ with martyrdom, and his blood, together with Peter's and that of many other Gospel witnesses, fertilized the Church of Rome which presides in charity over universal communion (cf. St. Ignatius of Antioch)."[2] Benedict's emphasis on both the Petrine and Pauline dimensions of the papacy — as opposed to an emphasis on papal power and rights — is rooted deeply in the church's tradition. Tillard and Pope John Paul II both wrote of how the memory of Peter and Paul as graced, forgiven sinners calls each pope to conversion and signals a desire for a leaner, more evangelical service to the church and to the world.[3]

And although it might seem counterintuitive in light of Benedict's support for the priority of the universal church to the local churches, his unassuming, self-effacing exercise of the papacy may help to foster decentralization and to strengthen the life of the local churches. His dislike for bureaucracy is well-known, as is his desire to simplify the church's administration. Benedict surely has shown little desire to create new synodal and collegial bodies, but he also seems — at least in the early stages of his pontificate — to be more willing to allow local bishops a greater role in the church's governance and perhaps to rein in some of the papal maximalization that occurred in recent decades.[4] If still unresolvable on an intellectual level, the Benedict-Kasper debate might yet find some pastoral resolution.

Benedict's ecclesiology, we have seen, is thoroughly eucharistic, and in his first post-conclave address to the College of Cardinals he stated that the eucharist is "the heart of Christian life and the source of the Church's evangelizing mission, [and] cannot but constitute the permanent center and source of the Petrine ministry that has been entrusted to me."[5] Moreover, as he reminded his congregation on the Solemnity of *Corpus Domini,* the eucharist gathers the church in adoration, while sending it forth in "procession . . . above and beyond the walls of our Churches. In this Sacrament, the Lord is always journeying to meet the world."[6] There can be little doubt that attentiveness to liturgy will mark Benedict's pontificate, and it will be revealing to see how Benedict extends this eucharistic dynamism of communion and mission into all aspects of the church's life.

The eucharist and the papacy are both intimately linked to the unity — and, sadly, the disunity — of the church. In his Sistine Chapel address to the College of Cardinals, delivered the day after his election, he stated that his "primary task [is] the duty to work tirelessly to rebuild the full and visible unity of all Christ's followers. This is his ambition, his impelling duty. He is aware that good intentions do not suffice for this. Concrete gestures that enter hearts and stir consciences are essential."[7] And he has reached out especially to the Orthodox, telling the representatives of the Ecumenical Patriarch of Constantinople, for instance, that "the unity we seek is neither absorption nor fusion, but respect for the many-faceted fullness of the church."[8] Time will tell how these words and thoughts translate into "concrete gestures" — for example, the invitation of twelve delegates from other Christian churches and communities to the October 2005 International Synod of Bishops on the eucharist, as well as the planned resumption of the international Orthodox-Catholic theological dialogue after a five-year suspension. But there are good grounds for hope — based on the continuity of his papal statements with his previous writings on, say, the first Christian millennium as a model for the future exercise of papal primacy in the East and the West—that Benedict will do much to revitalize the role of the local churches and to foster greater unity in the Christian church, especially with the Orthodox.

Nonetheless, it is clear that the ecumenical movement faces new, increasing difficulties. The Anglican Communion, for one, finds itself on the brink of schism, spurred by the Episcopal Church (USA)'s ordination to the episcopate of a gay man in a committed, sexual relationship and by the decision of the Canadian Diocese of New Westminster (British Columbia) to permit public liturgical blessings of same-sex unions. These longstanding Anglican tensions over matters of sexuality, authority, and tradition have found similar expression in mainline Protestant churches such as Lutheranism, Methodism, and Presbyterianism.

The "Windsor Report," a 2004 study on communion and authority commissioned by the archbishop of Canterbury in response to the aforementioned difficulties, has attempted to provide a theological and practical rationale for addressing these issues. It remains to be seen, though, how the churches of the Anglican Communion will respond to the report, and to what degree they will continue to act and pray together. The presently existing differences over the nature, structures, and exercise of Christian authority; the relationship of local autonomy and worldwide communion; and the interplay between unity and diversity, will likely continue to widen. It likewise is unclear how well both Anglicanism and Catholicism will respond to the Anglican–Roman Catholic International Commission's statement "The Gift of Authority" (1999), which addressed these very issues and challenged both churches to reform their structures and practices of authority.

Deeper still is the growing disagreement over the nature and purpose of the ecumenical movement. In 1961, the World Council of Churches (WCC) at its Third Assembly in New Delhi affirmed as its "basis" or foundational statement: "The World Council of Churches is a fellowship of churches which confess the Lord Jesus Christ as God and Savior according to the scriptures, and therefore seek to fulfill together their common calling to the glory of the one God, Father, Son and Holy Spirit." This common calling has traditionally been understood as involving a full, visible unity in faith, sacraments, and ministry.

However, a newer ecumenical vision proposed by Konrad Raiser, the former general secretary of the WCC, has given primacy to social concerns over doctrinal and doxological ones.[9] This newer "paradigm" (to use Raiser's word) holds that the churches' ecumenical efforts should be directed to combating such social problems as racism and economic inequality, in contrast to addressing more ecclesial matters as theology and ministry. Raiser, for one, thought that some previous understandings of ecumenism were introverted, dogmatic, and abstract. To some degree, this proposed shift reflects the perennial tensions between the WCC's two founding movements, "Life and Work" and "Faith and Order."

Tillard worried, though, that this newer ecumenical model, which seeks to build bridges not only within Christianity but also among the world religions, was often accompanied by the diminishment and even denial of Christ's divinity and unique salvific role. Tillard held that the Christian church, as God's chosen sacrament of reconciliation, must necessarily address global problems and foster interreligious harmony, but he insisted that such work would ultimately be fruitless if it were detached from explicit reference to Christ the Reconciler. This may seem like an obvious, even tautological point, but Tillard was deeply concerned about the spread in the WCC of what he called "an erosion of the basis of *koinonia* by a fragmentation of faith in Christ."[10] Such dissolution reveals itself not only in the denial of Christ's divinity (as with the "Jesus Seminar" and other movements), but also in the relativizing of Christ's salvific role. Responding to a comment he heard at a WCC meeting which called such relativizing a "defensible option," he wrote, "Anyone with any experience of the movement of ideas knows how very easily, especially where critical reticence in the face of what seems to be a generous doctrine [in this case, a desire to acknowledge the salvific potential of other religions, but at the unnecessary cost of Christ's unique mediation of salvation] is lacking, what is defensible becomes for many people what is true.... It is already finding a niche in the WCC."[11]

Ecumenism, he thought, was at a "double or quits" moment that would reveal which vision would prevail, and he had no doubt that the adoption of the newer *diakonia* model would effectively spell the end of the ecumenical movement as it had developed throughout the twentieth century. It would lead to the loss of Christ as the basis and purpose of all ecclesial communion and mission. Tillard suggested that ecumenism's — and Christianity's — greatest need was to return to the sources of Christian life and tradition, in order to renew a common faith in Christ:

> The pressing injunction of the founders of Faith and Order is more than ever relevant today. *Together* we must say afresh — and today that can only be done *together* — with intelligence but from within the faith, who Jesus Christ really is and what the Father's plan is, which was carried out through Christ. To do this we must put ourselves to school *together* to learn from the Scriptures, from the living Tradition, from the *sensus fidelium*. An arduous undertaking. But not more arduous than the undertaking which mobilized the Churches in the time of Arius.... It cannot be doubted that the urgent need to proclaim Christ *together* should become the chief purpose of the baptized, *hic et nunc*. It is a question of double or quits, life or death.[12]

Tillard's words found a recent echo in a homily delivered by Cardinal Walter Kasper at a Vespers service in Rome to mark the conclusion of the 2005 Week of Prayer for Christian Unity. He said there that the ecumenical movement, for all of its accomplishments, seemed to be "sliding toward a state of lethargy and losing its credibility." Noting that there was no lack of proposals for structural reforms, for the examination of urgent questions, or even for reflection on the very methods and purposes of the ecumenical movement, he called instead for all Christians to reflect on the one foundation of the church, Christ. With blunt, moving words, he stated:

> Faith in Jesus Christ, true God and true man, is the foundation of baptism, which makes us Christians by incorporating us into the church (cf. 1 Corinthians 12:13; Galatians 3:28). The Christological confession of faith in Jesus Christ as the *one* savior of *all* humanity is part of the World Council of Churches' basic formula and constitutes the fundamental agreement, the common denominator of all who participate in the ecumenical movement. And common missionary witness, which professes that salvation is found only in Jesus Christ (cf. Acts 4:12), before a world that does not yet know him or no longer knows him, is precisely the goal of ecumenical commitment. Thus, Jesus Christ is not only the foundation of our ecumenical commitment, but its goal. In him we will all be one. "All under one head, Jesus Christ," as the Lutheran founding fathers said in their confessional writings.
>
> But is this reality still clear enough to us? Do we take it into account enough in our debates and reflections? Don't we instead find ourselves in a situation where our foremost duty, our greatest challenge is recalling and strengthening our common foundation, lest it become fruitless in light of supposedly liberal interpretations that call themselves progressive, but in fact are subversive? Precisely today, when everything has become relative and arbitrary in postmodern society and each person creates his or her own religion *à la carte,* we need a solid foundation and a reliable common reference point for our personal lives and our ecumenical work. And what foundation can we have, if not Jesus Christ? Who can guide us better than he? Who can give us light and hope more than he? Where, if not in him, can we find the words of life (cf. John 6:68)?[13]

When reflecting on ecclesiology, it is always necessary to recall that Christ, not the church, is the *lumen gentium,* the light of the nations. He must always be the measure of the church's activity, and never what is measured. As *Gaudium et spes* stated, the church — local and universal — exists solely in order to carry on the work of Christ, its Founder and Risen Lord, and so to bring all of humanity into communion with him. All spiritual and structural reforms in the church should aim for this end alone. Jean-Marie Tillard's theology of the local church, built upon God's saving plan to bring humanity's histories and cultures to fullness in Christ, is a worthy witness to such divine and human communion.

Study questions for *The Local Church*

Chapter One
The Development of the Theology of the Local Church in Nineteenth- and Twentieth-Century Orthodoxy

1. What does Khomiakov mean by *sobornost*? How does it shape his entire conception of the church?
2. Why does Khomiakov think that Catholicism and Protestantism corrupt the essence of Christianity?
3. How does Afanasiev characterize eucharistic ecclesiology and universal ecclesiology, and why does he opt for the former?
4. What are some strengths and weaknesses of Afanasiev's eucharistic ecclesiology?
5. How does Zizioulas's understanding of God as triune communion shape his understanding of the church?
6. How does Zizioulas's theology of primacy and conciliarity offer a way forward for Catholic-Orthodox dialogue on church authority?

Chapter Two
The Development of the Theology of the Local Church in Nineteenth- and Twentieth-Century Catholicism

1. Möhler's early writing on the church is strongly Spirit-centered, while his later efforts are more Christ-centered. What are the advantages and disadvantages of each approach? How might one hold together both emphases in a single ecclesiology?
2. How does Congar distinguish between the "quantitative" and "qualitative" dimensions of catholicity? How does his understanding of catholicity shape his understanding of the relationship between unity and diversity in the church?
3. Like Afanasiev, Congar distinguishes between local and universal ecclesiologies. Unlike Afansiev, though, he thinks that the two are reconcilable. Why and how?

4. What are some of the "seeds" of Vatican II's theology of the local church? How well, in your opinion, did the council hold together the local and the universal dimensions of the church?
5. Is Hermann Pottmeyer correct in arguing that Vatican II's ecclesiology is, in some ways, more universalistic even than that of Vatican I?

Chapter Three
The Fundamental Principles of Jean-Marie Roger Tillard's Theology of the Local Church

1. Why does Tillard place Pentecost, rather than the call of the disciples or the Last Supper, at the heart of his ecclesiology? How does the event of Pentecost remain present today in the church?
2. Why is Jerusalem central to Tillard's theology of the local church? Why does he insist that the church at Pentecost is already universal and local?
3. How does Tillard affirm the church's holiness in light of its being marked by sinfulness?
4. How does Tillard understand catholicity? Why does he argue that catholicity and locality are not opposed, but express each other?
5. Why must the church always be "local"? Why is this local quality never just an "add-on" or "luxury" for the church?

Chapter Four
The Local Church Is a Communion of Faith and Sacrament

1. How does Tillard describe "communion," and how is it central to his ecclesiology?
2. Why does Tillard argue that the faith of the church precedes the faith of the believer? What are the implications of this communal priority?
3. Why is reception integral to the life of the church?
4. How does Tillard envision the relationship between the *sensus fidei,* the magisterium, and theologians? What are the tensions and possibilities inherent in that relationship?
5. Why does Tillard insist that baptism is foundational for his ecclesiology?
6. Why is the eucharist not simply what the local church *does,* but what it *is?*

Chapter Five
The Church of God Is a Communion of Local Churches

1. What difference does it make whether the universal church is "ontologically and temporally prior" to the local church, or the local and

universal churches are simultaneous? Why do both Pope Benedict XVI and the Congregation for the Doctrine of the Faith argue for universal priority, and why do they reject local priority?

2. Why does Tillard insist that synodality and episcopal collegiality are not simply administrative or bureaucratic realities, but belong to the very identity and mission of the church?
3. How does the pope exercise the "Petrine," "Pauline," and "Roman" dimensions of his office? Which dimensions seem to be emphasized more today? Which are less emphasized?
4. How well (or not) does Tillard's vision of the papacy cohere with the vision expressed in Pope John Paul II's *Ut unum sint*? How does Tillard see the papacy as exercising the "ministry of unity" in the church?

Chapter Six
Evaluation and Trajectories of Tillard's Theology of the Local Church

1. What are the merits of Avery Dulles's and Nicholas M. Healy's main criticisms of Tillard's ecclesiology? In your view, what are shortcomings of Tillard's ecclesiology, particularly of his theology of the local church?
2. How, if at all, does Tillard's understanding of primacy and synodality-collegiality help further the reception of Vatican II's teachings on the church? Why, in his view, are the contributions of the other churches and communities necessary for the full reception of Vatican II?
3. How might a renewed emphasis on the martyrological nature of the papacy help the papacy in its service of unity to the church and to the world?
4. How does Tillard see inculturation as intrinsic to evangelization? What are the possibilities and limits of inculturation?
5. How might the "*oikonomia* of patience" help the church as it faces its present tensions? What can a theology of the local church contribute to such patience?
6. What do you see as the primary challenges facing Catholicism today? How might Tillard's theology of the local church help in addressing them?

Notes

Introduction
Jean-Marie Roger Tillard and the Theology of the Local Church

1. For the sake of simplicity, I refer to the former cardinal Joseph Ratzinger as Pope Benedict XVI. Writings that preceded his election as pope, however, will be credited to him as (Cardinal) Joseph Ratzinger.

2. Joseph Ratzinger, "The Local Church and the Universal Church," *America* 185 (November 19, 2001): 7–11, at 8.

3. Walter Kasper, "On the Church," *The Tablet* 255 (June 23, 2001): 927–30, at 927.

4. Kasper, "On the Church," 930.

5. The best overview and evaluation of this conversation can be found in Kilian McDonnell, "The Ratzinger/Kasper Debate: The Universal Church and Local Churches," *Theological Studies* 63 (2002): 227–50; and ibid., "Walter Kasper on the Theology and Praxis of the Bishop's Office," *Theological Studies* 63 (2002): 711–29. See also Medard Kehl, "Der Disput der Kardinäle: Zum Verhältnis von Universalkirche und Ortskirchen," *Stimmen der Zeit* 221 (April 2003): 219–32.

6. *Christus Dominus* #11. This conciliar quotation, and all subsequent ones, are from *Vatican Council II: The Basic Sixteen Documents,* gen. ed. Austin Flannery (Northport, NY: Costello, 1996).

7. *Lumen gentium* #23.

8. *Lumen gentium* #26.

9. 1985 Extraordinary Synod of Bishops, "A Message to the People of God," *Origins* 15 (December 19, 1985): 441, 443–44, at 441.

10. 1985 Extraordinary Synod of Bishops, "The Final Report: The Church, in the Word of God, Celebrates the Mystery of Christ for the Salvation of the World," *Origins* 15 (December 19, 1985): 444–50, at 448.

11. See, for example, his 1989 Apostolic Exhortation on the Laity, *Christifideles laici* #19, which states, "The reality of the church as communion is, then, the integrating aspect, indeed the central content of the 'mystery,' or rather, the divine plan for the salvation of humanity" (Pope John Paul II, *Christifideles laici, Origins* 18 [February 9, 1989]: 561, 563–95, at 570). Also, in an address delivered at the closing of a special Jubilee-year symposium on Vatican II, John Paul stated, "*Communio* is the foundation on which the church's reality is based. It is a *koinonia* that has its source in the very mystery of the triune God and extends to all the baptized, who are therefore called to full unity in Christ. . . . The communion that the church lives with the Father, Son, and the Holy Spirit is a sign of how brothers and sisters are called to live together" ("Vatican Council II: Prophetic Message for the Church's Life," *Origins* 29 [May 4, 2000]: 753–55, at 755).

12. See the 1992 letter, "Some Aspects of the Church Understood as Communion": "The concept of communion (*koinonia*), which appears with a certain prominence in the texts of the Second Vatican Council, is very suitable for expressing the core of the mystery of the church and can certainly be a key for the renewal of Catholic ecclesiology" (Congregation for the Doctrine of the Faith, "Some Aspects of the Church Understood as a Communion," *Origins* 22 [June 25, 1992]: 108–12, at 108).

13. Jean-Marie Roger Tillard, "The Church of God Is a Communion: The Ecclesiological Perspective of Vatican II," *One in Christ* 17 (1981): 117–31.

14. Much of this biographical information is drawn from Gilles-Dominique Mailhiot's article "Le professeur," in *Communion et Réunion: Mélanges Jean-Marie Roger Tillard,* ed. Gillian R. Evans and Michel Gourgues (Leuven: Leuven University Press, 1995), 21–30.

15. *L'Eucharistie, Pâque de l'Église* (Paris: Cerf, 1964). English translation: *The Eucharist: Pasch of God's People,* trans. Dennis L. Wienk (Staten Island, NY: Alba House, 1967).

16. Tillard served as a *peritus* to the Canadian bishops at Vatican II, where he helped to prepare the council's Decree on the Up-to-Date Renewal of Religious Life (*Perfectae caritatis*).

17. *L'évêque de Rome* (Paris: Cerf, 1982). English translation: *The Bishop of Rome,* trans. John de Satgé (Wilmington, DE: Michael Glazier, 1983). *Église d'églises: L'ecclésiologie de communion* (Paris: Cerf, 1987). English translation: *Church of Churches: The Ecclesiology of Communion,* trans. R. C. De Peaux (Collegeville, MN: Liturgical Press/Michael Glazier, 1992); this translation is seriously deficient and will not be cited. *Chair de l'Église, chair du Christ: Aux sources de l'ecclésiologie de communion* (Paris: Cerf, 1992). English translation: *Flesh of the Church, Flesh of Christ: At the Source of the Ecclesiology of Communion,* trans. Madeleine Beaumont (Collegeville, MN: Liturgical Press/Pueblo, 2001). *L'Église locale: Ecclésiologie de communion et catholicité* (Paris: Cerf, 1995).

18. See *L'Eglise locale,* 263: "The eucharistic synaxis is therefore the normative expression par excellence of the local church, the Church of God in *such* a place, the catholic Church in *this* community *reconciled* by the Pasch." (All translations from the French original are the author's.)

19. *L'Eglise locale,* 53.

20. *L'Eglise locale,* 16. The phrase alludes to the French poet Charles Péguy's poem "Eve," which serves as the epigraph to the book: "Car le surnaturel est lui-même charnel / Et l'arbre de la grâce est raciné profond / Et plonge dans le sol et cherche jusqu'au fond / Et l'arbre de la race est lui-même éternal."

21. *L'Eglise locale,* 149: "The baptismal font is the maternal breast where the Spirit gives to the Church of God its children."

22. See n.18.

23. *L'Eglise locale,* 190–91: "Thus, by his presidency, integral to his *diakonia,* [the bishop] is, in his Church, the *sacramentum* of the *exousia* of divine *agapé.* It is this *exousia* which constitutes the Church in the *gift* of God, so that, in the Spirit, it may be entirely *given over* to the service of humanity."

24. *L'Eglise locale,* 250–51: "In the *katholou* of the *Church of God,* synodality (the *communion* of local churches with each other), collegiality (the *communion* of the bishops with each other), [and] the *communion* of the bishop and his local church are in fact inseparable."

25. *Église d'églises,* 399.
26. Tillard, "The Church of God Is a Communion," 117–18.
27. *Gaudium et spes* #1.
28. *L'Eglise locale,* 372–73.
29. Tillard, "Ecclésiologie de communion et exigence oecuménique," *Irénikon* 59 (1986): 201–30, at 217–18.
30. *Christus Dominus* #11, repeated verbatim in Canon 369. See also *Église d'églises,* 47.
31. *L'Eglise locale,* 290.
32. *L'Eglise locale,* 290.
33. *Église d'églises,* 48.

Chapter One
The Development of the Theology of the Local Church in Nineteenth- and Twentieth-Century Orthodoxy

1. Alongside him are the central figures of Georges Florovsky (1893–1979), Vladimir Lossky (1903–58), and Paul Evdokimov (1901–70).
2. Aidan Nichols, *Theology in the Russian Diaspora: Church, Fathers, Eucharist in Nikolai Afanas'ev* (Cambridge: Cambridge University Press, 1989), 176.
3. John Zizioulas, *Being as Communion: Studies in Personhood and the Church* (Crestwood, NY: St. Vladimir's Seminary Press, 1985).
4. Nicolas Zernov, Introduction to Alexei Khomiakov, *The Church Is One* (London: SPCK, 1948), 11.
5. Lewis Shaw, "John Meyendorff and the Heritage of the Russian Theological Tradition," in *New Perspectives on Historical Theology: Essays in Memory of John Meyendorff,* ed. Bradley Nassif (Grand Rapids, MI: Eerdmans, 1996), 16. Also Nicolas Zernov, *Three Russian Prophets: Khomiakov, Dostoevsky, Soloviev* (London: SCM Press, 1944), 44–55; John Meyendorff, "Visions of the Church: Russian Theological Thought in Modern Times," in *Rome, Constantinople, Moscow: Historical and Theological Studies* (Crestwood, NY: St. Vladimir's Seminary Press, 1996), 184–88. For general background, see the excellent work of Albert Gratieux, *A. S. Khomiakov et le mouvement slavophile,* 2 vols. (Paris: Cerf, 1939).
6. Nicolas Zernov, *Three Russian Prophets: Khomiakov, Dostoevsky, Soloviev* (London: SCM Press, 1944), 72. Also Shaw, "John Meyendorff and the Heritage of the Russian Theological Tradition," 18; Nichols, *Theology in the Russian Diaspora,* 18.
7. See Gratieux, *A. S. Khomiakov et le mouvement slavophile*: "The communitarian principle is thus essential to the Slavophile conception.... Khomiakov declared himself the fierce defender of the rural commune, *obchtchina* or *mir.* Khomiakov saw, in the Russian tradition, nothing more fundamental than this ancient custom... [of] the development of the social principle, to the detriment of the rights of the individual, [which were] neglected and even completely sacrificed.... In an article published by *Molva,* in 1857, he noted that... 'the Slavic race, and particularly the Russian people, are distinguished from all others by the distinctiveness of their communitarian life' " (2:173).
8. Nichols, *Theology in the Russian Diaspora,* 20. See also his related comment that Khomiakov's "primary intuition, at once philosophical and religious... consists in an awareness of the organic, quasi-natural unity of a faith-community, combined

with an insistence that this organic quality does not destroy but on the contrary supports the reasonable liberty of the individual spirit" (21). Joost van Rossum argues as well that "the two major themes of Khomiakov's ecclesiology are unity and freedom" ("A. S. Khomiakov and Orthodox Ecclesiology," *St. Vladimir's Theological Quarterly* 35 [1991]: 67–82, at 69).

9. This word, which "would become the rallying cry of his disciples . . . strangely enough, appears not in his own manuscripts but only in the Russian translation of the 'French Brochures' " (Nichols, *Theology in the Russian Diaspora,* 20). Nonetheless, other forms are used, such as *sobornoi,* which appears, for example, in Khomiakov's "Lettre au rédacteur de l'union chrétienne, à l'occasion d'un discours du Père Gagarine, Jésuite" (in *L'Église latine et le Protestantisme au point de vue de l'Église d'orient* (Lausanne: Benda, 1872), 391–400). Nichols writes that *sobornost* "lacks a single English equivalent," for "conciliarity" refers to institutional structures inimical to Khomiakov's thought, "communion" has no essential eucharistic reference in his writings, and "togetherness" is a primarily sociological claim, having no reference to the essentially invisible nature of the church (Nichols, *Theology in the Russian Diaspora,* 20).

10. For a helpful Catholic perspective on *sobornost,* see Yves Congar's concise and still masterful treatment in *Jalons pour une théologie du laicat* (Paris: Cerf, 1953), 380–86.

11. Khomiakov, *The Church Is One,* 28.

12. Khomiakov, *The Church Is One,* 16.

13. Khomiakov, *The Church Is One,* 17: "Neither individuals, nor a multitude of individuals within the Church, preserve tradition or write the Scriptures; but the Spirit of God, which lives in the whole body of the church. . . . To a man living outside the Church neither her scripture nor her tradition nor her works are comprehensible. But to the man who lives within the church and is united to the spirit of the Church, their unity is manifest by the grace which lives within her. . . .

"Every one that seeks for proof of the truth of the Church, by that very act either shows his doubt, and excludes himself from the Church, or assumes the appearance of one who doubts and at the same time preserves a hope of proving the truth and arriving at it by his own power of reason: but the powers of reason do not attain to the truth of God, and the weakness of man is made manifest by the weakness of his proofs. . . . For Christian knowledge is a matter, not of intellectual investigation, but of a living faith, which is a gift of grace."

14. Khomiakov, *The Church is One,* 27: "We know that when any one of us falls he falls alone; but no one is saved alone. He who is saved is saved in the Church, as a member of her, and in unity with all her other members. If any one believes, he is in the communion of faith. If he loves, he is in the communion of love; if he prays, he is in the communion of prayer. Wherefore no one can rest his hope on his own prayers."

15. Khomiakov, *The Church Is One,* 23.

16. Khomiakov, *The Church Is One,* 14.

17. Khomiakov, *The Church Is One,* 14, 24: "[The Church's] unity is, in reality, true and absolute. . . . Indeed the Church, the Body of Christ, is manifesting forth and fulfilling herself in time, without changing her essential unity or inward life of grace. . . . The Church, even upon earth, lives, not an earthly human life, but a life which is divine, and of grace. Wherefore not only each of her members, but she herself as a whole, solemnly calls herself 'Holy.' "

18. Khomiakov, *The Church Is One,* 15, 24.
19. Khomiakov, *The Church Is One,* 18.
20. Khomiakov, *L'Église latine et le Protestantisme,* 398.
21. Khomiakov, *L'Église latine et le Protestantisme,* 398.
22. Khomiakov, *The Church Is One,* 16.
23. Khomiakov, *The Church Is One,* 31.
24. John S. Romanides, "Orthodox Theology according to Alexis Khomiakov (1804–1860)," *Greek Orthodox Theology Review* 2 (1956): 57–73, at 68.
25. *L'Église latine et le Protestantisme,* 285–86: "Romanism, the revolt of a prideful freedom against the moral law of unity; Romanism, condemned by this law since its origin, has created, in order to escape its own consequences, an artificial unity by means of the authority which it accords to the pope over the consciences of its adherents. The hierarchy, personified in a single man, became tyrannical (I speak here not at all of Romanism's abuses, but of its law); Christians became slaves. They were no more than clumped on to Christianity.... They were obedient to a faith whose see was not at all within them, but outside of them."
26. Khomiakov, *L'Église latine et le Protestantisme,* 286–87: "Are the Reformers right, therefore, when they believe themselves to be representative of the principle of freedom? Not at all. It means nothing to say that man should be free in his belief: in this, Christian freedom would not be different from any other. If the fruits of this freedom are the interior discord of believers; avowed or inevitable subjectivism which, by itself, is doubt or rather unbelief; and the absence of objective faith, that is to say, of real knowledge, [then] this freedom has not received divine blessing. It is not the freedom to which God has revealed his mysteries; it is not the freedom that Christ has won for us by his death. The Reformers preach freedom, but they dishonor the freedom of the children of God, because of the blessing which has been accorded to it, and whose fruits are concord, faith, and fullness of life. Those who are free in Jesus Christ are one in him, and those who are not one are necessarily slaves of error and—appearing to be free in the eyes of men—are not so according to God. To deny Christian unity is to calumnize the Christian freedom of which it is the product and manifestation."
27. Khomiakov, *L'Église latine et le Protestantisme,* 287: "An exterior unity which rejects freedom and is not, by consequence, real unity: such is Romanism. An exterior freedom which does not yield unity and which, by consequence, is not real freedom: such is the Reform."
28. See Zernov, *Three Russian Prophets,* 67.
29. See Khomiakov, *L'Église latine et le Protestantisme,* 399: "The Church of the Apostles in the ninth century [the era of the *filioque* controversy] is neither the Church *kath'ekaston* (according to each) as with the Protestants, nor the Church *kata ton épiscopon tès Romés* (according to the Bishop of Rome), as with the Latins: but it is the Church *kath'olon* (according to all), as it had been before the Western schism, and as it still is with those whom God has preserved from schism, because schism, I repeat, is the heresy against the unity of the church."
30. Khomiakov, *L'Église latine et le Protestantisme,* 241. One must also note here the still greater tragedy, in Khomiakov's eyes, of Orthodoxy's own so-called Western Captivity, which, under Peter the Great's influence, imposed upon the Russian church what John Meyendorff has called a "Protestant model for church government and a Latin theology" (Meyendorff, "Visions of the Church," 184).

The Moscow patriarchate was abolished and replaced with a "Holy Synod" of state-appointed clerics, while seminaries and ecclesiastical academies were established — most notably in Kiev — in which Latin was the language of instruction and manuals were the content of study.

31. See, for example, Gratieux, *A. S. Khomiakov et le mouvement slavophile,* 2:95.

32. Romanides, "Orthodox Theology according to Alexis Khomiakov (1804–1860)," 73.

33. Khomiakov, *L'Église latine et le Protestantisme,* 398.

34. Khomiakov, *The Church Is One,* 31.

35. Khomiakov's lack of distinction between the earthly and heavenly churches also obscures any real sense of the church as either militant or pilgrimaging. See Congar, *Jalons,* 386.

36. Khomiakov, *L'Église latine et le Protestantisme,* 398.

37. See Romanides, "Orthodox Theology according to Alexis Khomiakov (1804–1860)," 57; Van Rossum, "A. S. Khomiakov and Orthodox Ecclesiology," 68, 78.

38. Khomiakov, *The Church Is One,* 22.

39. Shaw, "John Meyendorff and the Heritage of the Russian Theological Tradition," 16.

40. Nichols, *Theology in the Russian Diaspora,* 48.

41. See John Meyendorff, Review of Aidan Nichols, *Theology in the Russian Diaspora: Church, Fathers, Eucharist in Nikolai Afanas'ev (1893–1966), St. Vladimir's Theological Quarterly* 34 (1990): 363; also Michal Kaszowski, "Les sources de l'ecclésiologie eucharistique du P. Nicolas Afanassieff," *Ephemerides Theologicae Lovanienses* 52 (1976): 331–43, at 332.

42. Nichols, *Theology in the Russian Diaspora,* 55: "If Afanas'ev's Serbian experience be considered in terms of its lasting results for his ecclesiology, the dominant theme would undoubtedly be that of the jurisdictional conflicts in which the Russian Church of the Diaspora was caught up, with their disastrous consequences for the primitive Christian ideal of a single Eucharist and bishop in each local church."

43. Alexis Kniazeff, *L'Institut Saint-Serge: De l'academie d'autrefois au rayonnement d'aujourd'hui* (Paris: Editions Beauchesne, 1974), 47.

44. Alexander Schmemann, "Russian Theology: 1920–1972, An Introductory Survey," *St. Vladimir's Theological Quarterly* 16 (1972): 178. See also Kniazeff, *L'Institut Saint-Serge,* 63–69.

45. Kaszowski, "Les sources de l'ecclésiologie eucharistique du P. Nicolas Afanassieff," 337. Kaszowski notes that Bulgakov and Florovsky, among others, published works on the eucharist in 1929 and 1930, and that Russian theology as a whole had a eucharistic character; for example, the *Philokalia* recommended frequent communion.

46. Afanasiev, "Una Sancta," *Irénikon* 36 (1963): 436–75, at 440.

47. Afanasiev, "The Church Which Presides in Love," in *The Primacy of Peter,* ed. John Meyendorff (Crestwood, NY: St. Vladimir's Seminary Press, 1992), 94.

48. Afanasiev, "Una Sancta," 440.

49. Afanasiev, "Una Sancta," 452.

50. Cyprian, Letter 233, VII, 1, quoted in "Una Sancta," 449.

51. Afanasiev, "Una Sancta," 451.

52. Afanasiev, "*Statio Orbis,*" *Irénikon* 35 (1962): 65–75, at 71.

53. Afanasiev, "The Church Which Presides in Love," 105; also Afanasiev, "*Statio Orbis,*" 73.

54. Afanasiev even goes so far as to claim that the "fundamental difference" between the two types of ecclesiology consists precisely in their differences concerning attribution ("Una Sancta," 452). Universal ecclesiology can attribute the four "marks" only to the universal church, because the local churches are but parts of the universal church, possessing no independent ecclesial integrity. eucharistic ecclesiology sees each local church, in virtue of its eucharistic integrity and fullness, as being truly one, holy, catholic, and apostolic in its own right. This thoroughly eucharistic conception of the church's unity, holiness, catholicity, and apostolicity will become increasingly central in the writings of John Zizioulas and Jean-Marie Tillard.

55. Afanasiev, "Una Sancta," 453.

56. Afanasiev, "*Statio Orbis,*" 67.

57. Afanasiev, "Una Sancta," 453.

58. Afanasiev, "L'Eucharistie, principal lien entre les Catholiques et les Orthodoxes," *Irénikon* 38 (1965): 337–39, at 339.

59. Afanasiev, "L'Eucharistie, principal lien entre les Catholiques et les Orthodoxes," 338. Michael Plekon argues that Afanasiev is "formulating his own, more scriptural and patristic version of the Slavophiles' concept of the Church's catholic nature or *sobornost*" ("'Always Everyone and Always Together': The Eucharistic Ecclesiology of Nicolas Afanasiev's *The Lord's Supper* Revisited," *St. Vladimir's Theological Quarterly* 41 [1997]: 141–74, at 154).

60. Afanasiev, "The Church Which Presides in Love," 111; also "Una Sancta," 454.

61. Afanasiev, "The Church Which Presides in Love," 111–12.

62. Afanasiev, "The Church Which Presides in Love," 112.

63. Afanasiev, "La Concile dans la théologie orthodoxe russe," *Irénikon* 35 (1962): 316–39, at 316–17.

64. Afanasiev, "La Concile dans la théologie orthodoxe russe," 334.

65. Afanasiev, "La Concile dans la théologie orthodoxe russe," 318, 326.

66. Priority is thus a gift, a matter of grace. Historical contingencies such as "being in some special town, or being founded by Apostles, or having many adherents" are not inherently sufficient grounds for priority (Afanasiev, "The Church Which Presides in Love," 115).

67. Afanasiev, "The Church Which Presides in Love," 116. See also ibid., 141: "In spite of all the difference between these two types of ecclesiology, they agree in both accepting the idea that the whole church must follow a single directive. For the pattern of universal ecclesiology, a unique, personal power founded on rights is a necessity.... In the pattern of eucharistic theology, power of one single bishop does not exist in any case, because power based on right does not exist.... According to this doctrine [of eucharistic ecclesiology], one of the local churches possesses the priority, which is manifested in its greater authority of witness about events in other churches, that is, events in the Church of God in Christ, since every local church is the Church of God in Christ with all fullness. To put it otherwise, universal ecclesiology and eucharistic ecclesiology have different conceptions on the question of Church government: the first conceives this government as a matter of law and rights, and the second regards it as founded on grace." One hears echoes here of Rudolf Sohm's separation of law and spirit, law and grace.

68. Afanasiev, "The Church Which Presides in Love," 112–13.

69. Afanasiev, "The Church Which Presides in Love," 133.

70. Meyendorff, Review of Aidan Nichols, *Theology in the Russian Diaspora: Church, Fathers, Eucharist in Nikolai Afanas'ev (1893–1966)*: 363.

71. M. Edmund Hussey, "Nicholas Afanassiev's Eucharistic Ecclesiology: A Roman Catholic Viewpoint," *Journal of Ecumenical Studies* 12 (1975): 235–52, at 246–47. He notes also that Schmemann and Meyendorff are more balanced than Afanasiev in their treatment of ecclesial institutions.

72. For example, Meyendorff, "Review," 364; John Zizioulas, *Being as Communion: Studies in Personhood and the Church* (Crestwood, NY: St. Vladimir's Seminary Press, 1985), 144, 155–56, 200–203.

73. Hussey, "Nicholas Afanassiev's Eucharistic Ecclesiology: A Roman Catholic Viewpoint," 245.

74. Plekon, " 'Always Everyone and Always Together': The Eucharistic Ecclesiology of Nicolas Afanasiev's *The Lord's Supper* Revisited," 159.

75. Nichols, *Theology in the Russian Diaspora,* 219.

76. See Nichols, *Theology in the Russian Diaspora,* 166–221, esp. 173: "Three texts [nos. 3, 7, and 11] from the 'Dogmatic Constitution on the Church,' *Lumen Gentium,* may suffice to show the role of Afanas'ev's 'grosse Idee' in the ecclesiology of [the] council.... Afanas'ev's essay on 'The Church that Presides in Love,' with its sketch of his eucharistic ecclesiology... was mentioned in three of the 'General Congregations' where the documents of the Second Vatican Council were forged."

77. Nichols, *Theology in the Russian Diaspora,* 173; also Kniazeff, *L'Institut Saint-Serge,* 120.

78. Zizioulas, "Primacy in the Church: An Orthodox Approach," in *Petrine Ministry and the Unity of the Church: "Toward a Patient and Fraternal Dialogue,"* ed. James F. Puglisi, (Collegeville, MN: Michael Glazier/Liturgical, 1999), 115–25, at 117.

79. Zizioulas, *Being as Communion: Studies in Personhood and the Church* (Crestwood, NY: St. Vladimir's Seminary Press, 1985), 40–41.

80. Zizioulas, "Communion and Otherness," *St. Vladimir's Theological Quarterly* 38 (1994): 347–61, at 352–53. See, for instance: "otherness is inconceivable apart from relationship. Father, Son, and Spirit are all names indicating relationship. No Person can be different unless He is related. Communion does not threaten otherness; it generates it" (353).

81. Zizioulas, *Being as Communion,* 127–28.

82. Zizioulas, *Being as Communion,* 130.

83. Zizioulas, "Le Mystère de l'Église dans la tradition orthodoxe," *Irénikon* 60 (1987): 323–35, at 330. He adds that this "de-individualization" is "the stumbling block in all ecclesiological discussions in the ecumenical movement. The insistence of certain people on a sharp distinction between Christ and the Church presupposes an individualistic understanding of Christ. Such a Christ, however, could not be the spiritual being who incorporates all in himself. He could not be the first-born of many brothers, the first-born of all creation of which Colossians speaks. The 'one' without the 'many' would be an individual untouched by the Spirit. He would not be the Christ of our faith" (330).

84. Zizioulas, "The Church as Communion," *St. Vladimir's Theological Quarterly* 38 (1994): 3–16, at 6–7; "Communion and Otherness," 354; "Le Mystère de l'Église dans la tradition orthodoxe," 331.

85. Zizioulas,"Le Mystère de l'Église dans la tradition orthodoxe," 331: "The Mystery of the Church consists especially in the mystery of the 'one' who is 'many,'

not of a 'one' who is first 'one' and then — in the *eschata* — becomes 'many,' but really of a 'one' who is 'one,' that is to say, unique and 'other' precisely because it is in relation with the 'many.' "

86. Zizioulas, *Being as Communion,* 132.

87. Zizioulas, *Being as Communion,* 132.

88. Zizioulas, *Being as Communion,* 132.

89. Zizioulas, *Being as Communion,* 206.

90. Zizioulas, *Being as Communion,* 132–33.

91. Zizioulas, *Being as Communion,* 247.

92. Zizioulas, *Being as Communion,* 254.

93. See John S. Romanides, "Orthodox Ecclesiology according to Alexis Khomiakov (1804–1860)."

94. Zizioulas, *Being as Communion,* 154; also ibid., 157: "The whole Christ, the catholic Church, [is] present and incarnate in each eucharistic community."

95. Zizioulas, *Being as Communion,* 160–61.

96. Zizioulas, *Being as Communion,* 161.

97. Zizioulas, *Being as Communion,* 138: "The ecclesial institutions by being eschatologically conditioned become *sacramental* in the sense of being placed in the dialectic between history and eschatology, between the already and the not yet. They lose therefore their self-sufficiency, their individualistic ontology, and exist *epicletically,* that is, they depend for their efficacy constantly on prayer, the prayer of the community. It is not in history that the ecclesial institutions find their certainty (their validity) but in constant dependence on the Holy Spirit. This is what makes them 'sacramental,' which in the language of Orthodox theology may be called 'iconic.' " See also ibid., 185, and his "L'eucharistie: Quelques aspects bibliques" in *L'eucharistie,* ed. Jean Zizioulas, Jean-Marie Roger Tillard, and Jean-Jacques von Allmen (Paris: Maison Mame, 1970), 11–74, at 68: "And the eucharist cannot be an 'anamnesis' of Christ — that is to say, it cannot realize here and now not only what Christ *has done,* but also what he *will do* when he makes 'all things new' — if not by the coming of the Spirit. The eucharist becomes what it ought to be only by the *epiclesis,* and this is why it cannot rest solely on historical realities, but on *prayer.*"

98. Zizioulas, "Communion and Otherness," 355: "It is not by accident that the Church has given to the Eucharist the name of 'Communion.' For in the eucharist we can find all the dimensions of communion: God communicates himself to us, we enter into communion with Him, the participants of the Sacrament enter into communion with one another, and creation as a whole enters through man into communion with God. All this is taking place in Christ and the Spirit, Who bring the last days into history and offer to the world a foretaste of the Kingdom.

"But the Eucharist does not only affirm and sanctify communion; it also sanctifies otherness. It is the place where difference ceases to be divisive and becomes good. *Diaphora* does not lead to *diairesis,* and unity or communion does not destroy but affirms diversity and otherness in the Eucharist. Whenever this does not happen, the Eucharist is destroyed and even invalidated, even if all the other requirements for a 'valid' eucharist are met and satisfied. . . . A Church which does not celebrate the eucharist in this inclusive way risks losing her catholicity."

99. See Zizioulas, *Being as Communion,* 151–52, 255–56; "Communion and Otherness," 355; "L'Eucharistie," 39–40.

100. Zizioulas, *Being as Communion,* 149.

101. Gaëtan Baillargeon, "Jean Zizioulas, porte-parole de l'Orthodoxie contemporaine," *Nouvelle Revue Théologique* 111 (1989): 176–93, at 180.

102. Zizioulas, "Primacy in the Church: An Orthodox Approach," 118.

103. Zizioulas, "Primacy in the Church: An Orthodox Approach," 119. See especially *Being as Communion,* 24, 250–51. The bishop receives greater attention and prominence in Zizioulas than in Afanasiev, primarily because of the former's explicit linking of the local church with the diocese, not the parish (as Zizioulas asserts of Afanasiev); and this because Zizioulas sees eucharistic presidency as the primary task of the bishop, not the priest. He argues that "the proper ecclesiological status of the parish [is] one of the most fundamental problems in ecclesiology — both in the West and in the East," because its substitution of the priest for the bishop as eucharistic president (1) relegated the bishop to the role of administrator, and (2) "destroyed the image of the Church in which *all* orders are necessary as *constitutive* elements. The parish as it finally prevailed in history made redundant both the deacon and the bishop. (Later, with the private mass, it made redundant even the laity.)" (250–51).

104. Zizioulas, *Being as Communion,* 153; also ibid., 199.

105. Zizioulas, "The Church as Communion," 10.

106. Zizioulas, *Being as Communion,* 250.

107. Zizioulas, *Being as Communion,* 136–37; "The Church as Communion," 10. Also "Primacy in the Church," 119: "The bishop is the head, but as such he is conditioned by the 'body,' he cannot exercise authority without communion with his faithful. Just as he cannot perform the Eucharist without the *synaxis* of the people, his entire ministry requires the *consensus fidelium,* the 'Amen' of the community." And "Primacy in the Church," 121: "There is a primacy *within* each local church. The bishop is the *primus* at the local level. He is the head of the *collegium* of the presbyters, but at the same time he is the head of the eucharistic synaxis, which means that he is conditioned in his ministry by the entire community of which he is the head. The fact that there can be no eucharistic synaxis without his presidency (directly or indirectly through the authorized priest) shows that the *primus* is a *constitutive* element in the local church. Equally, however, the fact that the synaxis of the people is a condition for the bishop to function as the head of the community shows that his primacy requires the consent and participation of the community. . . . The 'many' cannot be a church without the 'one,' but equally the 'one' cannot be the *primus* without the 'many.' "

108. Zizioulas, *Being as Communion,* 202.

109. See Zizioulas, *Being as Communion,* 171–208, for a full discussion of apostolic continuity and succession. Zizioulas considers apostolic continuity as both historical (a largely retrospective continuity, which sees the apostles primarily as those individuals whose mission is to evangelize the world) and eschatological (a largely prospective continuity, in which the apostles are primarily a community, representing the Twelve gathered from the ends of the world, and pointing to the already-present Kingdom). Both dimensions are needed and must be integrated, so as to manifest the osmosis of history and eschatology in the church.

110. Zizioulas, "Primacy in the Church," 120.

111. Zizioulas, *Being as Communion,* 134–35.

112. Zizioulas, "Primacy in the Church," 120.

113. Zizioulas, *Being as Communion,* 157; also ibid., 258: "This is not to deny that there is only *one* Church in the world. But the oneness of the Church in the world

does not constitute a structure beside or *above* the local churches. Any ecclesial communion on the universal level should draw its forms from the local Church reality. It is not an accident that the synods according to Orthodox canon law are composed only of *diocesan* bishops. All forms of ministry of universal ecclesial communion should have some local Church as its basis."

114. In the Introduction to *Being as Communion,* Zizioulas writes that "the principle 'wherever the eucharist is, there is the Church' risks suggesting the idea that each Church could, *independently of other local Churches,* be the 'one, holy, catholic, and apostolic Church' " (*Being as Communion,* 25). Such a view is false both eucharistically and episcopally. In the former, a church is valid or genuine only if it is open to communion with others. A closed eucharist indicates a violation of the very nature of the eucharist, which destroys all boundaries of time and space through communion: "Just as *unus christianus nullus christianus,*... in the same way a eucharistic community which deliberately lives in isolation from the rest of the communities is not an ecclesial community" (ibid., 236). The seriousness with which the early church took this principle is evident in the fact that the early councils were devoted largely to questions of intercommunion and excommunication. Episcopally, the bishop of a given local church is related through his very ordination to other bishops and their churches, as he can be ordained validly only in the presence of at least two or three neighboring bishops (see ibid., 155); Zizioulas charges Afanasiev with ignorance of this requirement.

115. Zizioulas, "Primacy in the Church," 121–25; "The Church as Communion," 11.

116. The *Apostolic Canons,* a collection of eighty-five canons attributed to the Apostles but actually dating from the fourth century (c. 350–80), primarily concern the clergy's responsibilities and conduct. Taken together, they form the eighth, concluding book of the *Apostolic Constitutions,* which is itself a compilation of church law and discipline; much of this work is drawn from the *Didascalia, Didache,* and Hippolytus's *Apostolic Tradition.* See *The Oxford Dictionary of the Christian Church* for further information and references.

117. Zizioulas, "Primacy in the Church," 124–25.

118. Zizioulas, *Being as Communion,* 139; "The Church as Communion," 10, 16.

119. See Joost Van Rossum, "A. S. Khomiakov and Orthodox Ecclesiology," 81: "Zizioulas's ecclesiology has to be seen as a development, rather than a correction, of Afanasiev's insights, which found their first powerful expression (in Orthodox post-patristic theological literature) in the writings of Khomiakov."

120. As in Zizioulas, "Primacy in the Church," 120: "The local church could not ignore the consequences of its decisions and actions for the other churches, as if it were a 'catholic' church independently of its relations and communion with the rest of the churches. The catholicity of the local church cannot be turned into self-sufficiency."

121. See Zizioulas, "The Church as Communion," 12–13: "For quite a long time, Christian mission was regarded as a kind of sermon addressed *to* the world. It is, of course, true that the Church is not *of* this world and that the world hates Christ and his Church. But the relation of the Church to the world is not just negative: it is also positive. This is implied in the Incarnation and ideas such as the recapitulation of all in Christ to be found in the Bible (Ephesians, Colossians, etc.), and in the Fathers (Irenaeus, Maximus et al.). In the Orthodox tradition, in which the Eucharist is central, the world is brought into the Church in the form of the natural elements as

well as in the everyday preoccupations of the members of the Church. If communion is made a key idea in ecclesiology, mission is better understood and served not by placing the Gospel over against the world, but by inculturating it in it."

122. Zizioulas, *Being as Communion,* 254.

123. Zizioulas's understanding of the radical disintegration wrought by the Fall may preclude human culture and activity from being viewed as much more than fragments of divine goodness, unable to achieve any lasting coherence. In an interview with the author (December 2, 1999), Jean-Marie Tillard suggested that Zizioulas lacks a sense of *synderesis,* which would preserve an inclination toward the good, even if grace remains always the possibility and cause of human activity. One might ask as well if sanctifying or transforming grace extends to cultures and societies or is limited to individuals. That is, can human societies — especially non-Christian ones — achieve any substantial and lasting integration, truth, or permanence?

124. Zizioulas, "Communion and Otherness," 351.

125. Zizioulas, "Communion and Otherness," 351–52: "The Church is made of sinners, and she shares fully the ontological and cosmic dimension of sin which is death, the break of communion and final *diastasis* (separation and decomposition) of beings. And yet, we insist that the Church is in her essence holy and sinless.

"... The first thing that is implied in this position of the Orthodox is that the essence of Christian existence in the Church is *metanoia* (repentance).

"... The second implication of the Orthodox position concerning the holiness of the Church is that repentance can only be true and genuine if the Church and her members are aware of the *true nature* of the Church. We need a model by which to measure our existence. And the higher the model the deeper the repentance. This is why we need a maximalistic ecclesiology and a maximalistic anthropology — and even cosmology — resulting from it. Orthodox ecclesiology, by stressing the holiness of the Church, does not and should not lead to triumphalism but to a deep sense of compassion and *metanoia.*"

126. Zizioulas, "Primacy in the Church," 124.

127. Zizioulas, "The Church as Communion," 16.

Chapter Two
The Development of the Theology of the Local Church in Nineteenth- and Twentieth-Century Catholicism

1. Interestingly enough, Möhler and Khomiakov were acquainted with each other, and their ecclesiologies were deeply influenced by German Idealism.

2. See Olegario González de Cardenal, "Development of a Theology of the Local Church from the First to the Second Vatican Council" *The Jurist* 52 (1992): 11–43. Also see Yves Congar's comment that Gréa's work, in its understanding of the church as both trinitarian and local, is "a kind of *hapax* in the theology of the era" in *L'Église: De saint Augustin à l'époque moderne* (Paris: Cerf, 1970), 458.

3. Full title: *Unity in the Church, or the Principle of Catholicism: Presented in the Spirit of the Church Fathers of the First Three Centuries,* ed. and trans. Peter C. Erb (Washington, DC: Catholic University of America Press, 1996).

4. Full title: *Symbolism: Exposition of the Doctrinal Differences between Catholics and Protestants as Evidenced by Their Symbolical Writings,* trans. James Burton Robertson with intro. by Michael J. Himes (New York: Crossroad Herder, 1997).

5. Yves Congar, *L'Église: De saint Augustin à l'époque moderne* (Paris: Cerf, 1970), 416–23, at 423. See also Michael J. Himes, *Ongoing Incarnation: Johann Adam Möhler and the Beginnings of Modern Ecclesiology* (New York: Crossroad Herder, 1997), 326: "Möhler recast the church as an integral part of the mystery of faith and not merely the bearer of the mysteries.... [He] made the church one of the truths it proclaimed. It was no longer the bearer of revelation but the embodiment of revelation, no longer the possessor of God's self-communication but the extension of that communication."

6. Louis Bouyer, *The Church of God: Body of Christ and Temple of the Spirit,* trans. Charles Underhill Quinn (Chicago: Franciscan Herald, 1982), 93.

7. On these points, see Yves Congar, "La signification oecuménique de l'oeuvre de Möhler," *Irénikon* 15 (1938): 113–30, at 115–16; Bouyer, *The Church of God,* 91–105, esp. 93; Himes, *Ongoing Incarnation,* 47–49.

8. The definitive work is Josef Rupert Geiselmann, *Die Katholische Tübinger Schule: Ihre theologische Eigenart* (Freiburg: Herder, 1964). In English, see Himes, *Ongoing Incarnation,* esp. 28–42; Donald J. Dietrich and Michael J. Himes, eds. *The Legacy of the Tübingen School: The Relevance of Nineteenth-Century Theology for the Twenty-First Century* (New York: Crossroad Herder, 1997); and Thomas F. O'Meara, *Romantic Idealism and Roman Catholicism: Schelling and the Theologians* (Notre Dame, IN: University of Notre Dame Press, 1982), esp. chapter 7, "Between Schelling and Hegel: The Catholic Tübingen School."

9. The standard reference is O'Meara, *Romantic Idealism and Roman Catholicism: Schelling and the Theologians.*

10. Möhler, *Unity in the Church,* 210.

11. Möhler, *Unity in the Church,* 84.

12. Möhler, *Unity in the Church,* 246.

13. Möhler, *Unity in the Church,* 247.

14. Möhler, *Unity in the Church,* 77.

15. Möhler, *Unity in the Church,* 92.

16. Möhler, *Unity in the Church,* 86.

17. Möhler, *Unity in the Church, inter alia,* 89, 96–97, 102–3, 122, 175, 211, 218, and esp. 111: "Christianity does not consist in expressions, formulae, or figures of speech; it is an inner life, a holy power, and all doctrinal concepts and dogmas have value only insofar as they express the inner life that is present within them."

18. One notes the similarity here between Möhler and Khomiakov on the church as the locus of knowledge.

19. Möhler, *Unity in the Church,* 124, 143–44, 153.

20. Möhler, *Unity in the Church,* 128.

21. Möhler, *Unity in the Church,* 124.

22. See Möhler, *Unity in the Church,* 166: "The constant law for the common organism is the image for the Church body: an unconstrained unfolding of the characteristics of single individuals that is enlivened by the Spirit so that, although there are different gifts, there is only one Spirit"; also ibid., 186: "Since the Church can have in it members of differing individualities, the needs of all can be satisfied. She gives nourishment to all, all move freely and happily, working in each other and for each other, one member supporting the other. Faith and knowledge share themselves and flow into one another. All together form a great organic whole enlivened by one Spirit. Single individualities grow and the whole flourishes.

"No constraint of individuality comes from *the Spirit* of the Catholic Church. Rather, she forms individualities in virtue and power. This can be seen in the character of Catholic writers. No Church has brought forth so many great and influential persons as the Catholic [Church] has throughout the years of her existence. Great, weighty duties awaken the Spirit."

23. Möhler, *Unity in the Church,* 167.

24. Möhler, *Unity in the Church,* 190: "But this is the essence of egoism, which must construct everything according to itself and impress its essence on everything so that the total order of the world and of salvation becomes a reflection of its limitation. This is the essence of every heresy and the basis of its nothingness: it wishes to raise the limited individuality of its master to generality."

25. Möhler, *Unity in the Church,* 192.

26. Möhler, *Unity in the Church,* 281.

27. Möhler, *Unity in the Church,* 278.

28. Möhler, *Unity in the Church,* 278.

29. Möhler, *Unity in the Church,* 218.

30. Möhler, *Unity in the Church,* 220–21.

31. Möhler, *Unity in the Church,* 221.

32. Cyprian, Letter 66, as cited in Möhler, *Unity in the Church,* 218. Also ibid., 219, 226, 236.

33. Möhler, *Unity in the Church,* 239.

34. Möhler, *Unity in the Church,* 246–47.

35. Möhler, *Unity in the Church,* 256.

36. See Congar, *L'Eglise,* 421: "After the *Einheit,* which had exalted the *divine* principle of the Church, Möhler was concerned with better emphasizing its *human* principle, against the pantheistic evolutionism of Schleiermacher; his study of the history of Saint Athanasius (1827) made him understand better, on the one hand, the importance of the christological and the need for redemption and, on the other, the reality and role of the papacy. He also understood better that his initial pneumatological point of view did not allow him to oppose strongly enough the Protestant idea of the invisible Church. From then on he came to the resolutely *christological* vision that was affirmed in successive editions of the *Symbolik.*" See also Himes, *Ongoing Incarnation,* 152–208; Bradford E. Hinze, "The Holy Spirit and the Catholic Tradition: The Legacy of Johann Adam Möhler," in *The Legacy of the Tübingen School: The Relevance of Nineteenth-Century Theology for the Twenty-First Century,* ed. Donald J. Dietrich and Michael J. Himes (New York: Crossroad Herder, 1997), 75–94, at 83.

37. See, for example, Möhler, *Symbolism,* 258–59: "And as in the world nothing can attain to greatness but in society; so Christ established a community; and his divine word, his living will, and the love emanating from him exerted an internal, binding power upon his followers; so that an inclination implanted by him in the hearts of believers, corresponded to his outward institution. And thus a living, well-connected, visible association of the faithful sprang up, whereof it might be said—there they are, there is his Church, his institution wherein he continueth to live, his spirit continueth to work, and the word uttered by him eternally resounds." Ibid., 309: "the whole body is bound and joined together in a living organism: and as the tree, the deeper and wider it striketh its roots into the earth, the more goodly a summit of intertwining boughs and branches it beareth aloft unto the sky, it is so with the congregation of the Lord. For the more closely the community of believers

is established with him, and is enrooted in him, as the all-fruitful soil; the more vigorous and imposing is its outward manifestation."

38. Möhler, *Symbolism,* 258–59.

39. Möhler, *Symbolism,* 306.

40. Möhler, *Symbolism,* 307.

41. Möhler, *Symbolism,* 284.

42. An interesting parallel is seen in Bradford Hinze's argument that, from the *Unity* to the *Symbolism,* the role of the Holy Spirit shifts from the *genesis* of faith to the *defense* of faith (Hinze, "The Holy Spirit and the Catholic Tradition: The Legacy of Johann Adam Möhler," 86).

43. See Congar, *L'Eglise,* 428–33.

44. Congar, "La signification oecuménique de l'oeuvre de Möhler," 123.

45. For (auto)biographical information, see: Peter J. Bernardi, "A Passion for Unity: Yves Congar's Service to the Church," *America* 192 (April 4–11, 2005): 8–11; Yves Congar, *Fifty Years of Catholic Theology: Conversations with Yves Congar,* ed. and intro. Bernard Lauret, trans. John Bowden (Philadelphia, Fortress, 1988); idem, *Journal de la Guerre: 1914–1918,* ed. Stéphane Audoin-Rouzeau and Dominique Congar (Paris: Cerf, 1997); idem, *Journal d'un théologien, 1946–1956,* ed. Étienne Fouilloux, with Dominique Congar, André Duval and Bernard Montagnes (Paris: Cerf, 2000); idem, *Mon journal du Concile: 1960–1966,* ed. présenté et annoté par Éric Mahieu (Paris: Cerf, 2002); idem, "Preface: The Call and the Quest, 1929–1963," in *Dialogue between Christians: Catholic Contributions to Ecumenism,* trans. Philip Loretz (Westminster, MD: Newman, 1966), 1–51. Joseph Famerée, "L'ecclésiologie du Père Yves Congar: Essai de synthèse critique," *Revue des Sciences Philosophiques et Théologiques* 76 (1992): 377–419; idem, "Formation et ecclésiologie du 'premier' Congar," in *Yves Congar: 1904–1995,* ed. André Vauchez (Paris: Cerf, 1999), 51–70; idem, "Orthodox Influence on the Roman Catholic Theologian Yves Congar, O.P.: A Sketch," *St. Vladimir's Theological Quarterly* 39 (1995): 409–16; Etienne Fouilloux, "Frère Yves, Cardinal Congar, Dominican: Itinéraire d'un théologien," *Revue des Sciences Philosophiques et Théologiques* 79 (1995): 379–404; idem, *Les catholiques & l'unité chrétienne du xix au xx siècle: Itinéraires européens d'expression française* (Paris: Centurion, 1982), esp. 205–68; William Henn, "Yves Congar, O.P. (1904–95)" *America* 173 (August 12, 1995): 23–25; Jean-Pierre Jossua, "Yves Congar: Un portrait," *Études* 383 (1995): 211–18; Joseph Komonchak, "A Hero of Vatican II: Yves Congar," *Commonweal* 122 (December 1, 1995): 15–17; Hervé Legrand, "Yves Congar (1904–1995): Une passion pour unité: Note sur ses intuitions et son herméneutique oecuménique, à l'occasion du centenaire de sa naissance," *Nouvelle Revue Théologique* 126 (October–December 2004): 529–54; Jean Puyo, *Une vie pour la vérité: Jean Puyo interroge le Père Congar* (Paris: Centurion, 1975); Timothy Radcliffe, "La mort du cardinal Yves-Marie Congar: Homélie," *Documentation Catholique* 92 (July 16, 1995): 688–90; Bernard Sesboüé, "Le drame de la théologie au XXieme siècle: A propos du *Journal d'un théologien (1946–1956)* du P. Yves Congar," *Recherche de Science Religieuse* 89 (April–June 2001): 271–87; idem, "Un dur combat pour une Église conciliaire: *Mon journal du Concile,* de Yves Congar" *Recherche de Science Religieuse* 91 (April–June 2003): 259–72; Jared Wicks, "Yves Congar's Doctrinal Service of the People of God," *Gregorianum* 84 (2003): 499–550; Alain Woodrow, "Congar's Hard-Won Victory," *The Tablet* 255 (April 28, 2001): 604–5.

46. For background, see Fouilloux, *Une Église en quête de liberté: La pensée catholique française entre modernisme et Vatican II, 1914–1962* (Paris: Desclée de Brouwer, 1998), esp. 124–48; Marie-Dominique Chenu, *Une école de théologie: Le Saulchoir* (Paris: Cerf, 1985).

47. Puyo, *Une vie pour la vérité,* 47–48: "[Möhler offered] a more synthetic, more vital, more communitarian vision: it is in communion with other men that one can attain to a culture which would be that of a people, to a faith which would be that of the church. Möhler had been revealed to me, as with so many other things, by Father Chenu. I discovered in [Möhler] a source, the source I had needed. When, later, I founded the collection *Unam Sanctam,* I decided to begin it with a translation of a work of Möhler's, *Unity in the Church.* [This work] was to give the collection its spirit. Because of difficulties with translation, the work was only number two [in the series]. What Möhler had done in the nineteenth century became for me an ideal with which I wished to guide, in the twentieth century, my own thought."

48. See Fouilloux, *Les catholiques & l'unité chrétienne du xix au xx siècle* for an encyclopedic account of Catholic involvement in modern ecumenism. See also Famerée, "Orthodox Influence on the Roman Catholic Theologian Yves Congar, O.P.: A Sketch."

49. Fouilloux, "Frère Yves, Cardinal Congar, Dominican: Itinéraire d'un théologien," 391.

50. Puyo, *Une vie pour la vérité,* 117.

51. See François Leprieur, *Quand Rome condamne: Dominicains et prêtres-ouvriers* (Paris: Plon/Cerf, 1989).

52. Congar, *Dialogue between Christians,* 42–45. Also Congar, *Journal d'un théologien: 1946–56,* ed. Étienne Fouilloux (Paris: Cerf, 2000).

53. Fouilloux, "Frère Yves, Cardinal Congar, Dominican: Itinéraire d'un théologien," 400. See also Congar, *Mon journal du Concile: 1960–66,* 2 vols., ed. Éric Mahieu (Paris: Cerf, 2002), esp. 2:511.

54. Quite belatedly, one should add. He was originally scheduled to be the first theologian named a cardinal after the council (on account of both his service to the church and his friendship with Pope Paul VI), but his critical comments on *Humanae vitae* (1968) and his signing of a 1969 *Concilium* appeal supporting greater freedom of theological inquiry removed him from consideration. In his place, Jean Daniélou, the Jesuit patrologist and exegete, was named in 1969. For further information, see Fouilloux, "Frère Yves, Cardinal Congar, Dominican: Itinéraire d'un théologien," 401–2.

55. Congar, "La pensée de Möhler et l'Ecclésiologie orthodoxe," *Irénikon* 12 (1935): 321–29, at 321.

56. Congar, *Chrétiens désunis: Principes d'un "Oecuménisme" Catholique* (Paris: Cerf, 1937), 59–60.

57. Congar, *Chrétiens désunis,* 70–71.

58. Congar, *Chrétiens désunis,* 110.

59. Congar, *Chrétiens désunis,* 77.

60. Congar, "Conclusion," in *Le Concile et les Conciles* (Paris: Cerf, 1960), 285–334, at 305–6.

61. Congar, *Chrétiens désunis,* 148.

62. Congar, *Chrétiens désunis,* 148.

63. Congar, *Chrétiens désunis,* 180: "Catholicity is the integration of multiplicity in unity; or rather — since unity is already given, and predominates — [it] is unity

assimilating multiplicity. Unity, here, is primary: it is in relationship to [unity] that multiplicity can be understood and rightly valued: catholicity is '*extensio unitatis,*' '*universalis capacitas unitatis.*' What makes plurality into catholicity is that unity preexists [plurality] and can therefore incorporate it. . . . The Catholic Church fears that 'ecumenism' would be a temptation, for unity, to let itself be drawn into the logic of multiplicity, which is relativism, syncretism, concordism, private judgment. . . . [The Catholic Church] knows that it has the mission and the grace of unity and fullness, and that it does not bear in vain the name and responsibility of catholicity."

64. Joseph Famerée, "'*Chrétiens désunis*' du P. Congar 50 ans après," *Nouvelle Revue Théologique* 110 (1988): 666–86, at 680. See also Jossua, "L'oeuvre oecuménique du Père Congar," *Études* 357 (1982): 543–55.

65. For example, his 1949 entry on "catholicity" for the encyclopedia *Catholicisme* emphasizes that catholicity is not only universality and assimilation of human cultural richness, but also orthodoxy, i.e., the fullness of truth that is *in* the church and *is* the church. Catholicity is a "unity not of poverty, but of plenitude," involving the church's entire life (in Congar, *Sainte Eglise: Études et approches ecclésiologiques* [Paris: Cerf, 1963], 159).

66. Congar, *Sainte Eglise,* 125.

67. Congar, *Sainte Eglise,* 125.

68. Congar, *Sainte Eglise,* 126.

69. Congar, *Sainte Eglise,* 115.

70. Congar, "De la communion des Églises à une ecclésiologie de l'Église universelle," in *L'Épiscopat et l'Église universelle,* ed. Yves Congar and Bernard-Dominique Dupuy (Paris: Cerf, 1962), 227–60, at 251.

71. Congar, *After Nine Hundred Years: The Background of the Schism between the Eastern and Western Churches* (New York: Fordham University Press, 1959), 58.

72. Congar, "De la communion des Églises à une ecclésiologie de l'Église universelle," 250.

73. Congar, "De la communion des Églises à une ecclésiologie de l'Église universelle," 250.

74. Congar, "De la communion des Églises à une ecclésiologie de l'Église universelle," 252: "From the perspective of the spiritual goods of salvation, each local community gathered around its bishop is the Church of God [in that place]."

75. Although eucharistic ecclesiologies were developed most prominently and radically by (Russian) Orthodox theologians, Congar insists that the West also affirms the eucharistic nature of the church; one need look only at the "innumerable texts" of Aquinas on the eucharist, in which he holds that the *res* of the sacrament is the unity of the mystical body of Christ. Congar thus has no difficulty, then, in writing that, for the West, "each local unity of celebration possesses total [ecclesial] fullness" (Congar, "De la communion des Églises à une ecclésiologie de l'Église universelle," 250).

76. Congar, "De la communion des Églises à une ecclésiologie de l'Église universelle," 250.

77. Congar, "De la communion des Églises à une ecclésiologie de l'Église universelle," 252; also "Note on the Words 'Confession,' 'Church,' and 'Communion.'" In *Dialogue between Christians: Catholic Contributions to Ecumenism,* trans. Philip Loretz (Westminster, MD: Newman, 1966), 184–213, at 204.

78. See Congar, "Théologie de l'Église particulière," in *Mission sans frontières,* ed. Antonin M. Henry (Paris: Cerf, 1960), 17–52, at 39–46.

79. Congar, "De la communion des Églises à une ecclésiologie de l'Église universelle," 232.

80. Congar, "De la communion des Églises à une ecclésiologie de l'Église universelle," 252; also Congar, "Théologie de l'Église particulière," 21, 47: "the faithful are incorporated directly into the universal church. Then, in a second moment, being thus incorporated into the universal church, they are made part of a local church and they constitute a local church."

81. "De la communion des Églises à une ecclésiologie de l'Église universelle," 252–53, 257; also Congar, *After Nine Hundred Years,* 81: "But the Universal Church exists and, under God, possesses her structure as a Church Universal. If we say under God, we mean that it was instituted by Jesus Christ."

82. Congar, "Théologie de l'Église particulière," 20–21: "The Church is not composed essentially of local communities. There is certainly a sense where one can say this [that the church is composed of local communities], but, in my opinion, it is not the decisive sense.... The church is composed of persons who are converted and incorporated into this transcendent Church (in relation to earthly categories and particularities). Saint Paul always speaks in these terms. For him, each believer is incorporated to the universal, transcendent Church."

83. "Théologie de l'Église particulière," 23; Congar, "Conclusion," 307.

84. Congar, "De la communion des Églises à une ecclésiologie de l'Église universelle," 259; also Congar, "Théologie de l'Église particulière," 23.

85. Congar, "De la communion des Églises à une ecclésiologie de l'Église universelle," 234–35.

86. Congar, "De la communion des Églises à une ecclésiologie de l'Église universelle," 259.

87. Congar, "De la communion des Églises à une ecclésiologie de l'Église universelle," 248.

88. Congar, "De la communion des Églises à une ecclésiologie de l'Église universelle," 260.

89. See Joseph Famerée, "Orthodox Influence on the Roman Catholic Theologian Yves Congar, O.P.: A Sketch."

90. Congar, "Conclusion," 328–29.

91. For a concise account of Congar's involvement in Vatican II, see Joseph Komonchak, "A Hero of Vatican II: Yves Congar," *Commonweal* 122 (December 1, 1995): 15–17.

92. Antonio Acerbi, *Due ecclesiologie: ecclesiologia giuridica e ecclesiologia di comunione nella Lumen Gentium* (Bologna: Edizioni Dehoniane, 1976).

93. For example, Joseph Komonchak, "Ecclesiology of Vatican II," *Origins* 28 (April 22, 1999): 763–68, at 763–64.

94. It is mentioned forty-six times in *Lumen gentium* alone. See Kilian McDonnell, "Vatican II (1962–1964), Puebla (1979), Synod (1985): *Koinonia/Communio* as an Integral Ecclesiology," *Journal of Ecumenical Studies* 25 (1988): 399–427, at 426.

95. See Joseph Komonchak, "Ecclesiology of Vatican II," 764: "*Lumen gentium*'s second chapter is titled 'The People of God,' and some interpreters have misinterpreted the chapter and its theme as if the council were now moving to another topic; some have even seen it as in a certain tension with the first chapter and its theme of mystery. It was not rare soon after the council to read suggestions that one had to choose between *body of Christ* and *people of God,* and the last decades have seen a

shift away from *people of God* to *communion* as the key to the council ecclesiology, once again almost as if one had to choose one or the other.

"How far such intentions are from the council's intention is clear from the explanation offered by the doctrinal commission when it introduced this new second chapter. Chapter 2, it said, was an intrinsic part of the consideration of the mystery of the church and must not be separated from its inner nature and purpose; the material had been divided into two chapters simply because one chapter would have been too long."

96. Kilian McDonnell, "Vatican II (1962–1964), Puebla (1979), Synod (1985): *Koinonia/Communio* as an Integral Ecclesiology," 426. Also the Final Report of the 1985 Extraordinary Synod of Bishops, John Paul II's 1989 Apostolic Exhortation on the Laity, *Christifideles laici,* and the Congregation for the Doctrine of the Faith's 1992 Letter, "Some Aspects of the Church Understood as Communion."

97. Oskar Saier's *"Communio" in der Lehre des Zweiten Vatikanischen Konzils* (Munich: Max Huebner, 1973) is the most comprehensive study of the concept. He notes that communion is used but once, in *Unitatis redintegratio* #2, to describe the church itself. It does, however, have significant ecclesial overtones elsewhere in the conciliar documents, as will be indicated.

98. The most prominent passages are *Lumen gentium* # 1–4, 13; *Ad gentes divinitus* #2; and, most explicitly, *Unitatis redintegratio* #2: "The highest exemplar and source of this mystery [of the church's unity] is the unity, in the Trinity of Persons, of one God, the Father and the Son in the Holy Spirit." All references in this section to conciliar documents are illustrative, not exhaustive.

99. *Lumen gentium* #1; *Gaudium et spes* #40–45.

100. *Lumen gentium* #3, 7, 10, 11, 26; *Sacrosanctum concilium* #10; *Christus Dominus* #11; *Unitatis redintegratio* #4, 22.

101. *Lumen gentium* #26; *Sacrosanctum concilium* #41; *Christus Dominus* #11.

102. *Lumen gentium* #23.

103. *Lumen gentium* #8, 15; *Unitatis redintegratio* #1–4, 14–15, 20, 22.

104. *Lumen gentium* #13.

105. Komonchak, "Ecclesiology of Vatican II," 765.

106. *Lumen gentium* #13. This theme is virtually omnipresent. See also for example, *Lumen gentium* #17; *Ad gentes divinitus,* 6, 8, 9, 15, 22.

107. *Lumen gentium* #13.

108. *Ad gentes divinitus,* 19: "This work of implanting the church in a particular human community reaches a definite point when the assembly of the faithful, already rooted in the social life of the people and to some extent conformed to its culture, enjoys a certain stability and permanence."

109. *Ad gentes divinitus,* 21. See also *Ad gentes divinitus,* 11, 16, 18–22, 25–26.

110. *Ad gentes divinitus,* 8; *Gaudium et spes* #42.

111. *Ad gentes divinitus,* 6.

112. *Sacrosanctum concilium* #37–40.

113. *Lumen gentium* #23. Also *Ad gentes divinitus*, 22; *Orientalium ecclesiarum,* 2.

114. Karl Rahner, "Commentary on 'Chapter III: The Hierarchical Structure of the Church, with Special Reference to the Episcopate,'" in *Commentary on the Documents of Vatican II,* ed. Herbert Vorgrimler (New York: Herder and Herder, 1967–69), 1:216.

115. Kilian McDonnell, "Vatican II (1962–1964), Puebla (1979), Synod (1985): *Koinonia/Communio* as an Integral Ecclesiology," 408. Alfonso Carrasco Rouco notes that "Chapter 3 of *Lumen Gentium* recalls the role of the primacy more than fifty times"; see his "Vatican II's Reception of the Dogmatic Teaching on the Roman Primacy," *Communio* 25 (Winter 1998): 576–603, at 579.

116. *Sacrosanctum concilium* #10.

117. *Christus Dominus* #30.

118. *Presbyterorum ordinis* #6.

119. *Lumen gentium* #26.

120. *Christus Dominus* #11.

121. *Presbyterorum ordinis* #5.

122. On the "fullness of orders," see *Lumen gentium* #21, 26; *Christus Dominus* #15. On the bishop's ministry of unity, see *Lumen gentium* #23; *Christus Dominus* #16.

123. *Christus Dominus* #11. Also *Christus Dominus* #2; *Lumen gentium* #27: "The pastoral charge, that is, the permanent and daily care of their sheep, is entrusted to them fully; nor are they to be regarded as vicars of the Roman Pontiff; for they exercise a power which they possess in their own right and are most truly said to be at the head of the people whom they govern."

124. In addition to *Lumen gentium* #26 and *Christus Dominus* #11, see *Sacrosanctum concilium* #41: "The bishop is to be considered the high priest of his flock from whom the life of his people in Christ is in some way derived and on whom it in some way depends.

"Therefore, all should hold in the greatest esteem the liturgical life of the diocese centered around the bishop, especially in his cathedral church. They must be convinced that the principal manifestation of the church consists in the full, active participation of all God's holy people in the same liturgical celebrations, especially in the same eucharist, in one prayer, at one altar, at which the bishop presides, surrounded by his college of priests and by his ministers."

125. *Lumen gentium* #23; *Christus Dominus* #3, 6.

126. *Lumen gentium* #18–24; *Christus Dominus* #1–4.

127. The very structure of *Christus Dominus* bears witness to such ordering: Chapter I is titled "The Bishops in Relation to the Universal Church," while Chapter II is called "Bishops in Relation to Their Own Churches or Dioceses."

128. *Christus Dominus* #36–38; *Lumen gentium* #23.

129. *Lumen gentium* #18–25; *Christus Dominus* #1–4.

130. Chapter III of *Lumen gentium,* for example, refers to the pope as the "Roman Pontiff" in paragraphs 18, 22 (six times), 23, 25 (seven times), 27, 29; the "Supreme Pontiff": in paragraphs 22, 29; and "successor of Peter" in paragraphs 18, 22 (three times), 23 (two times), 24, 25 (two times). Not once is he called "bishop of Rome."

131. *Lumen gentium* #23; also *Lumen gentium* #18.

132. See *Lumen gentium* #22: "The college or body of bishops has no authority, however, other than the authority which it is acknowledged to have in union with the Roman Pontiff, Peter's successor, as its head, his primatial authority over everyone, pastors or faithful, remaining intact. For the Roman Pontiff, by reason of his office as Vicar of Christ and as pastor of the entire church, has full, supreme, and universal power over the whole church, a power which he can always exercise freely"; *Lumen gentium* #25: "[infallible papal] definitions are rightly said to be irreformable by their very nature and not by reason of the consent of the church, in as much as they

were made with the assistance of the Holy Spirit promised to him in blessed Peter; and as a consequence they are not in need of the approval of others, and do not admit of appeal to any other tribunal"; *Lumen gentium*, Preliminary Explanatory Note #3–4: "The Pope alone, in fact, being head of the college, is qualified to perform certain actions in which the bishops have no competence whatsoever, for example, the convocation and direction of the college, approval of the norms of its activity, and so on. . . . It is for the Pope, to whom the care of the whole flock of Christ has been entrusted, to decide the best manner of implementing this care, either personal or collegiate, in order to meet the changing needs of the church in the course of time. The Roman Pontiff undertakes the regulation, encouragement, and approval of the exercise of collegiality as he sees fit. The Pope, as supreme pastor of the church, may exercise his power at any time, as he sees fit, by reason of the demands of his office"; and *Christus Dominus* #2: "In this church of Christ the Roman Pontiff, as the successor of Peter, to whom Christ entrusted the care of his sheep and his lambs, has been granted by God supreme, full, immediate, and universal power in the care of souls. As pastor of all the faithful his mission is to promote the common good of the universal church and the particular good of all the churches. He is therefore endowed with the primacy of ordinary power over all the churches."

133. Hermann J. Pottmeyer, *Towards a Papacy in Communion: Perspectives from Vatican Councils I and II,* trans. Matthew J. O'Connell (New York: Crossroad/ Herder and Herder, 1998), 114.

134. *Christus Dominus* #30.

135. Walter Kasper, "Church as *Communio.*" *Communio* 12 (1986): 100–117, at 115.

136. Jean-Marie Tillard, "The Church of God Is a Communion: The Ecclesiological Perspective of Vatican II," *One in Christ* 17 (1981): 117–31, at 124.

Chapter Three
The Fundamental Principles of Jean-Marie Roger Tillard's Theology of the Local Church

1. Jean-Marie Tillard, *Église d'églises: L'ecclésiologie de communion* (Paris: Cerf, 1987).

2. *Église d'églises,* 10. J. N. D. Kelly's *Early Christian Creeds* (London: Longman, 1972), in part, traces the development of these four "marks" or "notes" of the church. While silent on the meaning of "one" and "apostolic," which were largely confined to Eastern creeds, most definitively in the Nicene-Constantinopolitan creed, he examines "holy" and "catholic" through their emergence in Western creeds — most notably the Old Roman Creed and the Apostles' Creed. In the Old Roman Creed, dating from the end of the second century, "holy" refers primarily to the church's election by God, its predestination to glory, and the abiding presence of the Holy Spirit. Kelly emphasizes that the profession of ecclesial holiness "has nothing to do, in the first instance at any rate, with *de facto* goodness of character or moral integrity" (159); it is more a statement about God than about God's people. The Apostles' Creed, dating from the end of the fourth century, adds "catholic" to the Old Roman Creed; while often present in Eastern creeds, "catholic" first appears in Western creeds only in the late fourth century. In the creed, "catholic" has several possible meanings. First, and most common, it refers simply to the universal reach of the church. More provocatively, Irenaeus will use it to distinguish the "Great

Church" from heretical sects. Later, "catholic" will be used to describe the "orthodox" church in distinction to heretical sects such as Arianism and Donatism. The geographic and orthodox meanings often blend, as when Augustine and Ildefonsus of Toledo envision the "orthodox" church as the one which is spread over all the earth, not limited to a locality or region.

In the East, Kelly is strangely silent about the Creed of Constantinople's (381) addition of the celebrated phrase, "one, holy, catholic, and apostolic church" to the Nicene Creed (325).

3. *Église d'églises,* 16.

4. Jean-Marie Tillard, *L'Église locale: Ecclésiologie de communion et catholicité* (Paris: Cerf, 1995).

5. Jean-Marie Tillard, "The Local Church within Catholicity," *The Jurist* 52 (1992): 448–54, at 449.

6. *Église d'églises,* 15–16.

7. See *L'Église locale,* 30–31: "Patristic ecclesiology is founded on a theological interpretation of history, that of Luke. One should not be astonished that other New Testament traditions do not agree perfectly with certain of these [patristic] views. We are in one of the domains in which the living Tradition pulls from the ensemble of Revelation what it perceives to be the axis by which it articulates and organizes the data that it *receives* from the first communities. It would be enlightening to show how, this time in regard to the Trinity, an analogous process slowly led to the confession of the divinity of the [Holy] Spirit. The scheme for the structuring of the church by the threefold ministry — bishop, presbyters, deacons — is [also] revealed in this manner."

8. Tillard's reading of Luke-Acts finds common acceptance, as, for instance, when Luke Timothy Johnson writes that "Luke's concern in the first part of Acts is to show that the birth of the church is really the restoration of Israel, in fulfillment of God's promise.... When the good news is extended (through God's initiative!) to the Gentiles, then, it is not a replacement for Israel but rather an extension of the restored and messianic people" (*Living Jesus: Learning the Heart of the Gospel* [San Francisco: HarperSanFrancisco, 1999], 170).

9. Tillard notes that the New Testament never uses the word *ekklesia* to describe the gathering of the disciples before the death of Jesus on the cross: "[The New Testament] does not make an exception even for the nucleus of the apostles. It speaks of the church only to describe the group of those who, after Easter, believe in the Resurrection.... Luke's case is typical: although the word '*ekklesia*' does not appear at all in his first book, he uses it at least sixteen times in Acts" (*Église d'églises,* 18). He holds that the two apparent exceptions — Matthew 16:18 and 18:17 — refer respectively to the future church and to a Syro-Palestinian community in the 80s C.E. and its disciplinary practices (See *Église d'églises,* 18, footnote 7). We will return to the nature of *ekklesia* in the following section.

10. *The Eucharist: Pasch of God's People,* trans. Dennis L. Wienk (Staten Island, NY: Alba House, 1967), 30. French original: *L'Eucharistie, Pâque de l'Église* (Paris: Cerf, 1964).

11. Writing of the book of Revelation, Tillard differentiates between the Greek *kainos,* which means a "radical mutation" or "total renewal," and *neos,* which means "radical newness" (*Église d'églises,* 118).

12. See, for example, *Église d'églises,* 24; "The Local Church within Catholicity," 448; *L'Église locale,* 32–34, 57.

13. *Église d'églises,* 24.

14. *Église d'églises,* 32–33: "And this God, although linked to a particular people, is the universal God. The tension between the particular and the universal is therefore already encountered at this depth. The Church of God which shoots forth at Pentecost has its roots there."

15. Note that the Pentecost narrative is immediately preceded by the election of Matthias as the twelfth apostle.

16. *Église d'églises,* 117, 122.

17. *Église d'églises,* 19.

18. *Église d'églises,* 194.

19. See "Corps du Christ et Esprit Saint: Les exigences de la communion," *Irénikon* 63 (1990): 163–85, at 166–67, 169, 174–75.

20. *Église d'églises,* 21–22.

21. *Église d'églises,* 29.

22. See Hervé Legrand's excellent article, "Inverser Babel, mission de l'Eglise," *Spiritus* 11 (1970): 323–46. Gustavo Gutiérrez treats the issue of unity-in-diversity from a more pointedly political and cultural perspective: "The episode of Pentecost, sometimes regarded as the paradigm of a universal language, illustrates this necessary communication out of diversity. It is not about speaking a single language, but about being able to understand one another. The story tells of persons who have come from different places and have heard the disciples of Jesus and understood them—three times, it says—in their own language (Acts 2:6, 8, 11). All are speaking their own language, but they understand one another. Hence Pentecost, far from being a paradigm of anti-Babel, signifies instead that each of the various ethnic groups in Jerusalem is prized. There is only one reservation: the legitimate linguistic differences between them must not only not hinder mutual understanding but must favor it. . . . It is not imposed uniformity that is required, but understanding in diversity" (*The Density of the Present: Selected Writings* [Maryknoll, NY: Orbis, 1999], 201). Also "The great cultural and ethnic variety of Latin America must be welcomed without trying to impose a single cultural form, the Western, which arrived very late, as *the* culture of the region. To claim that Western culture brings the Gospel is to ignore the Church's experience of Pentecost. According to the Acts of the Apostles the miracle of Pentecost did not consist in speaking a single language; rather, those who had come from different racial and cultural areas heard the apostles speaking 'each in *his own language*.' This was not uniformity, but dialogue and unity based on respect for difference. It was not imposed integration, but acceptance of otherness and ethnic and cultural heterogeneity. The process designated by the neologism 'inculturation' is highly necessary. For a Christian it also has resonances of incarnation, and therefore of authentic and profound presence in history" (ibid., 109). If one grants that the sin of Babel is not its plurality of languages, but its pride before God, then Tillard and Gutiérrez are clearly in agreement over Pentecost's reversal of Babel and its positive regard of cultural and linguistic diversity; Tillard sees the reversal of Babel not in the restoration of a single language, but in the renewal of a divinely willed unity-in-diversity, i.e., communion.

23. *Chair de l'Église, chair du Christ: Aux sources de l'ecclésiologie de communion* (Paris: Cerf, 1992), 22.

24. *Église d'églises,* 22.

25. *L'Église locale,* 483.

26. The references are numerous. See, for instance, *L'Église locale,* 40: "[Other churches] are not added to the Church of Jerusalem. . . . They enter into its grace, its 'once-for-all' (*ephapax*), its *kairos*"; *L'Église locale,* 553: "The Church is not multiplied. The Spirit integrates into the fullness of Pentecost the *places* of human destiny." And *L'Église locale,* 41: "[communion] means not addition . . . [but] entry into complete participation in a full and definitive (already eschatological) gift from God."

27. *Église d'églises,* 114. Also *Église d'églises,* 24; *The Eucharist,* 300.

28. *Église d'églises,* 115.

29. See *Église d'églises,* 24: "From the outset it is necessary to note that when Deuteronomy evokes the assembly of the People of God on the day of the promulgation of the Law or of the renewal of the Covenant, it uses the word *Qahal* (Dt 9: 10; 10: 4; 18: 16; also 4: 10; 23: 2–9)."

30. *L'Église locale,* 31; "The Local Church within Catholicity," 448.

31. See *Église d'églises,* 31–32, where Tillard outlines universalistic tendencies in the Old Testament — "the divine project of salvation in regard to humanity as such, caught up in its misery" — ranging from God's marking of Cain and the covenant with Noah to the Books of Isaiah (especially Deutero-Isaiah) and Tobit, where "the nations in the whole world will all be converted and worship God in truth" (Tb 14: 6). In *L'Église locale,* Tillard notes that several Rabbinic schools taught the universal destination of the Law. For example, the *Mekhilta,* a "relatively ancient Canaanite midrash," states that the Law is "destined for all peoples" (see *L'Église locale,* 31, esp. nn. 3–5).

32. *Église d'églises,* 114.

33. *Église d'églises,* 114–25; *L'Église locale,* 32–34; "The Local Church within Catholicity," 449.

34. *Église d'églises,* 139. Additional references are numerous, but see, for example: *Église d'églises,* 59: "the surpassing effected by Christ Jesus is not a rupture. It is a flowering. The short phrase of Paul to the Romans: 'All Israel will be saved' (Rom 11:26) can express the radicality of this continuity"; *Église d'églises,* 123: "For the Church of God, relationship with Israel is constitutive [of its being]"; and several references to the church as the completion, not rupture, of the covenant in *Église d'églises,* 118, 160; *Chair de l'Église, chair du Christ,* 124.

35. *Chair de l'Église, chair du Christ,* 27. For a succinct presentation of Tillard's christology, see "Jésus Christ Vie du monde (perspective oecuménique)," *Irénikon* 55 (1982): 332–49.

36. *Église d'églises,* 121; *L'Église locale,* 33.

37. *Église d'églises,* 28.

38. *Église d'églises,* 28.

39. See *The Eucharist,* 277; *The Bishop of Rome*, trans. John de Satgé (Wilmington, DE: Michael Glazier, 1983), 166. French original: *L'évêque de Rome* (Paris: Cerf, 1982). And see especially *L'Église locale,* 33. The church's possession by God is bound up with its holiness, which we will treat in a subsequent section of this chapter.

40. *The Eucharist,* 42; *Chair de l'Église, chair du Christ,* 46, 75; *Église d'églises,* 35, 48, 72–74, 101, 399; *L'Église locale,* 136.

41. *Église d'églises,* 73: "The communion of Christians is not separable from that of the Father, Son, and Spirit. All ecclesial reality, being and action, is understood only in this light."

42. Such ordering does not, however, necessarily involve conflict or competition between the two. Divine precedence does not preclude, but enables, a synergistic relationship.

43. *L'Église locale,* 483, 553.

44. See, among others, *Église d'églises,* 24–27; *L'Église locale,* 32; "The Local Church within Catholicity," 448–49. By situating the church of God's emergence in Jerusalem within the context of salvation history, Tillard wishes to understand "Jerusalem" in primarily historical terms; while not opposed to more patristic understandings — e.g., Jerusalem as symbol or figure of national and eschatological hope — the concretely historical sense is decisive for him.

45. See 2 Chronicles 3: 1, which states that Moriah, the site of the sacrifice, was in Jerusalem; Genesis 22:2 does not mention Jerusalem.

46. See *L'Église locale,* 35, which includes scriptural references for each of these events.

47. *L'Église locale,* 35: "The *Ekklesia* appears in the *place* [Jerusalem] where God willed that Christ die and be raised, because in this *place* beats the heart of Israel." See also *Église d'églises,* 116: "[Christ's] work is inserted in the covenant and the promise."

48. See *L'Église locale,* 33: "The community of Jerusalem . . . thus realizes the integrality, the *katholou* of the plan of God," and *L'Église locale,* 34: "It is thus the community where the divine *oikonomia* reaches its moment (*kairos*) of fullness."

49. *L'Église locale,* 557: "From the local Church, presence of the *ephapax* of Jerusalem, to the fullness of the heavenly Jerusalem, the *mysterion* (Rom 16: 26; Eph 3: 9) is accomplished by the communion of Christians in the once-for-all Pasch of Christ." Also *Église d'églises,* 91, 118; *L'Église locale,* 35.

50. *The Eucharist,* 201–2.

51. See *Église d'églises,* 32–33.

52. This section will present locality primarily through the perspective of Jerusalem. A fuller treatment will be found in our analysis of the church's catholicity.

53. *L'Église locale,* 15.

54. Joseph Komonchak's "The Local Church and the Church Catholic: The Contemporary Theological Problematic" *The Jurist* 52 (1992): 416–47, gives a perceptive account of the church's intrinsic engagement with culture and history. See especially p. 439: "It must also be asked whether it is even possible to speak of diverse Christian experiences without taking account of the total human experience in which the constitutive genetic principles [of the church] are received. As history amply demonstrates, social, cultural, and even geographical factors have been crucial determinations of the various legitimate diversities among local realizations of the Church. These factors, then, are not simply receptive 'matter'; they have also served as the 'formal principle' of local churches. It is, of course, true that the gospel does effect a *discretio spirituum* within particular cultures, and it is the gospel and not the cultural particularities which primarily generate a Church. But a local church arises out of the encounter between the gospel and a particular culture, a set of specific social and historical experiences, and this encounter, as it differs from other encounters of gospel and culture, must also generate a constitutively different local church." And p. 447: "For the objective principles of the Church's realization do not constitute the Church except insofar as they are received in the acts of faith, hope, and love of the human members of the Church. Under the Word and by the power of the Spirit men and women are also the subjects of the Church's self-realization.

Thus the formal principle of the Church's genesis includes not only the gifts of God but also the freedom of men and women with which they receive them.

"When the human subjects of the Church's realization are introduced into ecclesiology, the focus begins to shift to include also the local communities in which alone the Church is realized, since human freedom is never realized except in particular individuals and communities and as a moment in their historical self-projects. This does *not* mean an option for the local in place of the universal; in fact, it represents the basic methodological shift required in order to understand why it is a fatal mistake to counterpose the two adjectives. But it does mean that a general ecclesiology of the formal elements of the Church has to include as a necessary and intrinsic dimension a consideration of the co-constituting freedom of the human subjects of the Church's realization."

55. *L'Église locale,* 35.

56. See *L'Église locale,* 16–17: "However, thus linked to the earth, [the church] is, in the grace of the Spirit, the citizen of a world to come, of a future city already its own (Phil 3:20; see Eph 2:6, 19). It comes from it. It draws its very being from it. Certainly, it does not yet see it and sighs toward it (Heb 13:14), as a pilgrim. Nonetheless, it lives from its goods. It makes of this even the experience — that of the communion in Christ of the *totality* of the fellow-citizens (Eph 2:19) of the City of God — of the eucharistic synaxis. It already celebrates there the great Liturgy of the Lamb, the eternal communion that the Apocalypse exalts. It is, at the Eucharist, the *already* of that to which it sighs, although it is so only in faith.

"The Church is thus found at the conjunction of the *earth* (with all that this implies for its relation to history, culture, suffering and joy, the problems of societies and their projects) and of the eschatological *future* (which has already found its fullness in the Lord Jesus Christ). [It is] the meeting of the *place* of history (which God takes seriously) and of the *beyond* of time (where the *totality* of the gift of God is unfurled for the *totality* of the People who welcome it). [It is] the meeting, in the glorified Lord, of that which rises from the 'earthly Adam' (in communion with his 'places of humanity') and of that which descends from the Father (giving communion with the *fullness* of his goods, with their *totality*).

"[It is] impossible, therefore, to understand the Church of God without seeing that in it the 'human' *place* is found seized in a *totality* which stems from an entirely other register than that of the world, since it has its source in the *fullness* of the Lord exalted by the Father, therefore in the eschatological beyond. This is why the Church is inseparably local and catholic. One cannot look for it elsewhere than there where the *katholou* (the whole, fullness) of the eschatological gift of the Spirit comes, *in* the places of history, to plant the reality of the new (*kainè*) humanity, that which is not *of* this world." This tension between the historical and the eschatological, so present at Pentecost, will be a central theme in our subsequent treatment of the "marks" of the church.

57. *Église d'églises,* 122–23: "One does not break with the Promise; one enlarges it. One does not deny the figure of Abraham; one is focused on his faith and by this on his interiority. His heritage is no longer limited by race, by the circumcision attached to it, but it is opened onto a faith rooted in his faith as the 'father of believers' (Rom 4:9–12, 16–25). And this faith binds in unity Jews and Greeks (Gal 3:28–29).

"The Church of God thus becomes, in Christ Jesus, the fundamental and radical communion of pagans with the 'heritage of Abraham,' with the Promise, with the blessing joined to Abraham's faith. One finds there an essential and primary dimension of *koinonia,* too little underlined."

58. *L'Église locale,* 133.

59. See *Église d'églises,* 73: "The communion of Christians is not separable from that of the Father, Son, and Spirit. All ecclesial reality, being and action, is understood only in this light."

60. See *The Eucharist,* 42; *Chair de l'Église, chair du Christ,* 46, 75; *Église d'églises,* 35, 48, 72–74, 101, 399; *L'Église locale,* 136.

61. See *L'Église locale,* 34, 36, 39–41.

62. Tillard, "Preparing for Unity — A Pastoral Approach to Ecumenism," *One in Christ* 16 (1980): 2–18, at 4.

63. See *L'Église locale,* 40, 553, 558.

64. *L'Église locale,* 41.

65. *Église d'églises,* 298.

66. References are numerous. See, for instance, "Corps du Christ et Esprit Saint: Les exigences de la communion," 180–81; *Chair de l'Église, chair du Christ,* 22–24.

67. *L'Église locale,* 553. Also *L'Église locale,* 75: "How is the Church *multiple* and not *multiplied?* Extending Augustine's intuition of the homogeneity between the eucharistic body and the ecclesial body, one may say that in one hundred Churches there is no more of the Church of God than in the Church of Jerusalem, just as in one hundred eucharistic breads there is no more of the body of the Lord than in one single eucharistic bread."

68. This is a favorite theme of Tillard. See *Église d'églises,* 38, 298; *Chair de l'Église, chair du Christ,* 64; *L'Église locale,* 81.

69. On the confluence of baptismal and ecclesial grace, see *The Eucharist,* 67–68.

70. *Summa theologiae* III, 69, 5.

71. *Summa theologiae* III, 69, 2.

72. Tillard, "One Church of God: The Church Broken in Pieces," *One in Christ* 17 (1981): 2–12, at 5. Also *Chair de l'Église, chair du Christ,* 52: "The West affirms moreover with conviction that this unity of Christians has nothing of a simple psychological unity, of an exterior unanimity, of a concord founded on purely human sentiments. Hilary of Poitiers... will say this well in his *De Trinitate:* this unity is founded in God. Such is the fruit of baptism, which the eucharist leads to its fulfillment."

73. This theme dominates Tillard's first major work, *The Eucharist,* and remains prominent in all of his subsequent writings. Representative of this current is *Chair de l'Église, chair du Christ,* 53: "The principal effect of the eucharist — the scholastic would say the *res eucharistiae* — is therefore full insertion into the Body of Christ, the Body of which the risen Lord is the Head, the Body formed of this Head and of its members who are the baptized, the Body which the Spirit — given by Christ, who receives it from the Father — vivifies." The nature and effects of the eucharist will be developed in greater detail in chapter 4.

74. *Église d'églises,* 57.

75. In addition to note 68, see *Église d'églises,* 239: "From the Last Supper to the last eucharist that the Church will celebrate in history, there is only one eucharist." Tillard bases his argument on the principle that the eucharistic liturgy does not "re-do" or "renew" Christ's *ephapax* sacrifice, but rather "re-presents" it. This is a seriously complicated issue with immense repercussions, not only for the Catholic

Church, but also for its ecumenical dialogues, especially with Anglicans and Protestants. Clear presentations of the theme may be found in ARCIC-I's agreed statement on the eucharist (which Tillard helped to draft), as well as in Tillard's articles "Liturgical Reform and Christian Unity," *One in Christ* 19 (1983): 227–49, and especially "Sacrificial Terminology and the Eucharist," *One in Christ* 17 (1981): 306–23. The latter argues that recent changes in sacrificial terminology brought about by the ecclesial, liturgical, and sacramental renewal of Vatican II — particularly the "rejection of *renovare* and the choice of *perpetuare* to indicate properly the unity with the sacrifice of the Cross" (322) — are actually more faithful to the Council of Trent than is most post-Tridentine theology, which tended to obscure the *ephapax* nature of Christ's sacrifice through its use of terms like *renovatio* and *repetitio* (318).

76. "Preparing for Unity — A Pastoral Approach to Ecumenism," 4.

77. "Preparing for Unity — A Pastoral Approach to Ecumenism," 4.

78. See "We Are Different," *One in Christ* 22 (1986): 62–72, at 63–64. Tillard contrasts the wholly eschatological ethos of Orthodoxy with the more historical one of Catholicism; the former refuses to separate the sacraments of initiation, while the latter construes them more developmentally.

79. *Unitatis redintegratio,* Vatican II's Decree on Ecumenism, states "For those who believe in Christ and have been properly baptized are put in some, though imperfect, communion with the Catholic Church.... They therefore have a right to be called Christians, and with good reason are accepted as sisters and brothers in the Lord by the children of the Catholic Church" (#3), and, more tortuously, "Nevertheless, the divisions among Christians prevent the church from realizing the fullness of catholicity proper to her in those of her children who, though joined to her baptism, are yet separated from full communion with her" (#4).

80. For example, see the landmark 1982 statement of the Faith and Order Commission of the World Council of Churches, "Baptism, Eucharist, and Ministry." Tillard was a vice-president of Faith and Order during its drafting.

81. Tillard, "Ecumenism Enters a New Phase," 11–12. Delivered in September 1999 in Cambridge, England, on the occasion of the launching of a new center for ecumenism, this paper is as yet unpublished.

82. See "Preparing for Unity — A Pastoral Approach to Ecumenism," 17: "The 'evangelical space' is a space of patience as well as one of conversion. Patience guarantees the seriousness of conversion; this in its turn guarantees the authenticity of the unity which is being built up.

"More profoundly still, this 'space' is one of poverty. For in the gospel nothing is accomplished without acceptance of the principle of loss. This is true even of the Son: according to the Letter to the Philippians *kenosis* is the very heart of his mission. Here we ought to draw attention to an ecclesiology of *harpagmos*.... No unity will be possible unless the Churches who are richest in doctrine and theology — I do not say faith — and who are the proudest of their traditions are the first to be ready to renounce, *if it is necessary,* some of their particular features for the sake of *communion*."

Also Tillard, "A New Age in Ecumenism," *One in Christ* 27 (1991): 320–31, at 331: "If we accept going beyond our immediate experience and joining up in hope with the pioneers once more, then the coming age will be one of ecumenism at depth. To put it in uncushioned terms, it will require us to go to the extent of the demand involved in faithfulness to God himself. Many of our contemporaries accuse the Churches of double-talk, declaring in and out of season that they hold progress toward unity to be one of their priorities, and simultaneously baring their teeth if any precious points of their confessional tradition are challenged. From now on we must act quite frankly in all the Churches.... The grace of the coming age may well be this: to do for unity all that faith in Christ requires, to die to sterile enclosure in our own selves and to all its egoistic claims."

83. *The Eucharist,* 284.

84. Tillard, "The Church of God Is a Communion: The Ecclesiological Perspective of Vatican II," *One in Christ* 17 (1981): 117–31, at 120.

85. *Église d'églises,* 134.

86. See notes 40 and 41.

87. See *Église d'églises,* 134, and "The Church of God Is a Communion: The Ecclesiological Perspective of Vatican II," 120.

88. *The Bishop of Rome,* 166.

89. *Église d'églises,* 28.

90. *The Eucharist,* 21.

91. See *The Eucharist,* 314: "By the expression Pasch of Christ, we designate here the Paschal Mystery of Jesus, his passage from this world to the world of the Father, realized historically by the events of his death and of his resurrection and ascension. This traditional designation recovers a theological foundation which is more than ample. The Pasch of Jesus, realized at the moment when the Jewish People celebrated the memorial... of its passage from the slavery of Egypt to the freedom of the Promised Land, accomplishes... what was only preparation and prefiguration of his own Mystery. In this passage he trains the whole Church after him."

92. *The Eucharist,* 21.

93. *Chair de l'Église, chair du Christ,* 133.

94. *The Eucharist,* 67. In the same work Tillard notes: "The mystery of salvation necessarily binds together these two moments, these two powerful interventions of God, being at once redemption (rooting out of sin) and communion.... Medieval theology will express this in distinguishing two effects of grace, one of cure (*gratia sanans*) and another of super-elevation (*gratia elevans*). We must regret that current theological teaching has lost a bit of the dynamic connection between these two effects of grace (so clearly underlined by Saint Thomas in his scheme of the *justificatio impii*). Man, if we keep the balance of the mystery, is not pardoned and sanctified, redeemed and super-elevated. He is pardoned, redeemed in order to be sanctified, super-elevated. A genuine theology of salvation will have to take into account without loss these two moments: Salvation does not consist only of redemption, nor only of sanctification. It consists of a redemption opening into the communion of life, in a communion of life rooted in redemption" (39–40).

95. *The Eucharist,* 197.

96. *Chair de l'Église, chair du Christ,* 133.

97. Augustine, *Sermo* 362, cited in *Chair de l'Église, chair du Christ,* 144.

98. Augustine, *De Doctrina Christiana,* III, 32, 45, cited in *Église d'églises,* 52.

99. These two ecclesial moments are the heart of Tillard's thesis in *The Eucharist.* See especially, *The Eucharist,* 129, 276.

100. *The Eucharist,* 278: "The wandering church can then be defined as the communion of life of men with the Father and among themselves in Jesus the Lord, already realized, but, however, still in a state of hope, of tension toward the definitive enjoyment of the good possessed now in the modalities of a not total bloom, of a simple seed, proper to the Christian condition in the stage of faith."

101. *The Eucharist,* 315.

102. *The Eucharist,* 202.

103. *Lumen gentium* #8.

104. *The Eucharist,* 199.

105. *The Eucharist,* 203. One hears echoes of Aquinas's teaching on the eucharist, where he writes of how "this sacrament foreshadows the divine fruition, which shall come to pass in heaven; and according to this it is called *viaticum,* because it supplies the way of winning thither" (*Summa theologiae* III, 73, 4).

106. *Église d'églises,* 50.

107. *The Eucharist,* 129.

108. *Église d'églises,* 51.

109. *Église d'églises,* 51. This phrase is Augustine's, but no source is given.

110. *L'Église locale,* 9–10.

111. See, for instance, *L'Église locale,* 36: "The *Ekklesia* is therefore catholic more by the possession of integrality of the goods 'of the Promise' (Acts 2:39) than by their extension," and *L'Église locale,* 393: "the notion of catholicity taken in its traditional sense denotes, in effect, inseparably both the fullness of the divine gift spread out (of which the local Church is the fruit) and the totality of times and human places taken up in this fullness."

112. Avery Dulles, *The Catholicity of the Church* (Oxford: Clarendon, 1985). Dulles presents catholicity "from above" as "the fullness of God in Christ," which involves the plenitude of God's trinitarian unity and diversity; "from below" as "the aspirations of nature," in which that fullness of divine grace reaches down into creation in order to heal and transform it; "in breadth" as "mission and communion," whereby the church spreads itself throughout the world to all peoples and cultures; and "in length," which refers to the development and reform in time of the church and its tradition.

113. *L'Église locale,* 126.

114. For bibliography and references, see *L'Église locale,* 17–29. See also Wolfgang Beinert, *Um das dritte Kirchenattribut: Die Katholizität der Kirche im Verständnis der evangelische-lutherischen und römisch-katholischen Theologie der Gegenwart* (Essen: Ludgerus-Verlag Hubert Wingen KG, 1964), 1:13–92, esp. 36–77.

115. Avery Dulles states that the nearest scriptural equivalent for catholicity is the Greek *pleroma,* meaning "fullness" (*The Catholicity of the Church,* 31).

116. *L'Église locale,* 21–22.

117. *See Chair de l'Église, chair du Christ,* 53–76.

118. See Thomas Aquinas, *The Sermon-Conferences of St. Thomas Aquinas on the Apostles' Creed,* trans. and intro. Nicholas Ayo (Notre Dame, IN: University of Notre Dame Press, 1988).

119. See Gustave Thils's still-definitive *Les notes de l'Église dans l'apologétique catholique depuis la Réforme* (Louvain: Gembloux, 1937).

120. *L'Église locale,* 34.

121. *L'Église locale,* 41.

122. See n. 64.

123. "The Local Church within Catholicity," 449–51.

124. Joseph Komonchak, "The Local Church and the Church Catholic: The Contemporary Theological Problematic," 419.

125. Komonchak, "The Local Church and the Church Catholic: The Contemporary Theological Problematic," 436.

126. See Tillard, "L'Universal et le Local: Réflexion sur Église universelle et Églises locales," *Irénikon* 60 (1987): 483–94, at 486: "We have often said, and written, that one of the most important fruits of Vatican II has been its correction of the Catholic Church's allergy in the last centuries toward diversity. The council put a brake on the will to Romanize Catholicism at any cost, orchestrated (since the arrival of various Ultramontanisms) by influential persons convinced that there was salvation only in Roman centralization. Unity and centralization, centralization and mimicry in regard to Rome became synonyms. All resistance to Romanization appeared suspect. In the West 'difference' was tolerated; it was not welcomed as a gift from God to be guarded and promoted."

127. For "unity-in-diversity," see, among others, *The Bishop of Rome,* 152, 181; *Église d'églises,* 22, 174–75, 181–83, 214, 401.

128. See, for instance, *Lumen gentium* #23: "This multiplicity of local churches, unified in a common effort, shows all the more resplendently the catholicity of the undivided church."

129. One might think of Karl Barth's analogous comment that "[Jesus Christ's] way into the spaciousness of the world leads out from the narrowness of Israel" (*Dogmatics in Outline,* trans. G. T. Thomson [New York: Harper & Row, 1959], 73).

130. See *L'Église locale,* 77: "The local church of Ephesus is *wholly* the Church, but it is not the *whole* church." The English translation loses some of the French's wordplay: "L'Église locale d'Éphèse a *le tout* de l'Église mais elle n'est pas *toute* l'Église."

131. *L'Église locale,* 41.

132. *Église d'églises,* 362.

133. *L'Église locale,* 83–88. For instance, *L'Église locale,* 88: "Such is the church: communion *restored* by the reconciliation in Christ of humanity with *all* of itself, *all* its destiny and its origin, even with *all* the cosmos, and supremely with God." Recapitulation will be presented at greater length in chapter r.

134. See *Église d'églises,* 44–45, 47, 57, 60, 211; *L'Église locale,* 142.

135. *Église d'églises,* 57.

136. Inculturation will be examined more fully in chapter 6, where Tillard's thought will be evaluated for its reception of Vatican II.

137. Tillard, "Évangéliser l'humanité," 6. This paper is not yet published.

138. Tillard, "Reception — Communion," *One in Christ* 28 (1992): 307–22, at 321. Also *L'Église locale,* 93–105.

139. *Lumen gentium* #13. For Tillard, see *The Eucharist,* 198; *Église d'églises,* 183; *Chair de l'Église, chair du Christ,* 97; *L'Église locale,* 126.

140. For instance, *L'Église locale,* 102–4.

141. *Lumen gentium* #13.

142. *Chair de l'Église, chair du Christ,* 22. Also *Chair de l'Église, chair du Christ,* 23–24; *L'Église locale,* 105ff.; "L'Universal et le Local: Réflexion sur Église universelle et Églises locales," 492, 494.

143. Tillard finds support for his position in such papal documents as Paul VI's *Evangelii nuntiandi* (1975), as well as John Paul II's *Slavorum apostoli* (1985) and especially his 1986 address at Alice Springs to Australian Aborigines. As will be seen in chapter 6, this last document is central to Tillard's theology and ecclesiology.

144. See, for instance, Tillard, "Dogmatic Development and *Koinonia.*" In *New Perspectives in Historical Theology: Essays in Memory of John Meyendorff,* ed. Bradley Nassif (Grand Rapids, MI: Eerdmans, 1996), 172–85.

145. *Lumen gentium* #8.

146. See *The Eucharist,* 45, 198; *Église d'églises,* 59, 118–19, 185; *Chair de l'Église, chair du Christ,* 124.

147. Dulles, *The Catholicity of the Church,* 105.

148. *Église d'églises,* 184.

149. *Église d'églises,* 174.

150. *L'Église locale,* 74.

151. See *Église d'églises,* 226: "It is through the apostolic witness, borne in the power of the Spirit, that one knows what has arrived in Jesus, what God has accomplished in him, . . . Salvation is therefore recognized as a gift coming not from a vague and abstract source, but from the Father in and through Jesus Christ, the faithful servant of the Gospel of God. This relation to the *acta* and *dicta* of Christ Jesus is essential. It is fundamentally for this reason that the church is said to be founded on the Apostles (Eph 2:20)."

152. *Église d'églises,* 117.

153. *Église d'églises,* 20.

154. See note 64. Also "The Local Church within Catholicity," 449–50; Tillard, "The Apostolic Foundations of Christian Ministry," *Worship* 63 (1989): 290–300, at 293.

155. *Église d'églises,* 28; *L'Église locale,* 408, 553; "The Church of God Is a Communion: The Ecclesiological Perspective of Vatican II," 121; "The Local Church within Catholicity," 449; "The Apostolic Foundations of Christian Ministry," 293.

156. Tillard, "Ecclésiologie de communion et exigence oecuménique," *Irénikon* 59 (1986): 201–30, at 226; "The Apostolic Foundations of Christian Ministry," 294.

157. Tillard, "The Presence of Peter in the Ministry of the Bishop of Rome," *One in Christ* 27 (1991): 101–20, at 105.

158. "The Apostolic Foundations of Christian Ministry," 294.

159. "The Presence of Peter in the Ministry of the Bishop of Rome," 106.

160. "The Apostolic Foundations of Christian Ministry," 293.

161. For succinct overviews, see *Église d'églises,* 241; Tillard, "Sacraments et communion ecclésiale," *Nouvelle Revue Théologique* 111 (1989): 641–63, esp. 641–43; Tillard, "The Eucharist in Apostolic Continuity," *One in Christ* 24 (1988): 14–24, at 14–17.

162. See *Église d'églises,* 241.

163. *Église d'églises,* 182.

164. *Église d'églises,* 228. See also *L'Église locale,* 525; "The Presence of Peter in the Ministry of the Bishop of Rome," 118.

165. Tillard, "Reception — Communion," *One in Christ* 28 (1992): 307–22, at 319. Also *L'Église locale,* 525; "The Apostolic Foundations of Christian Ministry," 296; Tillard, "Autorité et mémoire dans l'Église," *Irénikon* 61 (1988): 332–46, 481–84, esp. 344.

166. The contrast between "successor" and "vicar" is a constant theme in Tillard's ecclesiology, especially in regard to the papacy. See, for instance, "The Presence of Peter in the Ministry of the Bishop of Rome," 106: "The apostolic group was to be replaced by nobody. It was to have 'vicars.' " For a presentation of the dual function

of the apostolic college—its intransmissible function of *witness*, its transmissible one of *judgment* for the preservation of communion—see *Église d'églises*, 254–56.

167. *L'Église locale*, 553.
168. *Église d'églises*, 384.
169. *Église d'églises*, 58.
170. "The Apostolic Foundations of Christian Ministry," 291.
171. "The Local Church within Catholicity," 449.
172. *L'Église locale*, 53.
173. *L'Église locale*, 16.

Chapter Four
The Local Church Is a Communion of Faith and Sacrament

1. *Lumen gentium* #26.

2. Tillard, "How Is Christian Truth Taught in the Roman Catholic Church?" *One in Christ* 34 (1998): 293–306, at 294.

3. *L'Église locale*, 263.

4. *Chair de l'Église, chair du Christ*, 151.

5. See *Presbyterorum ordinis* #18: "Christians are nourished by the word of God from the double table of holy scripture and the eucharist." See also the analogous statements of *Dei verbum* #21: "[the church] never ceases, above all in the sacred liturgy, to partake of the bread of life and to offer it to the faithful from the one table of the word of God and the body of Christ," and *Perfectae caritatis* #6: "Thus, refreshed at the table of the divine law and of the sacred altar, let [professed religious] love the members of Christ as sisters and brothers." Tillard was a *peritus* on the commission that prepared this last conciliar document. See also *Sacrosanctum concilium* #51 and *Ad gentes divinitus* #6.

6. *L'Église locale*, 354.

7. *Chair de l'Église, chair du Christ*, 150.

8. Tillard, "The Apostolic Foundations of Christian Ministry," *Worship* 63 (1989): 290–300, at 290.

9. *Chair de l'Église, chair du Christ*, 147.

10. *Chair de l'Église, chair du Christ*, 147.

11. *Église d'églises*, 140.

12. See Tillard, "Faith: The Believer and the Church," *Mid-Stream* 34 (1995): 45–60, at 47.

13. *Église d'églises*, 31–32.

14. The written Gospel is essential, however, for the life of the church: "Without these writings—including the *kerygma* and its echo in the life of the communities and persons which 'receive' it—the *euaggelion* would not be communicated in a human way, and its transmission would be reduced to a kind of enthusiastic experience based on feelings more than on the knowledge of what God really did in Christ Jesus. Hence the authority of Scriptures as sources of the knowledge of Christ in whom the *euaggelion tou Theou* is fulfilled, the 'hope' realized. This collection of human writings, 'recognized' as inspired, is 'received' as the fundamental norm of the faith, prayer commitment, mission and life of the disciples of Christ, whoever they may be. It is impossible to be a Christian community and a Christian person without 'receiving' at least their authority and message" (Tillard, "The Gospel of God and the Church of God," *Mid-Stream* 35 (1996): 363–75, at 366.)

15. Tillard, "Faith: The Believer and the Church," 47.

16. On joys and sorrows, see *Chair de l'Église, chair du Christ,* 150: "Yet, the Word becomes, effectively, the dynamism of life, with the Spirit, only when the community — which the eucharistic synaxis gathers and welds together — knows to make of it not an archival piece of a sacred book but an ever-present reality questioning humanity to the quick of its hopes and failures, its joys and tears, its happiness and suffering."

The motif *Ecclesia iam ab Abel justo* has deep patristic roots — for example, Gregory the Great and Augustine — and received conciliar approbation at Vatican II in *Lumen gentium* #2, due, in large measure, to the research of Yves Congar; see his "Ecclesia ab Abel," in *Festschrift Karl Adam,* ed. Marcel Reding (Düsseldorf: Patmos, 1952), 79–110. Tillard uses the motif to express the continual reach of God's mercifulness to all humanity. See Tillard, "The Gospel of God and the Church of God," 364, and *Église d'églises,* 31–33.

17. *L'Église locale,* 55.

18. For a creative and profound study of salvation, see David F. Ford's *Self and Salvation: Being Transformed* (New York: Cambridge University Press, 1999). Ford insists that Christian salvation embraces every dimension of human life, culminating in eucharistic feasting which engages all the physical and spiritual senses: "Christian vocation can be summed up as being called to the feast of the Kingdom of God. The salvation of selves is in responding to that invitation. The book's themes of joy and responsibility here come together in the most complete way: the responsibility to respond to an invitation into joy. The book's menu of a limited number of dialogues [Levinas, Jüngel, Ricoeur], themes [worship, hospitality, service, feasting], and saints [Thérèse of Lisieux and Dietrich Bonhoeffer] has focussed on a theology of the face of Jesus Christ leading into a spirituality of feasting before that face" (272).

19. *Église d'églises,* 188–91.

20. *Chair de l'Église, chair du Christ,* 27.

21. As explained in chapter 3, the plan of God reaches its fullness, its catholicity at Pentecost, where all peoples are gathered into the church of God. Accordingly, the church stands not as the rejection, but as the fulfillment of the salvific covenant formed at Sinai; the Christian faith and church are absurd apart from their relationship to Judaism. In unpublished class notes for a course on memory, Tillard states: "The Gentiles do not replace Israel in the plan of God (which is guarded in the memory of the People). They are joined to the Holy People and open it unto the ends of the entire world.... The Church of God is built and develops in remembering its origin in Israel.... A thorough study of the ensemble of Christian ritual shows that the Church has not repudiated its roots, but that it is aware of flourishing on them and because of them. The grave tension between Gentile Christians and Jewish Christians, of which Acts 15 is the echo, does not undercut this rooting and dependence: the Church of the Gentiles is born in the wake of the great Pentecost [in Jerusalem]. Thus built on the memory of its origin, the Church of God cannot remain indifferent to the lot of Israel" (unpublished class notes, 49–50).

22. *Église d'églises,* 33–35: "Were it necessary to sum up in a single word the concrete content of the salvation, individual as well as collective, announced in the Gospel of God, we would use — following many of the Fathers — *communion,* the word which sums up the 'summaries' of Acts. For biblical thought, such as the first centuries understood it, salvation is called communion.... In many Pauline and Johannine passages, the word *koinonia* appears as that which best expresses what

founds and envelops such communion.... In brief, *koinonia* in the New Testament designates, in its depth, the entrance of each baptized and of each believing community into the space of reconciliation opened by Christ on his cross and that the Spirit causes to appear through... Pentecost. And this space is situated within the eternal mystery of communion which marks the existence of God himself."

23. *Église d'églises,* 74. Also *Église d'églises,* 72: "Christians have fraternal communion (1 John 1:3, 6–7) because all share in—as it has transpired in the economy of salvation—the total communion of Christ Jesus with the will of the Father, itself rooted in the eternal 'circumincession' of the Father and the Son."

24. See *Église d'églises,* 199: "The origin, the cause, the ultimate foundation of our communion is none other than the Father, in God. Even if it does not use the word *koinonia,* but the expression 'to be one,' the Johannine gospel is more audacious still. According to it, the unity of the disciples is that which corresponds to the unity existing between Jesus and the Father, and which is founded on the reality of God," *The Eucharist,* Tillard's first book, goes still further: "[John 17:21–26 is] perhaps... the most beautiful and most compact text of the whole Bible.... Here is the ultimate goal of salvation.... This is the most intimate communion possible between God and man. Here it is a question of a real communion of Life: divine energy traverses the believer in order that his works be those of God himself" (50–51).

25. See Tillard, " 'Communion' and Salvation," *One in Christ* 28 (1992): 1–12.

26. See *Église d'églises,* 68: "The Church of God appears as the realization of the *mystery,* that is to say, the accomplishment in Jesus of the eternal plan which forms the story of Revelation and has for its object the reconciliation of humanity, the reunification of the universe. It therefore belongs, we might say, to the very reality of *humanity-according-to-God.*"

27. *Église d'églises,* 33.

28. Tillard, " 'Communion' and Salvation," 2.

29. *The Eucharist,* 21.

30. See *L'Église locale,* 86.

31. *The Eucharist,* 21 and 39.

32. See Aquinas, *Summa theologiae* III, qq. 68 and 69 on the recipients and effects of baptism, respectively.

33. *The Eucharist,* 203: "The eucharist is truly the paschal food of the church, at once the joyous entry of the People of the Covenant into the Promised Land, and the break with the land of trial."

34. See *Église d'églises,* 41: "The letter to the Ephesians—also written, it seems, in a context of intra-ecclesial tensions—is the key document on this unitive function of the Body of Christ. In effect, it puts at the heart of its meditation on the Church—which has for its Head Christ the ruler of the entire universe (Eph 1:20–23)—the affirmation that hatred, division, separation, estrangement have been abolished, killed, annihilated by the blood of the Cross."

35. Likewise, *Chair de l'Église, chair du Christ,* 20: "The author of [Ephesians] puts at the heart of faith the abolition of division through the Cross by which Christ has killed hatred." For a christological analysis of the soteriology of Ephesians, see Tillard, "Jésus Christ Vie du monde (perspective oecuménique)," *Irénikon* 55 (1982): 332–49.

36. See *L'Église locale,* 93: read in the light of Ephesians, "[the theology of mission] ceases to be a theology of the Church's extension, becoming rather a theology of

the entrance of *all* human richness and *all* creation into Christ." Linked to a primarily qualitative sense of catholicity, this conception of ecclesial mission has profound implications for evangelization and inculturation, whereby the church aims to spread not a monolithic Christianity, but one that will take flesh in the diversity of human cultures. These themes will be examined in depth in chapter 6.

37. *L'Église locale,* 87–88.

38. *The Eucharist,* 30.

39. *Église d'églises,* 30.

40. *Chair de l'Église, chair du Christ,* 155.

41. *L'Église locale,* 104.

42. *Église d'églises,* 70.

43. *Église d'églises,* 34, 66.

44. *Lumen gentium* #5.

45. *Église d'églises,* 100.

46. Tillard sees their relationship as Christocentric: "The church as body of Christ and the Kingdom present, from two different angles, the same relationship between Christ and his own; the former concerns belonging to Christ, the latter the consequence of this belonging. The church will inherit the kingdom. However, to the degree that the baptized, participating in the grace of the resurrection, are *already* 'hidden with Christ in God' (Col 3:3), one can say that the church *already* has within itself the substance of its heritage, the heart of the Kingdom. It is inaugurated in it" (*Église d'églises,* 79). Such grounding helps to allay the concerns expressed by the Roman Congregation for the Doctrine of the Faith in its declaration *Dominus Iesus* (August 6, 2000) regarding the Christ-Church-Kingdom relationship. Sections #18, 19, and 21 of that document criticize those theologies and ecclesiologies that would replace a Christocentric approach to the Kingdom and to salvation with a "theocentric" one, whereby the knowability of Christ by non-Christians, the necessity of Christ for salvation, the need for an integration of the mystery of creation with the mystery of redemption, and the essential salvific role of the church are all obscured or even denied in an attempt to find "common ground in the one divine reality, by whatever name it is called" (#19). These are wholly legitimate concerns, but the adequacy of the CDF's argumentation is a different matter. At the very least, one may ask why its presentation of the Church-Kingdom relationship makes no reference to, say, *Lumen gentium*'s affirmation that the "pilgrim church, in its sacraments and its institutions, which belong to this present age, carries the mark of this world which will pass, and it takes its place among the creatures which groan and until now suffer the pains of childbirth and await the revelation of the children of God" (#45). That is, the CDF, while rightly affirming with Vatican II that the church is the "seed and beginning of that Kingdom," fails to affirm explicitly with the same council that the church remains a *corpus permixtum,* a church "at once holy and always in need in purification" (*Lumen gentium* #8). The church's relationship to the Kingdom is not simply that of grace to glory, but involves a passage through sin and a real, but as yet incomplete, manifestation of the Kingdom. Tillard's thought on the interplay of the church's inalienable, divinely given unity and holiness with its presently imperfect response to those gifts would serve as a useful corrective to idealistic, even unwittingly triumphalistic ecclesiologies.

47. *Église d'églises,* 87–88.

48. *Église d'églises,* 92.

49. See *The Eucharist,* esp. 20–21.

50. *L'Église locale,* 318.

51. See *Église d'églises,* 142; *Chair de l'Église, chair du Christ,* 150.

52. Tillard's *Chair de l'Église, chair du Christ* is an extended study of the intrinsically ecclesial nature of Christian existence: life in Christ necessarily involves life with others in Christ's body. In this work's opening lines, Tillard writes: "In effect, we affirm that for the common Tradition of the first centuries, Christian existence, in all its aspects and parts, is integrally an existence of the *church.* It has struck us that nothing — from the act of faith to vision, from private prayer to the eternal Liturgy evoked in the Apocalypse, from personal witness to communal engagement, from the respect of one's own person to the defense of the rights of the oppressed — escapes the purview of the communion which baptism inaugurates and the eucharist seals and signifies" (7).

53. "Faith: The Believer and the Church," 49.

54. *Église d'églises,* 308.

55. See "Faith: The Believer and the Church," 49–51. In the same article Tillard, drawing upon Congar's *Tradition and Traditions,* also describes the church's role in the formation of scripture through a distinction between "Tradition," which refers to the content of revelation, and "traditions," which are "the way[s] the revealed message has been actualized, perceived, unfolded, transmitted in specific ecclesiastical contexts, according to the needs, the culture, the circumstances of the people" (49). See also *Église d'églises,* 183: "Many [*les*] traditions enter therefore into the very texture of what *the* [*la*] Tradition guards, transmits, explicates. If [Tradition] transcends [traditions], it does not deny them: it depends on them."

56. See *Église d'églises,* 184; "Faith: The Believer and the Church," 52; "The Gospel of God and the Church of God," 367.

57. "Faith: The Believer and the Church," 48.

58. "The Gospel of God and the Church of God," 367–75.

59. "Faith: The Believer and the Church," 50–51.

60. For example, faith is: "trustful adherence to what the Word presents" ("We Believe," *One in Christ* 27 [1991]: 3–7, at 4); the "welcome extended to the Word" ("The Church of God Is a Communion: The Ecclesiological Perspective of Vatican II," *One in Christ* 17 [1981]: 117–31, at 118); "the welcome of the free gift of God" (*Chair de l'Église, chair du Christ,* 147); and the "duty of each person to give oneself entirely to God" (*Chair de l'Église, chair du Christ,* 147).

61. *The Eucharist,* 282.

62. *Chair de l'Église, chair du Christ,* 147.

63. "Faith: The Believer and the Church," 56.

64. "Faith: The Believer and the Church," 57.

65. *Église d'églises,* 166. Tillard continues, "When Irenaeus wrote that the Spirit of God is the water that makes of the dusty wheat a single dough for a single loaf of bread, he was probably thinking of this communal reality of faith. One believes personally, but one does so only in the church."

66. *Lumen gentium* #12.

67. *Église d'églises,* 167.

68. In *Église d'églises,* Tillard provides an extensive bibliography on reception covering the years 1961–85 (see pp. 156–57). For a comprehensive historical, theological, and canonical analysis of the current state of affairs, see "Reception and Communion among Churches," *The Jurist* 57 (1997). Especially helpful are the

articles of Gilles Routhier, "Reception in the Current Theological Debate," 17–52; Emmanuel Lanne, "Reception in the Early Church: Fundamental Processes of Communication and Communion," 53–72; Klaus Schatz, "The Gregorian Reform and the Beginning of a Universalist Ecclesiology," 123–36; Joseph Komonchak, "The Epistemology of Reception," 180–203; Wolfgang Beinert, "The Subjects of Ecclesial Reception," 324–46; William Henn, "The Reception of Ecumenical Documents,"362–95; and Hervé Legrand, "Reception, *Sensus Fidelium,* and Synodal Life: An Effort at Articulation," 405–31.

69. *Église d'églises,* 155. See *Église d'églises* 140–86, for a fuller presentation of reception. Also Tillard, "Théologie et vie ecclésiale," in *Initiation à la pratique de la théologie,* vol. 1, ed. Bernard Lauret and François Refoulé (Paris: Cerf, 1982), 160–82; and Tillard, "Reception-Communion," *One in Christ* 28 (1992): 307–22.

70. *Église d'églises,* 168.

71. *L'Église locale,* 318.

72. *L'Église locale,* 318.

73. See *Église d'églises,* 169: "[Reception] gives to the apostolic tradition its catholic richness, in making [that tradition] flourish in a new context." Also *Église d'églises,* 175: "Reception is built on the conviction which founds catholicity: unity of faith and of ecclesial life does not demand a uniformity bracketing or denying the riches proper to each race, each temperament, each culture, each religious terrain, each history."

74. Yves Congar, *Vraie et fausse réforme dans l'Église* (Paris: Cerf, 1968), 250–61; an English translation is in preparation. See, for example, 251–52: "Most often, initiative comes not from the center, but from the periphery; from below more often than from on high.

"The Church, as with any living thing, is at once continuity and progress: progress in continuity. It is wholly continuity and wholly progress. However, in it, as with all living things — especially higher ones — functions tend to be specialized, such that there are parts of the Church which are more organs of movement and parts which are more organs of continuity. In this ensemble, initiative and newness come especially from the periphery, from the church at its frontiers. The central organs fill especially a function of unity and of continuity; they exercise, par excellence, the charisms which ensure apostolicity.... If one refers to the distinction already made between the *structure* of the church and its *life,* one sees that the central organs in the church, and, more exactly, the hierarchy, have first of all the charge of the church's continuity with its foundations and principles, the charge of conserving the essential form or structure."

See also 261: "The two poles are peripheral initiative and central sanction.... The concrete life of the church is realized in a perpetual exchange between *Urbs* and *Orbis*. Ceaselessly the *Orbis* brings to the *Urbs* its aspirations, its problems, its call; ceaselessly the *Urbs* cares for the entire universe. The *Orbis* brings to the *Urbs* its movement; the *Urbs* gives to it its measure and its rule. The *Orbis* brings to the *Urbs* the voices of the world, multiple and impetuous, sometimes violent or discordant; and the *Urbs* repeats to the *Orbis* the apostolic word of unity: its grace is of harmonizing the voices of the parts with the voice of the whole, not simply through space (catholicity-unity), but through time (apostolicity-unity), and of ensuring, in an immense body all of whose parts are active, that all, however, 'be united in the same mind and the same purpose' (1 Cor 1:10)."

75. *L'Église locale,* 318.

76. *Église d'églises,* 228.

77. On scripture, see *Église d'églises,* 141–42: "The Gospel writings hand to us not the words of Jesus in a pure, direct state, but what the apostolic churches understood and retained of the deep meaning and purpose of his life, of his preaching, of his work, of his person. This understanding passed through the filter of their milieux, their cultures, their concerns."

On the canon, see *Église d'églises,* 143–44: "The ultimate goal of this canon will be the preservation of all communities in the communion of the same faith, rooted in the apostolic witnesses 'recognized' as authentic."

On creeds, see "We Believe," *One in Christ* 27 (1991): 3–7, at 6–7: "The creeds, whatever form they take, are always the work of communities, not of isolated individuals. And it may be that the deep concern to which they respond is of an ecclesiological nature. A Church cannot exist without feeling itself *hic et nunc* in communion with the long line of generations which have preceded it and prepared it. For it is not a spiritual 'happening' which results from a sudden experience on the part of some personality or group. It is the presence, today, of an experience which has the sheen of centuries on it, since it is inseparable from the experience of the apostles, even of Israel. So it must be possible to say again today, usually in the same words and with the same resonances, what has never ceased to bring the group into being, from its very first beginnings. When I say the creed I do so along with all the men and women who, as they prepared themselves for baptism in the church of Caesarea or elsewhere, saw in it 'the definition of Christian identity.' I sing it with them, exactly as they sang it with the apostolic generation. This community of words, of formulas, of 'memory,' makes heard from the inner recesses of history what Augustine perceived as a voice 'always the same, and always different,' 'never altered and yet issuing from throats which are never the same,' the voice of the one and indivisible Body of Christ, a response to the living Word of God, which says 'I believe,' carrying on Peter's confession until the Parousia."

78. "Reception-Communion," 314.

79. "Reception-Communion," 321.

80. "How Is Christian Truth Taught," 298–99: "There is, between pastors and other members of the local Churches, a two-way dynamism.... Each side 'receives' and gives. But usually this exchange and communion occurs more through reflection on the experience of daily life and participation in the sacramental (liturgical) celebrations of the community than through direct academic study of the Scriptures. This is typical of the Catholic *ethos.* The discernment of the authentic meaning of the Word of God is never made outside the concreteness and sacramentality of the church's life. It is never an abstract achievement insensitive to pastoral situations, forgetting that God reveals himself through his action in the Catholic *ethos;* the 'memory' of Christ's deeds and works is not to be searched for outside his whole Body made up of living persons. Before 'receiving' a new idea, bishops feel obliged to look at their congregations in order to 'receive' from them an awareness of what can and must be said. This belongs to their pastoral *prudence.*"

81. For a brief, lucid analysis of Vatican II's teaching on the *sensus fidei,* see Francis A. Sullivan, *Magisterium: Teaching Authority in the Church* (New York: Paulist, 1983), 21–23. See also Richard R. Gaillardetz, *By What Authority?: A Primer on Scripture, the Magisterium, and the Sense of the Faithful* (Collegeville, MN: Liturgical Press, 2003), especially 107–19.

82. *L'Église locale,* 314.

83. "Théologie et vie ecclésiale," 163.

84. *L'Église locale,* 315.

85. *L'Église locale,* 319: "By ministry of the Word, one does not therefore intend to designate simply—nor even primarily—a ministry which speaks (preaches, catechizes, exhorts). Formally, it concerns a ministry which, at the heart of the community, has the mission of guarding the 'memory' of the church, and therefore of the Word which is its content."

86. Tillard defines the magisterium's role as "permitting the Word to shine in all its brilliance and, in the power of the Spirit, of imposing itself. Obedience to [its] judgments, acquiescence to [its] decisions come fundamentally from listening to the truth in question, not primarily from consideration of [its] hierarchical rank and power" (*Église d'églises,* 150). In this context, Tillard follows Congar in quoting the errant words of the sixteenth-century English Catholic apologist Thomas Stapleton: "In what concerns the doctrine of the faith, the faithful should consider not what is said but who is speaking" (Stapleton, *De principiis fidei doctrinalibus,* 1572, lib. X, cap. 5, quoted in Congar, *L'Église: De saint Augustin à l'époque moderne* [Paris: Cerf, 1970], 371.

87. *L'Église locale,* 182.

88. See "Reception-Communion," 313, 319–20.

89. See *Église d'églises,* 147; also chapter 1 of this book.

90. *Église d'églises,* 167: "Certainly it is the minister who, by the epiclesis and the recalling of the words of the Lord, can give to the faithful the body and blood of Christ. But his act is enveloped in the act of the entire assembly, culminating in the *Amen* which accompanies the reception and which is prolonged in the reception of the eucharistic bread and cup. Without the welcome of faith expressed by the *Amen,* there is not—Augustine and Thomas Aquinas wrote—full communion, and therefore not the full effect of the sacrament despite the presence of the Lord in the eucharistic species: *crede et manducasti.* It is likewise with the 'reception' of the Bread of God that is the Word." Also *Église d'églises,* 214.

91. See *Église d'églises,* 152–54 and "How Is Christian Truth Taught," 299, both of which cite Aquinas, *Quodlibet* III, 9. Standard treatments of the topic are Raymond Brown, "The Dilemma of the Magisterium vs. the Theologians: Debunking Some Fictions," *Chicago Studies* 17 (1978): 282–99; and Avery Dulles, "The Two Magisteria: An Interim Reflection," *Proceedings of the Catholic Theological Society of America* 35 (1980): 155–69.

92. "How Is Christian Truth Taught," 300.

93. "How Is Christian Truth Taught," 300.

94. "How Is Christian Truth Taught," 300. Tillard sounds here a theme developed at length by Yves Congar in *Vraie et fausse réforme dans l'Église.* In this work, Congar outlines four conditions for authentic reform in the church: the primacy of charity and pastoral concerns over purely intellectual concerns (228–40); the need to remain in communion of truth and life with the entire church (241–76); patience (277–300); and a true renewal founded not on novelty, but on a return to the sources of the tradition (301–17). For a very brief translation, see "Yves Congar on Patience," trans. Christopher Ruddy, *Commonweal* 126 (January 29, 1999): 14–15.

95. *L'Église locale,* 323.

96. See *Église d'églises,* 153–54: "The tension between the more pragmatic function of the *cathedra pastoralis* and the more contemplative one of the *cathedra*

magistralis subsides in privileged moments, of which Vatican II is the most recent example. The 'discord' (in Newman's words) — expressed at times by the condemnation of certain theologians — of the turbulent inquiry of previous decades became 'concord' in the texts of the hierarchical magisterium of the episcopal college as such. Theology had been 'received' by the organ through which the entire church is kept in the succession of the apostolic faith. No one would deny that in this marvelous event of communion the questions and interpretations of theologians of the local churches, in tension with those of the Roman commissions but, all the same, heard by the ensemble of the Catholic episcopate, and pondered and judged in open dialogue, played not only an invaluable (as it has become fashionable to say) role, but a necessary one. On the occasion of the 1985 Synod of Bishops one heard it said over and again, rightly, that Vatican II had been an 'event of episcopal communion.' One must add that it was also an event of communion of all the perceptions, soundings, inquiries, and tensions by which the Church of God is preserved in the apostolic faith, all in being open to the problems, needs, and suffering of the world to which it is sent for the purpose of salvation. Vatican II was in large part an event of welcome. It confirmed a long quest, guided in theological honesty.

"This recent experience shows that, beyond the narrow realm of theologians, what concerns the truth of the faith is the concern of all the People of God. In the decision of bishops, as in the inquiries of theologians, it is the entire ecclesial body which seeks and speaks the truth which gives it life."

97. See *Église d'églises,* 186–215.

98. *L'Église locale,* 301.

99. Tillard, "We Are Different," *One in Christ* 22 (1986): 62–72, at 65. The word "door" is taken from *Lumen gentium* #14.

100. *Summa theologiae* III, 8, 5.

101. *Summa theologiae* III, 69, 3.

102. Tillard, "Les Sacraments de l'Église," in *Initiation à la pratique de la théologie,* vol. 3, ed. Bernard Lauret and François Refoulé (Paris: Cerf, 1982), 387–466, at 426–28.

103. Tillard notes that the *General Introduction* to the *Roman Missal* insists so strongly upon the bond between faith and baptism that it specifies that "the rite of the baptism of children in danger of death should not lack the confession of faith of those present" (Tillard, "Liturgical Reform and Christian Unity" *One in Christ* 19 [1983]: 227–49, at 239).

104. *Église d'églises,* 324.

105. *The Eucharist,* 197.

106. Groupe Pascal Thomas, *Ces chrétiens qu'on appelle laics* (Paris: Les Éditions ouvrières, 1988), 97, 106. Cited in *L'Église locale,* 365–66.

107. For example, *Unitatis redintegratio* #3: "For those who believe in Christ and have been properly baptized are put in some, though imperfect, communion with the Catholic Church. . . . It remains true that all who have been justified by faith in baptism are incorporated into Christ; they therefore have a right to be called Christians, and with good reason are accepted as sisters and brothers in the Lord by the children of the Catholic Church." Also *Lumen gentium* #15.

108. Tillard, "The Roman Catholic Church and Bilateral Dialogues," *One in Christ* 19 (1983): 368–77, at 369.

109. *Chair de l'Église, chair du Christ,* 52.

110. *L'Église locale,* 376–77.

111. *L'Église locale,* 303. In this work Tillard outlines briefly the development of the distinction between clergy and laity. The New Testament is silent on the matter, and the distinction emerges only toward the end of the second century. The word *laikos* entered into common Christian usage at the turn of the third century, referring primarily to once married men who could administer baptism in an emergency. In the fourth century it was applied to all non-clerical faithful. Eventually, it came to refer to those Christians outside the sphere of "powers." For background and fuller exposition, see *L'Église locale,* 302–6.

112. See *L'Église locale,* 307: "The *hierateuma hagion* of [this Petrine priesthood] is not equivalent therefore to the sum total of a collection of priesthoods. On the contrary, it designates the organic totality that constitutes the body of the faithful *as such.* The *christifideles* thus have priestly character and responsibility only to the degree to which they are *in* the 'priestly body.' "

113. *L'Église locale,* 220. See also *L'Église locale,* 309, 372.

114. *L'Église locale,* 332. See *L'Église locale,* 331: "The running of the local church is therefore ruled neither in a hierarchical mode where one imposes his will, nor in a democratic or 'parliamentary' mode where everything is done in a collective manner . . . by the majority of voices. It is ruled according to what is called a synodal mode where, at every level, the entire community is active, but in regard to their proper functions, certain of which are given with the sacrament of ministry. One of the difficulties of our time comes precisely from the democratic mores of the Western world. There . . . common utility grounds distinctions between citizens. . . . Everything occurs on the same level. In the local church, on the contrary, everything is located at the intersection of two levels whose point of communion is relation to Christ: in one case Christ understood in his members, in the other Christ heard in the *sacramentum* of his transcendent function as the Head who enlivens and unifies his members. This properly synodal articulation is essential to the life of the local church."

115. Code of Canon Law, canon 204.1: "The Christian faithful are those who, inasmuch as they have been incorporated in Christ through baptism, have been constituted as the people of God; for this reason, since they have become sharers in Christ's priestly, prophetic, and royal office in their own manner, they are called to exercise the mission which God has entrusted to the Church to fulfill in the world, in accord with the condition proper to each one" (*The Code of Canon Law: A Text and Commentary,* ed. James A. Coriden, Thomas J. Green, and Donald Heintschel [New York: Paulist, 1985], 122). For background and references, see *L'Église locale,* 306.

116. *The Eucharist,* 197. As we have seen, in this work Tillard avoids ecclesial triumphalism through his complementary insistence upon the pilgrim church, whose members all remain sinners and in need of forgiveness. In speaking of the "saints," then, Tillard is simply elaborating upon the liturgical invitation "holy things for holy people" and insisting that those who participate in the "sacrament of communion" already be joined together in Christ through baptism: "The Lord's meal can unite only those who, having received the Word of God, 'are no longer strangers or guests' but are become by baptism 'fellow citizens of the saints, of the household of God' (Eph 2:19). To whomever is not yet part of the Church in this full and explicit manner or has been rejected from it, access to this table of the festival meal is forbidden" (196).

117. Tillard, "Ecclésiologie de communion et exigence oecuménique," *Irénikon* 59 (1986): 201–30, at 225.

118. *Chair de l'Église, chair du Christ,* 63–64.

119. The view of Anscar Vonier in his *Key to the Doctrine of the Eucharist* (Newman Press, 1959); cited in *The Eucharist,* 71–72.

120. *Chair de l'Église, chair du Christ,* 73–74.

121. *The Eucharist,* 127.

122. *Chair de l'Église, chair du Christ,* 76.

123. *Chair de l'Église, chair du Christ,* 93: "Perhaps more than Augustine and John Chrysostom, Cyril makes known the source and nature of ecclesial unity. This source is none other than Christ, in his body as the New Adam. This nature is essentially christological. It has nothing to do with a pure and simple concord of spirits, even of a pure and simple union of charity. The eucharist fuses together the church in fusing it to Christ in what Cyril calls a physical unity, doubtlessly understanding by this the communion of being that the presence of the eucharistic body effects in the spiritual and corporeal reality of the baptized.

"...Eucharistic communion leaves in the believer's flesh the imprint of Christ's flesh, in the Spirit. From this imprint in all the Church of God is born."

124. *The Eucharist,* 105.

125. *Chair de l'Église, chair du Christ,* 58.

126. Augustine, *Sermon* 272. Cited in *Chair de l'Église, chair du Christ,* 56.

127. *Chair de l'Église, chair du Christ,* 155.

128. See *L'Eglise locale,* 263: "The eucharistic synaxis is therefore the normative expression par excellence of the local church, the Church of God in *such* a place, the Catholic Church in *this* community *reconciled* by the Pasch."

129. See *L'Église locale,* 256: "The essential thing is that, around the eucharistic Table, most especially at the moment where it is nourished by the Body and Blood of the Lord, the community of all the baptized who 'inhabit this place,' Jews and Gentiles, rich and poor, whites and blacks, men and women, children and the elderly, Christians of easy-going holiness and Christians who are ceaselessly struggling under the burden of evil, are enveloped in the mystery of the paschal reconciliation. They do not form a group cemented together simply by some natural affinity, 'a group linked by some historical event,' but—this changes things entirely—a community of humanity *reconciled* with God and itself, where the *Gospel of God* is actualized. Certainly, grace never recreates innocence. The eucharistic community remains a community healed but still marked by its wounds. In effect, the divine pardon itself does not permit one to say that 'what *has been* done has *not been.*' That would be absurd. Ecclesial communion, in its pilgrim stage, is not identified with total harmony. It remains, in certain aspects, fragile, even precarious. The aftermath of human evil inhabits it and shapes it. However, in the eucharist, the local church lets itself be grasped, with its scars and wounds, for the duration of the synaxis (and called also to radiate into its daily life) in the unity which Christ gives. This synaxis itself thus becomes the sign of something wholly unusual in our world. Instead of putting up walls between themselves, men and women of all stripes are gathered *for* and *in agape,* in the name of the God and Father of Jesus." This passage's conjunction of the local church's sinfulness and graced being helps to alleviate concerns that the "high," Pentecostal character of Tillard's theology of the local church obscures the church of God's pilgrim status on earth.

130. *L'Église locale,* 257; *The Bishop of Rome,* 151.

131. *Église d'églises,* 57.

132. Tillard, "L'Eucharistie: La Communion à la Pâque du Seigneur," 39.

133. *L'Église locale,* 190.

134. Tillard, "L'Eucharistie: La Communion à la Pâque du Seigneur," 36. Also: "The grace of the eucharist is inseparably a rooting in the ecclesial body charged with being in the world the *sacramentum* of the reconciliation obtained on the cross and each [believer's] deeper entry into the intimacy of God. Sentimental deviations or inward retreats into the 'delicacies of my life with Jesus' should not lead one to forget or even reject this more mystical dimension of the eucharist and of all sacramental life. Moreover, if the eucharist is the *anamnesis,* the memorial, the *zikkaron* of the great work of God, of his *mirabilia* throughout the ages, it is also, in every single one of its dimensions, the privileged moment where, in being mingled with the great act of thanksgiving of the entire church, the believer remembers his own thanksgiving, his own reasons to praise God, but also his own needs, his own anguishes, his own torments — spiritual as well as physical. That is, one remains at the very periphery of communion with God if one does not plunge all these motifs of joy or pain into the memory of Jesus Christ, the memory of what he lived in his life and his Passion, the memory of what he worked in his ministry with the poor and the sinful, the memory of what he taught in his sermons or his parables, the memory of what the authors of the New Testament... understood and revealed of what God accomplished in Jesus Christ. I praise, I implore, I cry out my need in remembering Jesus before Lazarus, Jairus's daughter, the man born blind, the blind Bartimaeus, the ten lepers, or his parable of the prodigal son, the Samaritan, the publican.... In other words, in the first order of the 'interior life,' one is before God by being one who remembers Jesus Christ" (unpublished class notes on memory, 39).

135. *L'Église locale,* 265.

136. *L'Église locale,* 264. See also *Chair de l'Église, chair du Christ,* 143: "In the 'sacrament of the altar,' the diverse 'sacrifices' are therefore found together in osmosis. They are all grasped in the sacramental presence of the paschal Sacrifice that Christ offered 'once for all' and in which all the forms of his own sacrifice found their fullness: 'sacrifice of charity and mutual aid,' 'spiritual sacrifice of the holy life,' 'sacrifice of praise,' 'sacrifice of the lips,' especially sacrifice of the 'self-dispossession' of his own life. Thus, in their passage in the power of the Paschal sacrifice of the communion of Christ, the hearts and words of those whom the synaxis gathers form but one unique and radically indivisible 'sacrifice,' that of the Church, Body and Head."

137. Tillard argues that the deepest meaning of *episkopè* is "visit" or "visitation." He notes that the Septuagint uses *episkopè* to translate the Hebrew *paqad,* which means "visit." The more common translation of *episkopè* as "oversight" is certainly legitimate, but secondary. The bishop, then, is the one who is charged with keeping his local church in the grace of God's visit to his people, which has culminated in Jesus Christ; this visit's defining characteristic is mercy, as with the Benedictus in Luke's Gospel (see *L'Église locale,* 168–72). For a vision of how this understanding of *episkopè* shapes the bishop's ministry, see the intervention at the 2001 Synod of Bishops by Bishop Raymond Lahey, then of St. George's, Newfoundland (presently bishop of Antigonish, Nova Scotia), "Understanding the Bishop's Role from a Fresh Perspective," *Origins* 31 (October 18, 2001).

138. *L'Église locale,* 525.

139. See *L'Église locale,* 153, 220.

140. *L'Église locale,* 219–20.

141. See *L'Église locale,* 222–23; *The Bishop of Rome,* 69–71.

142. *L'Église locale,* 223.

143. *L'Église locale,* 225.
144. *L'Église locale,* 228.
145. *Église d'églises,* 235–36.
146. *L'Église locale,* 148.
147. For a vision of this synergy in the life and ministry of the local church, see Cardinal Roger Mahony and the Priests of the Los Angeles Archdiocese, "'As I Have Done for You': Pastoral Letter on Ministry," *Origins* 29 (May 4, 2000): 741, 743–53. See also the "Green Paper" released in May 2005 by the Archdiocese of Westminster (London): *www.rcdow.org.uk/greenpaper.pdf.* This report is the product of several years of prayer and consultation through the archdiocesan-wide pastoral plan, "Graced by the Spirit." Cardinal Cormac Murphy-O'Connor's final report, the "White Paper," is scheduled for release in November 2005.
148. *L'Église locale,* 148–49.
149. *L'Église locale,* 171–74, at 174.
150. Ultimately, the entire church is under the episcopacy of the Father. See Ignatius of Antioch, Letter to Polycarp, VIII, 3; cited in *L'Église locale,* 160–61.
151. Tillard, "The Eucharist in Apostolic Continuity," *One in Christ* 24 (1988): 14–24, at 16.
152. See *Église d'églises,* 254–56.
153. *Église d'églises,* 232.
154. *Église d'églises,* 236.
155. Tillard, "Reception-Communion," 319. Tillard has gone so far as to say that "memory is everything" in Christianity (interview with author, December 2, 1999).
156. *L'Église locale,* 319.
157. *L'Église locale,* 319.
158. *The Bishop of Rome,* 151. Also *Église d'églises,* 236–37.
159. See *Église d'églises,* 47.
160. *Église d'églises,* 210.
161. *L'Église locale,* 142.
162. *L'Église locale,* 257.
163. The phrase is Jeffrey VanderWilt's. See his *A Church Without Borders: The Eucharist and the Church in Ecumenical Perspective* (Collegeville, MN: Michael Glazier/Liturgical Press, 1998). This work is a revision of his doctoral dissertation, "The Eucharist as Sacrament of Ecclesial *Koinonia* with Reference to the Contribution of Jean-Marie Tillard to Ecumenical Consensus on the Eucharist," Ph.D. dissertation, University of Notre Dame, 1996. Although borrowing his title, I disagree with the theology behind it: a belief that the eucharist synaxis should be open unconditionally to all baptized Christians, regardless of confessional background. Rather, I use the title to suggest that the eucharistic nature of the church necessarily points to the limitless love of God and to the communion that spans all time and space.

Chapter Five
The Church of God Is a Communion of Local Churches

1. *L'Église locale,* 394.
2. *L'Église locale,* 244; Tillard, "The Local Church within Catholicity," *The Jurist* 52 (1992): 448–54, at 451.
3. "The Local Church within Catholicity," 454.

4. *L'Église locale,* 250–51.

5. *L'Église locale,* 503.

6. *Église d'églises,* 284.

7. *L'Église locale,* 380.

8. See *L'Église locale,* 250.

9. See *L'Église locale,* 40: "The *churches of God* or the *churches of the saints* are not added to the church of Jerusalem. . . . They enter into its grace, its 'once-for-all' (*ephapax*), its *kairos*. They commune with it. There, moreover, is rooted their necessary *apostolicity*. The Spirit makes them commune (in the full sense of the term) in the fullness of grace that God made emerge from his holy people (*Qahal*), at Jerusalem, on the day of Pentecost in the apostolic community."

10. "The Local Church within Catholicity," 453.

11. Pope John Paul II, "Address to the Roman Curia (December 21, 1984)," *Acta Apostolicae Sedis* 77 (1985): 503–14, at 506; cited in Joseph Komonchak, "The Local Church and the Church Catholic: The Contemporary Theological Problematic," *The Jurist* 52 (1992): 416–47, at 441.

12. *L'Église locale,* 91.

13. An obvious parallel to Tillard's understanding of recognition is Karl Rahner's typology of the three eras of Christianity: the first, "short period of Judaeo-Christianity," the second of Gentile-Hellenistic-European Christianity, and the third of the "world-church." Rahner, like Tillard, sees the matter of Gentile circumcision as the crucial issue in the transformation of the early church's self-understanding, leading to a epochal "caesura." Rahner likewise views Vatican II as another "caesura," marking the beginning of a movement — by no means assured — from a largely European Christianity to a genuinely global one. Strikingly, he, too, sees the central issue as one of recognition: "with comparatively slight exceptions . . . Christianity as a western export has not in practice made any impact on the advanced civilizations of the East or in the world of Islam. It made no impact because it was western Christianity and sought to establish itself as such in the rest of the world without the risk of a really new beginning. . . . *This, then, is the situation: either the church sees and recognizes these essential differences of the other cultures, into which it has to enter as world-church, and accepts with a Pauline boldness the necessary consequences of this recognition or it remains a western church and thus in the last resort betrays the meaning of Vatican II*" (86; italics added). Although Rahner does not say so, a theology of the local church is essential for any such recognition of (ecclesial and human) diversity. See his "Basic Theological Interpretation of the Second Vatican Council," *Concern for the Church,* Theological Investigations 20 (New York: Crossroad, 1981), 77–89.

14. *Église d'églises,* 284.

15. "The Local Church within Catholicity," 453

16. *L'Église locale,* 388.

17. *L'Église locale,* 380; see also *L'Église locale,* 90.

18. *Lumen gentium* #23.

19. Congregation for the Doctrine of the Faith, "Some Aspects of the Church Understood as Communion," *Origins* 22 (June 25, 1992): 108–12, at 109.

20. Congregation for the Doctrine of the Faith, "Some Aspects of the Church Understood as Communion," 109. The internal quotation is from John Paul II's September 16, 1987, address to the bishops of the United States; see footnote 41 of "Some Aspects."

21. Congregation for the Doctrine of the Faith, "Some Aspects of the Church Understood as Communion," 109.

22. For background, see Edward Yarnold, "The Church as Communion," *The Tablet* 246 (December 12, 1992): 1564–65; and Brian Daley, "Some Reflections on the Ecclesiology of Communion in the Roman Catholic Church Today," unpublished paper presented to the May 1994 meeting of the North American Orthodox-Roman Catholic Consultation. Daley denies that Tillard is an intended target of the Congregation's criticism, suggesting instead Leonardo Boff and Edward Schillebeeckx. Yarnold, while noting a "surprising correspondence" on the papacy between Tillard and the Congregation, nonetheless argues that an "at least verbal" variance exists between the two concerning the questions of ecclesial priority and mutual recognition (Yarnold, 1565). I agree more with Yarnold. While the accuracy and adequacy of the Congregation's account of recognition is debatable (and, so, with Daley, Tillard may not hold the position seemingly attributed to him), it seems likely that Tillard is one of the objects of its criticism. Part of the burden of this chapter will be to address whether such critique of Tillard is justified.

23. Joseph Komonchak, "The Theology of the Local Church: The State of the Question," in *The Multicultural Church,* ed. William Cenkner (New York: Paulist, 1996), 35–53, at 43.

24. See Tillard's respectful, but fundamentally critical, study of Aquinas in *L'Église locale,* 489–98.

25. Even Leonardo Boff, the theologian most commonly held to be representative of local priority in the form of ecclesial base communities, in fact upholds the priority of the universal church to the local church: "The church universal—the mystery of salvation, the *ecclesia deorsum,* the church-from-above — enjoys a primacy over the particular churches because it is this church-from-above that exists in them all" (Leonardo Boff, *Ecclesiogenesis: The Base Communities Reinvent the Church,* trans. Robert R. Barr [Maryknoll, NY: Orbis, 1986], 19).

26. The standard introduction to his thought is, Aidan Nichols, *The Theology of Joseph Ratzinger* (Edinburgh: T&T Clark, 1988). For a brief overview of his theology in light of his election to the papacy, see Christopher Ruddy, "No Restorationist: Ratzinger's Theological Journey," *Commonweal* 132 (June 3, 2005): 15–18.

27. Thomas Weiler. *Volk Gottes — Leib Christi: Die Ekklesiologie Joseph Ratzingers und ihr Einfluß auf das Zweite Vatikanische Konzil* (Mainz: Matthias-Grünewald-Verlag, 1997), 351.

28. "The Church year gave time its rhythm, and I experienced that with great gratitude and joy already as a child, indeed, above all as a child. . . . I received the complete missal for every day of the year. Every new step into the liturgy was a great event for me. Each new book I was given was something precious to me, and I could not dream of anything more beautiful. It was a riveting adventure to move by degrees into the mysterious world of the liturgy, which was being enacted before us and for us there on the altar. It was becoming more and more clear that here I was encountering a reality that no one had simply thought up, a reality that no official authority or great individual had created. This mysterious fabric of texts and actions had grown from the faith of the Church over the centuries. It bore the whole weight of history within itself, and yet, at the same time, it was much more than the product of human history. Every century had left its mark upon it. The introductory notes informed us about what came from the early Church, what from the Middle Ages, and what from modern times. Not everything was logical. Things sometimes

got complicated, and it was not always easy to find one's way. But precisely this is what made the whole edifice wonderful, like one's own home. Naturally, the child I then was did not grasp every aspect of this, but I started down the road of the liturgy, and this became a continuous process of growth into a grand reality transcending all particular individuals and generations, a reality that became an occasion for me of ever-new amazement and discovery. The inexhaustible reality of the Catholic liturgy has accompanied me through all phases of life, and so I shall have to speak of it time and again" (Joseph Ratzinger, *Milestones: Memoirs 1927–1977,* trans. Erasmo Leiva-Merikakis [San Francisco: Ignatius Press, 1998], 18–20).

Also, "The maker is the opposite of the wonderer (*ammiratore*). He narrows the scope of reason and thus loses sight of the mystery. The more men themselves decide and do in the Church, the more cramped it becomes for us all. What is great and liberating about the Church is not something self-made but the gift that is given to us all. This gift is not the product of our own will and inventions but precedes us and comes to meet us at the incomprehensible reality that is 'greater that our heart' (cf. 1 Jn 3:20). The reform that is needed at all times does not consist in constantly remodelling 'our' Church according to our taste, or in inventing her ourselves, but in ceaselessly clearing away our subsidiary constructions to let in the pure light that comes from above and that is also the dawning of pure freedom" (Ratzinger, *Called to Communion: Understanding the Church Today,* trans. Adrian Walker [San Francisco: Ignatius Press, 1996], 140).

29. Ratzinger, *Called to Communion,* 75–76.

30. Ratzinger, *Called to Communion,* 79.

31. Ratzinger, *Principles of Catholic Theology: Building Stones for a Fundamental Theology,* trans. Sister Mary Frances McCarthy (San Francisco: Ignatius Press, 1987), 308.

32. See Ratzinger, *Church, Ecumenism, and Politics: New Essays in Ecclesiology,* trans. Robert Nowell and Dame Frideswide Sandemann (New York: Crossroad, 1988), 12–13: "The bishop is not a bishop on his own but only in the Catholic community of those who were bishops before him, who are bishops with him and who will be bishops after him. The dimension of time is also included in the meaning of this term: the Church is not something we make today but something that we receive from the history of those who believe and that we pass on as something as yet incomplete, only to be fulfilled when the Lord shall come again."

33. Ratzinger, *The Nature and Mission of Theology: Essays to Orient Theology in Today's Debates,* trans. Adrian Walker (San Francisco: Ignatius Press, 1995), 86.

34. Ratzinger, *The Nature and Mission of Theology,* 85.

35. Ratzinger, *Called to Communion,* 29.

36. Afanasiev, "The Church Which Presides in Love," in *The Primacy of Peter,* ed. John Meyendorff (Crestwood, NY: St. Vladimir's Seminary Press, 1992), 91–143, at 111; also Afanasiev, "Una Sancta," *Irénikon* 36 (1963): 436–75, at 454.

37. Congregation for the Doctrine of the Faith, "Some Aspects of the Church Understood as Communion," 109.

38. Ratzinger, *Principles of Catholic Theology,* 292. Also *Church, Ecumenism and Politics,* 9: "The idea of eucharistic ecclesiology was expressed first of all in the Orthodox theology developed by Russian theologians in exile and was thus contrasted with supposed Roman centralism. Every eucharistic community, it was being said, is already completely the Church because it possesses Christ completely. Hence external unity with the other communities is not constitutive for the Church, nor, it

was concluded, can unity with Rome be constitutive for the Church. This kind of unity is good, because it shows the fullness of Christ to the outside world, but it does not really belong to the essence of the Church, because one cannot add anything to the completeness of Christ."

39. Ratzinger, *The Nature and Mission of Theology,* 86: "We . . . possess him in his entirety only when we possess him together with others, when we possess him in unity." See also *Principles of Catholic Theology,* 293: "Unity with all other communities is not just something that may or may not be added to the Eucharist at some later time; rather, it is an *inner constitutive element* of the eucharistic celebration. Being one with others is the inner foundation of the Eucharist without which it does not come into being. To celebrate the Eucharist means to enter into union with the universal Church—that is, with the one Lord and his one Body" (italics added).

40. Ratzinger, *Called to Communion,* 99–100.

41. Ratzinger, *The Nature and Mission of Theology,* 86.

42. Congregation for the Doctrine of the Faith, "Some Aspects of the Church Understood as Communion," 109, 111.

43. Congregation for the Doctrine of the Faith, "Some Aspects of the Church Understood as Communion," 110, 111. In his own writings, Benedict again criticizes those such as Afanasiev who see the Petrine office as a "resort to a worldly pattern of unity that is opposed to the sacramental unity represented in the Church's eucharistic constitution" (*Called to Communion,* 80); Benedict is clearly thinking here of Afanasiev's opposition of primacy-as-power to priority-as-witness, as examined in our first chapter. In contrast, Benedict holds that the successor of Peter, properly understood, does not stand over against the particular churches, but "must discharge his office in such a way that it does not stifle the special gifts of the single local Churches or compel them into a false uniformity but, rather, allows them to play an active part in the vital exchange of the whole" (*Called to Communion,* 100).

44. Ratzinger, *Called to Communion,* 44.

45. Congregation for the Doctrine of the Faith, "Some Aspects of the Church Understood as Communion," 109.

46. Ratzinger, *Called to Communion,* 44.

47. *Église d'églises,* 48. See also *L'Église locale,* 429, 483, 548.

48. *L'Église locale,* 310.

49. Tillard, "Ecclésiologie de communion et exigence oecuménique," *Irénikon* 59 (1986): 201–30, at 207.

50. *L'Église locale,* 497–98.

51. *L'Église locale,* 491.

52. *L'Église locale,* 490, 491.

53. Aquinas, *Contra errores Graec.,* pars altera, prol., cited in *L'Église locale,* 491.

54. *L'Église locale,* 495–96.

55. It should be noted that Aquinas's 'universalistic' thought on papal primacy is shaped by the Great Schism, as well as by the conflicts between the secular clergy and the newly emergent mendicant orders. He accordingly takes pains to affirm papal authority and its necessary role in the church. In this sense, the metaphysical meets the historical.

56. *L'Église locale,* 492.

57. In fairness, Tillard does note that the "centralism" or "universalism" of Aquinas's thought has nothing to do — and should not be confused — with the

extremism of an Augustino Trionfo (d. 1328), who "extended the primatial power to pagans, Jews, the church triumphant, purgatory; only hell and limbo fall outside his jurisdiction" (*L'Église locale,* 498).

58. Tillard, "L'Universal et le Local: Réflexion sur Église universelle et Églises locales," *Irénikon* 61 (1988): 28–40, at 30.

59. *L'Église locale,* 79.

60. Irenaeus, Augustine, and Fulgentius of Ruspe offer classic reflections on this theme. Is it mere coincidence that both Tillard and the CDF make reference to the same passages in Fulgentius: for example, "in truth I speak all languages because I am in the Body of Christ, the Church, which speaks all languages" (*Sermo 8 in Pentecoste,* 2–3 [PL 65, 743–44]).

61. *L'Église locale,* 391.

62. *L'Église locale,* 35: "This place has nothing of the accidental. The *Ekklesia* appears in the place where God willed that Christ die and rise, because in this place beats the heart of Israel. The cross has been planted in this heart.... The church springs forth as catholic, but of a catholicity whose nature is marked by the place where the Spirit of God effects [the church's] birth by Israel. In brief, it is born a *catholic local church*—catholic in its place, which is the pivotal place of the divine plan for the whole of humanity." Chapter 3 develops more extensively this interplay of locality and universality in the church of Jerusalem.

63. The CDF, for example, writes: "The church-mystery, the church that is one and unique, precedes creation and gives birth to the particular churches as her daughters. She expresses herself in them; she is the mother and not the offspring of the particular churches. Furthermore, the church is manifested temporally on the day of Pentecost in the community of the 120 gathered around Mary and the Twelve Apostles, the representatives of the one unique church and the founders-to-be of the local churches, who have a mission directed to the world. From the first the church speaks all languages.

"From the church, which in its origin and its first manifestation is universal, have arisen the different local churches as particular expressions of the one unique church of Jesus Christ. Arising within and out of the universal church, they have their ecclesiality in her and from her" (Congregation for the Doctrine of the Faith, "Some Aspects of the Church Understood as Communion," 109).

64. See *L'Église locale,* 35, 41, 53, 92, 246, 503.

65. *The Bishop of Rome,* 150–51. See also *The Bishop of Rome,* 37–38: "The movement from an ecclesiology starting with the idea of the universal Church divided into portions called dioceses, to an ecclesiology which understands the Church as the communion of all the local churches... this is the great new insight of Vatican II compared with Vatican I.... The Church of God, seen in its universality, is the communion of local or particular churches. The universal Church is not to be identified as a vast whole, divided into portions each one of which is imperfect on its own." Also *Église d'églises,* 44, 273, 337; *L'Église locale,* 227–28, 250, 279, 392.

66. "L'Universal et le Local: Réflexion sur Église universelle et Églises locales," *Irénikon* 61 (1988): 28–40, at 30.

67. *L'Église locale,* 391–92.

68. Congregation for the Doctrine of the Faith, "La Chiesa come Comunione," *L'Osservatore Romano* (June 23, 1993), cited in Joseph Komonchak, "The Epistemology of Reception," *The Jurist* 57 (1997): 180–203, at 199.

69. Congregation for the Doctrine of the Faith, "Some Aspects of the Church Understood as Communion," 109.

70. *L'Église locale,* 228.

71. *L'Église locale,* 227. In this section, Tillard quotes, in part, the following selection from Louis Bouyer: "Certainly [the localist tendencies of Congregationalist and Orthodox-eucharistic ecclesiologies] can still become the pretext of aberrant developments which ignore the unity and unicity of the Church, and we have seen how essential these two qualities are for the Church. But all the aberrations that can be attached to poorly understood truths could not excuse us from misunderstanding the obvious. And this is that the Church does not exist from the outset as a kind of enormous universal extension device: a *Gesellschaft* destined to set up branches everywhere... On the contrary, she proceeds from essentially local communities and has never, truly speaking, any real existence except in these communities: in the *Gemeinschaften* in which concrete men concretely live a common life of shared faith, unanimous prayer, and fellowship in praise and charity. Everything else in the Church is only in service of these communities and has no real spiritual existence except in their actual life.... The Church of all times and all places was founded, then, in the first local church, that of Jerusalem, and she was propagated from this Church in similar local churches by planting cuttings, as it were, from the main shoot (*The Church of God: Body of Christ and Temple of the Spirit,* trans. Charles Underhill Quinn [Chicago: Franciscan Herald, 1982], 278).

72. Ratzinger, *Called to Communion,* 44.

73. Joseph Komonchak, "The Ecclesiology of Vatican II," *Origins* 28 (April 22, 1999): 763–68, at 768. Komonchak comments that many of those who critique "merely sociological" ecclesiologies are themselves in danger of a "new monophysitism," wherein "the human responses of faith, hope, and love and the intersubjectivity they enable and embody are not considered constitutive of the church, and when it is forgotten that this communion is realized in a people of God still on pilgrimage in history.... An ontology of the church that neglects the human history-shaped and history-shaping element falls short of the properly theological meaning of the word *mystery.* I think we still lack an ecclesiology adequate to *Lumen Gentium,* 8."

74. Joseph Komonchak, "The Local Church and the Church Catholic," 436.

75. Ratzinger, *Church, Ecumenism, and Politics,* 52.

76. Ratzinger, *Called to Communion,* 94, 99–100.

77. *L'Église locale,* 228.

78. Tillard, "In Search of Vatican II: Archbishop Quinn's 'The Reform of the Papacy.'" *One in Christ* 36 (2000): 176–84, at 179. He goes on to say: "Is the bishop of a diocese such as Poitiers or Arundel bishop in the same way as the Archbishop Nuncio in Ottawa, who has no actual diocese, no 'faithful,' and who celebrates the sacred mysteries not in a cathedral but in a private chapel, and does not preside over any priestly or diocesan council? So it occurred to me that this was a quasi-analogous idea of the episcopate. Of course, I was told to keep quiet about that!... This is not a frivolous or otiose question. It goes to the heart of an ecclesiology of communion" (180).

79. It should be noted at this point that Vatican II is ambiguous on priority, but does have a universalist cast. *Lumen gentium* #23 has a balanced (or simply juxtaposed?) statement on interplay of the universal and particular churches, which leaves unexplained and unanswered how they interact. Our second chapter argued

that *Christus Dominus* clearly affirms the priority of the universal church both in its structure (its first chapter treats of bishops in relation to the universal church, its second the bishops in relation to the particular churches) and substance (the bishops are seen first as successors of the apostles, second as heads of particular churches). *Apostolos suos,* Pope John Paul II's 1998 *motu proprio* on episcopal conferences, is decidedly universalistic. It reaffirms the ontological and temporal priority of the universal church, and states, "as an essential element of the universal church [the college of bishops] is a reality which precedes the office of being the head of a particular church"; in a footnote appended to this comment, John Paul says, "Besides, as is clearly evident, there are many bishops who are not heads of particular churches, although they perform tasks proper to bishops" ("*Apostolos suos:* The Theological and Juridical Nature of Episcopal Conferences," *Origins* 28 [July 30, 1998]: 152–58, at 154, 158). The exact nature of these tasks is left unspecified.

80. *L'Église locale,* 278.

81. *L'Église locale,* 380.

82. *L'Église locale,* 279; Tillard, "In Search of Vatican II," 179.

83. Tillard, "In Search of Vatican II," 179: "Which is the more important reality: the communion of the Churches or the *collegium?* It would appear to be the latter. The new Code of Canon Law lends credit to this by speaking of the local Church only after dealing with the *Romanus pontifex* and the *collegium* (then the synod, the college of cardinals, the curia, the legates) (canons 331–67). Here the *collegium* precedes the communion of local Churches."

84. *The Bishop of Rome,* 69; *Église d'églises,* 222, 273, 356; *L'Église locale,* 222.

85. *L'Église locale,* 278, 395, 471, 474. This dependence is logical rather than ontological or temporal, as it is clear that synodality and collegiality cannot exist without each other—just as there can be no church without a bishop and vice versa: "a bishop without a local church would be, for the Great Tradition, as monstrous as a parent without a child, a husband without a wife, a professor without students" (*Église d'églises,* 273).

86. Tillard, "The Primacy-Conciliarity Tension," *Theology Digest* 41 (Spring 1994): 41–45, at 41.

87. Tillard takes up Alexander Schmemann's argument that synodality be understood in terms of the communion of all believers and their respective charisms, rather than as an attempt to "democratize" the church along a balance-of-powers model, whereby increased lay participation is promoted as a counterweight to clerical power (*Église d'églises,* 274–75). The Code of Canon Law defines the diocesan synod as follows: "A diocesan synod is a group of selected priests and other Christian faithful of a particular church which offers assistance to the diocesan bishop for the good of the entire diocesan community" (Canon 460). The Code further specifies that laity "are to be called to the diocesan synod as its members and are obliged to participate in it" (Canon 463); Tillard sees in this "banal, at first glance," requirement the beginnings of "a return to the authentic nature of the local church" (*L'Église locale,* 353).

88. *L'Église locale,* 333–34, 361, 556.

89. *L'Église locale,* 361; also *L'Église locale,* 332, 440. Tillard notes that the 1595 Pontifical, 1600 Ceremonial, and 1984 Ceremonial of Bishops all call for various prayers and liturgies to be celebrated before and during a synod (*L'Église locale,* 360–61).

90. *L'Église locale,* 557.

91. *L'Église locale,* 348, 410, 428.

92. *L'Église locale,* 411–12.

93. *L'Église locale,* 349.

94. *L'Église locale,* 355. In contrast, Tillard notes that John XXIII's 1959 Roman synod was conceived of as "the reunion of the bishop and his priests" (*L'Église locale,* 354).

95. *L'Église locale,* 358.

96. For a helpful study of reception in the life of the church, see Gilles Routhier, *La réception d'un concile* (Paris: Cerf, 1993).

97. *L'Église locale,* 358, 449. John Paul II's apostolic letter, *Novo millennio ineunte* (January 6, 2001), provides explicit support for the contemporary exercise of synodality: "With its universal and indispensable provisions, the program of the Gospel must continue to take root, as it has always done, in the life of the Church everywhere. It is *in the local churches* that the specific features of a detailed pastoral plan can be identified — goals and methods, formation and enrichment of the people involved, the search for the necessary resources — which will enable the proclamation of Christ to reach people, mold communities, and have a deep and incisive influence in bringing Gospel values to bear in society and culture.

"I therefore earnestly exhort the Pastors of the particular churches, with the help of all sectors of God's people, confidently to plan the stages of the journey ahead, harmonizing the choices of each diocesan community with those of neighboring Churches and of the universal Church.

"This harmonization will certainly be facilitated by the collegial work which bishops now regularly undertake in episcopal conferences and synods. Was this not the point of the continental assemblies of the synods of bishops which prepared for the Jubilee, and which forged important directives for the present-day proclamation of the Gospel in so many different cultures? This rich legacy of reflection must not be allowed to disappear, but must be implemented in practical ways" (#29).

98. *L'Église locale,* 483.

99. *Église d'églises,* 273; *L'Église locale,* 475. Tillard notes that one of the flaws of *Lumen gentium* is its failure to place episcopal collegiality in the context of synodality.

100. Tillard, "The Presence of Peter in the Ministry of the Bishop of Rome," *One in Christ* 27 (1991): 101–20, at 115. See also *Église d'églises,* 173; *L'Église locale,* 483.

101. Tillard, "The Mission of the Bishop of Rome: What Is Essential, What Is Expected?" *One in Christ* 34 (1998): 198–211, at 203.

102. *L'Église locale,* 248: "There is no more of the episcopate in one hundred bishops than in one bishop, but one would not be a bishop were he not in communion with the one hundred."

103. Although continuing the apostles' role of judgment in matters of faith, the bishops cannot succeed their role as witnesses to Christ's resurrection. Instead, the bishops guard the church's memory of that unrepeatable witness (*L'Église locale,* 174–75).

104. *L'Église locale,* 175.

105. *L'Église locale,* 249.

106. Canon 447.

107. *L'Église locale,* 475. Tillard sees a clear, paradigmatic affirmation of the teaching mission of episcopal conferences in Pope Pius IX's reception in 1875 of

the German episcopate's statement, against Bismarck's charge that bishops are mere legates of the pope, that Vatican I does not uphold the pope's absolute sovereignty. Pius IX, in his letter to the German episcopate, stated, "You have again upheld the glory of the Church, venerable Brothers, when you undertook to expound the true meaning of the decrees of the Vatican Council . . . and thus prevented the faithful from developing wrong ideas. . . . Your corporate decision is marked by clarity and exactness so that it leaves nothing to be desired, that it has been a great source of joy to us and that there is no need for us to add anything to it. . . . Your declaration gives the pure Catholic doctrine, and therefore that of the Holy Council and the Holy See, perfectly grounded and clearly developed by evident and irrefutable arguments." For background, see *The Bishop of Rome,* 138–41; *Église d'églises,* 335–37; and *L'Église locale,* 470.

108. *L'Église locale,* 472.

109. Tillard, "The Theological Significance of Local Churches for Episcopal Conferences," *The Jurist* 48 (1988): 220–26, at 225. Also *L'Église locale,* 477: "The space where a conference exercises, in solidarity, its *episkope* is therefore much larger than the sum of the parishes of its dioceses. It is, we might say, a segment of humanity possessed of the same problems, the same sufferings, the same hopes, the same joys, the same riches, the same patrimony, the same common good."

110. Tillard, "The Theological Significance of Local Churches for Episcopal Conferences," 223, 224.

111. Tillard, "The Theological Significance of Local Churches for Episcopal Conferences," 223: "[Episcopal conferences] are to assure the place of what is local, cultural, regional, particular, or one would say today (in the jargon of Geneva) the 'contextual,' within unity itself. We would rather say that it is important ecclesiologically to assure diversity or difference. Without this, in fact, not only does unity turn into uniformity, but what is infinitely more serious, catholicity is reduced to its geographic dimension. A study of sermons and catechisms from the last century and the beginning of the twentieth century reveals how much in fact at that time catholicity appeared only as its territorial form. Episcopal conferences, approved and even encouraged by Rome, have safeguarded in a concrete and realistic fashion the rooting of the one Church in the variety and differences of cultures, human settings, and traditions. . . . They have permitted unity to be realized in a respect and welcome for the riches and needs of people. They have, at this essential level, maintained the foundation for catholicity in *koinonia.*"

112. In light of Tillard's vision of the bishop as representative of a segment of humanity, one wonders how titular bishops, who lack presently existing churches, exercise such a function.

113. *L'Église locale,* 477.

114. For a concise overview of the synod's history and operation, see Thomas J. Reese, *Inside the Vatican: The Politics and Organization of the Catholic Church* (Cambridge, MA: Harvard University Press, 1996), 42–65.

115. *L'Église locale,* 481.

116. Tillard's unpublished paper "Évangéliser l'humanité" comments: "[At the Asian Synod, the local bishops] emphasized before all else the necessity of a real and not simply verbal inculturation, sometimes demanding very concrete measures, the nature and urgency of which only the episcopal conferences can appreciate. . . . They demanded a greater leeway of initiative, in virtue of the *exousia* received at their episcopal ordination. Are they not those who, 'eminently and visibly, take the place

of Christ himself, teacher, shepherd, and priest, and act in his person' (*Lumen gentium* #21)? The contrast [of the local bishops' interventions] with the interventions of certain members of the Vatican curia present at the synod is striking. These latter, seeming to place little trust in the analyses of theologians, barely insisted on the role of episcopal conferences. The unity of the Church around the ministry of the bishop of Rome, in absolute unanimity, preoccupied them above all else. One sensed the implicit desire to 'calm the fever of inculturation,' because it upsets matters. Only what comes from the center is absolutely sure for the good of the Church" (15–16).

117. *L'Église locale,* 481.

118. Pope John Paul II, *Ut unum sint* #95. *Origins* 25 (June 8, 1995): 49, 51–72, at 69.

119. Tillard, "The Mission of the Bishop of Rome," 205, 202.

120. *The Bishop of Rome,* 186.

121. *L'Église locale,* 147.

122. The standard reference is Klaus Schatz, *Papal Primacy: From Its Origins to the Present,* trans. John A. Otto and Linda M. Maloney (Collegeville, MN: Michael Glazier/Liturgical Press, 1996). Also William Henn, *The Honor of My Brothers: A Brief History of the Relation between the Pope and the Bishops* (New York: Herder and Herder, 2000); and Brian E. Daley, "The Ministry of Primacy and the Communion of Churches," in *Church Unity and the Papal Office: An Ecumenical Dialogue on John Paul II's Encyclical* Ut unum sint. Ed. Carl E. Braaten and Robert W. Jenson (Grand Rapids, MI: Eerdmans, 2001), 27–58. Tillard's account of papal primacy coheres with these three works.

123. *Église d'églises,* 368–69.

124. *Église d'églises,* 368, 375.

125. *Église d'églises,* 376. Klaus Schatz writes that although the New Testament witness testifies "to Peter's position as leader of the Twelve and of the primitive community in Jerusalem, a role conferred on him by Jesus," it likely does not "in purely historical terms" attest to "an enduring office beyond Peter's lifetime" (Schatz, *Papal Primacy,* 1). Schatz does not claim, however, that scripture excludes the possibility and legitimacy of the development of such an office. Schatz's position concurs with, and builds upon, the work of both Oscar Cullmann, *Peter: Disciple, Apostle, Martyr,* 2nd ed. (Grand Rapids, MI: Eerdmans, 1968; original English edition: London: SCM Press, 1953); and R. E. Brown, K. P. Donfried, and J. Reumann, eds., *Peter in the New Testament* (New York: Paulist, 1973).

126. *L'Église locale,* 438–39, 454–56.

127. *The Bishop of Rome,* 53–54. See Schatz, *Papal Primacy,* 86, 89: "The underlying tone of the entire document emerges in the statement that the pope alone can do everything in the Church; without him, nothing can be validly or legally done; there appear to be absolutely no limits to papal authority. . . . A 'mysticism of Peter' [is] the true kernel of Gregory's notion of primacy. He believes that he stands in a mystical union with Peter, who acts, thinks, and speaks through him. The pope is Peter present on earth. His own authority is thus also and immediately that of Peter. Obedience to Peter now becomes the epitome of ecclesiality."

128. *The Bishop of Rome,* 55–57.

129. *The Bishop of Rome,* 53, 55.

130. Bellarmine, *Controversiae* V, c.4, cited in *The Bishop of Rome,* 100. Also *The Bishop of Rome,* 59.

131. *The Bishop of Rome,* 18–25.

132. *The Bishop of Rome,* 26. For a concise account and interpretation of Vatican I, see Hermann J. Pottmeyer, *Towards a Papacy in Communion: Perspectives from Vatican Councils I and II,* trans. Matthew J. O'Connell (New York: Herder and Herder, 1998).

133. *Lumen gentium* #27: "The bishops [are] vicars and legates of Christ.... The pastoral charge, that is, the permanent and daily care of their sheep, is entrusted to them fully; nor are they to be regarded as vicars of the Roman pontiff; for they exercise a power which they possess in their own right and are most truly said to be at the head of the people whom they govern."

134. *Lumen gentium* #18–19.

135. See *The Bishop of Rome,* 45: "Putting it briefly, one has the impression that the new institutions [episcopal conferences, synods of bishops] responsible for translating Vatican II into the dynamics of church life have not so far succeeded in jointing together the *munus* of the Roman pontiff with the *munus* of the whole college of bishops; or the freedom of the Roman pontiff, claimed so firmly by Vatican I though not without ultramontane overtones, with the demands of collegiality which Vatican II reasserted, but too vaguely; or the privilege of the Roman pontiff, so deeply engraved on the Roman Catholic consciousness by ultramontane mystique, and the rights of the college of bishops claimed throughout history but still under suspicion for Gallican leanings. Concern for safety has made us continue to revolve round a monarchical view without realizing that expressions of collegiality become something more than a means of serving the primacy. In so doing we turn our backs on Vatican II. Putting collegiality at the service of the pope's power reverts to making him 'more than a pope.' Primacy in the Great Tradition is at the service of collegiality, not the other way round. It is a serious problem, for it perpetuates a hesitation and an ambiguity which could slowly lead on to wither the fruits of Vatican II."

136. Pope John Paul II, *Ut unum sint* #97.

137. Pope John Paul II, *Ut unum sint* #94.

138. Pope John Paul II, *Ut unum sint* #95–96.

139. *Unitatis redintegratio* #14, cited in Pope John Paul II, *Ut unum sint* #95.

140. See, for example, the published results of the Congregation for the Doctrine of the Faith's 1996 symposium on the encyclical, *Il Primato del Successore di Pietro, Atti del Simposio Teologico* (Vatican City: Libreria Editrice Vaticana, 1998), and those of the 1997 symposium organized in Rome by the Friars of the Atonement, *Petrine Ministry and the Unity of the Church: "Toward a Patient and Fraternal Dialogue,"* ed. James F. Puglisi, (Collegeville, MN: Michael Glazier/Liturgical Press, 1999). Also Carl E. Braaten and Robert W. Jenson, eds., *Church Unity and the Papal Office: An Ecumenical Dialogue on John Paul II's Encyclical* Ut unum sint (Grand Rapids, MI: Eerdmans, 2001).

Also Congregation for the Doctrine of the Faith, "Reflections on the Primacy of Peter," *Origins* 28 (January 28, 1999): 560–63. Hermann J. Pottmeyer, "Primacy in Communion," *America* 182 (June 3–10, 2000): 15–18. Avery Dulles, "The Papacy for a Global Church," *America* 183 (July 15–22, 2000): 6–11. Ladislas Orsy, "The Papacy for an Ecumenical Age: A Response to Avery Dulles," *America* 183 (October 21, 2000): 9–15. Avery Dulles and Ladislas Orsy, "In Dialogue," *America* 183 (November 25, 2000): 12–15.

Finally, Crossroad Herder has initiated a series, "*Ut Unum Sint:* Studies on Papal Primacy," featuring works by such scholars as Michael Buckley, William Henn, Hermann Pottmeyer, and Archbishop John Quinn.

141. *L'Église locale,* 522.

142. Jerome, *Epist.* 15, 2 (CSEL 54, 63), cited in *L'Église locale,* 524.

143. *The Bishop of Rome,* 105. Also *The Bishop of Rome,* 111: "Peter's preeminence, which explains his primacy among the twelve, comes from his confession of the apostolic faith. And it is in his act of confession that he becomes the first among those upon whom the Lord founds his Church."

144. Augustine, Sermon 295, in *Sermons* vol. III/8 (273–305A), *The Works of Saint Augustine: A Translation for the 21st Century,* trans. and notes Edmund Hill, ed. John E. Rotelle (Hyde Park, NY: New City Press, 1994), 197–98, 199.

145. *The Bishop of Rome,* 115. In an ecumenical context, the matter of Rome's "primacy of honor" is inevitable. The East, valuing the sacramental equality of all bishops, usually sees primacy as a matter of *taxis,* of right ordering; its talk of "primacy of honor" often has, in Tillard's words, a certain "fuzziness" (*flou*) about it, and tends to a largely ceremonial role devoid of jurisdictional power. Tillard, drawing upon the work of Brian Daley, argues that primacy (Gr., *presbeia;* Lat., *primatus*) literally means "privileges" or "prerogatives," often based upon the wisdom and experience which founds authority; it is more than a "recognition of moral authority." Honor (Gr., *timè;* Lat., *honos*) is "the recognition not only of a citizen's inner qualities, but also of the concrete service that he renders to society and which reveals his 'worth' " (*L'Église locale,* 486). Primacy of honor, properly understood in its classical and ecclesial contexts, is therefore a real, effective primacy of patronage and protection, not simply a ceremonial honorific. For a fuller exposition, see *L'Église locale,* 484–89. Brian Daley's study is "Position and Patronage in the Early Church: The Original Meaning of Primacy of Honour," *Journal of Theological Studies* 44 (1993): 529–53.

146. *L'Église locale,* 526.

147. *The Bishop of Rome,* 100.

148. *L'Église locale,* 525.

149. See *L'Église locale,* 503–4, 523–26, 554. Also *The Bishop of Rome,* 100.

150. Tillard, "The Presence of Peter in the Ministry of the Bishop of Rome," 113; also *L'Église locale,* 519.

151. *Église d'églises,* 362. Also *Église d'églises,* 357; *L'Église locale,* 435–36.

152. *The Bishop of Rome,* 74–75: "The hierarchy of the Churches was thus determined in relation not to the story of Jesus, but to the apostolic mission and witness. It derives from the apostolicity of the Church. Its great centers are therefore not the holy places of the Lord's life, ministry, and Passion, but those points on the map of the world where in the power of the Spirit the gospel of God took root in order to spread out among all the peoples of the world. The local church at Rome is first among all the churches because the martyrdom of Peter and Paul there made it the supreme place of apostolic witness, not because it was established before the others."

153. *L'Église locale,* 516. Also *Église d'églises,* 357–58; and *The Bishop of Rome,* 81: "Martyrdom itself is important because it represents the supreme test of Christian genuineness, the absolute seal on the witness to the gospel. By his death the witness to the faith enters into communion with the glory of Christ Jesus himself. He makes in some way the journey through the cross his own."

154. *Église d'églises,* 362–63.

155. *The Bishop of Rome,* 79: "The joint commemoration of the apostles Peter and Paul at Rome is attested from the year 258. An interesting point, explained by what we have seen, is that this is one of the rare commemorations which the West has

given to the East. From the fifth century at Rome there were two separate synaxes celebrated, one at the Vatican and the other at St. Paul-outside-the-Walls; but in them both, the two apostles were honored together. The East does not separate them in its liturgy either. . . . It is therefore important that the *Missale Romanum* promulgated by Paul VI in 1970 has joined Peter and Paul in the Eucharist for the vigil and the feast, thereby renewing an ancient tradition buried in the Church's memory; the separate celebration of Paul on 30 June is replaced by that of the first Roman martyrs."

156. For a fuller account than this chart allows, see *The Bishop of Rome,* 81–83, 93, 115–17; *Église d'églises,* 361–63, 381–83; *L'Église locale,* 533–43.

157. *The Bishop of Rome,* 69, 71, 86; *Église d'églises,* 328, 356.

158. *Église d'églises,* 324. The Code of Canon Law affirms this episcopal character, specifying that episcopal ordination is necessary for the exercise of the papal office: "The Roman Pontiff obtains full and supreme power in the Church by means of legitimate election accepted by him together with episcopal consecration; therefore, one who is already a bishop obtains this same power from the moment he accepts election to the pontificate, but if the one elected lacks the episcopal character, he is to be ordained a bishop immediately" (Canon 332.1).

159. *The Bishop of Rome,* 142; *Église d'églises,* 328, 333.

160. *The Bishop of Rome,* 1, 3, 18.

161. *L'Église locale,* 543.

162. *The Bishop of Rome,* 125.

163. *The Bishop of Rome,* 154.

164. "The Local Church within Catholicity," 454.

165. *The Bishop of Rome,* 193.

166. *Église d'églises,* 380. It is clear that Tillard's argument depends upon a classically "Catholic" understanding of the interplay of scripture and tradition, as well as the church's role vis-à-vis the interpretation of scripture.

167. Tillard, "The Ecumenical Kairos and the Primacy," in *Petrine Ministry and the Unity of the Church: "Toward a Patient and Fraternal Dialogue,"* ed. James F. Puglisi, (Collegeville, MN: Michael Glazier/Liturgical, 1999), 185–96, at 195.

168. *The Bishop of Rome,* 49. See Pierre Batiffol, *Cathedra Petri* (Paris: Cerf, 1938); Yves Congar, *After Nine Hundred Years: The Background of the Schism between the Eastern and Western Churches* (New York: Fordham University Press, 1959), 63ff.

169. *Église d'églises,* 338–39. Also *The Bishop of Rome,* 49–52, 123.

170. "The Local Church within Catholicity," 454.

171. *The Bishop of Rome,* 154; *L'Église locale,* 554.

172. *The Bishop of Rome,* 90. Also *The Bishop of Rome,* 84, 92, 165, 168, and 193: "the bishop of Rome's mission remained that of a watchman or sentinel in the service of the apostolic witness which Peter and Paul gave to make the foundation of their local church, which has now become touchstone, point of reference, and memorial of the faith."

173. *L'Église locale,* 459.

174. *L'Église locale,* 526.

175. Even the most "universal" of papal acts, the exercise of infallibility *"ex cathedra,"* proceeds from the pope's local, episcopal ministry as head of the church of Rome and as occupant of the Chair of Peter.

176. See *Constitutions apostoliques* VIII, 47, 34 (*Sources chretiénnes*, 336, 285).

177. *L'Église locale,* 428–31.

178. Tillard, "In Search of Vatican II," 183. Tillard comments elsewhere: "If the primate happens to cut himself off from the episcopal college, he is no longer primate; he is no more than a solitary pastor" ("The Ecumenical Kairos and the Primacy," 190).

179. Tillard, "The Mission of the Bishop of Rome," 207.

180. *The Bishop of Rome,* 41.

181. *L'Église locale,* 544.

182. The concept of sovereignty is examined in detail in Hermann J. Pottmeyer, *Unfehlbarkeit und Souveränität: Die päpstliche Unfehlbarkeit im System der ultramontanen Ekklesiologie des 19. Jahrhunderts* (Mainz: Grünewald, 1975). A shorter presentation is found in Hermann J. Pottmeyer, *Towards a Papacy in Communion,* 41–45.

183. Cited in *The Bishop of Rome,* 27.

184. *L'Église locale,* 503.

Chapter Six
Evaluation and Trajectories of Tillard's Theology of the Local Church

1. David Carter, review of *L'Église locale, One in Christ* 32 (1996): 378–85, at 378.

2. *Église d'églises,* 275.

3. *Chair de l'Église,* 7–10.

4. *L'Église locale,* 8.

5. Avery Dulles, "A Half Century of Ecclesiology," *Theological Studies* 50 (1989): 419–42, at 437.

6. *L'Église locale,* 543.

7. Tillard, "Towards an Ecumenical Ecclesiology of Communion," in *Ecumenism: Present Realities and Future Prospects,* ed. Lawrence S. Cunningham (Notre Dame, IN: University of Notre Dame Press, 1998), 133–48, at 146. See also Tillard, "The Roman Catholic Church and Bilateral Dialogues," *One in Christ* 19 (1983): 368–77, at 372–73: "Since the historical conditions are no longer those of the undivided Church, it seems to me that the dialogue will be driven into a cul-de-sac if its aim is set out unconditionally as a return to the type of relations with the See of Rome (both in East and West) which prevailed in that epoch. The function of the bishop of Rome cannot be seen with those eyes. It is clear that neither Vatican I nor Vatican II said the last word on this subject. It will be necessary that the East says what it has to say and, above all, that its sister Church of the West takes concrete account of it. So it will be necessary that the East does not read *Pastor Aeternus* with the eyes of Photius and Cerularius.

"... The Roman Catholic Church cannot then, in its judgment of a bilateral agreement, try to rediscover its own doctrines, its theology, especially those explicated since the breach with the group who is its dialogue partner. It would be absolutely to fall back into an 'ecumenism of return' to make the affirmations of Trent or of Vatican I, taken in the letter alone without being submitted to a serious hermeneutic, the norm of such a judgment.... It must be able to *re-cognize* in the ARCIC Report its faith in the Lord's presence in the bread truly become his Body and the wine truly become his Blood. It does not have the right to demand to rediscover the doctrine of transubstantiation or its cultic practice *extra missam.* It must be able to *re-cognize* its faith in a concrete primacy of the See of Rome, guarantee of the unity of the *koinonia;* it does not have the right to demand that everyone should take on its conception of and manner of exercising the jurisdiction of the Bishop of Rome."

8. Tillard, "Preparing for Unity — A Pastoral Approach to Ecumenism," *One in Christ* 16 (1980): 2–18, at 17.

9. Nicholas M. Healy, *Church, World and Christian Life: Practical-Prophetic Ecclesiology* (Cambridge: Cambridge University Press, 2000), 50. Healy's argument was first presented in "The Logic of Modern Ecclesiology: Four Case Studies and a Suggestion from St. Thomas Aquinas," Ph.D. dissertation, Yale University, 1992, 55–95, and "Communion Ecclesiology: A Cautionary Note," *Pro Ecclesia* 4 (1995): 442–53.

10. Healy, *Church, World and Christian Life,* 38.

11. Healy, *Church, World and Christian Life,* 30–32.

12. Healy, *Church, World and Christian Life,* 37–38.

13. Healy, *Church, World and Christian Life,* 142–44.

14. Healy, *Church, World and Christian Life,* 44–46.

15. Healy, *Church, World and Christian Life,* 45.

16. Healy, *Church, World and Christian Life,* 45–46.

17. Healy, *Church, World and Christian Life,* 177. It should be noted that Healy does not spare himself from this critique.

18. Healy, *Church, World and Christian Life,* 36.

19. Healy argues that "blueprint ecclesiologies frequently display a curious inability to acknowledge the complexities of ecclesial life in its pilgrim state. To take just one instance, we noted how Tillard believes that the Eucharist is the most perfect expression of 'communion.' While that may well be true, Eucharists are concretely and frequently divided by race, class, gender and political ideology, to say nothing of denominational divisions. Does not the presence of such flaws so obscure the expression of perfection that it becomes the contrary, namely an expression of the loss of communion? Should we not understand the very brokenness of the Body of Christ as an expression of the church's true reality prior to the eschaton?" (*Church, World and Christian Life,* 37–38)

However, Tillard's normative-ideal vision of the eucharistic osmosis of Christ and the church (outlined in *Chair de l'Église, chair du Christ*) does not prevent him from acknowledging the 'pilgrim' character of each eucharistic celebration; see, for instance, *L'Église locale,* 256: "[The community of all the baptized] do not form a group cemented together simply by some natural affinity, 'a group linked by some historical event,' but — this changes things entirely — a community of humanity *reconciled* with God and itself, where the *Gospel of God* is actualized. Certainly, grace never recreates innocence. The eucharistic community remains a community healed but still marked by its wounds. In effect, the divine pardon itself does not permit one to say that 'what *has been* done has *not been.*' That would be absurd. Ecclesial communion, in its pilgrim stage, is not identified with total harmony. It remains, in certain aspects, fragile, even precarious. The aftermath of human evil inhabits it and shapes it. However, in the eucharist, the local church lets itself be grasped, with its scars and wounds, for the duration of the synaxis (and called also to radiate into its daily life) in the unity which Christ gives. This synaxis itself thus becomes the sign of something wholly unusual in our world. Instead of putting up walls between themselves, men and women of all stripes are gathered *for* and *in agape,* in the name of the God and Father of Jesus."

20. See, for instance, Tillard, "Ecumenism: The Church's Costly Hope," *One in Christ* 35 (1999): 218–27, at 220. This essay, which sets forth the scope of the Father's plan for humanity and the scandal ecclesial division presents to it, is one of Tillard's finest efforts. Combining immense despair and hope for the future of an increasingly divided Christianity, it was prompted by Tillard's experiences at the 1998 General Assembly of the World Council of Churches in Harare, Zimbabwe.

21. Healy, *Church, World and Christian Life,* 50, 25.

22. Tillard, "The Mission of the Bishop of Rome: What Is Essential, What Is Expected?" *One in Christ* 34 (1998): 198–211, at 209.

23. *Lumen gentium* #27; also *Christus Dominus* #11.

24. *Lumen gentium* #27.

25. *Lumen gentium* #23.

26. *Lumen gentium* #22.

27. Tillard, "In Search of Vatican II: Archbishop Quinn's 'The Reform of the Papacy.' " *One in Christ* 36 (2000): 176–84, at 183.

28. *The Bishop of Rome,* 27–28, 41–42; *Église d'églises,* 341.

29. *Ad gentes divinitus* #4.

30. For an Orthodox conception of primatial witness as rooted in martyrdom, see Olivier Clément, *Rome, autrement: Une réflexion orthodoxe sur la papauté* (Paris: Desclée de Brouwer, 1997), especially chapter 12, "Le mystère de la primauté." For a largely sympathetic review of Clément's book, see Avery Dulles, "A New Orthodox View of the Papacy," *Pro Ecclesia* 12 (2003): 345–58.

31. See *Lumen gentium* #18–23.

32. "It is towards the Roman church, on account of its superior origin, that it has always been necessary for every Church, that is, for the faithful from everywhere, to turn in order that they should be made one body only in that holy see from which flow all the rights of the venerable communion," *Pastor aeternus,* cited in *The Bishop of Rome,* 26.

33. For helpful background and reflections, see Lawrence S. Cunningham, "Saints and Martyrs: Some Contemporary Concerns," *Theological Studies* 60 (1999): 529–37, esp. 534–37; idem, "On Contemporary Martyrs: Some Recent Literature," *Theological Studies* 63 (2002): 374–81; idem, "The Universal Call to Holiness: Martyrs of Charity and Witnesses of Truth," in *The New Catholic Encyclopedia Jubilee Volume: The Wojtyla Years* (Washington, DC: Catholic University of America, 2001), 109–16. Also Sven-Erik Brødd, "A Communion of Martyrs: Perspectives on the Papal Encyclical Letter *Ut unum sint,*" *Ecumenical Review* 52 (April 2000): 223–33.

34. George Weigel, *Witness to Hope: The Biography of Pope John Paul II* (New York: Cliff Street Books/HarperCollins, 1999), 846.

35. George Weigel, "Papacy and Power," *First Things* 110 (February 2001): 18–25, at 23–24.

36. Pope John Paul II, *Tertio millennio adveniente* #37, *Origins* 24 (November 24, 1994): 401, 403–16, at 411, 412. In this same section, he adds: "Perhaps the most convincing form of ecumenism is the ecumenism of the saints and of the martyrs. The *communio sanctorum* speaks louder than the things which divide us," *Veritatis splendor,* the pope's 1993 encyclical on moral theology, also probes the nature and meaning of martyrdom; see #89–94.

37. See the following passages of *Ut unum sint, Origins* 25 (June 8, 1995): 49, 51–72: "The courageous witness of so many martyrs of our century, including members of churches and ecclesial communities not in full communion with the Catholic Church, gives new vigor to the council's call [*Ut unum sint!*] and reminds us of our duty to listen and put into practice its exhortation. These brothers and sisters of ours, united in the selfless offering of their lives for the kingdom of God, are the most powerful proof that every factor of division can be transcended and overcome in the total gift of self for the sake of the Gospel.

"Christ calls all his disciples to unity. My earnest desire is to renew this call today, to propose it once more with determination, repeating what I said at the Roman Colosseum on Good Friday 1994 at the end of the meditation on the *via crucis* prepared by my venerable brother Bartholomew, the ecumenical patriarch of Constantinople. There I stated that believers in Christ, united in following in the footsteps of the martyrs, cannot remain divided" (#1).

"Is not the 20th century a time of great witness, which extends 'even to the shedding of blood'? And does not this witness also involve the various churches and ecclesial communities which take their name from Christ, crucified and risen?

"Such a joint witness of holiness, as fidelity to the one Lord, has an ecumenical potential extraordinarily rich in grace" (#48).

"In a theocentric vision, we Christians already have a common martyrology. This also includes the martyrs of our own century, more numerous than one might think, and it shows how, at a profound level, God preserves communion among the baptized in the supreme demand of faith, manifested in the sacrifice of life itself. The fact that one can die for the faith shows that other demands of the faith can also be met. I have already remarked and with deep joy, how an imperfect and real communion is preserved and is growing at many levels of ecclesial life. I now add that this communion is already perfect in what we all consider the highest point of the life of grace, *martyria* unto death, the truest communion possible with Christ who shed his blood, and by that sacrifice brings near those who once were far off (cf. Eph. 2:13)" (#84).

38. Pope John Paul II, *Ut unum sint* #90, 92, 94, 103. The Congregation for the Doctrine of the Faith's "Reflections on the Primacy of Peter," a set of summary reflections occasioned by its symposium in 1996 on the encyclical, likewise affirms "the martyrological nature of [the pope's] primacy," its origin in Peter and Paul, and states that "the primacy of the bishop of Rome is first of all expressed in transmitting the word of God" ("Reflections on the Primacy of Peter," *Origins* 28 [January 28, 1999]: 560–63, at 562.)

This vision of papal primacy is also ecumenically promising. "The Gift of Authority," the 1999 agreed statement of ARCIC-II, speaks not of the "pope" or the "pontiff," but of the "bishop of Rome" and the "chair of Peter in the church of Peter and Paul." Quoting Luke 22 and *Ut unum sint,* the statement highlights Peter's fragility and weakness, noting that "authority is exercised by fragile Christians for the sake of other fragile Christians. This is no less true of the ministry of Peter" (#48). And yet (or, perhaps, because of this admission), the document is notable for its unprecedented common affirmation that, under certain clearly defined conditions, the "church may teach infallibly" (#42, also #47; ARCIC-II, "The Gift of Authority," *Origins* 29 [May 27, 1999]: 17, 19–29).

39. Tillard, "Évangéliser l'humanité," 19–20. See also Avery Dulles and Ladislas Orsy, "In Dialogue," *America* 183 (November 25, 2000): 12–15. Orsy, in response to

Dulles's vision of a "stronger office of unity" in "our electronic, global age," argues: "Globalization is a secular phenomenon driven strongly by the powerful forces of the market — and greed; it tends to destroy what is 'small and beautiful.' In no way must it touch, still less diminish, theological realities, such as the God-given diversity and dignity of the particular churches, the energy of the Spirit in the bishops' gatherings in synods and conferences, the appreciation for the sense of faith of the people in the provinces. Such realities, and their functions, must be determined exclusively from traditional theological sources.... Today the global corporations are on the horizon and shine as tempting images for neatly ordered efficiency. The 'multinationals' are internally unified and disciplined; they are shaped and governed from the center down to the last details. Their way of doing business, however, is utterly unsuitable for any Christian communion that honors God's gifts in their diversity no less than it respects God's design in their unity. Wisdom tells us: here is a temptation to be watched and resisted."

40. Tillard, "Évangéliser l'humanité," 20.

41. It is significant that *Lumen gentium* #25, which contains the council's most explicit statement on ecclesial teaching authority and infallibility, begins by declaring that "among the more important duties of bishops, that of preaching the Gospel has pride of place." All genuine authority in the church is evangelical.

42. Tillard, 'The Ministry of Unity," *One in Christ* 33 (1997): 97–111, at 107.

43. Tillard, "The Ministry of Unity," 108; "The Mission of the Bishop of Rome: What Is Essential, What Is Expected?" *One in Christ* 34 (1998): 198–211, at 202, 209.

44. *Église d'églises,* 324.

45. ARCIC-II, "The Gift of Authority" #38, 39, 47. For a helpful, concise overview of the history of Anglican-Catholic dialogue on authority, see Adelbert Denaux, "The Anglican–Roman Catholic Dialogue about Authority in the Church," *Louvain Studies* 24 (1999): 291–318.

46. Tillard, "The Ministry of Unity," 98.

47. Pope John Paul II, *Ut unum sint* #95.

48. Pope John Paul II, *Ut unum sint* #94.

49. "The Mission of the Bishop of Rome," 210.

50. Tillard, "The Church of God Is a Communion: The Ecclesiological Perspective of Vatican II," *One in Christ* 17 (1981): 117–31, at 127.

51. *The Bishop of Rome,* 123.

52. *Christus Dominus* #11, 2.

53. Tillard, "The Primacy-Conciliarity Tension," *Theology Digest* 41 (Spring 1994): 41–45, at 43–44. It is ironic that some of those prone to such confusion are likely to insist, with the CDF, that the universal church must not be understood as the sum or federation of local churches!

54. Tillard, "Papal Primacy," in *The HarperCollins Encyclopedia of Catholicism,* ed. Richard P. McBrien (San Francisco: HarperSanFrancisco, 1995), 1051–53, at 1052.

55. *Lumen gentium* #22: "Together with its head, the Supreme Pontiff, and never apart from him, [the episcopal college] is the subject of supreme and full authority over the universal church; but this power cannot be exercised without the consent of the Roman Pontiff."

56. Tillard, "In Search of Vatican II," 181.

57. Tillard, "In Search of Vatican II," 182.

58. Tillard, "In Search of Vatican II," 182–83.

59. See *The Bishop of Rome,* 49: "In a word, the file on the dogmatic theology of the papacy is not closed. One of its most complex chapters has still to be written. This chapter cannot be written by the Catholic Church alone. It will take shape only in so far as that church sets herself to listen to the other Christian communities who are eager to reconstruct with her the unity of the Body of Christ, notably those whom she continues to regard as sister churches. Only in this way will the ultramontane temptation be overcome, for its roots are strong." Ibid., 67: "We have earlier expressed our belief that the solemn affirmations of the two Vatican Councils are among those which need 'ecumenical interpretation' to bring them to that degree of purity from distorting factors and of fullness of meaning which will be sealed only when they are 'received' by the whole body of Churches rooted in the apostolic tradition."

60. Pope John Paul II, *Ut unum sint* #96.

61. Tillard, "The Mission of the Bishop of Rome," 209.

62. Tillard, "The Mission of the Bishop of Rome," 204–5.

63. Tillard, "The Mission of the Bishop of Rome," 208.

64. Tillard, "The Mission of the Bishop of Rome," 209.

65. Tillard, "The Mission of the Bishop of Rome," 209.

66. Tillard, "The Mission of the Bishop of Rome," 208.

67. Congregation for the Doctrine of the Faith, "Reflections on the Primacy of Peter," 561. The qualification of "monarchy" by "political" seems both unnecessary and slightly troubling: would a "religious monarchy" be acceptable?

68. Tillard, "The Mission of the Bishop of Rome," 208.

69. Tillard, "The Mission of the Bishop of Rome," 208.

70. *Unitatis redintegratio* #14: "For many centuries the churches of the east and of the west went their separate ways, though a communion of faith and sacramental life bound them together. If disagreements in faith and discipline arose among them, the Roman See acted by common consent as moderator."

71. Tillard, "The Mission of the Bishop of Rome," 209.

72. Tillard, "Roman Catholics and Anglicans: Is There a Future for Ecumenism?" *One in Christ* 32 (1996): 106–17, at 114.

73. Tillard, "Roman Catholics and Anglicans: Is There a Future for Ecumenism?" 114–16.

74. ARCIC-II, "The Gift of Authority" #59. The preceding section states: "Anglicans and Roman Catholics are already facing these issues [of authority and ministry], but their resolution may well take some time. However, there is no turning back in our journey toward full ecclesial communion. In light of our agreement, the commission believes our two communions should make more visible the *koinonia* we already have. Theological dialogue must continue at all levels in the churches, but is not of itself sufficient.

"For the sake of *koinonia* and a united Christian witness to the world, Anglican and Roman Catholic bishops should find ways of cooperating and developing relationships of mutual accountability in their exercise of oversight. At this new stage we have not only to *do* together whatever we can, but also to *be* together all that our existing *koinonia* allows" (#58).

Also see section #60: "The commission's work has resulted in sufficient agreement on universal primacy as a gift to be shared for us to propose that such a primacy could be offered and received even before our churches are in full communion. Both

Roman Catholics and Anglicans look to this ministry being exercised in collegiality and synodality — a ministry of *servus servorum Dei*.... This sort of primacy will already assist the church on earth to be the authentic catholic *koinonia* in which unity does not curtail diversity, and diversity does not endanger but enhances unity."

75. *The Bishop of Rome*, 48.

76. John Zizioulas, "The Institution of Episcopal Conferences: An Orthodox Reflection," *The Jurist* 48 (1988): 376–83, at 377.

77. Cardinal Roger Mahony and the Priests of the Los Angeles Archdiocese, " 'As I Have Done for You': Pastoral Letter on Ministry," *Origins* 29 (May 4, 2000): 741, 743–53, at 747.

78. Tillard, "Évangéliser l'humanité," 16–17.

79. John R. Quinn, *The Reform of the Papacy: The Costly Call to Christian Unity* (New York: Crossroad, 1999), 113; Richard R. Gaillardetz, *Teaching with Authority: A Theology of the Magisterium in the Church* (Collegeville, MN: Michael Glazier/Liturgical, 1997), 284; Reese, *Inside the Vatican*, 64.

80. Gaillardetz, *Teaching With Authority*, 283–84.

81. Reese, *Inside the Vatican*, 61, 64.

82. Archbishop Quinn writes that, at the 1998 Asian Synod, use of the word "subsidiarity" was forbidden by the curia (John R. Quinn, *The Reform of the Papacy: The Costly Call to Christian Unity* [New York: Crossroad, 1999], 113). Michael A. Fahey likewise has said that such topics as "liberation theology, basic Christian communities, the responsibilities of collegiality for the regional bishops, the restoration of the diaconate for women in the Church, the serious shortage of priests in most countries, and the need for theological research" were all proscribed in advance by the Secretariat of the 1997 Synod of America (Fahey, "The Synod of America: Reflections of a Nonparticipant," *Theological Studies* 59 [1998]: 486–504, at 503).

83. Ladislas Orsy, "The Papacy for an Ecumenical Age: A Response to Avery Dulles," *America* 183 (October 21, 2000): 9–15, at 11.

84. Francis A. Sullivan, "The Magisterium in the New Millennium," *America* 185 (August 27–September 3, 2001): 12–16.

85. Joseph Komonchak, "Consensus or Unanimity?: On the Authority of Bishops' Conferences," *America* 179 (September 12, 1998): 7–10, at 10.

86. For a critique of these critiques as beholden to flawed notions of "democratization," see George Weigel, "The Church's Teaching Authority and the Call for Democracy in North Atlantic Catholicism," in *Church Unity and the Papal Office: An Ecumenical Dialogue on John Paul II's Encyclical* Ut unum sint, ed. Carl E. Braaten and Robert W. Jenson (Grand Rapids, MI: Eerdmans, 2001), 142–58.

87. The standard reference is Joseph Komonchak, "Subsidiarity in the Church: The State of the Question," *The Jurist* 48 (1988): 298–349. Also Ad Leys, *Ecclesiological Impacts of the Principle of Subsidiarity* (Kampen: Kok, 1995); idem, "Structuring Communion: The Importance of the Principle of Subsidiarity," *The Jurist* 58 (1998): 84–123. This last article makes a helpful distinction, often overlooked by critics and supporters of subsidiarity alike: "But one should not see the principle of subsidiarity and decentralization as equivalent in content.... In decentralization the position of the highest authority prevails; it is a concession. But the principle of subsidiarity presupposes an original right of the person or the smaller community" (85). Too often, I think, talk of "decentralization" runs the risk of construing

ecclesial relationships solely along "power-sharing" models, which reduce otherwise legitimate sacramental claims to political tactics.

88. See Avery Dulles, "The Papacy for a Global Church," *America* 183 (July 15–22, 2000): 6–11, at 8–9. Ladislas Orsy replies that "the grace that pervades the church does not take away its humanity" ("The Papacy for an Ecumenical Age: A Response to Avery Dulles," 11). More broadly, Joseph Komonchak's entire ecclesiological corpus may be seen as an ongoing effort to explore, on the grounds of *Lumen gentium* #8, the meaning and consequences of the inseparability of the divine and human elements in the church, i.e., the church as both "God's gift" and "our achievement." One must therefore avoid "reductionisms" of all stripes, be they "sociological" or "theological." For a concise, accessible presentation of this theme, see his "The Church: God's Gift and Our Task," *Origins* 16 (April 2, 1987): 735–41.

89. *The Bishop of Rome,* 186.

90. This passage reads, in part: "In the face of such widely varying situations it is difficult for us to utter a unified message and to put forward a solution which has universal validity. Such is not our ambition, nor is it our mission. It is up to the Christian communities to analyze with objectivity the situation which is proper to their own country, to shed on it the light of the Gospel's unalterable words and to draw principles of reflection, norms of judgment and directive for action from the social teaching of the Church.... It is up to these Christian communities, with the help of the Holy Spirit, in communion with the bishops who hold responsibility and in dialogue with other Christian brethren and all men of good will, to discern the options and commitments which are called for in order to bring about the social, political, and economic changes seen in many cases to be urgently needed." For background and analysis, see Mary Elsbernd, "What Ever Happened to *Octogesima Adveniens?*" *Theological Studies* 56 (1995): 39–60.

91. *The Bishop of Rome,* 67.

92. *The Bishop of Rome,* 32.

93. Tillard, "The Mission of the Bishop of Rome," 199.

94. ARCIC-II, "The Gift of Authority" #54–57.

95. For an overview and analysis, see Peter C. Phan, *The Asian Synod: Texts and Commentaries* (Maryknoll, NY: Orbis, 2002). See also Thomas C. Fox, *Pentecost in Asia: A New Way of Being Church* (Maryknoll, NY: Orbis, 2002), esp. 149–97.

96. Cardinal Paul Shan Kuo-hsi, "Opening Report" [these titles are the editors', not the authors'] *Origins* 27 (April 30, 1998): 752–53, at 752.

97. Archbishop Leo Jun Ikenaga, "Asian Ways of Expression," *Origins* 27 (May 7, 1998): 769–70, at 770. He states elsewhere: "In Christianity, clear boundaries are given; God, the universe, the eternity of heaven and hell, sin, punishment, charity is rewarded and so forth. When we look at Buddhism, we find many of its Japanese, Indian, and East Asian members are pantheists, believe in the transmigration of souls, and there is a feeling that we cannot sort good from bad in the actions of man. Put in another way, we can say that in the West paternal characteristics are dominant, while in Asia, particularly East Asia, it is maternal traits that are operative. The fatherly figure divides and selects; the motherly figure unites and embraces all.... In the East we need to give greater expression to the feminine aspects of God: God who permeates the universe, lives in us through faith, receives all people in his embrace, the God of universal love, infinite tenderness, always ready to forgive, Christ atoning for all the sins of mankind on the cross. If our theology, art,

preaching, and evangelization move along these lines, then Christianity will take on a gentler, more approachable face for Asian people."

98. Bishop Francis Hadisumarta, "Enhanced Role for Bishops' Conferences," *Origins* 27 (May 7, 1998): 773–74.

99. Cardinal Angelo Sodano, "The Roman Curia's Role," *Origins* 27 (May 7, 1998): 774–75, at 775.

100. Cardinal William Baum, "Proclaiming the Truth about Jesus Christ," *Origins* 27 (May 7, 1998): 772–73.

101. Cardinal Julius Riyadi Darmaatmadja, "A Church with a Truly Asian Face," *Origins* 28 (May 28, 1998): 24–28, at 26.

102. *Lumen gentium* #13.

103. Tillard, "L'Universal et le Local: Réflexion sur Église universelle et Églises locales," *Irénikon* 60 (1987): 483–94, at 486.

104. Paul VI, *Evangelii nuntiandi* #14, 20.

105. Paul VI, *Evangelii nuntiandi* #20.

106. Paul VI, *Evangelii nuntiandi* #63.

107. See John Paul II, *Slavorum apostoli* #13–15. *Origins* 15 (July 18, 1985): 113, 115–25, at 119–20.

108. John Paul II, *Slavorum apostoli* #12, 17.

109. Commenting upon *Lumen gentium* #13, John Paul writes: "We can say without fear of contradiction that such a traditional and at the same time extremely up-to-date vision of the catholicity of the church — like a symphony of the various liturgies in all the world's languages united in one single liturgy or a melodious chorus sustained by the voices of unnumbered multitudes rising in countless modulations, tones, and harmonies for the praise of God from every part of the globe, at every moment of history — this vision corresponds in a particular way to the theological and pastoral vision which inspired the apostolic and missionary work of Constantine the Philosopher and of Methodius, and which sustained their mission among the Slav nations.

"In Venice, before the representatives of the ecclesiastical world, who held a rather narrow idea of the church and were opposed to this vision, St. Cyril defended it with courage" (*Slavorum apostoli* #17).

110. See *Slavorum apostoli* #21. Also *Redemptoris missio* #52 *Origins* 20 (January 31, 1991): 541, 543–68, at 556.

111. Pope John Paul II, "A Defense of the Rights of Aborigines," *Origins* 16 (December 11, 1986): 473, 475–77, at 476–77.

112. John Paul II, *Redemptoris missio* #52.

113. John Paul II, *Redemptoris missio* #54.

114. Pope John Paul II, *Novo millennio ineunte* #40, *Origins* 30 (January 18, 2001): 489, 491–508, at 502.

115. *Église d'églises,* 30.

116. I do not consider as major the schism effected by Archbishop Marcel Lefebvre and his followers.

117. Tillard, "Was the Holy Spirit at Canberra?" *One in Christ* 29 (1993): 34–64, at 40.

118. Tillard, "Was the Holy Spirit at Canberra?" 43.

119. Tillard, "Ecumenism: The Church's Costly Hope," 223.

120. Tillard, "Ecumenism: The Church's Costly Hope," 226.

121. *L'Église locale,* 93.

122. Tillard, "A New Age in Ecumenism," *One in Christ* 27 (1991): 320–31, at 329.

123. Tillard, "L'Universal et le Local: Réflexion sur Église universelle et Églises locales," *Irénikon* 61 (1988): 28–40, at 37.

124. Tillard, "L'Universal et le Local: Réflexion sur Église universelle et Églises locales," *Irénikon* 60 (1987): 483–94, at 492.

125. *L'Église locale,* 387–88.

126. See *L'Église locale,* 388. Also Tillard, " 'Communion' and Salvation," *One in Christ* 28 (1992): 1–12, at 8: "And catholicity would not be an essential qualification of the redeemed community if it consisted only in a recognition of diversity, without a simultaneous recognition of the oneness which Christ made real through the grace of his cross."

127. Tillard, "L'avenir de Foi et Constitution," *Irénikon* 66 (1993): 357–66, at 363–64. John Erickson has argued similarly, calling for a "baptismal ecclesiology" to balance the possible triumphalism of eucharistic ecclesiologies: "Is the Church's catholicity to be located simply in its radical openness to every value, its capacity to be comprehensive and embracing toward the rich variety and diversity of human experience and culture? The answer clearly is no.... The Church is a eucharistic organism, but only because the Church is a baptismal organism.

"Modern ecclesiology, like modern church practice, has tended to ignore the significance of baptism. Emphasis has been on eucharistic fellowship, with relatively little concern for the preconditions for this fellowship.

"...In our churches today we talk a great deal about the need for 'building community.' Early Christians knew that this community could be nothing other than a community of faith. Hence the importance of the catechumenate. It was not a matter of acquiring certain vital information. It involved a complete orientation to life, the exorcism of demons and renunciation of false gods, and above all the *traditio* and *redditio* — the receiving and giving back — of the Church's confession of faith. In this perspective the long-standing Orthodox insistence on the true faith as the content of catholicity takes on new meaning. It does not mean simply preserving the creed and other aspects of the teaching of the seven ecumenical councils as an inert deposit.... It means making one's own the very content of this faith — the revelation of the Holy Trinity — and expressing this content in all aspects of life.... These members [of the church] become catholic only in and through Christian initiation.

"...Exploration of the ecclesiological significance of baptism would also help to correct the present imbalance by reminding us that baptism is of vital importance not just for the individual on whom it is performed but for the Church as a whole, which sees itself in the penitent, the catechumen, the baptizand, the neophyte" (John H. Erickson, "The Local Churches and Catholicity: An Orthodox Perspective," *The Jurist* 52 (1992): 490–508, at 505–6, 508). Erickson reminds one that catholicity is fullness of life only in the Christ who dies and rises — as his followers do in baptism.

128. Tillard, " 'Communion' and Salvation," 8: "This fullness, this *katholou,* of the Lordship itself consists essentially in the conjunction of the power of the Redeemer overcoming the forces which lead humanity to division, and of the power of the Creator permitting all the diversities to blossom."

129. See "L'Universal et le Local," 485; "The Local Church within Catholicity," 452; "Évangéliser l'humanité," 6.

130. Tillard, "La catholicité de la mission," *Spiritus* 30 (1989): 347–64, at 349; "A New Age in Ecuemenism," 329; "Faith and Order after Canberra," *One in Christ* 27 (1991): 379–82, at 381; "'Communion' and Salvation," 7.

131. Tillard, "La catholicité de la mission," 349. See also "'Communion' and Salvation," 7: "Through Chrysostom, Basil, Ambrose we would be confirmed in our view that catholicity is related *en Christo* to the *pleroma*, the plenitude, of God's grace as it is related to the *pleroma* of human suffering and misery. Indeed, this misery cannot be identified with a kind of abstract, universal situation.... Thus, through each local Church authentically committed to its milieu, the Lordship of compassion, of mercifulness, of the 'sympathy' of Christ is exercised, in diverse ways according to the variety of needs and situations."

132. Tillard, "Reception-Communion," *One in Christ* 28 (1992): 307–22, at 321.

133. Tillard, "Ecumenism after Bangalore," *One in Christ* 15 (1979): 322–33, at 329. The interventions of the Asian Synod are particularly relevant here, in regard to both the supporters and critics of inculturation. One thinks of Bishop Hadisumarta's dismissal of "adaptation" as insufficient for the challenges facing the church in Asia, as well as curial conceptions of inculturation as a matter of "clothing" or "skin color."

134. Tillard, "La catholicité de la mission," 355: "Every culture stands in need of being evaluated and scrutinized in the light of the Gospel and its fundamental implications. Catholicity never receives indiscriminately what culture conveys, because this, too, is the object of salvation. And the 'inculturation' of faith has precisely the function of plunging culture into the efficacy of the Gospel, in 'saving' its riches. The local Church, in its specificity, is therefore not the mere mirror of society. And the Gospel does not confirm all that the cultural, social, ethnic milieu desires or pushes. Between the People of God and the people a threshold always exists. And this is not simply that which separates nature and supernature."

135. Tillard, "Was the Holy Spirit at Canberra?" 43.

136. Tillard, "Was the Holy Spirit at Canberra?" 44–45.

137. See Joseph Komonchak, "The Local Church and the Church Catholic: The Contemporary Theological Problematic," *The Jurist* 52 (1992): 416–47.

138. See, for instance, John Paul II, *Ut unum sint* #80: "It is the same Spirit who assists the magisterium and awakens the *sensus fidei.*"

139. Tillard's conception of inculturation is paralleled by his understanding of doctrinal truth: it "unfolds," rather than develops like a seed: "Normally, Christian Truth is unfolded in a 'catholic way,' that is, through its diverse expressions — remaining in *communion* — in the plurality of cultures, histories, and situations. In some places and some periods this actualization may be splendid, in other places and periods very weak. Moreover it happens that sometimes the spiritual life and quality of sacramental celebrations are regressing in some local churches.

"... But this concrete existence shows that the condition of this truth is not that of a seed led by its inner force toward an always more perfect development. It is the condition of a transcendent reality, delivered once for all (*ephapax*) with its whole richness (*katholou*) in the *kairos* of Christ Jesus, always *re-received* in the *communion* of all the local churches of God, remaining the same in its inner perfection (*katholou*) but expressed in the complex and constantly changing situation of humanity, sometimes advancing, sometimes regressing" ("Dogmatic Development and *Koinonia.*" In *New Perspectives in Historical Theology: Essays in Memory of John*

Meyendorff, ed. Bradley Nassif. [Grand Rapids, MI: Eerdmans, 1996], 172–85, at 185). Inculturation, like the apostolic witness, has its origin in the Pentecostal event. Such a "high" view of ecclesial and doctrinal fullness need not lead to triumphalism or to a fully realized eschatology, as "regression" and sinfulness remain ever-present in the church's pilgrimage in history.

140. See Tillard, "A New Age in Ecumenism," 329–31.

141. Tillard, "How Is Christian Truth Taught in the Roman Catholic Church?" *One in Christ* 34 (1998): 293–306, at 298–99.

142. John Paul II, *Redemptoris missio* #54.

143. John Paul II, *Redemptoris missio* #54.

144. Tillard, "The Fidelity of the Roman Catholic Church to the Faith of the Fathers," *One in Christ* 18 (1982): 131–40, at 137.

145. Tillard, "The Mission of the Bishop of Rome," 209.

146. See Ghislain Lafont's comment that "the Church can be truly ecumenical and open to religions *ad extra* only if it succeeds in determining fair norms in regard to its plurality *ad intra*" (*Imagining the Catholic Church: Structured Communion in the Spirit,* trans. John J. Burkhard. [Collegeville, MN: Michael Glazier/Liturgical, 2000], 87).

147. John Paul II, *Novo millennio ineunte* #57.

148. John Paul II, *Novo millennio ineunte* #2.

149. John Paul II, *Novo millennio ineunte* #3.

150. John Paul II, *Novo millennio ineunte* #29.

Conclusion

1. Pope Benedict XVI, "Homily at Mass of Possession of the Chair of the Bishop of Rome," online at:

http://212.77.1.245/holy_father/benedict_xvi/homilies/2005/documents/hf_ben-xvi_hom_20050507_san-giovanni-laterano_en.html.

2. Pope Benedict XVI, "Homily at Visit to the Roman Basilica of St. Paul-Outside-the-Walls," online at:

http://212.77.1.245/holy_father/benedict_xvi/homilies/2005/documents/hf_ben-xvi_hom_20050425_san-paolo_en.html.

3. Seen in this light, even a minor detail like the replacement on Benedict's papal coat-of-arms of the papal tiara with a bishop's miter indicates his hope for a simpler, less "powerful" ministry.

4. The Vatican reporter John L. Allen Jr. makes this point in his recent book *The Rise of Benedict XVI:* "Speaking on deepest background, two cardinals said they felt Ratzinger heard them [during the daily General Congregations of the cardinals held in the interregnum between John Paul II and Benedict XVI] in a way that John Paul II did not always manage; one, for example, said that while John Paul II always recognized him, he sometimes had to be prompted to recall his name, something that never happened with Ratzinger. Perhaps as pope, some of them found themselves ruminating, Ratzinger would be less tempted to personalize his reign, less given to imposing his own devotional, liturgical, and stylistic tastes, and more willing to surround himself with strong collaborators who would be able to provide him with a stronger, albeit informal, system of 'checks and balances' " (*The Rise of Benedict XVI: The Inside Story of How the Pope Was Elected and Where He Will Take the Catholic Church* [New York: Doubleday, 2005], 95).

5. Pope Benedict XVI, "First Message of His Holiness Benedict XVI at the End of the Eucharistic Concelebration with the Members of the College of Cardinals in the Sistine Chapel," online at:
http://212.77.1.245/holy_father/benedict_xvi/messages/pont-messages/2005/documents/hf_ben-xvi_mes_20050420_missa-pro-ecclesia_en.html.

6. Pope Benedict XVI, "Homily at Mass and Eucharistic Procession on the Solemnity of Corpus Domini," online at:
http://212.77.1.245/holy_father/benedict_xvi/homilies/2005/documents/hf_ben-xvi_hom_20050526_corpus-domini_en.html.

7. Pope Benedict XVI, "First Message of His Holiness Benedict XVI at the End of the Eucharistic Concelebration with the Members of the College of Cardinals in the Sistine Chapel," online at:
http://212.77.1.245/holy_father/benedict_xvi/messages/pont-messages/2005/documents/hf_ben-xvi_mes_20050420_missa-pro-ecclesia_en.html.

8. Pope Benedict XVI, "Discorso di Sua Santità Benedetto XVI alla Delegazione del Patriarchato Ecumenico di Costantinopoli," online at:
http://212.77.1.245/holy_father/benedict_xvi/speeches/2005/june/documents/hf_ben-xvi_spe_20050630_deleg-costantinopoli_it.html.
See also Ronald G. Roberson, "Facing East: New Initiatives toward the Orthodox," *America* 192 (May 16, 2005): 7–10.

9. Konrad Raiser, *Ecumenism in Transition: A Paradigm Shift in the Ecumenical Movement?* (Geneva: WCC Publications, 1991).

10. Jean-Marie Tillard, "Ecumenism: The Church's Costly Hope," 224. See also his "Crise dans les Églises: peut-on encore faire confiance au temps passé?" *Science et Esprit* 53 (2001): 219–31, esp. 226–29.

11. "Ecumenism: The Church's Costly Hope," 225.

12. "Ecumenism: The Church's Costly Hope," 226.

13. Cardinal Walter Kasper, "Homily to Conclude Christian Unity Week," at:
http://212.77.1.245/roman_curia/pontifical_councils/chrstuni/card-kasper-docs/rc_pc_chrstuni_doc_20050125_kasper-vespers_en.html [translation amended].

Bibliography

Primary Sources

Books

Tillard, Jean-Marie R. *Appel du Christ... Appels du monde: les religieux relisent leur appel.* Paris: Cerf, 1978. English translation: *Dilemmas of Modern Religious Life.* Wilmington, DE: Michael Glazier, 1984.

———. *Chair de l'Église, chair du Christ: Aux sources de l'ecclésiologie de communion.* Paris: Cerf, 1992. English translation: *Flesh of the Church, Flesh of Christ: At the Source of the Ecclesiology of Communion.* Translated by Madeleine Beaumont. Collegeville, MN: Liturgical Press/Pueblo, 2001.

———. *Devant Dieu et pour le monde: le projet des religieux.* Paris: Cerf, 1975.

———. *Église d'églises: L'ecclésiologie de communion.* Paris: Cerf, 1987. English translation: *Church of Churches: The Ecclesiology of Communion.* Translated by R. C. De Peaux. Collegeville, MN: Liturgical Press/Michael Glazier, 1992.

———. *L'Église locale: Ecclésiologie de communion et catholicité.* Paris: Cerf, 1995.

———. *L'Eucharistie, Pâque de l'Église.* Paris: Cerf, 1964. English translation: *The Eucharist: Pasch of God's People.* Translated by Dennis L. Wienk. Staten Island, NY: Alba House, 1967.

———. *L'évêque de Rome.* Paris: Cerf, 1982. English translation: *The Bishop of Rome.* Translated by John de Satgé. Wilmington, DE: Michael Glazier, 1983.

———. *Il y a charisme et charisme: La vie religieuse.* Bruxelles: Editions Lumen Vitae, 1977. English translation: *There Are Charisms and Charisms: The Religious Life.* Brussels: Lumen Vitae Press, 1977.

———. *Je crois en dépit de tout: Entretiens d'hiver avec Francesco Strazzari.* Paris: Cerf, 2001. English translation: *I Believe, Despite Everything,* ed. William G. Rusch. Collegeville, MN: Liturgical Press/Unitas, 2003.

———. *The Mystery of Religious Life.* Translated by George Courtright and R. F. Smith. St. Louis: B. Herder, 1967.

———. *Religieux, un chemin d'évangile.* Bruxelles: Editions Lumen Vitae, 1975. English translation: *A Gospel Path: The Religious Life.* Translated by Olga Prendergast. Brussels: Lumen Vitae Press, 1977.

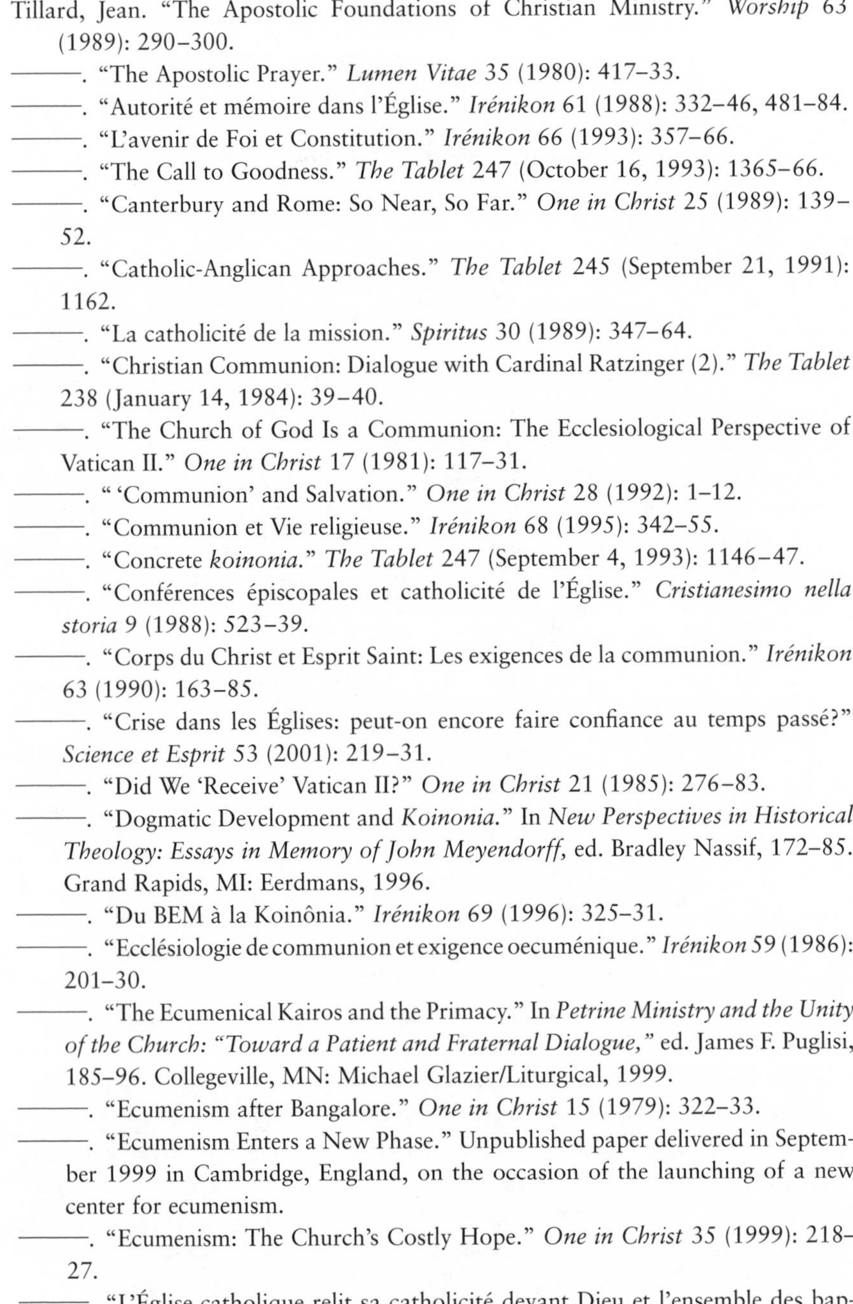

Articles

Tillard, Jean. "The Apostolic Foundations of Christian Ministry." *Worship* 63 (1989): 290–300.

———. "The Apostolic Prayer." *Lumen Vitae* 35 (1980): 417–33.

———. "Autorité et mémoire dans l'Église." *Irénikon* 61 (1988): 332–46, 481–84.

———. "L'avenir de Foi et Constitution." *Irénikon* 66 (1993): 357–66.

———. "The Call to Goodness." *The Tablet* 247 (October 16, 1993): 1365–66.

———. "Canterbury and Rome: So Near, So Far." *One in Christ* 25 (1989): 139–52.

———. "Catholic-Anglican Approaches." *The Tablet* 245 (September 21, 1991): 1162.

———. "La catholicité de la mission." *Spiritus* 30 (1989): 347–64.

———. "Christian Communion: Dialogue with Cardinal Ratzinger (2)." *The Tablet* 238 (January 14, 1984): 39–40.

———. "The Church of God Is a Communion: The Ecclesiological Perspective of Vatican II." *One in Christ* 17 (1981): 117–31.

———. " 'Communion' and Salvation." *One in Christ* 28 (1992): 1–12.

———. "Communion et Vie religieuse." *Irénikon* 68 (1995): 342–55.

———. "Concrete *koinonia*." *The Tablet* 247 (September 4, 1993): 1146–47.

———. "Conférences épiscopales et catholicité de l'Église." *Cristianesimo nella storia* 9 (1988): 523–39.

———. "Corps du Christ et Esprit Saint: Les exigences de la communion." *Irénikon* 63 (1990): 163–85.

———. "Crise dans les Églises: peut-on encore faire confiance au temps passé?" *Science et Esprit* 53 (2001): 219–31.

———. "Did We 'Receive' Vatican II?" *One in Christ* 21 (1985): 276–83.

———. "Dogmatic Development and *Koinonia*." In *New Perspectives in Historical Theology: Essays in Memory of John Meyendorff*, ed. Bradley Nassif, 172–85. Grand Rapids, MI: Eerdmans, 1996.

———. "Du BEM à la Koinônia." *Irénikon* 69 (1996): 325–31.

———. "Ecclésiologie de communion et exigence oecuménique." *Irénikon* 59 (1986): 201–30.

———. "The Ecumenical Kairos and the Primacy." In *Petrine Ministry and the Unity of the Church: "Toward a Patient and Fraternal Dialogue,"* ed. James F. Puglisi, 185–96. Collegeville, MN: Michael Glazier/Liturgical, 1999.

———. "Ecumenism after Bangalore." *One in Christ* 15 (1979): 322–33.

———. "Ecumenism Enters a New Phase." Unpublished paper delivered in September 1999 in Cambridge, England, on the occasion of the launching of a new center for ecumenism.

———. "Ecumenism: The Church's Costly Hope." *One in Christ* 35 (1999): 218–27.

———. "L'Église catholique relit sa catholicité devant Dieu et l'ensemble des baptisés." In *Vatican II and Its Legacy*, ed. M. Lamberigts and L. Kenis, 107–27. Leuven: Leuven University Press, 2002.

———. "Eglise et Salut: sur la sacramentalité de l'église." *Nouvelle Revue Théologique* 106 (1984): 658–85.
———. "L'Esprit Saint et la question oecuménique de l'institution ecclésiale: Point de vue de l'Occident latin." *Irénikon* 71 (1998): 17–41.
———. "Évangéliser l'humanité." Unpublished paper.
———. "The Eucharist in Apostolic Continuity." *One in Christ* 24 (1988): 14–24.
———. "Faith and Order after Canberra." *One in Christ* 27 (1991): 379–82.
———. "Faith: The Believer and the Church." *Mid-Stream* 34 (1995): 45–60.
———. "The Fidelity of the Roman Catholic Church to the Faith of the Fathers." *One in Christ* 18 (1982): 131–40.
———. "Final Report of the Last Synod." In *Synod 1985 — An Evaluation,* ed. Giuseppe Alberigo and James Provost, 64–77. Edinburgh: T&T Clark, 1986.
———. "From *Unitatis Redintegratio* to *Ut Unum Sint:* The Church's 'Reception' of the Ecumenical Implications of the Theology of *Communio.*" *Catholic International* 7 (1996): 76–80.
———. "The Gospel of God and the Church of God." *Mid-Stream* 35 (1996): 363–75.
———. "Les grandes lois de la rénovation de la vie religieuse (commentaire de la première partie)." In *L'adaptation et la rénovation de la vie religieuse,* ed. J. M. R. Tillard and Yves Congar, 77–158. Paris: Cerf, 1967.
———. "Hope from ARCIC." *The Tablet* 246 (October 3, 1992): 1243.
———. "How Is Christian Truth Taught in the Roman Catholic Church?" *One in Christ* 34 (1998): 293–306.
———. "In Search of Vatican II: Archbishop Quinn's 'The Reform of the Papacy.' " *One in Christ* 36 (2000): 176–84.
———. "Jésus Christ Vie du monde (perspective oecuménique)." *Irénikon* 55 (1982): 332–49.
———. "La justice, la paix, le respect de la Création: quel engagement pour l'Église catholique?" *Irénikon* 60 (1987): 5–15.
———. "*Koinonia*-Sacrament." *One in Christ* 22 (1986): 104–14.
———. "Liturgical Reform and Christian Unity." *One in Christ* 19 (1983): 227–49.
———. "The Local Church within Catholicity." *The Jurist* 52 (1992): 448–54.
———. "The Ministry of Unity." *One in Christ* 33 (1997): 97–111.
———. "The Mission of the Bishop of Rome: What Is Essential, What Is Expected?" *One in Christ* 34 (1998): 198–211.
———. "A New Age in Ecumenism." *One in Christ* 27 (1991): 320–31.
———. "L'obéissance religieuse." In *L'adaptation et la rénovation de la vie religieuse,* ed. J. M. R. Tillard and Yves Congar, 449–84. Paris: Cerf, 1967.
———. "One Church of God: The Church Broken in Pieces." *One in Christ* 17 (1981): 2–12.
———. "Our Goal: Full and Visible Communion." *One in Christ* 39 (2004): 39–50.
———. "Preparing for Unity — A Pastoral Approach to Ecumenism." *One in Christ* 16 (1980): 2–18.
———. "The Presence of Peter in the Ministry of the Bishop of Rome." *One in Christ* 27 (1991): 101–20.

———. "The Primacy-Conciliarity Tension." *Theology Digest* 41 (Spring 1994): 41–45.
———. "The Problem of Justification: a new context for study." *One in Christ* 26 (1990): 328–38.
———. "Reception — Communion." *One in Christ* 28 (1992): 307–22.
———. "Recognition of ministries: what is the real question?" *One in Christ* 21 (1985): 31–39.
———. "The Roman Catholic Church and Bilateral Dialogues." *One in Christ* 19 (1983): 368–77.
———. "The Roman Catholic Church and Education of Conscience." *One in Christ* 35 (1999): 313–25.
———. "Roman Catholics and Anglicans: Is There a Future for Ecumenism?" *One in Christ* 32 (1996): 106–17.
———. "Les Sacraments de l'Église." In *Initiation à la pratique de la théologie,* vol. 3, ed. Bernard Lauret and François Refoulé, 387–466. Paris: Cerf, 1982.
———. "Sacraments et communion ecclésiale." *Nouvelle Revue Théologique* 111 (1989): 641–63.
———. "Sacrificial Terminology and the Eucharist." *One in Christ* 17 (1981): 306–23.
———. "The Theological Significance of Local Churches for Episcopal Conferences." *The Jurist* 48 (1988): 220–26.
———. "Théologie et vie ecclésiale." In *Initiation à la pratique de la théologie,* vol. 1, ed. Bernard Lauret and François Refoulé, 160–82. Paris: Cerf, 1982.
———. "Théologies et 'dévotions' au pape depuis le Moyen Age. De Jean XXIII à . . . Jean XXIII." *Cristianesimo nella Storia* 22 (February 2001): 191–211.
———. "Towards an Ecumenical Ecclesiology of Communion." In *Ecumenism: Present Realities and Future Prospects,* ed. Lawrence S. Cunningham, 133–48. Notre Dame, IN: University of Notre Dame Press, 1998.
———. "Tradition and Authority: Dialogue with Cardinal Ratzinger (1)." *The Tablet* 238 (January 7, 1984): 15–17.
———. "L'Universal et le Local: Réflexion sur Église universelle et Églises locales." *Irénikon* 60 (1987): 483–94; 61 (1988): 28–40.
———. "Vatican II et l'après-concile: espoirs et craintes." In *Les Églises après Vatican II: dynamisme et prospective: actes du colloque international de Bologne — 1980,* ed. Giuseppe Alberigo. Paris: Beauchesne, 1981.
———. "The Voice of an Ecumenist." *Priests & People* 9 (1995): 27.
———. "Was the Holy Spirit at Canberra?" *One in Christ* 29 (1993): 34–64.
———. "We Are Different." *One in Christ* 22 (1986): 62–72.
———. "We Believe." *One in Christ* 27 (1991): 3–7.
———. "World Council Adrift." *The Tablet* 246 (September 26, 1992): 1194–96.
———. "The World Council of Churches in Quest of Its Identity." *Ecumenical Review* 50 (1998): 390–98.

Secondary Sources

Afanasieff, Nicolas. "The Church Which Presides in Love." In *The Primacy of Peter*, edited by John Meyendorff. Crestwood, NY: St. Vladimir's Seminary Press, 1992, 91–143.

———. "La Concile dans la théologie orthodoxe russe." *Irénikon* 35 (1962): 316–39.

———. "L'Eucharistie, principal lien entre les Catholiques et les Orthodoxes." *Irénikon* 38 (1965): 337–39.

———. "*Statio Orbis.*" *Irénikon* 35 (1962): 65–75.

———. "Una Sancta." *Irénikon* 36 (1963): 436–75.

Alberigo, Giuseppe. "The Local Church in the West (1500–1945)." *Heythrop Journal* 28 (1987): 125–43.

———. "Réforme et unité de l'Église." In *Yves Congar: 1904–1995*, edited by André Vauchez, 9–25. Paris: Cerf, 1999.

Anglican–Roman Catholic International Commission II. "The Church as Communion." *One in Christ* 27 (1991): 78–97.

———. "The Gift of Authority." *Origins* 29 (May 27, 1999): 17, 19–29.

Aquinas, Thomas. *The Sermon-Conferences of St. Thomas Aquinas on the Apostles' Creed.* Translation and introduction by Nicholas Ayo. Notre Dame, IN: University of Notre Dame Press, 1988.

Avis, Paul. "Don't Ask Too Much . . . " *The Tablet* 257 (January 25, 2003): 12–13.

Baillargeon, Gaëtan. "Jean Zizioulas, porte-parole de l'Orthodoxie contemporaine." *Nouvelle Revue Théologique* 111 (1989): 176–93.

Barr, Robert B. "The Changing Face of 'Sobornost.' " *Sciences Ecclésiastiques* 15 (1963): 59–71.

The Basic Sixteen Documents: Vatican Council II. Edited by Austin Flannery. Northport, NY: Costello, 1996.

Baum, Cardinal William. "Proclaiming the Truth about Jesus Christ." *Origins* 27 (May 7, 1998): 772–73.

Baycroft, John. "Memory as Ecumenical Motive and Method." In *Communion et Réunion: Mélanges Jean-Marie Roger Tillard,* edited by Gillian R. Evans and Michel Gourgues, 63–73. Leuven: Leuven University Press, 1995.

Beinert, Wolfgang. "Catholicity as a Property of the Church." *The Jurist* 52 (1992): 455–83.

———. *Um das dritte Kirchenattribut: Die Katholizität der Kirche im Verständnis der evangelische-lutherischen und römisch-katholischen Theologie der Gegenwart.* Essen: Ludgerus-Verlag Hubert Wingen KG, 1964.

Boff, Leonardo. *Church: Charism and Power.* Translated by John W. Diercksmeier. New York: Crossroad, 1985.

———. *Ecclesiogenesis: The Base Communities Reinvent the Church.* Translated by Robert R. Barr. Maryknoll, NY: Orbis, 1986.

Bouyer, Louis. *The Church of God: Body of Christ and Temple of the Spirit.* Translated by Charles Underhill Quinn. Chicago: Franciscan Herald, 1982.

Braaten, Carl E., and Robert W. Jenson, editors. *Church Unity and the Papal Office: An Ecumenical Dialogue on John Paul II's Encyclical* Ut unum sint. Grand Rapids, MI: Eerdmans, 2001.

Brødd, Sven-Erik. "A Communion of Martyrs: Perspectives on the Papal Encyclical Letter *Ut unum sint.*" *Ecumenical Review* 52 (April 2000): 223–33.

Brown, Raymond E. "New Testament Background for the Concept of Local Church." *Proceedings of the Catholic Theological Society of America* 36 (1981): 1–14.

Buckley, Michael J. *Papal Primacy and the Episcopate: Towards a Relational Understanding.* New York: Crossroad Herder, 1998.

Butler, Bishop Christopher. "The Bishop of Rome." *The Tablet* 236 (March 6, 1982): 222–24.

———. Review of *The Bishop of Rome. The Tablet* 237 (June 18, 1983): 585–86.

Carrasco Rouco, Alfonso. "Vatican II's Reception of the Dogmatic Teaching on the Roman Primacy." *Communio* 25 (Winter 1998): 576–603.

Carter, David. Review of *L'Église locale. One in Christ* 32 (1996): 378–85.

Caza, Lorraine. "Le théologien." In *Communion et Réunion: Mélanges Jean-Marie Roger Tillard,* edited by Gillian R. Evans and Michel Gourgues, 31–45. Leuven: Leuven University Press, 1995.

Chaput, Charles J. "Reflections on Walter Kasper's 'On the Church.'" *America* 185 (July 30–August 6, 2001): 18–19.

Charley, Julian. "A Passion for unity." *The Tablet* 257 (January 25, 2003): 10–11.

———. "*In Memoriam:* Jean Tillard, O.P." *Doctrine and Life* 51 (January 2001): 23–26.

Church Authority in American Culture: The Second Cardinal Bernardin Conference. Intro. Philip J. Murnion. New York: Herder & Herder, 1999.

Clément, Olivier. *Rome, autrement: Une réflexion orthodoxe sur la papauté.* Paris: Desclée de Brouwer, 1997.

Congar, Yves. *After Nine Hundred Years: The Background of the Schism between the Eastern and Western Churches.* New York: Fordham University Press, 1959.

———. *Chrétiens Désunis: Principes d'un "Oecuménisme" Catholique.* Paris: Cerf, 1937.

———. "Conclusion." In *Le Concile et les Conciles.* Paris: Cerf, 1960, 285–334.

———. "Conscience ecclésiologique en Orient et en Occident du VIe au XIe siècle." *Istina* 6 (1959): 187–236.

———. "De la communion des Églises à une ecclésiologie de l'Église universelle." In *L'Épiscopat et l'Église universelle,* edited by Yves Congar and Bernard-Dominique Dupuy, 227–60. Paris: Cerf, 1962.

———. *Jalons pour une théologie du laicat.* Paris: Cerf, 1953.

———. *Journal d'un théologien, 1946–1956,* edited by Étienne Fouilloux, with Dominique Congar, André Duval, and Bernard Montagnes. Paris: Cerf, 2000.

———. "La pensée de Möhler et l'Ecclésiologie orthodoxe." *Irénikon* 12 (1935): 321–29.

———. "La signification oecuménique de l'oeuvre de Möhler." *Irénikon* 15 (1938): 113–30.

———. *L'Église: De saint Augustin à l'époque moderne.* Paris: Cerf, 1970.

———. *Mon journal du Concile: 1960–66.* 2 vols. Edited by Éric Mahieu. Paris: Cerf, 2002.

———. "Note on the Words 'Confession,' 'Church,' and 'Communion.'" In *Dialogue between Christians: Catholic Contributions to Ecumenism.* Translated by Philip Loretz, 184–213. Westminster, MD: Newman, 1966.

———. "Preface: The Call and the Quest, 1929–1963." In *Dialogue between Christians: Catholic Contributions to Ecumenism,* translated by Philip Loretz, 1–51. Westminster, MD: Newman, 1966.

———. *Sainte Église: Études et approches ecclésiologiques.* Paris: Cerf, 1963.

———. "Sur l'évolution et l'interprétation de la pensée de Moehler." *Revue des Sciences Philosophiques et Théologiques* 27 (1938): 205–12.

———. "Théologie de l'Église particulière." In *Mission sans frontières,* edited by Antonin M. Henry, 17–52. Paris: Cerf, 1960.

———. *Vraie et fausse réforme dans l'Église.* Paris: Cerf, 1968.

Congregation for the Doctrine of the Faith. "The Expression 'Sister Churches.'" *Origins* 30 (September 14, 2000): 222–24.

———. "Reflections on the Primacy of Peter." *Origins* 28 (January 28, 1999): 560–63.

———. "Some Aspects of the Church Understood as Communion." *Origins* 22 (June 25, 1992): 108–12.

Cornwell, Peter. ". . . but Love Takes Risks." *The Tablet* 257 (January 25, 2003): 13.

Cunningham, Agnes. "A Roman Catholic Response [to *The Bishop of Rome*]." *Ecumenical Trends* 13 (1984): 116–17.

Cunningham, Lawrence S. "On Contemporary Martyrs: Some Recent Literature." *Theological Studies* 63 (2002): 374–81.

———. "Saints and Martyrs: Some Contemporary Considerations." *Theological Studies* 60 (1999): 529–37.

———. "The Universal Call to Holiness: Martyrs of Charity and Witnesses of Truth." In *The New Catholic Encyclopedia Jubilee Volume: The Wojtyla Years.* Washington, DC: Catholic University of America Press, 2001, 109–16.

Daley, Brian E. "Headship and Communion: American Orthodox-Catholic Dialogue on Synodality and Primacy in the Church." *Pro Ecclesia* 5 (1996): 55–72.

———. "The Ministry of Primacy and the Communion of Churches." In *Church Unity and the Papal Office: An Ecumenical Dialogue on John Paul II's Encyclical* Ut unum sint. Edited by Carl E. Braaten and Robert W. Jenson, 27–58. Grand Rapids, MI: Eerdmans, 2001.

———. "Position and Patronage in the Early Church: The Original Meaning of 'Primacy of Honour.'" *Journal of Theological Studies* 44 (1993): 529–53.

———. "Some Reflections on the Ecclesiology of Communion in the Roman Catholic Church Today." Unpublished paper presented to the May 1994 meeting of the American Orthodox-Roman Catholic Consultation.

———. "Structures of Charity: Bishops' Gatherings and the See of Rome in the Early Church." In *Episcopal Conferences: Historical, Canonical, and Theological Studies,* edited by Thomas J. Reese, 25–58. Washington, DC: Georgetown University Press, 1989.

Danneels, Godfried. "The Contemporary Person and the Church: An Intervention at the Consistory." *America* 185 (July 30–August 6, 2001): 6–9.

Darmaatmadja, Cardinal Julius Riyadi. "A Church with a Truly Asian Face." *Origins* 28 (May 28, 1998): 24–28.

Denaux, Adelbert. "The Anglican–Roman Catholic Dialogue about Authority in the Church." *Louvain Studies* 24 (1999): 291–318.

———. "L'Église comme communion: réflexions à propos du rapport final du synode extraordinaire de 1985." *Nouvelle Revue Théologique* 110 (1988): 16–37, 161–80.

Doyle, Dennis M. "Book Essay: Communion Ecclesiology." *Church* 12 (Spring 1996): 41–44.

———. *Communion Ecclesiology: Visions and Versions.* Maryknoll, NY: Orbis, 2000.

———. "Communion Ecclesiology and the Silencing of Boff." *America* 187 (September 10, 1992): 139–43.

———. "Communion Ecclesiology: Beyond Left-Right Dichotomies?" *Pro Ecclesia* 6 (1997): 7–12.

———. "Henri de Lubac and the Roots of Communion Ecclesiology." *Theological Studies* 60 (1999): 209–27.

———. "Journet, Congar, and the Roots of Communion Ecclesiology." *Theological Studies* 58 (1997): 461–79.

———. "Möhler, Schleiermacher, and the Roots of Communion Ecclesiology." *Theological Studies* 57 (1996): 467–80.

Dulles, Avery. "A Half Century of Ecclesiology." *Theological Studies* 50 (1989): 419–42.

———. *The Catholicity of the Church.* Oxford: Clarendon, 1985.

———. "The Church as Communion." In *New Perspectives in Historical Theology: Essays in Memory of John Meyendorff,* edited by Bradley Nassif, 125–39. Grand Rapids, MI: Eerdmans, 1996.

———. "Doctrinal Authority of Episcopal Conferences." In *Episcopal Conferences: Historical, Canonical, and Theological Studies,* edited by Thomas J. Reese, 207–31. Washington, DC: Georgetown University Press, 1989.

———. "The Ecclesiology of John Paul II." *Origins* 28 (April 22, 1999): 759–63.

———. "A New Orthodox View of the Papacy." *Pro Ecclesia* 12 (2003): 345–58.

———. "The Papacy for a Global Church." *America* 183 (July 15–22, 2000): 6–11.

———. "The Petrine Office at the Service of Unity." *Origins* 31 (April 4, 2002): 704–8.

Dulles, Avery, and Ladislas Orsy. "In Dialogue." *America* 183 (November 25, 2000): 12–15.

Elsbernd, Mary. "What Ever Happened to *Octogesima Adveniens?*" *Theological Studies* 56 (1995): 39–60.

Erickson, John H. "The Local Churches and Catholicity: An Orthodox Perspective." *The Jurist* 52 (1992): 490–508.

Evans, Gillian R. Review of *Church of Churches: The Ecclesiology of Communion. Heythrop Journal* 35 (1994): 211.

Evdokimov, Paul. *L'Orthodoxie.* Paris: Delachaux et Niestlé, 1959.

Extraordinary Synod of Bishops (1985). "The Final Report: The Church, in the Word of God, Celebrates the Mystery of Christ for the Salvation of the World." *Origins* 15 (December 19, 1985): 444–50.

———. "A Message to the People of God." *Origins* 15 (December 19, 1985): 441, 443–44.

Fabry, Michael B. "*Communio* and the Local Community: Recapturing Traditional Understandings of Church." Ph.D. dissertation, Graduate Theological Union, 1998.

Fahey, Michael A. "Am I My Sister's Keeper?: The Vatican's New Letter on 'Sister Churches.' " *America* 183 (October 28, 2000): 12–15.

———. "The Synod of America: Reflections of a Nonparticipant." *Theological Studies* 59 (1998): 486–504.

Famerée, Joseph. "*'Chrétiens désunis'* du P. Congar 50 ans après." *Nouvelle Revue Théologique* 110 (1988): 666–86.

———. "Communion in Baptism: A Catholic Viewpoint and Ecumenical Questions." *One in Christ* 36 (2000): 205–22.

———. "L'ecclésiologie du Père Yves Congar: Essai de synthèse critique." *Revue des Sciences Philosophiques et Théologiques* 76 (1992): 377–419.

———. *L'ecclésiologie d'Yves Congar avant Vatican II: Analyse et reprise.* Leuven: Leuven University Press, 1992.

———. "Formation et ecclésiologie du 'premier' Congar." In *Yves Congar: 1904–1995,* edited by André Vauchez, 51–70. Paris: Cerf, 1999.

———. "Orthodox Influence on the Roman Catholic Theologian Yves Congar, O.P.: A Sketch." *St. Vladimir's Theological Quarterly* 39 (1995): 409–16.

Florovsky, Georges. "The Catholicity of the Church." In *Bible, Church, Tradition: An Eastern Orthodox View.* Collected Works, vol. 1: 37–55. Belmont, MA: Nordland, 1972.

———. "The Church: Her Nature and Task." In *Bible, Church, Tradition: An Eastern Orthodox View.* Collected Works, vol. 1: 57–72. Belmont, MA: Nordland, 1972.

Fois, Mario. "Il vescovo di Roma." *Civiltà Cattolica* 139 (September 1988): 502–7.

Fouilloux, Etienne. "Frère Yves, Cardinal Congar, Dominican: Itinéraire d'un théologien." *Revue des Sciences Philosophiques et Théologiques* 79 (1995): 379–404.

———. *Les catholiques & l'unité chrétienne du xix au xx siècle: Itinéraires européens d'expression française.* Paris: Centurion, 1982.

———. *Une Église en quête de liberté: La pensée catholique française entre modernisme et Vatican II, 1914–1962* Paris: Desclée de Brouwer, 1998.

Fox, Thomas C. *Pentecost in Asia: A New Way of Being Church.* Maryknoll, NY: Orbis, 2002.

Gaillardetz, Richard R. *By What Authority?: A Primer on Scripture, the Magisterium, and the Sense of the Faithful.* Collegeville, MN: Liturgical Press, 2003.

———. *Teaching with Authority: A Theology of the Magisterium in the Church.* Collegeville, MN: Michael Glazier/Liturgical, 1997.

Galot, Jean. Review of *L'Église locale. Gregorianum* 78 (1997): 384–85.

Galvin, John P. "The Church as Communion: Comments on a Letter of the Congregation for the Doctrine of the Faith." *One in Christ* 29 (1993): 310–17.

Geernaert, Donna. "*Koinonia:* Integrating Issues of Faith and Justice in Ecumenical Dialogue." In *Communion et Réunion: Mélanges Jean-Marie Roger Tillard,* edited by Gillian R. Evans and Michel Gourgues, 139–47. Leuven: Leuven University Press, 1995.

George, Cardinal Francis. "Episcopal Conferences: Theological Bases." *Communio* 26 (1999): 393–409.

González de Cardenal, Olegario. "Development of a Theology of the Local Church from the First to the Second Vatican Council." *The Jurist* 52 (1992): 11–43.

Granfield, Patrick. "The Concept of the Church as Communion." *Origins* 28 (April 22, 1999): 753, 755–58.

Gratieux. Albert. *A. S. Khomiakov et le Mouvement Slavophile: Les Doctrines.* Paris: Cerf, 1939.

———. *A. S. Khomiakov et le Mouvement Slavophile: Les Hommes.* Paris: Cerf, 1939.

Greatrex, Joan. "*Koinonia* as the Key to the Church's Self-Understanding and to Ecumenical Rapprochement." In *Communion et Réunion: Mélanges Jean-Marie Roger Tillard,* edited by Gillian R. Evans and Michel Gourgues, 149–56. Leuven: Leuven University Press, 1995.

Grimes, Donald J. Review of *The Bishop of Rome. Theological Studies* 45 (1984): 369–70.

Gros, Jeffrey. Review of *Chair de l'Église, chair du Christ. St. Vladimir's Theological Quarterly* 39 (1995): 315–17.

Gutiérrez, Gustavo. *The Density of the Present: Selected Writings.* Maryknoll, NY: Orbis, 1999.

Hadisumarta, Bishop Francis. "Enhanced Role for Bishops' Conferences." *Origins* 27 (May 7, 1998): 773–74.

Hamer, Jérôme. *L'Église est une communion.* Paris: Cerf, 1962.

Hatt, Harold. Review of *Église d'Églises. Journal of Ecumenical Studies* 25 (1989): 122–23.

Healy, Nicholas Martin. *Church, World and Christian Life: Practical-Prophetic Ecclesiology.* Cambridge: Cambridge University Press, 2000.

———. "Communion Ecclesiology: A Cautionary Note." *Pro Ecclesia* 4 (1995): 442–53.

———. "The Logic of Modern Ecclesiology: Four Case Studies and a Suggestion from St. Thomas Aquinas." Ph.D. dissertation, Yale University, 1992: 55–95.

Hebblethwaite, Peter. "Successor of Peter." *The Tablet* 238 (July 14, 1984): 669–70.

Henn, William. *The Honor of My Brothers: A Brief History of the Relation between the Pope and the Bishops.* New York: Herder and Herder, 2000.

———. "Yves Congar, O.P. (1904–95)" *America* 173 (August 12, 1995): 23–25.

Himes, Michael J. *Ongoing Incarnation: Johann Adam Möhler and the Beginnings of Modern Ecclesiology.* New York: Crossroad Herder, 1997).

Hinze, Bradford E. "The Holy Spirit and the Catholic Tradition: The Legacy of Johann Adam Möhler." In *The Legacy of the Tübingen School: The Relevance of Nineteenth-Century Theology for the Twenty-First Century,* edited by Donald J. Dietrich and Michael J. Himes, 75–94. New York: Crossroad Herder, 1997.

Hume, Cardinal Basil. "A Bishop's Relation to the Universal Church and His Fellow Bishops." *Origins* 29 (July 1, 1999): 108–12.

Hussey, M. Edmund. "Nicholas Afanassiev's Eucharistic Ecclesiology: A Roman Catholic Viewpoint." *Journal of Ecumenical Studies* 12 (1975): 235–52.

Ikenaga, Archbishop Leo Jun. "Asian Ways of Expression." *Origins* 27 (May 7, 1998): 769–70.

John Paul II, Pope. *Christifideles laici. Origins* 18 (February 9, 1989): 561, 563–95.

———. "A Defense of the Rights of Aborigines." *Origins* 16 (December 11, 1986): 473, 475–77.

———. "*Dominus Iesus.*" *Origins* 30 (September 14, 2000): 209, 211–19.

———. *Novo millennio ineunte. Origins* 30 (January 18, 2001): 489, 491–508.

———. *Redemptoris missio. Origins* 20 (January 31, 1991): 541, 543–68.

———. *Slavorum apostoli. Origins* 15 (July 18, 1985): 113, 115–25.

———. *Tertio millennio adveniente. Origins* 24 (November 24, 1994): 401, 403–16.

———. "The Theological and Juridical Nature of Episcopal Conferences (*Apostolos suos*)." *Origins* 28 (July 30, 1998): 152–58.

———. *Ut unum sint. Origins* 25 (June 8, 1995): 49, 51–72.

———. "Vatican Council II: Prophetic Message for the Church's Life." *Origins* 29 (May 4, 2000): 753–55.

Johnson, Luke Timothy. "*Koinonia:* Diversity and Unity in Early Christianity." *Theology Digest* 46 (1999): 303–13.

Jossua, Jean-Pierre. "L'oeuvre oecuménique du Père Congar." *Études* 357 (1982): 543–55.

———. "Yves Congar: Un portrait." *Études* 383 (1995): 211–18.

Kasper, Walter. "Church as *Communio.*" *Communio* 12 (1986): 100–117.

———. "On the Church." *The Tablet* 255 (June 23, 2001): 927–30.

———. *Theology and Church.* New York: Crossroad, 1989.

Kaszowski, Michal. "Les sources de l'ecclésiologie eucharistique du P. Nicolas Afanassieff." *Ephemerides Theologicae Lovanienses* 52 (1976): 331–43.

Kehl, Medard. "Der Disput der Kardinäle: Zum Verhältnis von Universalkirche und Ortskirchen." *Stimmen der Zeit* 221 (April 2003): 219–32.

Kelly, Gerard. *Recognition: Advancing Ecumenical Thinking.* New York: Peter Lang, 1996.

Kelly, J. N. D. *Early Christian Creeds.* London: Longman, 1972.

Khomiakov, Alexei Stepanovich. *The Church Is One.* London: SPCK, 1948.

———. *L'Église latine et le Protestantisme au point de vue de l'Église d'orient* (Lausanne: Benda, 1872).

Kilian, Sabbas J. "The Meaning and Nature of the Local Church." *Proceedings of the Catholic Theological Society of America* 35 (1980): 244–55.

———. "Pope Paul VI's Theology of the Local Church." *Proceedings of the Catholic Theological Society of America* 36 (1981): 130–34.

Kniazeff, Alexis. *L'Institut Saint-Serge: De l'academie d'autrefois au rayonnement d'aujourd'hui.* Paris: Editions Beauchesne, 1974.

Komonchak, Joseph A. "The Church: God's Gift and Our Task." *Origins* 16 (April 2, 1987): 735–41.

———. "The Church Is a Communion." *Liturgy* 3/2 (1983): 7–11.

———. "Consensus or Unanimity?: On the Authority of Bishops' Conferences." *America* 179 (September 12, 1998): 7–10.

———. "Ecclesiology and Social Theory: A Methodological Essay." *The Thomist* 45 (1981): 262–83.

———. "Ecclesiology of Vatican II." *Origins* 28 (April 22, 1999): 763–68.

———. "The Epistemology of Reception." *The Jurist* 57 (1997): 180–203.

———. "A Hero of Vatican II: Yves Congar." *Commonweal* 122 (December 1, 1995): 15–17.

———. "Introduction: Episcopal Conferences under Criticism." In *Episcopal Conferences: Historical, Canonical, and Theological Studies,* edited by Thomas J. Reese, 1–22. Washington, DC: Georgetown University Press, 1989.

———. "The Local Church and the Church Catholic: The Contemporary Theological Problematic." *The Jurist* 52 (1992): 416–47.

———. "Ministry and the Local Church." *Proceedings of the Catholic Theological Society of America* 36 (1981): 56–82.

———. "Missing Person: Review of *Heart of the World, Center of the Church.*" *Commonweal* 124 (September 12, 1997): 34–35.

———. "The Roman Working Paper on Episcopal Conferences." In *Episcopal Conferences: Historical, Canonical, and Theological Studies,* edited by Thomas J. Reese, 177–204. Washington, DC: Georgetown University Press, 1989.

———. "The Significance of Vatican Council II for Ecclesiology." In *The Gift of the Church: Essays on Ecclesiology in Honor of Patrick Granfield, O.S.B.* edited by Peter Phan, 69–92. Collegeville, MN: Michael Glazier/Liturgical Press, 2000.

———. "Subsidiarity in the Church: The State of the Question." *The Jurist* 48 (1988): 298–349.

———. "The Theological Debate." In *Synod 1985 — An Evaluation,* edited by Giuseppe Alberigo and James Provost, 53–63. Edinburgh: T&T Clark, 1986.

———. "The Theology of the Local Church: The State of the Question." In *The Multicultural Church,* edited by William Cenkner, 35–53. New York: Paulist, 1996.

———. "Vatican II as an 'Event.' " *Theology Digest* 46 (1999): 337–52.

Lafont, Ghislain. *Imagining the Catholic Church: Structured Communion in the Spirit.* Translated by John J. Burkhard. Collegeville, MN: Michael Glazier/Liturgical, 2000.

Lanne, Emmanuel. "The Local Church: Its Catholicity and Apostolicity." *One in Christ* 6 (1970): 288–313.

———. Review of *Chair de l'Église, chair du Christ. Irénikon* 65 (1992): 157–58.

———. Review of *Église d'Églises. Irénikon* 60 (1987): 317–18.

———. Review of *L'Église locale. Irénikon* 68 (1995): 593.

———. Review of *L'évêque de Rome. Irénikon* 55 (1982): 153.

Legrand, Hervé. "Collégialité des évêques et communion des Églises dans la réception de Vatican II." *Revue des Sciences Philosophiques et Théologiques* 75 (1991): 545–68.

———. "La réalization de l'Église en un lieu." In *Initiation à la pratique de la théologie,* vol. 3, edited by Bernard Lauret and François Refoulé, 143–345. Paris: Cerf, 1982.

———. "Les évêques, les Églises locales et l'Église entière." *Revue des Sciences Philosophiques et Théologiques* 85 (2001): 461–509.

———. " 'One Bishop per City': Tensions Around the Expression of the Catholicity of the Local Church since Vatican II." *The Jurist* 52 (1992): 369–400.

———. "Reception, *Sensus Fidelium,* and Synodal Life: An Effort at Articulation." *The Jurist* 57 (1997): 405–31.

Leys, Ad. "Structuring Communion: The Importance of the Principle of Subsidiarity." *The Jurist* 58 (1998): 84–123.

Lossky, Nicolas. "Conciliarity-Primacy in a Russian Orthodox Perspective." In *Petrine Ministry and the Unity of the Church: "Toward a Patient and Fraternal Dialogue,"* edited by James F. Puglisi, 127–35. Collegeville, MN: Michael Glazier/Liturgical, 1999.

———. "J.-M. R. Tillard op." *Contacts: Revue Française de Orthodoxy* 194 (April 2001): 98–106.

Lossky, Vladimir. "Catholic Consciousness: Anthropological Implications of the Dogma of the Church." In *The Image and Likeness of God,* edited by John H. Erickson and Thomas E. Bird, 183–94. Crestwood, NY: St. Vladimir's Seminary Press, 1974.

———. "Concerning the Third Mark of the Church: Catholicity." In *The Image and Likeness of God.* Crestwood, NY: St. Vladimir's Seminary Press, 1974, 169–81.

———. "Two Aspects of the Church." In *The Mystical Theology of the Eastern Church.* Crestwood, NY: St. Vladimir's Seminary Press, 1976, 174–95.

Lubac, Henri de. *At the Service of the Church: Henri de Lubac Reflects on the Circumstances That Occasioned His Writings.* Translated by Anne Elizabeth Englund. San Francisco: Ignatius Press, 1993.

———. *Catholicism: Christ and the Common Destiny of Man.* Translated by Lancelot C. Sheppard and Sister Elizabeth Englund, O.C.D. San Francisco: Ignatius Press, 1988.

———. *Corpus Mysticum: L'Eucharistie et L'Église au Moyen Age.* 2d ed. Paris: Aubier, 1949.

———. *The Motherhood of the Church Followed by Particular Churches in the Universal Church.* Translated by Sr. Sergia Englund, O.C.D. San Francisco: Ignatius Press, 1982.

———. *The Splendour of the Church.* Translated by Michael Mason. New York: Sheed and Ward, 1956.

Mahony, Cardinal Roger, and the Priests of the Los Angeles Archdiocese. "'As I Have Done for You': Pastoral Letter on Ministry." *Origins* 29 (May 4, 2000): 741, 743–53.

Mailhiot, Gilles-Dominique. "Le professeur." In *Communion et Réunion: Mélanges Jean-Marie Roger Tillard,* edited by Gillian R. Evans and Michel Gourgues, 21–30. Leuven: Leuven University Press, 1995.

Manna, Salvatore. "L'oecuméniste." In *Communion et Réunion: Mélanges Jean-Marie Roger Tillard,* edited by Gillian R. Evans and Michel Gourgues, 47–59. Leuven: Leuven University Press, 1995.

Markey, John Joseph. "Community and Communion: An Analysis of the Understandings of Community in Some 'Communion Ecclesiologies' in Post–Vatican II Roman Catholic Thought and a Proposal for Clarification and Further Dialogue." Ph.D. dissertation, Graduate Theological Union, 1997.

McBrien, Richard P. Review of *Church of Churches. Worship* 67 (1993): 381–83.

McDonnell, Kilian. "Our Dysfunctional Church." *The Tablet* 255 (September 8, 2001): 1260–61.

———. "The Ratzinger/Kasper Debate: The Universal Church and Local Churches." *Theological Studies* 63 (June 2002): 227–50.

———. "Vatican II (1962–1964), Puebla (1979), Synod (1985): *Koinonia/Communio* as an Integral Ecclesiology." *Journal of Ecumenical Studies* 25 (1988): 399–427.

———. "Walter Kasper on the Theology and Praxis of the Bishop's Office." *Theological Studies* 63 (December 2002): 711–29.

McGoldrick, Terence. "Episcopal Conferences Worldwide on Catholic Social Teaching." *Theological Studies* 59 (1998): 22–50.

McManus, Eamon. "Aspects of Primacy according to Two Orthodox Theologians." *One in Christ* 36 (2000): 234–50.

McPartlan, Paul. *The Eucharist Makes the Church: Henri de Lubac and John Zizioulas in Dialogue.* Edinburgh: T&T Clark, 1993.

———. *The Sacrament of Salvation: An Introduction to Eucharistic Ecclesiology.* Edinburgh: T&T Clark, 1995.

Medina, Cardinal Jorge A. "Cardinal Jorge A. Medina on the ICEL Controversy." *America* 182 (May 13, 2000): 17–19.

Meyendorff, John. "An Orthodox Response [to *The Bishop of Rome*]." *Ecumenical Trends* 13 (1984): 119–20.

———. "The Catholicity of the Church." In *Living Tradition.* Crestwood, NY: St. Vladimir's Seminary Press, 1978, 81–97.

———. "One Bishop in One City." In *Orthodoxy and Catholicity.* New York: Sheed and Ward, 1966, 107–18.

———. Review of Aidan Nichols, *Theology in the Russian Diaspora: Church, Fathers, Eucharist in Nikolai Afanas'ev (1893–1966)." St. Vladimir's Theological Quarterly* 34 (1990): 361–64.

———. "Visions of the Church: Russian Theological Thought in Modern Times." In *Rome, Constantinople, Moscow: Historical and Theological Studies.* Crestwood, NY: St. Vladimir's Seminary Press, 1996, 183–91.

Möhler, Johann Adam. *Symbolism: Exposition of the Doctrinal Differences between Catholics and Protestants as Evidenced by their Symbolical Writings.* Translated by James Burton Robertson with Intro. by Michael J. Himes. New York: Crossroad Herder, 1997.

———. *Unity in the Church, or the Principle of Catholicism: Presented in the Spirit of the Church Fathers of the First Three Centuries.* Edited and translated by Peter C. Erb. Washington, DC: Catholic University of America Press, 1996.

Mucci, G. Review of *Église d'Églises. Civiltà Cattolica* 139 (July 2, 1988): 95–96.

Müller, Hubert. "How the Local Church Lives and Affirms Its Catholicity." *The Jurist* 52 (1992): 340–64.

Nichols, Aidan. *Theology in the Russian Diaspora: Church, Fathers, Eucharist in Nikolai Afanas'ev.* Cambridge: Cambridge University Press, 1989.

———. *The Theology of Joseph Ratzinger.* Edinburgh: T&T Clark, 1988.

O'Connor, Michael. "The Holy Spirit and the Church in Catholic Theology: A Study in the Ecclesiology of J.-M. R. Tillard." *One in Christ* 28 (1992): 331–41.

O'Malley, John W. "The Millennium and the Papalization of Catholicism." *America* 182 (April 8, 2000): 8–16.

O'Meara, Thomas F. "Beyond 'Hierarchology': Johann Adam Möhler and Yves Congar." In *The Legacy of the Tübingen School: The Relevance of Nineteenth-Century Theology for the Twenty-First Century,* edited by Donald J. Dietrich and Michael J. Himes, 173–91. New York: Crossroad Herder, 1997.

———. *Church and Culture: German Catholic Theology, 1860–1914.* Notre Dame, IN: University of Notre Dame Press, 1991.

———. *Romantic Idealism and Roman Catholicism: Schelling and the Theologians.* Notre Dame, IN: University of Notre Dame Press, 1982.

Orsy, Ladislas. "The Papacy for an Ecumenical Age: A Response to Avery Dulles." *America* 183 (October 21, 2000): 9–15.

———. "Reflections on the Teaching Authority of the Episcopal Conferences." In *Episcopal Conferences: Historical, Canonical, and Theological Studies,* edited by Thomas J. Reese, 233–52. Washington, DC: Georgetown University Press, 1989.

Phan, Peter C. *The Asian Synod: Texts and Commentaries* (Maryknoll, NY: Orbis, 2002.

Plekon, Michael. "'Always Everyone and Always Together': The Eucharistic Ecclesiology of Nicolas Afanasiev's *The Lord's Supper* Revisited." *St. Vladimir's Theological Quarterly* 41 (1997): 141–74.

Pottmeyer, Hermann J. "The Church as Mysterium and as Institution." In *Synod 1985 — An Evaluation,* edited by Giuseppe Alberigo and James Provost, 99–109. Edinburgh: T&T Clark, 1986.

———. "Primacy in Communion." *America* 182 (June 3–10, 2000): 15–18.

———. *Towards a Papacy in Communion: Perspectives from Vatican Councils I and II*. Translated by Matthew J. O'Connell. New York: Herder and Herder, 1998.

Provost, James H. "Episcopal Conferences as an Expression of the Communion of Churches." In *Episcopal Conferences: Historical, Canonical, and Theological Studies,* edited by Thomas J. Reese, 267–89. Washington, DC: Georgetown University Press, 1989.

Prusak, Bernard P. "The Theology of the Local Church in Historical Development." *Proceedings of the Catholic Theological Society of America* 35 (1980): 287–308.

Puyo, Jean. *Une vie pour la vérité: Jean Puyo interroge le Père Congar*. Paris: Centurion, 1975.

The Quest for Unity: Orthodox and Catholics in Dialogue: Documents of the Joint International Commission and Official Dialogues in the United States, 1965–1995. Edited by John Borelli and John H. Erickson. Crestwood, NY: St. Vladimir's Seminary Press, and Washington, DC: United States Catholic Conference, 1996)

Quinn, John R. "A Permanent Synod? Reflections on Collegiality." *Origins* 31 (April 18, 2002): 730–36.

———. *The Reform of the Papacy: The Costly Call to Christian Unity.* New York: Crossroad, 1999.

Radcliffe, Timothy. "La mort du cardinal Yves-Marie Congar: Homélie." *Documentation Catholique* 92 (July 16, 1995): 688–90.

Rahner, Karl. "Basic Theological Interpretation of the Second Vatican Council." In *Concern for the Church,* Theological Investigations 20, pp. 77–89. New York: Crossroad, 1981.

Ratzinger, Joseph Cardinal. *Called to Communion: Understanding the Church Today.* Translated by Adrian Walker. San Francisco: Ignatius Press, 1996.

———. *Church, Ecumenism, and Politics: New Essays in Ecclesiology.* Translated by Robert Nowell and Dame Frideswide Sandemann. New York: Crossroad, 1988.

———. "The Ecclesiology of the Second Vatican Council." *Communio* 13 (1986): 239–52.

———. "The Local Church and the Universal Church: A Response to Walter Kasper." *America* 185 (November 19, 2001): 7–11.

———. *Milestones: Memoirs 1927–1977*. Translated by Erasmo Leiva-Merikakis. San Francisco: Ignatius Press, 1998.

———. *The Nature and Mission of Theology: Essays to Orient Theology in Today's Debates*. Translated by Adrian Walker. San Francisco, Ignatius Press, 1995.

———. *Principles of Catholic Theology: Building Stones for a Fundamental Theology.* Translated by Sister Mary Frances McCarthy. San Francisco: Ignatius Press, 1987.

Reese, Thomas J. *Inside the Vatican: The Politics and Organization of the Catholic Church*. Cambridge, MA: Harvard University Press, 1996.

Rigal, Jean. *L'ecclésiologie de communion — Son évolution historique et ses fondements*. Paris: Cerf, 1997.

———. *Le mystère de l'Église: Fondements théologiques et perspectives pastorales.* Paris: Cerf, 1992.

Romanides, John S. "Orthodox Ecclesiology according to Alexis Khomiakov (1804–1860)." *Greek Orthodox Theological Review* 2 (1956): 57–73.

Rousseau, Olivier. "*In memoriam:* le R. P. Nicolas Afanassieff." *Irénikon* 40 (1967): 291–97.

Routhier, Gilles. " 'Église locale' ou 'Église particulière': querelle sémantique ou option théologique?" *Studia canonica* 25 (1991): 277–334.

———. *La réception d'un concile.* Paris: Cerf, 1993.

———. "Reception in the Current Theological Debate." *The Jurist* 57 (1997): 17–52.

Sagovsky, Nicholas. *Ecumenism, Christian Origins, and the Practice of Communion.* Cambridge: Cambridge University Press, 2000.

Schatz, Klaus. *Papal Primacy: From Its Origins to the Present.* Translated by John A. Otto and Linda M. Maloney. Collegeville, MN: Michael Glazier/Liturgical Press, 1996.

Schmemann, Alexander. "Russian Theology: 1920–1972, An Introductory Survey." *St. Vladimir's Theological Quarterly* 16 (1972): 172–94.

Sesboüé, Bernard. "Le drame de la théologie au XXieme siècle: A propos du *Journal d'un théologien (1946–1956)* du P. Yves Congar." *Recherche de Science Religieuse* 89 (April–June 2001): 271–87.

———. "Un dur combat pour une Église conciliaire: *Mon journal du Concile,* de Yves Congar" *Recherche de Science Religieuse* 91 (April–June 2003): 259–72.

Shan, Cardinal Paul Kuo-hsi. "Opening Report." *Origins* 27 (April 30, 1998): 752–53.

Shaw, Lewis. "John Meyendorff and the Heritage of the Russian Theological Tradition." In *New Perspectives on Historical Theology: Essays in Memory of John Meyendorff,* edited by Bradley Nassif, 10–42. Grand Rapids, MI: Eerdmans, 1996.

Sicouly, Pablo. "Yves Congar und Johann Adam Möhler: Ein theologisches Gespräch zwischen den Zeiten." *Catholica* 45 (1991): 36–43.

Sodano, Cardinal Angelo. "The Roman Curia's Role." *Origins* 27 (May 7, 1998): 774–75.

Staudt, Brian. "Book Review: The Lay-Cleric Distinction: Tragedy or Comedy?" *Church* 12 (Fall 1996): 47–50.

Sullivan, Francis A. "The Impact of *Dominus Iesus* on Ecumenism." *America* 183 (October 28, 2000): 8–11.

———. "The Magisterium in the New Millennium." *America* 185 (August 27–September 3, 2001): 12–16.

———. *Magisterium: Teaching Authority in the Church.* New York: Paulist, 1983.

———. "Response to Wolfgang Beinert." *The Jurist* 52 (1992): 484–89.

Tanner, Mary. "In Memoriam: Jean-Marie Roger Tillard, O.P. (1927–2000)." *One in Christ* 36 (2000): 378–81.

Tavard, George H. "The Gift of Authority: The Latest Report of the Anglican–Roman Catholic International Commission." *America* 181 (July 3, 1999): 10–12.

———. Review of *Chair de l'Église, chair du Christ: Aux sources de l'ecclésiologie de communion. Theological Studies* 54 (1993): 200.

———. Review of *Église d'Églises: L'ecclésiologie de communion. Theological Studies* 49 (1988): 349–51.

Toubeau, A. Review of *Chair de l'Église, chair du Christ: Aux sources de l'ecclésiologie de communion. Nouvelle Revue Théologique* 114 (1992): 901–2.

———. Review of *Église d'Églises: L'ecclésiologie de communion. Nouvelle Revue Théologique* 110 (1988): 426–28.

Trautman, Bishop Donald W. "Rome and ICEL." *America* 182 (March 4, 2000): 7–11.

VanderWilt, Jeffrey T. *A Church without Borders: The Eucharist and the Church in Ecumenical Perspective.* Collegeville, MN: Michael Glazier/Liturgical Press, 1998.

———. "The Eucharist as Sacrament of Ecclesial *Koinonia* with Reference to the Contribution of Jean-Marie Tillard to Ecumenical Consensus on the Eucharist." Ph.D. dissertation, University of Notre Dame, 1996.

Van Rossum, Joost. "A. S. Khomiakov and Orthodox Ecclesiology." *St. Vladimir's Theological Quarterly* 35 (1991): 67–82.

Vatican Council II: The Basic Sixteen Documents. General editor Austin Flannery. Northport, NY: Costello, 1996.

Vercruysse, J. E. Review of *Chair de l'Église, chair du Christ: Aux sources de l'ecclésiologie de communion. Ephemerides Theologicae Lovanienses* 70 (1994): 191–93.

Villar, José R. *Teología de la Iglesia Particular: El tema en la literatura de lengua francesa hasta el Concilio Vaticano II.* Pamplona: Ediciones Universidad de Navarra, 1989.

Vorgrimler, Herbert, general editor. *Commentary on the Documents of Vatican II.* New York: Herder and Herder, 1967–69.

Wainwright, Geoffrey. "A Protestant Response [to *The Bishop of Rome*]." *Ecumenical Trends* 13 (1984): 118.

Weigel, George. "The Church's Teaching Authority and the Call for Democracy in North Atlantic Catholicism." In *Church Unity and the Papal Office: An Ecumenical Dialogue on John Paul II's Encyclical* Ut unum sint. Edited by Carl E. Braaten and Robert W. Jenson, 142–58. Grand Rapids, MI: Eerdmans, 2001.

———. "Papacy and Power." *First Things* 110 (February 2001): 18–25.

———. *Witness to Hope: The Biography of Pope John Paul II.* New York: Cliff Street Books/HarperCollins, 1999.

Weiler, Thomas. *Volk Gottes — Leib Christi: Die Ekklesiologie Joseph Ratzingers und ihr Einfluß auf das Zweite Vatikanische Konzil.* Mainz: Matthias-Grünewald-Verlag, 1997.

Wicks, Jared. "Yves Congar's Doctrinal Service of the People of God." *Gregorianum* 84 (2003): 499–550.

Willebrands, Cardinal Jan. "Vatican II's Ecclesiology of Communion." *Origins* 17 (May 28, 1987): 27–33.

Wood, Susan K. "The Church as Communion." In *The Gift of the Church: Essays on Ecclesiology in Honor of Patrick Granfield, O.S.B.* edited by Peter Phan, 159–76. Collegeville, MN: Michael Glazier/Liturgical Press, 2000.

———. "Communion Ecclesiology: Source of Hope, Source of Controversy." *Pro Ecclesia* 2 (1993): 424–32.

Woodrow, Alain. "Congar's Hard-Won Victory." *The Tablet* 255 (April 28, 2001): 604–5.

Yarnold, Edward. "The Church as Communion." *The Tablet* 246 (December 12, 1992): 1564–65.

Zernov, Nicolas. *The Russian Religious Renaissance of the Twentieth Century.* New York: Harper & Row, 1963.

———. *Three Russian Prophets: Khomiakov, Dostoevsky, Soloviev.* London: SCM Press, 1944.

Zizioulas, John. *Being as Communion: Studies in Personhood and the Church.* Crestwood, NY: St. Vladimir's Seminary Press, 1985.

———. "The Church as Communion." *St. Vladimir's Theological Quarterly* 38 (1994): 3–16.

———. "Communion and Otherness." *St. Vladimir's Theological Quarterly* 38 (1994): 347–61.

———. "L'eucharistie: Quelques aspects bibliques" in Jean Zizioulas, Jean-Marie Roger Tillard, and Jean-Jacques von Allmen, *L'eucharistie.* Paris: Maison Mame, 1970, 11–74.

———. "The Institution of Episcopal Conferences: An Orthodox Reflection." *The Jurist* 48 (1988): 376–83.

———. "Le Mystère de l'Église dans la tradition orthodoxe." *Irénikon* 60 (1987): 323–35.

———. "Primacy in the Church: An Orthodox Approach." In *Petrine Ministry and the Unity of the Church: "Toward a Patient and Fraternal Dialogue,"* edited by James F. Puglisi, 115–25. Collegeville, MN: Michael Glazier/Liturgical Press, 1999.

Index

Of Related Interest

Christopher Steck
THE ETHICAL THOUGHT OF HANS URS VON BALTHASAR

In contemporary theology, the thought of Hans Urs von Balthasar (1905–1988) exerts ever-greater influence, as readers discover that his thought is too subtle and rich to be pigeonholed into categories as simple as "neopatristic" or "conservative." In the emerging discussion of his contributions to key themes in theology, however, surprisingly little attention has been paid to his view of ethics. In this remarkable study, the first of its kind in any language, Christopher Steck uncovers the ethical dimension of von Balthasar's thought, showing its relation to other key issues in his works, and to key figures such as Ignatius Loyola, Karl Barth, and especially Karl Rahner. Steck shows both the importance of ethics in von Balthasar's thinking and how it exposes limitations of current ethical reflection. This clear, authoritative introduction is indispensable for von Balthasar scholars and students of contemporary Catholic theology, as well as all interested in major trends in contemporary conversations about religious ethics. Winner of the Book of the Year Award from the College Theology Society!

0-8245-1915-9, $35.00, paperback

crossroad

Of Related Interest

Kevin Mongrain
THE SYSTEMATIC THOUGHT OF HANS URS VON BALTHASAR
An Irenaean Retrieval

Mongrain's comprehensive study of von Balthasar's thought suggests that von Balthasar intended his theology to be a retrieval of several themes in the theology of the church father Irenaeus of Lyons. One key element is the idea of the *corpus triforme* christology, which views the incarnate Word as a complex expression of divine mystery. This mystery interprets itself as a number of unities — the unity of the Old and New Covenants, the unity of creation and redemption, and the unity of Christ and Church. Irenaeus also offers von Balthasar ways to resist the danger of gnosticism, which he saw as an ongoing temptation in modern theology and philosophy. Unifying several of these elements, von Balthasar uses "doxology" as a rule for guiding Christian theology. Mongrain concludes this exploration of von Balthasar with a critique of his thought from within, showing additional ways that von Balthasar could have carried out his own rule of theological resistance to gnosticism.

0-8245-1927-2, $29.95, paperback

Check your local bookstore for availability.
To order directly from the publisher,
please call 1-800-707-0670 for Customer Service
or visit our website at *www.cpcbooks.com.*
For catalog orders, please send your request to the address below.

THE CROSSROAD PUBLISHING COMPANY
16 Penn Plaza, Suite 1550
New York, NY 10001

All prices subject to change.

About the Author

Herder & Herder is delighted to welcome Christopher Ruddy to our community of Catholic constructive theologians. Dr. Ruddy is an assistant professor of theology at the University of St. Thomas in St. Paul, Minnesota. He taught previously at St. John's University and the College of St. Benedict in Minnesota. A graduate of Yale College and Harvard Divinity School, he received his doctorate in systematic theology from the University of Notre Dame. His writing has appeared in *America, Christian Century, Commonweal*, and *Logos*; his article "No Restorationist: Ratzinger's Theological Journey" was a cover story for the June 3, 2005, issue of *Commonweal.* His theological interests include ecclesiology, ecumenism, and the relationship of Christ and culture. He is presently working on books on the Catholic priesthood and on "la nouvelle théologie" and its influence upon Vatican II. A native of New York City, he lives in St. Paul with his wife, Deborah, and their two sons, Peter and Luke.